SPAIN, EUROPE & THE WIDER WORLD
1500–1800

Georg Wezeler, *Atlas Supporting the Armillary Sphere,* Brussels, *c.* 1530, after a cartoon attributed to Bernard van Orley. Originally created for the king of Portugal, this tapestry passed into the collection of the kings of Spain, who, as rulers of a world-wide empire, appropriated for themselves the image of Atlas bearing the burden of the globe.

SPAIN, EUROPE

& THE

WIDER WORLD

1500–1800

J. H. ELLIOTT

YALE UNIVERSITY PRESS
NEW HAVEN AND LONDON

Published with assistance from the Annie Burr Lewis Fund.

For information about this and other Yale University Press publications, please contact:
U.S. Office: sales.press@yale.edu   www.yalebooks.com
Europe Office: sales @yaleup.co.uk   www.yaleup.co.uk

Set in Minion by IDSUK (DataConnection) Ltd
Printed in the United States of America.

Library of Congress Cataloging-in-Publication Data

Elliott, John Huxtable.
   Spain, Europe and the wider world, 1500-1800 / J.H. Elliott.
      p. cm.
   Includes bibliographical references and index.
   ISBN 978-0-300-14537-3 (ci : alk. paper)
   1. Spain—History—House of Austria, 1516-1700. 2. Spain—History—Bourbons,
1700- 3. Spain—Relations—Europe. 4. Europe—Relations—Spain. 5. Spain—
Colonies—America. 6. Europe—History—1492-1648. 7. Europe—History—1648-1789.
8. Painting, Spanish. 9. Spain—Civilization. I. Title.
   DP171.E423 2009
   940.2—dc22
                                                                                    2009004214
A catalogue record for this book is available from the British Library.

10 9 8 7 6 5 4 3 2 1

For Jonathan Brown

CONTENTS

ACKNOWLEDGEMENTS

I 'A Europe of Composite Monarchies' from *Past and Present: A Journal of Historical Studies*, no. 137 (November 1992). By permission of The Past and Present Society, 175 Banbury Road, Oxford.

II 'Learning from the Enemy: Early Modern Britain and Spain', Dacre Lecture, Oxford, 2007, Trustees of the Dacre Trust and the Oxford History Faculty.

III 'The General Crisis in Retrospect: A Debate without End' in *Early Modern Europe: From Crisis to Stability*, ed. Philip Benedict and Myron P. Gutmann (University of Delaware, 2005).

IV 'A Non-Revolutionary Society: Castile in the 1640s' in *Etudes d'Histoire Européenne. Mélanges offerts à René et Suzanne Pillorget* (Presses de l'Université d'Angers, 1990).

V 'Europe After the Peace of Westphalia' in *1648: Paix de Westphalie, l'art entre la guerre et la paix* (Musée de Louvre éditions/Westfälisches Landesmuseum Für Kunst und Kulturgeschichte/Klincksieck, Paris, 1999). By permission of Musée de Louvre éditions, Westfälisches Landesmuseum für Kunst und Kulturgeschichte and Editions Klincksieck.

VI 'The Seizure of Overseas Territories by the European Powers' in *The European Discovery of the World and its Economic Effects on Pre-Industrial Society, 1500–1800*, ed. Hans Pohl (Stuttgart, 1990), and reprinted in *Theories of Empire, 1450–1800*, ed. David Armitage (Ashgate, Kent, 1998, Variorum, vol. 20).

VII 'Illusion and Disillusionment: Spain and the Indies', Creighton Lecture, 1991 (University of London, 1992).

VIII 'Britain and Spain in America: Colonists and Colonized', Stenton Lecture, 1994 (University of Reading, 1994).

IX 'King and *Patria* in the Hispanic World' in *El Imperio Sublevado. Monarquía y naciones en España e Hispanoamérica*, ed. Victor Mínguez and Manuel Chust (Consejo Superior de Investigaciones Científicas, Madrid, 2004).

X 'The Same World, Different Worlds', in *Mezclado y sospechoso*, ed. Gregorio Salinero (Casa de Velázquez, Madrid, 2005).

XI 'Starting Afresh? The Eclipse of Empire in British and Spanish America', conference paper given as part of 'Imperial Models in the Early Modern World', UCLA Center for 17th- & 18th-Century Studies, Los Angeles, 2007.

XII 'El Greco's Mediterranean: The Encounter of Civilizations', in David Davies, ed., *El Greco* (National Gallery Publications, London 2003). With permission of the National Gallery.

XIII 'Court Society in Seventeenth-Century Europe: Madrid, Brussels, London', in *Velázquez, Rubens y Van Dyck* (Museo del Prado/Ediciones El Viso, Madrid, 1999).

XIV 'Appearance and Reality in the Spain of Velázquez', in Dawson W. Carr, *Velázquez* (National Gallery Publications, London, 2006). With permission of the National Gallery.

FIGURES

PREFACE

In 1989 I published a volume of selected essays, *Spain and its World, 1500–1700*, which was designed to illustrate different aspects of my interest in the Hispanic world over the course of two critical centuries in which the history of Europe was overshadowed by the power of Spain.[1] The reception accorded that volume has encouraged me to publish this sequel, containing a selection of essays based on articles or lectures dating from 1990 onwards. Most of these were *pièces d'occasion*, originally prepared as conference papers or named lectures, or alternatively as essays in honour of a historical colleague. In publishing them here, I have usually removed local and personal references which were appropriate for the occasion but are of no direct relevance to the theme. Otherwise, with the exception of a few changes to vocabulary, and some updating of bibliographical references where this seemed appropriate, I have left the pieces more or less as they were. Inevitably there will be some overlap between essays that are intended to be self-contained but share common ground. Although I have sought to eliminate unnecessary repetition, some allusions and examples are bound to recur, although in different contexts. To search for alternatives, perhaps of less relevance or immediacy, would be a pointless exercise.

'Ought one to reprint historical essays which have already been published once?' This was the question somewhat defensively posed by Hugh Trevor-Roper in the foreword to a volume of essays that abundantly testifies to his own mastery of the historical essay as an art-form.[2] In the present volume one

---

[1] J. H. Elliott, *Spain and its World, 1500–1700* (New Haven, Conn. and London, 1989).
[2] H. R. Trevor-Roper, *Historical Essays* (London, 1957), p. v.

exception to pieces that have previously been published, sometimes in English and sometimes in Spanish, is a lecture delivered in Oxford in October 2007 as the first in a series of annual Dacre lectures set up to honour Trevor-Roper's memory. I have chosen to keep this in its original lecture form because it is so closely related to some of Trevor-Roper's principal concerns and is at least in part inspired by his work (see Chapter 2). Answering his own question, he argued that 'essays . . . various in time, depth and subject, can only bear republication if they receive an underlying unity from the philosophy of the writer.' In the present instance I do not know to what extent, if at all, these essays can be said to express an underlying philosophy, but in so far as they possess a unity it is because they arise out of my engagement with a number of themes that have long interested me, and reflect what I hope is a unified vision of the ways in which those themes relate to each other, and to the historical process as a whole. Beyond this, all the essays seek to present my reflections and the results of my research in a form that I hope will be accessible to readers who do not necessarily share my specialist concerns.

While the essays in this volume range well beyond Spain itself, its history, especially during the early modern period, has remained central to those concerns. As I explained in *Spain and its World, 1500–1700,* I first became interested in Spain and Spanish civilisation as the result of a six-week tour of the Iberian Peninsula with a group of fellow Cambridge undergraduates during the summer vacation of 1950.[3] In the aftermath of the Spanish Civil War, in spite of the efforts of a handful of outstanding historians working in isolation under conditions of great difficulty, Spanish historical writing was backward by international standards, and the country's rich archives were relatively under-explored. Fernand Braudel, in his epoch-making *La Méditerranée et le monde méditerranéen à l'époque de Philippe II,* first published in 1949, had revealed something of the treasures that were waiting to be unearthed, but researchers at that time were few on the ground. Consequently, when I embarked in the early 1950s on archival research into the history of Spain in the first half of the seventeenth century—the Spain of the Count-Duke of Olivares—I had the field almost to myself. If the problems involved in research were considerable, so too were the opportunities.

The half-century since then has seen an amazing transformation. Spain's transition to democracy in the mid-1970s was accompanied by the emergence of a new generation of historians who travelled abroad with a frequency impossible for the Civil War generation, and who made it their business to

---

[3] Elliott, *Spain and its World,* p. ix.

catch up with the dominant trends in international historiography. The expansion of universities, made possible by a renovated and buoyant economy, led to a proliferation of research. As a result of these developments Spanish historical writing now competes on a level playing field with that of other countries, and native Spanish historians share the attitudes, the approaches and the language of an international historical community into which they are fully integrated.

The transformation of Spanish historiography has naturally brought with it a transformation of the part that foreign scholars can be expected to play in writing the history of a country that is not their own. Many such scholars, collectively known in Spain as *hispanistas*, have made impressive contributions over the years to the knowledge and understanding of Spanish literature, history and art, and will no doubt continue to do so in the years to come. But the amount of research currently being undertaken by Spanish scholars, and their readiness to turn their backs on the traditional preoccupation of Spanish scholarship with what was perceived to be the 'difference', or the 'problem', of Spain, has effectively brought the age of the *hispanista* to an end. There is no longer any need to look to foreign researchers to fill the gaps in knowledge, or to offer interpretations generated by the latest developments in international scholarship. Spanish scholars are perfectly capable of doing this for themselves.

It has been both a pleasure and a privilege to witness, and live through, this process of transformation—a process that has left its own marks on the selection and treatment of the themes studied in this book. Yet I remain grateful for the formative experience of those early years when great tracts of the Spanish past were relatively under-studied. The challenge back then was to break through the constraints of traditional interpretations, and come up with new ones that would resonate both in the closed Spain of Franco and in an outside world with a different set of historical preoccupations, along with an often distorted view of Spain and its history.

The distortion derived from a longstanding sense of Spanish exceptionalism. While this was partly inspired by nineteenth-century Romanticism, much of it was home-grown, and was the outcome in particular of national agonising over what was perceived as the continuing inability of Spain to make the transition to modernity long since achieved by other nation states. By a neat inversion, the regime of General Franco reinterpreted failure as success. Spain alone had resisted the temptation of succumbing to the siren songs of liberalism and atheism, and had remained true to the eternal values it had traditionally sought to uphold. The regime therefore took pride in proclaiming that 'Spain is different'. Every country in fact sees itself as in some way exceptional, but Spanish exceptionalism, used as an explanatory device for Spain's deviation, for good or ill, from the path taken by other societies of the western world, was deeply entrenched at the time when I first began to research in Spanish archives. The results of that research, together with my extensive reading in British and European history for the purposes of university teaching, persuaded me that in reality the Spain of the seventeenth century had many points of affinity with other European states. In examining aspects of Spanish history, whether in books or in articles, I have therefore consistently sought, wherever appropriate, to set them into the wider context of the western world.

The attempt to do so made me reflect on the nature of national history and how best to approach it. No nation is an island unto itself, in spite of the efforts of many of its historians to treat it as such. Early modern Spain formed part of a European community that was a patchwork of polities ranging from city states and republics to supranational composite monarchies, the subject of one of the essays in this book (Chapter 1). Indeed, the Spanish Monarchy—the monarchy governed by Philip II and his Habsburg successors—was itself Europe's preeminent composite monarchy, consisting as it did of a complex of Iberian and European kingdoms and provinces, and an American empire, the 'empire of the Indies' (Chapter 9). Spain also formed part of a developing Atlantic community that initially was largely its own creation as it took the lead in seizing, subjugating and colonising vast areas of transatlantic territory (Chapter 6). The European world in which Spain played a leading role, and the overseas world that it sought to bring within its orbit, are two of the worlds explored from various angles in these essays. Spain, Europe and the Americas were all interlocking communities, and their histories should not be kept apart.

The search for connections is an essential part of the historical enterprise, and is one way of countering the exceptionalism that bedevils the writing of national history. A network of connections—diplomatic, religious, commercial, personal—linked the lands and the peoples of early modern Europe, transcending frontiers and spanning political and ideological divides. It also extended across the Atlantic as settler communities were established and grew to maturity in the Americas, and sought to define their place in the world (Chapter 10). A rapidly developing print culture made Europeans more aware of each other, and of the lands beyond the boundaries of Christendom. Princes and statesmen kept an increasingly close eye on the activities of their rivals and contemporaries, and had no hesitation in copying one another's methods and practices when it suited their purposes. In the highly competitive world of a developing European state-system, imitation was natural, especially among those who felt themselves at a comparative disadvantage. Therefore, learning from the enemy, as my discussion of the Anglo-Spanish relationship indicates (Chapter 2), became a characteristic of international life.

The predisposition to imitate neighbours and rivals was made all the stronger by the fact that the printing press allowed novel doctrines and ideas, like the neo-stoic philosophy of Justus Lipsius or the theories of Giovanni Botero about the nature of power and the conservation of states, to find a European-wide audience, and mould the attitudes of an entire generation, irrespective of national or religious affiliation. Europe's governing classes, drawing on a shared Christian and classical heritage, and subject to a common set of influences, operated within the same intellectual context. As a consequence, their attitudes and responses, and the policies they followed, tended to move along broadly similar lines. While the post-Westphalian Europe that emerged from the upheavals of the mid-seventeenth century remained in many respects a divided continent, it was also one possessing many traits in common (Chapter 5). Not only the elites, however, were exposed to the impact of new information and ideas. To what extent were those mid-century upheavals, now collectively known as the 'general crisis of the seventeenth century' (Chapters 3 and 4), the outcome of a revolutionary virus spreading across the continent and creating pockets of infection from which no social group was immune?

If the tracing of connections can help to break down the exceptionalism to which the writing of national history is all too liable to succumb, the drawing of comparisons can perform a similar service.[4] As long ago as 1928 Marc Bloch made an eloquent appeal for a comparative history of European societies.[5] Since then, historians have been more inclined to praise the virtues of comparative history than to practise it. Their hesitation, while regrettable, is understandable. The writing of comparative history presents many problems, both technical and conceptual.[6] An enormous, and rapidly growing, literature has to be mastered, not just for one society or state, but for two or more. The literature itself is inevitably uneven in quality and depth, thus complicating the task of making

---

[4] See my *National and Comparative History: An Inaugural Lecture Delivered before the University of Oxford on 10 May 1991* (Oxford, 1991). The number of local references in this Inaugural Lecture makes it inappropriate for republication in this volume, but I have drawn on some of the points made in it in writing this preface.

[5] Marc Bloch, 'Pour une histoire comparée des sociétés européennes', *Revue de synthèse historique*, 46 (1928), pp. 15–50. By an unfortunate slip, the date wrongly appears as 1925 in the published text of my Inaugural Lecture.

[6] See George M. Frederickson, 'Comparative History', in Michael Kammen, ed., *The Past Before Us* (Ithaca, N.Y., 1980), ch. 19.

comparisons that will be free of bias and distortion. Nor is it always clear which units are best selected for comparative purposes, although the choice between broadly based comparisons ranging widely across time and space, and comparisons restricted to societies within a roughly similar temporal and geographical frame, will presumably be determined by the kind of questions to be asked. Social scientists may tend to favour the former and historians the latter, but both choices have validity within their own terms of reference.

Whatever the choice, there hovers over every attempt at comparison the danger that the search for commonality will lead to an underestimation of the differences. Yet in all comparative work, the identification of differences is at least as important as the discovery of resemblances. The realisation that Spain was in many respects not as different from other contemporary European states as was traditionally assumed has helped to bring it back into the mainstream of European history and historical writing, with obvious benefits to our understanding of Spanish and European history alike. Yet a blurring of differences can lead to as much distortion as their exaggeration through an excessive emphasis on the exceptional character of national experience. In recent approaches to the history of Spain, the pendulum is now in danger of swinging too far the other way. Sixteenth-century Spain was, after all, unique among the states of western Europe in having within its borders a large, and for the most part unassimilated, ethnic minority which, in spite of nominal conversion to Christianity, still clung to many of its traditional Islamic beliefs and practices. It was also unique in its possession of an overseas empire populated by millions of indigenous inhabitants with their own belief-systems and forms of social organisation—an empire, moreover, that was found to contain the silver and gold so coveted by Europeans on a scale that exceeded their wildest dreams, but that all too often turned to dross in the eyes of Spaniards themselves (Chapter 7). These two differences alone had profound consequences for Spanish government and Spanish society, and did much to set early modern Spain on a path distinctive from that of neighbouring states.

The identification of differences is, by itself, not enough. Once identified, both difference and similarity need to be explained, and the comparative approach, by leading on from identification to the search for explanation, is a valuable device for testing standard hypotheses, putting forward new ones, and subverting traditional assumptions that may be deeply ingrained in a society's perception of itself.[7] It is an approach that runs through many of the

---

[7] For the comparative method as a means of hypothesis testing, see William H. Sewell, Jr, 'Marc Bloch and the Logic of Comparative History', *History and Theory*, 6 (1967), pp. 208–18.

essays in this book. It inspired my attempt to study in parallel the careers of the two statesmen who directed the fortunes of France and Spain in the 1620s and 1630s, Cardinal Richelieu and the Count-Duke of Olivares,[8] and more recently has led me to undertake a systematic and large-scale comparison of the empires of Britain and Spain in the Americas, for which the essay in this volume on colonists and colonised (Chapter 8) served as a trial run.[9] I would like to think that the exercise has brought into closer relationship a quartet of worlds too often compartmentalised—the European and the American, the British and the Hispanic—without at the same time underplaying the many differences between them. In Chapter 11 on the eclipse of empire in British and Spanish America, I attempt to identify some of these differences and seek explanations for them.

If these essays explore aspects of these four worlds, at once similar and different, they also touch on another that has long been of interest to me, the world of art. My first visit to the Prado Museum in the summer of 1950 was a revelation, not least because it opened my eyes to the greatness of Velázquez. I appreciated from an early stage of my researches that art and culture were an integral part of the story I wanted to tell, since the age traditionally seen as that of Spain's decline is also known as the Golden Age of its creative arts. It was not, however, easy to see how to achieve the integration of these two very different faces of the Spanish seventeenth century. The exact nature of the relationship between a society's cultural achievements and its political and economic fortunes, or misfortunes, has always been elusive, and the problem had not seriously engaged my attention until I moved to the Institute for Advanced Study in Princeton in 1973. The prominence of art history at Princeton acted as a spur, and brought home to me the importance of approaching the past through its images as well as more conventionally through the written word.

I was fortunate in having as a near neighbour in Princeton the leading expert on Velázquez in the United States. After many enjoyable discussions about different aspects of the art and history of seventeenth-century Spain, Jonathan Brown and I decided to undertake a collaborative project that would allow us to pool our respective skills. We chose as our subject the palace of the Buen Retiro, the pleasure palace built by the Count-Duke of Olivares for Philip IV on the outskirts of Madrid in the 1630s. The resulting book, *A Palace for a King:*

---

[8] J. H. Elliott, *Richelieu and Olivares* (Cambridge, 1984; repr. 1991).
[9] J. H. Elliott, *Empires of the Atlantic World: Britain and Spain in America, 1492–1830* (New Haven, Conn. and London, 2006).

The Buen Retiro and the Court of Philip IV,[10] was an attempt to produce a 'total history', embracing not simply the palace itself but also the context, in its widest sense, in which the palace was constructed and used. It involved the study not just of the economics and politics of palace-building, but also of court culture and patronage, and the relationship of artists and men of letters to the Crown, the elite and the society of which they formed a part.

Since the publication of that book, art history has massively extended its territory, and the contextualisation of the lives and works of artists has become routine. In consequence, I have been asked to contribute to the catalogues of a number of major international exhibitions. On each occasion the request was for an accessible account of the social, political and cultural environment in which the artist lived and worked—an account that would enhance the public's understanding and appreciation of the works on display. Three of these catalogue contributions are reprinted in this volume, two of them written for exhibitions held at the National Gallery in London (Chapters 12 and 14), and one in the Prado Museum in Madrid (Chapter 13). While they make no claim to originality, they all seek to assemble and integrate information that is often disconnected.

If there is a *leitmotif* to the essays in this volume, I hope it will be found in my aspiration both to connect and compare. In recent years, the proliferation of research coupled with an excessive degree of specialisation has all too often led to a narrowing of focus, and a degree of concentration on the minutiae that makes it difficult to appreciate their relationship to the wider scene. More recently still, and at least partly in reaction, we have been offered macro-historical studies that sweep excitingly, if vertiginously, over continents and peoples, at the expense of some of that definition which can only come from an examination conducted closer to the ground. My hope in these essays is to have achieved some sort of balance between these two approaches, addressing problems that I believe to be of general interest and importance, while anchoring them in specific historical contexts shaped by time and place. The distinguished French historian Emmanuel Le Roy Ladurie once famously divided historians into parachutists and truffle hunters.[11] I should like to think that this volume is the work of a parachutist with a few truffles in his bag.

---

[10] Jonathan Brown and John H. Elliott, *A Palace for a King: The Buen Retiro and the Court of Philip IV* (New Haven, Conn. and London, 1980; rev. and expanded edn, 2003).

[11] When I asked Ladurie for the reference some years ago, he was unable to come up with it, but assured me that I could cite him with confidence (letter to the author, 4 May 1999). The contrast is between parachutists who, like French soldiers in Algeria around 1960, scour large areas of territory, and truffle hunters who unearth a buried treasure.

SPAIN, EUROPE & THE WIDER WORLD
1500–1800

PART I

EUROPE

CHAPTER I

A EUROPE OF COMPOSITE MONARCHIES

The concept of Europe implies unity. The reality of Europe, especially as it has developed over the past five hundred years or so, reveals a marked degree of disunity, deriving from the establishment of what has come to be regarded as the characteristic feature of European political organisation as against that of other civilisations: a competitive system of sovereign, territorial nation states. 'By 1300', wrote Joseph Strayer in a highly perceptive little book, 'it was evident that the dominant political form in Western Europe was going to be the sovereign state. The universal Empire had never been anything but a dream; the universal Church had to admit that the defense of the individual state took precedence over the liberties of the Church or the claims of the Christian commonwealth. Loyalty to the state was stronger than any other loyalty, and for a few individuals (largely government officials) loyalty to the state was taking on some of the overtones of patriotism.'[1]

Here in embryo we have the themes that form the agenda for the bulk of nineteenth- and twentieth-century historical writing on the political history of early modern and modern Europe: the collapse of any prospect of European unity based on dominion by a 'universal Empire' or a 'universal Church', followed by the preordained failure of all subsequent attempts to achieve such unity through one or other of these two agencies; and the long, slow and often tortuous process by which a number of independent sovereign states succeeded in defining their territorial boundaries against their neighbours and in establishing a centralised authority over their subject populations, while at the same

---

[1] Joseph R. Strayer, *On the Medieval Origins of the Modern State* (Princeton N.J., 1970), p. 57.

time providing a focus of allegiance through the establishment of a national consensus that transcended local loyalties.

As a result of this process, a Europe that in 1500 included 'some five hundred more or less independent political units' had been transformed by 1900 into a Europe of 'about twenty-five',[2] of which the strongest were judged to be those that had reached the highest degree of integration as fully fledged nation states. Anomalies still survived—not least the Austro-Hungarian monarchy—but that they were anomalies was amply confirmed by the cataclysmic events of the First World War. The subsequent triumph of the 'principle of nationality' in the Versailles settlement of 1919[3] appeared to set the seal on the nation state as the logical, and indeed necessary, culmination of a thousand years of European history.

Different ages bring different perspectives. What seemed logical, necessary and even desirable at the end of the nineteenth century looks less logical and necessary, and somewhat less desirable, from the vantage point of the early years of the twenty-first. The development, on the one hand, of multinational political and economic organisations, and the revival, on the other, of 'suppressed' nationalities and of half-submerged regional and local identities, have simultaneously placed pressures on the nation state from above and beneath. These two processes, no doubt connected in ways that it will be for future generations of historians to trace, are bound to call into question standard interpretations of European history conceived in terms of an inexorable advance towards a system of sovereign nation states.

This process of historical reinterpretation clearly involves a fresh assessment of earlier attempts to organise supranational polities. Indeed, one such attempt, the empire of Charles V in the sixteenth century, received a semi-endorsement from an unexpected quarter shortly after the Second World War, when Fernand Braudel argued in 1949 that, with the economic revival of the fifteenth and sixteenth centuries, the conjuncture had become 'consistently favourable to the large and very large state, to the "super-states" which today are once again seen as the pattern of the future as they seemed to be briefly at the beginning of the eighteenth century, when Russia was expanding under Peter the Great, and when a dynastic union at least was projected between Louis XIV's France and Spain under Philip V'.[4]

---

[2] C. Tilly, 'Reflections on the History of European State-Making', in C. Tilly, ed., *The Formation of National States in Western Europe* (Princeton, N.J., 1975), p. 15.

[3] E. J. Hobsbawm, *Nations and Nationalism since 1780* (Cambridge, 1990), p. 131.

[4] Fernand Braudel, *The Mediterranean and the Mediterranean World in the Age of Philip II*, trans. Siàn Reynolds, 2 vols (London, 1972–3), ii, p. 660.

Braudel's perception that history is in turn favourable and unfavourable to vast political formations does not seem to have stimulated much enquiry among political and economic historians, perhaps because of the inherent difficulty in assessing the optimum size of a territorial unit at any given historical moment. Nor do historians of political thought seem to have accepted fully the implications of Frances Yates's insistence on the importance of Charles V's revival of the imperial idea.[5] Ideas about the sovereign territorial state remain the principal focus of attention in surveys of early modern political theory, at the expense of other traditions concerned with alternative forms of political organisation subsequently regarded as anachronistic in a Europe that had turned its back on universal monarchy[6] and had subsumed its local particularisms into unitary nation states.

Of these alternative forms of political organisation, one that has aroused particular interest in recent years has been the 'composite state'.[7] This interest certainly owes something to Europe's current preoccupation with federal or confederal union, as submerged nationalities resurface to claim their share of the sunlight.[8] But it also reflects a growing historical appreciation of the truth behind H. G. Koenigsberger's assertion that 'most states in the early modern period were composite states, including more than one country under the sovereignty of one ruler'. He divides these states into two categories: first, composite states separated from each other by other states, or by the sea, like the Spanish Habsburg monarchy, the Hohenzollern monarchy of Brandenburg–Prussia, and

---

[5] Frances Yates, 'Charles V and the Idea of the Empire', in her *Astraea: The Imperial Theme in the Sixteenth Century* (London, 1975), p. 1.

[6] For a treatment of the theme of universal monarchy, see F. Bosbach, *Monarchia Universalis: Ein politischer Leitbegriff der frühen Neuzeit* (Schriftenreihe der historischen Kommission bei der Bayerischen Akademie der Wissenschaften, xxxii, Göttingen, 1988).

[7] 'Composite state' was the term used by Koenigsberger in his 1975 Inaugural Lecture to the Chair of History at King's College London: H. G. Koenigsberger, '*Dominium Regale* or *Dominium Politicum et regale*', in his *Politicians and Virtuosi: Essays in Early Modern History* (London, 1986). Conrad Russell, in applying the concept to British history, prefers to speak of 'multiple kingdoms': see, for example, Conrad Russell, *The Causes of the English Civil War* (Oxford, 1990), p. 27. More recently, John Morrill, arguing that 'the notion of composite monarchy conveys all too settled and institutional a feel', has opted for the ungainly 'dynastic agglomerate', as giving a better sense of 'how unstable the evolving composite was'. See John Morrill, ' "Uneasy Lies the Head that Wears a Crown". Dynastic Crises in Tudor and Stewart Britain, 1504–1746', the Stenton Lecture 2003 (University of Reading, 2005), pp. 10–11.

[8] See, for instance, the reference to contemporary European developments in the preface to Mark Greengrass, ed., *Conquest and Coalescence: The Shaping of the State in Early Modern Europe* (London, 1991), a collection of essays presenting case studies of mergers, or attempted mergers, between larger and smaller political units in early modern Europe.

England and Ireland; and, second, contiguous composite states, like England and Wales, Piedmont and Savoy, and Poland and Lithuania.[9]

By the time of the early modern period of which Koenigsberger is writing, some composite states, like Burgundy and the Scandinavian Union of Kalmar, had already dissolved or were on the point of dissolution, while others, like the Holy Roman Empire, were struggling for survival. On the other hand, it was Charles V's imperial successors, drawn from the Austrian branch of the Habsburgs, who were to fashion from their own inherited kingdoms and patrimonial lands a state whose composite character would stay with it to the end. While some early modern states were clearly more composite than others, the mosaic of *pays d'élections* and *pays d'états* in Valois and Bourbon France is a reminder of a historical process that was to be repeated once again when Louis XIII formally united the principality of Béarn to France in 1620.[10] A state that was still essentially composite in character was only adding one further component to those already in place.

If sixteenth-century Europe was a Europe of composite states, coexisting with a myriad of smaller territorial and jurisdictional units jealously guarding their independent status, its history needs to be assessed from this standpoint rather than from that of the society of unitary nation states that it was later to become. It is easy enough to assume that the composite state of the early modern period was no more than a necessary but rather unsatisfactory way-station on the road that led to unitary statehood; but it should not automatically be taken for granted that at the turn of the fifteenth and sixteenth centuries this was already the destined end of the road.

The creation in medieval western Europe of a number of large political units—France, England, Castile—which had succeeded in building up and maintaining a relatively strong administrative apparatus, and had at once drawn strength from, and fostered, some sense of collective identity, certainly pointed strongly in a unitary direction. But dynastic ambition, deriving from the deeply rooted European sense of family and patrimony, cut across unitary tendencies and constantly threatened, through the continuing pursuit of new territorial acquisitions, to dilute the internal cohesion that was so laboriously being achieved.

For monarchs concerned with aggrandisement, the creation of composite states seemed a natural and easy way forward. New territorial acquisitions

---

[9] Koenigsberger, '*Dominium Regale* or *Dominium Politicum et Regale*', p. 12.

[10] For a succinct recent account of the events of 1620, see Christian Desplat, 'Louis XIII and the Union of Béarn to France', in Greengrass, ed., *Conquest and Coalescence*.

meant enhanced prestige and potentially valuable new sources of wealth. They were all the more to be prized if they possessed the additional advantages of contiguity and what was known as 'conformity'. James VI (of Scotland) and I (of England and Ireland) would use the argument of contiguity to strengthen the case for the union of the Crowns of England and Scotland.[11] It was also considered easier to make the new union stick where there were marked similarities in 'language, customs and institutions', as Machiavelli observed in the third chapter of *The Prince*.[12] Francesco Guicciardini made the same point when he spoke of the *conformità* that made the newly conquered kingdom of Navarre such a fine acquisition for Ferdinand the Catholic.[13] Yet contiguity and conformity did not necessarily of themselves lead on to integral union. Spanish Navarre remained in many respects a kingdom apart, and saw no major transformation of its traditional laws, institutions and customs before 1841.

According to the seventeenth-century Spanish jurist Juan de Solórzano Pereira, there were two ways in which newly acquired territory might be united to a king's other dominions. One was 'accessory' union, whereby a kingdom or province, on union with another, was regarded juridically as part and parcel of it, with its inhabitants possessing the same rights and subject to the same laws. The outstanding example of this kind of union in the Spanish Monarchy was provided by the Spanish Indies, which were juridically incorporated into the Crown of Castile. The incorporation of Wales with England by the Acts of Union of 1536 and 1543 may also be regarded as an accessory union.

There was also, according to Solórzano, the form of union known as *aeque principaliter*, under which the constituent kingdoms continued after their union to be treated as distinct entities, preserving their own laws, *fueros* and privileges. 'These kingdoms', wrote Solórzano, 'must be ruled and governed as if the king who holds them all together were king only of each one of them.'[14] Most of the kingdoms and provinces of the Spanish Monarchy—Aragon, Valencia, the principality of Catalonia, the kingdoms of Sicily and Naples, and the different provinces of the Netherlands—fell more or less squarely into this

---

[11] See Brian P. Levack, *The Formation of the British State: England, Scotland and the Union, 1603–1707* (Oxford, 1987), p. 6.
[12] Machiavelli, *The Prince*, ed. Quentin Skinner and Russell Price (Cambridge, 1990), p. 8.
[13] Francesco Guicciardini, *Legazione di Spagna* (Pisa, 1825), pp. 61–2 (letter xvi, 17 Sept. 1512).
[14] Juan de Solórzano y Pereira, *Obras pósthumas* (Madrid, 1776), pp. 188–9; Juan de Solórzano y Pereira, *Política indiana* (Madrid, 1647; repr. Madrid, 1930), bk iv, ch. 19, s. 37. See also J. H. Elliott, *The Revolt of the Catalans* (Cambridge, 1963), p. 8; F. Javier de Ayala, *Ideas políticas de Juan de Solórzano* (Seville, 1946), ch. 5.

second category.[15] In all of them the king was expected, and indeed obliged, to maintain their distinctive identity and status.

This second method of union possessed certain clear advantages for rulers and ruled in the circumstances of early modern Europe, although Francis Bacon, in *A Brief Discourse Touching the Happy Union of the Kingdoms of England and Scotland*, would later comment on its inadequacies.[16] In any union, the problem was how to hold on to such new acquisitions in a ruthlessly competitive world. Of the two recommendations offered by Machiavelli in his laconic piece of advice about the treatment of conquered republics—'destroy them or else go to live there'—the first was liable to be self-defeating and the second impracticable. But he also suggested letting conquered states 'continue to live under their own laws, exacting tribute and setting up an oligarchical government that will keep the state friendly towards you'.[17] This method was a natural consequence of union *aeque principaliter*, and was employed with considerable success by the Spanish Habsburgs over the course of the sixteenth century to hold their enormous Spanish Monarchy together.

The greatest advantage of union *aeque principaliter* was that by ensuring the survival of their customary laws and institutions it made more palatable to the inhabitants the kind of transfer of territory that was inherent in the international dynastic game. No doubt they often felt considerable initial resentment at finding themselves subordinated to a 'foreign' ruler. But a promise by the ruler to observe traditional laws, customs and practices could mitigate the pains of these dynastic transactions, and help reconcile elites to the change of masters. The observance of traditional laws and customs involved in particular the perpetuation of Estates and representative institutions. Since sixteenth-century rulers were generally used to working with such bodies, this was not in itself an insuperable difficulty, although it could in time lead to complications, as it did with the union of the Crowns of Castile and Aragon. The traditional institutional restraints on kingship were so much stronger in the Aragonese territories than in sixteenth-century Castile that it became difficult for a Crown grown accustomed to relative freedom of action in one part of its dominions to accept that its powers were so curtailed in another. The disparity between the

---

[15] The kingdom of Naples was something of an anomaly, since it constituted part of the medieval Aragonese inheritance, but had also, more recently, been conquered from the French. In practice it was classed in the *aeque principaliter* category.
[16] Francis Bacon, 'A Brief Discourse Touching the Happy Union of the Kingdoms of England and Scotland', in *The Works of Francis Bacon*, ed. James Spedding, 14 vols (London, 1858–74), x, p. 96.
[17] Machiavelli, *Prince*, pp. 19, 17–18.

two constitutional systems was also conducive to friction between the constituent parts of the union when friction expressed itself in a widening disparity between their fiscal contributions. The difficulty of extracting subsidies from the Cortes of the Crown of Aragon naturally persuaded monarchs to turn for financial assistance with increasing frequency to the Cortes of Castile, which were more amenable to royal direction. Castilians came to resent the higher tax burden they were called on to bear, while the Aragonese, Catalans and Valencians complained at the diminishing frequency with which their Cortes were summoned, and feared that their constitutions were being silently subverted.

Yet the alternative, which was to reduce newly united realms to the status of conquered provinces, was too risky for most sixteenth-century rulers to contemplate. Few early modern rulers were as well placed as Emmanuel Philibert of Savoy, who, after recovering his war-devastated territories in 1559, was in a position to begin the construction of a Savoyard state almost from scratch, and passed on to his successors a centralising bureaucratic tradition which would make Piedmont–Savoy, at least by the standards of early modern Europe, an unusually integrated state.[18] In general it seemed safer, when taking over a new kingdom or province in reasonable working order, to accept the status quo and keep the machinery functioning. Some institutional innovations might be possible, like the creation in Spanish Naples of a collateral council,[19] but it was important to avoid alienating the province's elite by introducing too many changes too soon.

On the other hand, some initial degree of integration was called for if the monarch were to take effective control of his new territory. What instruments were available to secure this? Coercion played its part in establishing certain early modern unions, like the union of Portugal with Castile in 1580; but the maintenance of an army of occupation was not only an expensive business, as the English found in Ireland, but could also militate against the very policy of integration that the Crown was attempting to pursue, as the Austrians were to discover towards the end of the seventeenth century in their attempts to bring Hungary under royal control.[20]

Failing a more or less permanent military presence, the choice came down to the creation of new institutional organs at the highest level of government,

---

[18] For a brief summary of the fate of Piedmont and its representative institutions, see H. G. Koenigsberger, 'The Italian Parliaments from their Origins to the End of the Eighteenth Century', in Koenigsberger, *Politicians and Virtuosi*, pp. 54–9.

[19] I am grateful to Giovanni Muto of the University of Milan for his guidance on the affairs of Naples.

[20] John P. Spielman, *Leopold I of Austria* (New Brunswick, N.J., 1977), pp. 67, 132.

and the use of patronage to win and retain the loyalty of the old administrative and political elites. Since royal absenteeism was an inescapable feature of composite monarchies, the first and most important change likely to be experienced by a kingdom or province brought into union with another more powerful than itself was the departure of the court, the loss of capital status for its principal city and the replacement of the monarch by a governor or viceroy. No viceroy could fully compensate for the absence of the monarch in the face-to-face societies of early modern Europe. But the Spanish solution of appointing a council of native councillors attendant on the king went some way towards alleviating the problem, by providing a forum in which local opinions and grievances could be voiced at court, and local knowledge could be used in the determination of policy. At a higher level, a council of state, composed largely, but not always exclusively, of Castilian councillors, stood in reserve as at least a nominal instrument for final policy decisions and coordination in the light of the interests of the Spanish Monarchy as a whole. A council of state was something notably absent in the British composite monarchy of the seventeenth century. Here the privy councils of Scotland and Ireland operated in Edinburgh and Dublin rather than at court, and neither James I nor Charles I attempted to create a council for all Britain.[21]

At the lower levels of administration the patrimonial approach to office in early modern Europe made it difficult to replace existing officials with others who might be regarded as more loyal to the new regime. Moreover, there could well be strict constitutional rules governing appointment to office, as there were in parts of the Spanish Monarchy. In the Crown of Aragon, laws and constitutions forbade the appointment of non-native officials, and regulated the size of the bureaucracy. In Sicily, too, secular offices were reserved for natives of the island.[22] In mainland Italy the Crown had more room for manoeuvre, and it was possible to infiltrate Spanish officials into the administration of Milan and Naples. But here, as everywhere, there was no alternative to heavy dependence on provincial elites, whose loyalty could only be won, and kept, by patronage. This in turn gave provincial elites, like that of Naples,[23]

---

[21] Levack, *Formation of the British State*, p. 61; Conrad Russell, *The Fall of the British Monarchies, 1637–1642* (Oxford, 1991), p. 30.

[22] H. G. Koenigsberger, *The Government of Sicily under Philip II of Spain* (London, 1951), pp. 47–8.

[23] Rosario Villari, *La rivolta antispagnola a Napoli* (Bari, 1967). The degree to which the old nobility retained their dominance after the Neapolitan revolt of 1647–8 is the subject of current debate. See especially Pier Luigi Rovito, 'La rivoluzione costituzionale di Napoli, 1647–48', *Rivista storica italiana*, xcviii (1986), pp. 367–462. But provincial elites that included a strong component of *togati* also possessed ample opportunities for political leverage.

substantial leverage, which could be used on the one hand to exert pressure on the Crown, and on the other to extend their social and economic dominance over their own communities.

This suggests a brittleness about composite monarchies which is bound to raise questions about their long-term viability. There can be no doubt that for all of them royal absenteeism constituted a major structural problem, which not even the energetic itinerancy of that indefatigable traveller, Charles V, could entirely resolve. But those constant complaints of sixteenth-century Catalans or Aragonese about being deprived of the light of the sun,[24] while no doubt expressing a legitimate sense of grievance, may also be seen as useful strategies for getting more of what they wanted. The Catalans, after all, as partners in a medieval confederation, were no strangers to absentee kingship, and had learnt to accommodate themselves to this not always unfortunate fact of life even before the union of the Crowns.

In return for a degree of benign neglect, local elites enjoyed a measure of self-government which left them without any urgent need to challenge the status quo. In other words, composite monarchies were built on a mutual compact between the Crown and the ruling class of their different provinces, which gave even the most arbitrary and artificial of unions a certain stability and resilience. If the monarch could then go on from here to foster, especially among the higher nobility of his different kingdoms, a sense of personal loyalty to the dynasty, transcending provincial boundaries, the chances of stability were still further improved. This was something that Charles V sought to achieve when he opened the Burgundian Order of the Golden Fleece to aristo-crats from the various kingdoms of his composite monarchy. It was also some-thing that the Austrian Habsburgs of the seventeenth century would accomplish on a much more lavish and systematic scale through their develop-ment of a spectacular court culture.[25]

It was easier to generate a sense of loyalty to a transcendent monarch than to a wider community created by political union, although it no doubt helped if the wider community was acceptably named. Monarchs uniting the crowns of Castile and Aragon sought to revive shadowy memories of a Roman or Visigothic *Hispania* in order to suggest a wider potential focus of loyalty in the form of a historically revived 'Spain'. But 'Union in Name', as Bacon called it,[26]

---

[24] Elliott, *Revolt of the Catalans*, pp. 12–14.
[25] See R. J. W. Evans, *The Making of the Habsburg Monarchy* (Oxford, 1979), esp. pp. 152–4.
[26] Bacon, 'Brief Discourse', p. 96.

was not easily achieved. For some seventeenth-century Scots, the name 'Britain' still possessed negative connotations.[27]

Closer association, especially where it brought economic or other benefits, could help promote this wider loyalty, as it did among the Scots in the eighteenth century. So, too, could the magnetic attraction for local nobilities of a dominant court culture and language; as early as 1495 an Aragonese noble translating a book from Catalan into Castilian spoke of the latter as the language of 'nuestra Hyspaña'.[28] But 'Spain', although capable of arousing loyalty in certain contexts, remained distant in comparison with the more immediate reality of Castile or Aragon.

Yet a community's sense of identity is neither static nor uniform.[29] Strong loyalty to the home community—the sixteenth-century *patria*[30]—was not inherently incompatible with the extension of loyalty to a wider community, so long as the advantages of political union could be considered, at least by influential groups in society, as outweighing the drawbacks. But the stability and survival prospects of sixteenth-century composite monarchies based on a tacit mutual acceptance of each other by the contracting parties were to be jeopardised by a number of developments during the course of the century. Potentially the most dangerous of these was the religious division of Europe, pitting subject against monarch and subject against subject. If the great religious changes of the century constituted a threat to every kind of state, the larger composite states were especially at risk, although the Polish–Lithuanian commonwealth, fortified by the 1569 Union of Lublin, and based on a high degree of aristocratic consensus, successfully weathered the storm. The awareness of this risk encouraged the increasingly desperate search of the later sixteenth-century Austrian Habsburgs for an ecumenical solution to the problems of religious division—a solution that would not only reunite a divided Christendom, but would also save their own patrimony from irreparable disintegration.

---

[27] See Roger A. Mason, 'Scotching the Brut: Politics, History and National Myth in Sixteenth-Century Britain', in Roger A. Mason, ed., *Scotland and England, 1286–1815* (Edinburgh, 1987). I am indebted to John Robertson for this reference, and also for his helpful comments on an early draft of this essay.

[28] Cited in Alain Milhou, *Colón y su mentalidad mesiánica en el ambiente franciscanista español* (Valladolid, 1983), p. 14.

[29] For a suggestive discussion of the multifaceted character of a sense of identity in the process of European state-building, see Peter Sahlins, *Boundaries: The Making of France and Spain in the Pyrenees* (Berkeley, Calif., 1989), esp. pp. 110–13.

[30] See J. H. Elliott, 'Revolution and Continuity in Early Modern Europe', *Past and Present*, 42 (1969), pp. 35–56; repr. in J. H. Elliott, *Spain and its World, 1500–1700* (New Haven, Conn., and London, 1989), ch. 5.

The effect of the religious changes of the sixteenth century was to add a new, and highly charged, additional component to those elements—geographical, historical, institutional and, in some instances, linguistic—which together helped constitute the collective sense of a province's identity in relation to the wider community of the composite state and to the dominant territory within it. Protestantism sharpened the sense of distinctive identity in a Netherlands always conscious of the differences that set it apart from Spain, just as Catholicism sharpened the sense of distinctive identity among an Irish population subject to Protestant English rule. Pressures from the centre to secure religious conformity were therefore liable to produce explosive reactions in communities that, for one reason or another, already felt their identities at risk. When the explosion occurred, the rebels could hope to exploit the new international network of confessional alliances to secure outside help. Here the rulers of extended composite states were highly vulnerable, since outlying provinces under imperfect control, like the Netherlands or Ireland, offered tempting opportunities for foreign intervention.

The consequences of the new religious dynamics of the sixteenth century, however, were not confined to peripheral provinces anxious to conserve their distinctive identities against pressures from the centre. Both Castile and England, as strong core states of composite monarchies, sharpened their own distinctive identities during the religious upheavals of the sixteenth century, developing an acute, and aggressive, sense of their unique place in God's providential design. In helping to define their own position in the world, their aggressive religious nationalism inevitably had its impact on relationships within the composite monarchies of which they formed a part. Unique responsibilities carried with them unique privileges. The Castilians, wrote a Catalan in 1557, 'want to be so absolute, and put so high a value on their own achievements and so low a value on everyone else's, that they give the impression that they alone are descended from heaven, and the rest of mankind are mud'.[31]

The sense of self-worth was increased, in both Castile and England, by the acquisition of overseas empire, a further indication of divine favour. The Castilians, by acquiring an empire in the Indies and reserving its benefits for themselves, enormously enhanced their own wealth and power in relation to the other kingdoms and provinces. The English, too, in acquiring an American empire, widened the gulf between themselves on one side and the Scots and the Irish on the other. The kings of Scotland had earlier sought to counter English

---

[31] Cristòfol Despuig, quoted in Elliott, *Revolt of the Catalans*, p. 13.

claims to an imperial Crown by adopting one of their own;[32] in the seventeenth century, as 'empire' came to include the possession of overseas dominions, Scottish colonisation projects in the New World might serve to reinforce the counterclaim to 'empire' in its new, more modern, sense. In general, imperialism and composite monarchy made uncomfortable bedfellows. The possession of overseas empire by one party to a union encouraged it to think in terms of domination and subordination in a way that militated against the whole conception of a composite monarchy united *aeque principaliter*.[33]

Where one component part of a composite monarchy is not only obviously superior to the others in power and resources, but also behaves as if it is, the other parts will naturally feel their identities to be increasingly under attack. This is what happened in the Spanish Monarchy in the sixteenth and early seventeenth centuries, as the non-Castilian kingdoms and provinces saw themselves at a growing disadvantage in relation to Castile. Levels of anxiety were raised by the disparaging or threatening comments of highly placed Castilians, and by the tightening Castilian grip on office after Madrid became the permanent home of the court in 1561. The financial needs of a king who more and more tended to be perceived as exclusively Castilian were also a source of growing disquiet. Even where, as in the Crown of Aragon, the presence of representative institutions and assemblies acted as an effective restraint on new fiscal initiatives, there was widespread and understandable suspicion of Madrid's long-term intentions. Kingdoms that feared for the erosion of their liberties scrutinised every move by royal officials which might be interpreted as a violation of their laws, and fortified their constitutional defences whenever possible. It is not by chance that the famous 'medieval' Aragonese oath of allegiance, with its resounding formula 'If not, not', was in fact a mid-sixteenth-century invention.[34] Jurists in Aragon, as in other parts of Europe,[35] were hard at work rediscovering or inventing customary laws and constitutions. The Aragonese revolt of 1591 was the revolt of a ruling elite, or a section of it, which sought and found the justification for its resistance to the Crown in a defence of the just (but not always justly interpreted) Aragonese liberties.

---

[32] I am grateful to David Stevenson for advice on this point.
[33] Campare the equation between Italians and Indians made by an official of Philip II, as cited in Koenigsberger, *Government of Sicily*, p. 48.
[34] See Ralph A. Giesey, *If Not, Not* (Princeton, N.J., 1968).
[35] See Donald R. Kelley, *Foundations of Modern Historical Scholarship: Language, Law and History in the French Renaissance* (New York, 1970).

Philip II's response to that same revolt was framed with a restraint which no doubt owed something to natural caution reinforced by the experience of the revolt of the Netherlands in the 1560s. But it also seems expressive of the dynastic and moral attitudes that governed the traditional Habsburg vision of the world. In spite of contemporary and later assumptions to the contrary, the kingdom of Aragon, although shorn of some of its privileges and institutional arrangements, retained its essentially constitutionalist and contractual character.[36] A few years earlier a similar willingness to accept existing constitutional and institutional arrangements had informed Philip's policies for union between Castile and Portugal. In the traditional Habsburg style this union of the Crowns in 1580 was another dynastic union, *aeque principaliter*, carefully designed to ensure the survival of Portugal's separate identity, along with that of its empire. The only specifically integrating measure was the abolition of customs posts between the two kingdoms, and this attempt at a customs union was abandoned in 1592.[37]

It is significant that Sir Henry Savile, in considering a series of historical examples of union in 1604 when discussing Jacobean projects for Anglo-Scottish union (Lithuania and Poland, Norway and Sweden, Aragon and Castile, Brittany and France, and the England of Mary Tudor with Spain), should have singled out the union between Castile and Portugal in 1580 as 'in mine opinion the likest to ours'.[38] While hardly the kind of perfect union to which James I aspired, a dynastic union, *aeque principaliter*, preserving the separate identities of the uniting kingdoms, remained the form of union most easily achieved, and its most far-reaching integrationist measure—the abolition of customs barriers—proved as impossible to maintain in the Scottish union as in the Portuguese.[39]

The test of kingship thereafter, as James I was wise enough to realise, was to seek out every opportunity to nudge the two uniting kingdoms towards closer uniformity—in law, religion and government—while working, above all, to

---

[36] For the survival of Aragonese constitutionalism, see Xavier Gil Pujol, 'Las cortes de Aragón en la edad moderna: comparación y reevaluación', *Revista de las Cortes Generales*, no. 22 (1991), pp. 79–119.

[37] For a brief survey of the sixty years' union between Castile and Portugal, see J. H. Elliott, 'The Spanish Monarchy and the Kingdom of Portugal, 1580–1640', in Greengrass, ed., *Conquest and Coalescence*.

[38] Sir Henry Savile, 'Historicall Collections', repr. in *The Jacobean Union: Six Tracts of 1604*, ed. Bruce R. Galloway and Brian P. Levack (Edinburgh, 1985), p. 229.

[39] Levack, *Formation of the British State*, p. 148. The commercial reciprocity between England and Scotland, introduced in 1604, had to be abandoned in 1611.

suppress the mutual hostility that accompanied every union of independent states. This same pragmatic policy was to be pursued by Louis XIII in the 1620 union of Béarn with France,[40] and was very much in line with contemporary thinking in, and about, the Spanish Monarchy. Theorists like Giovanni Botero, Tommaso Campanella and Baltasar Álamos de Barrientos were much exercised by the problem of how to conserve a composite monarchy, and were well primed with suggestions, like the intermarriage of nobilities and an equitable distribution of offices, which would conduce to 'fair correspondence and friendship' between the peoples of Spain, and would allow them to be 'brought to a familiarity one with another'.[41] This idea of 'familiarising'[42] the peoples of the Spanish Monarchy with each other, in order to end what he called their 'dryness and separation of hearts',[43] was to be taken up by the Count-Duke of Olivares in his great reform projects of the 1620s, which included closer union through mutual defence. A union of hearts—James I's 'union of love'[44]—was to be the natural consequence of a Union of Arms.[45]

Seventeenth-century rulers, imbued with Lipsian teachings about the ordered and disciplined state, in which unity of religion was seen as indispensable for the maintenance of political and social cohesion,[46] were everywhere talking the language of union. But Justus Lipsius had also warned against undue zeal in introducing change.[47] Yet by the 1620s there are indications among these rulers of growing impatience with the system of union *aeque principaliter*, and its corollary of unification by slow, pragmatic methods. A new generation of statesmen had come to power, with high notions of the royal prerogative and with less tolerance than their predecessors for a diversity that was felt to stand in the way of effective government. The activities of Protestant-dominated estates in the Austrian patrimonial lands, culminating in 1618–20 in the revolt of Bohemia, reinforced in the eyes of Ferdinand II and his advisers the fundamental importance of religious unity for the survival of their own composite

---

[40] Desplat, 'Louis XIII and the Union of Béarn to France'.

[41] Thomas Campanella, *A Discourse Touching the Spanish Monarchy* (London, 1654), p. 125.

[42] Elliott, *Revolt of the Catalans*, p. 204 n. 2.

[43] *Memoriales y cartas del Conde Duque de Olivares*, ed. J. H. Elliott and J. F. de la Peña, 2 vols (Madrid, 1978–80), i, p. 187.

[44] 'Introduction' to *Jacobean Union*, ed. Galloway and Levack, p. xli.

[45] For the Union of Arms, see J. H. Elliott, *The Count-Duke of Olivares: The Statesman in an Age of Decline* (New Haven, Conn., and London, 1986), ch. 7.

[46] 'Therefore this is my unshakeable opinion: that one religion be observed in one kingdom': *Iusti Lipsi politicorum sive civilis doctrinae libri sex* (Leiden, 1589), iv. 3, cited in Mark Morford, *Stoics and Neostoics: Rubens and the Circle of Lipsius* (Princeton, N.J., 1991), p. 108.

[47] Gerhard Oestreich, *Neostoicism and the Early Modern State* (Cambridge, 1982), p. 47.

state; and even if post-revolt Bohemia was permitted to preserve some measure of its earlier autonomy,[48] the pursuit of uniformity of religious belief and practice seemed—as it seemed to Charles I in Scotland—a natural concomitant to the proper exercise of princely power.

Above all, war and economic depression appeared to strengthen the case for the concentration of power. Resources had to be mobilised, economic activity directed, and Crown revenues increased to meet the costs of defence. All this made a higher degree of union the order of the day. For Michel de Marillac, the Keeper of the Seals in the France of Louis XIII, and probably, too, for Cardinal Richelieu—at least until he seems to have had second thoughts in the 1630s[49]—the system of the *pays d'élections* needed to be extended to the *pays d'états*. For Olivares, always ready with his aphorism 'many kingdoms but one law',[50] the institutional and legal diversity of the kingdoms of the Spanish Monarchy represented an intolerable impediment to his plans to maximise resources and ensure the military cooperation among them that was essential to survival.

These moves in the direction of a more unitary state structure, with union conceived primarily in terms of uniformity of religion, laws and taxation, vindicated the warning given by Bacon that 'unnatural hasting thereof doth disturb the work, and not dispatch it'.[51] By appearing to challenge outlying kingdoms and provinces at their most sensitive point, their sense of distinctive identity, these moves unleashed counter-revolutionary movements, above all in the British and Spanish monarchies. The Earl of Bedford, for one, showed himself aware of the parallels between the revolts of Scotland and Portugal.[52] The parallels, of course, were not entirely exact. Religion, although it played its part in the Portuguese revolt, as also in the contemporaneous revolt of Catalonia against the government of Olivares, was not at issue in Portugal as it was in Scotland. But the revolt of the Scots against the government of Charles I was more than a purely religious revolt. Essentially it was a revolt to defend the integrity of a historic, and to some extent idealised, community, which perceived itself in mortal danger from the actions of a dominant partner to

---

[48] See Evans, *Making of the Habsburg Monarchy*, ch. 6; R. J. W. Evans, 'The Habsburg Monarchy and Bohemia, 1526–1848', in Greengrass, ed., *Conquest and Coalescence*. I am indebted to Professor Evans for his comments on this and other points made in this essay.
[49] See R. J. Knecht, *Richelieu* (London, 1991), pp. 139–41, for a brief and balanced survey of the current debate over Richelieu's intentions.
[50] Elliott, *Count-Duke of Olivares*, p. 197.
[51] Bacon, 'Brief Discourse', p. 98.
[52] Russell, *Fall of the British Monarchies*, p. 240.

which it had been somewhat uneasily united within living memory. In this fundamental respect it closely resembled the Portuguese revolt.

Composite monarchies based on loose dynastic union, *aeque principaliter*, could only hope to survive if systems of patronage were maintained in careful working order, and if both parties kept close to the ground rules laid down in the original agreement of union. In both respects the governments of Philip IV and Charles I had failed disastrously. They had drawn up, for reasons good or bad, agendas dictated by a set of priorities which made more sense in Madrid and London than in Lisbon and Edinburgh. Then, by failing to keep open adequate lines of communication and patronage, they had deprived themselves of the local knowledge required to save them from egregious mistakes of execution. Once those mistakes had been made, the range of options was reduced to two: retreat, or a conquering, integrative, union in the style of Bohemia, in which a greater or lesser degree of uniformity was imposed by force of arms.

In his dealings with Scotland, Charles I was driven into humiliating retreat, while Cromwell's later attempt at a forced, integrative union—a union designed to bring about legal and religious conformity among the British kingdoms—not only failed to survive his own regime, but destroyed any future prospects for such a comprehensive style of union by reinforcing the very sense of separate Scottish and Irish identities that he had been so anxious to efface.[53] In the Iberian Peninsula, Castile, the core state, similarly proved incapable of imposing a permanent integrative solution by force of arms, and with comparable results. Catalonia, after twelve years of separation, returned to allegiance, but with the same constitutional rights as before its revolt. Portugal, with assistance at different moments from the French, the Dutch and the English, survived twenty-eight years of warfare to achieve definitive independence from Castile. In both instances the collective sense of separate identity had been strengthened by the shared experiences and memories of Castilian oppression and of the struggle for survival.

The disastrous failure of Olivares's experiment with a closer integration of the kingdoms and provinces of the Iberian Peninsula appeared to vindicate the wisdom of the traditional Habsburg approach to provincial rights and

---

[53] H. R. Trevor-Roper, 'The Union of Britain in the Seventeenth Century', in his *Religion, the Reformation and Social Change, and Other Essays* (London, 1967), p. 464. On the other hand, however, as John Robertson pointed out to me, the Cromwellian 'conquest' in some respects facilitated the later union of the Crowns, not least by sweeping away the independent hereditary jurisdictions of the great nobility, and encouraging a climate in which the Scots would be able to reassess the case for union.

privileges. It is significant that a younger generation formed in the Olivares school—men like Bishop Juan de Palafox and the diplomat and man of letters Diego Saavedra Fajardo—now insisted on the recognition of diversity as a necessary condition of successful government. If God, they argued, had created provinces that were naturally different from each other, it was important that the laws by which they were governed should conform to their distinctive character.[54] The argument from nature, therefore, which had been used by Francis Bacon at the beginning of the seventeenth century in favour of union, was now being employed in the middle of the century by Spanish theorists in favour of the acceptance of diversity.

Yet continuing diversity was beginning to look like an expensive luxury in a competitive state system in which the most powerful state, France, was also the most united. Seventeenth-century France in practice shared many of the problems of the more obviously composite monarchies. But, once religious unity had been restored and the Crown had overcome its mid-century troubles, it was well placed to bind outlying provinces more closely to the centre. Much of this process of national unification was achieved, as in Languedoc,[55] by the skilful use of patronage, but in his treatment of newly acquired provinces Louis XIV adopted a conscious policy of political, administrative and cultural Gallicisation. 'In order', he wrote in his memoirs, 'to strengthen my conquests by closer union with my existing territories . . . I tried to establish French customs in them.'[56] This policy, never as systematic as the memoirs would suggest, was more successful in some provinces than others. In French-occupied Flanders it seems to have been counter-productive until the Anglo-Dutch occupation of 1708–13 proved to the inhabitants that the alternatives were worse.[57] In the Pyrenean region of Cerdagne, acquired in the peace settlement of 1659, political and administrative uniformity were imposed, but policies of cultural and linguistic assimilation—at best tentatively pursued—were to be abandoned after the War of the Spanish Succession of 1701–13.[58]

---

[54] Diego Saavedra Fajardo, *Empresas políticas. Idea de un príncipe político-cristiano*, ed. Quintín Aldea Vaquero, 2 vols (Madrid, 1976), ii, p. 614 (*empresa* 61); Juan de Palafox y Mendoza, 'Juicio interior y secreto de la monarquía para mí solo', appended to José María Jover Zamora, 'Sobre los conceptos de monarquía y nación en el pensamiento político español del XVII', *Cuadernos de historia de España*, xiii (1950), pp. 138–50.

[55] See William Beik, *Absolutism and Society in Seventeenth-Century France: State Power and Provincial Aristocracy in Languedoc* (Cambridge, 1985).

[56] Cited in Sahlins, *Boundaries*, p. 117.

[57] Alain Lottin, 'Louis XIV and Flanders', in Greengrass, ed., *Conquest and Coalescence*, ch. 5.

[58] Sahlins, *Boundaries*, pp. 113–23.

The relative degree of national unity achieved by the France of Louis XIV contrasted sharply with the markedly composite character of its rivals, Great Britain, the United Provinces, and the Spanish and Austrian monarchies. The pressures for unification, therefore, were once again building, as in the 1620s. The first ruler to respond, although with all the ambiguities associated both with his Habsburg inheritance and with the conflicting demands of war with France on the one hand and the Ottoman empire on the other, was the Emperor Leopold I of Austria.[59] As Hungary was recaptured from the Turks between 1684 and 1699, a lobby in Vienna pressed for it to be treated, like Bohemia in the 1620s, as a conquered kingdom. But magnates and gentry were too strong, and the imperial administration too weak, for the traditional Magyar liberties to be easily suppressed; and the Rácócki rebellion of 1703–11, in defence of those liberties, drove home the message that the Hungarians should be handled with care.

Neither the government of Charles II of England nor that of Carlos II of Spain, both of them haunted by memories of the 1640s, was in a position to move more than obliquely towards a closer union of their disunited kingdoms, although revolt in Sicily in 1674–8 provided an opportunity for the Spanish Crown to reduce Messina's privileges.[60] It would take the accession of the new Bourbon dynasty to the Spanish throne in 1700, and the subsequent refusal of the Catalans, Aragonese and Valencians to accept its legitimacy, to create a situation in which the abolition of the traditional constitutional arrangements of the Crown of Aragon could once again be seriously contemplated by Madrid.

In Scotland Charles II had recourse to the well-tried techniques of patronage employed to such effect by his grandfather, James VI and I, but could get no further.[61] As in Spain, dynastic upheaval was to provide the catalyst in Britain for new moves towards unification. The need to protect the Glorious Revolution and the Protestant settlement of 1688–9, and the continuing anxiety over national security in time of warfare as long as the union of the Crowns remained incomplete, combined to create the conditions in which a more firmly grounded Anglo-Scottish union could again be seriously discussed. Ireland, as a savagely reconquered kingdom, remained a different matter.

Given the vast differences in their internal balance of forces and their international situation, it is not surprising that these three composite monarchies— the Austrian, the Spanish and the British—should have reordered themselves

---

[59] See Spielman, *Leopold I*, ch. 6; Evans, *Habsburg Monarchy*, ch. 7.
[60] For the background to these Sicilian troubles, see Luis Ribot Garcia, *La revuelta antiespañola de Mesina. Causas y antecedentes, 1591–1674* (Valladolid, 1982).
[61] Trevor-Roper, 'Union of Britain', p. 466.

in very different ways. But this general reordering, which occurred between 1707 and 1716, was in each instance one that bound their component parts closer to each other. The Austrian solution of 1711 was to strike a deal with the Hungarians, the Peace of Szatmár, in which continuing religious diversity and the survival of the Magyar constitution were guaranteed in return for acknowledgement of hereditary succession in the Habsburg male line. The road now lay open to the Dual Monarchy of 1867. In 1707 the English, too, had struck a deal, by which the Scots, like the Magyars, preserved their own laws and religious identity. But in its unique establishment of a parliamentary union, and in its measures to promote economic unification, the Anglo-Scottish union went much further than the Peace of Szatmár towards the creation of a cohesive and unitary state.

The most unitary solution of the three was that adopted by Madrid. Its victory over the rebels of Aragon, Valencia and Catalonia had given it a free hand, and the *Nueva Planta* of 1707–16 suppressed for ever the distinctive regimes of the provinces of the Crown of Aragon. But even here the measures for unification, which included the suppression of old institutions and the abolition of customs barriers, were not all-embracing. The Catalans, in spite of their preeminent role in the rebellion, kept their civil, and most of their penal, laws; and the compulsory use of the Castilian language was confined to the world of official acts and correspondence.[62]

In spite of such survivals, and in part because of them, there would be an accelerating European trend over the next two centuries towards the creation of unitary nation states. Composite monarchy, by contrast, looked weak and unimpressive. Its weaknesses were obvious, and have indeed been much emphasised in recent accounts: the inevitable resentments over royal absenteeism; the distribution of offices and exclusion from domestic and colonial markets; the difficulties inherent in securing an equitable apportionment of the costs of war and defence; the problem of religious diversity in kingdoms owing allegiance to a single monarch; and the danger of foreign intervention when grievances accumulated.[63]

Yet for all these weaknesses the composite monarchies of the sixteenth and seventeenth centuries had shown a remarkable resilience and capacity for survival. It is striking that over the period between the dissolution of the

---

[62] For the *Nueva Planta* in Aragon and Valencia, see Henry Kamen, *The War of Succession in Spain, 1700–1715* (London, 1969), chs 12–13; for Catalonia, see Joan Mercader i Riba, *Felip V i Catalunya*, 2nd edn (Barcelona, 1985).
[63] See Conrad Russell, 'The British Problem and the English Civil War', *History*, lxxii (1987), pp. 395–415.

Scandanavian Union of Kalmar in 1523 and the establishment of the Anglo-Scottish union of 1707, there were only three successful secessions from a composite monarchy—those of the northern provinces of the Netherlands from Spain in the 1570s; that of Sweden from Poland, with the renunciation of allegiance to Sigismund III in 1599; and that of Portugal from Spain in 1640.

How did unions so artificial in conception and so loose in articulation hold together for so long? Contiguity, as contemporaries asserted, was obviously a help, but it proved insufficient to keep Portugal within the Spanish Monarchy. 'Conformity', no doubt, was also a help; but conformity is a vague and ambiguous term. Did Scotland—another partner in a contiguous union—have more conformity with England than Portugal with Castile? Was the permanency of Scotland's union with England inevitable, in a way that Portugal's union with Castile was not? This seems hard to believe.

If we look at the general character of early modern Europe, with its profound respect for corporate structures and for traditional rights, privileges and customs, the union of provinces to each other *aeque principaliter* seems to fit well with the needs of the times. The very looseness of the association was in a sense its greatest strength. It allowed for a high degree of continuing local self-government at a time when monarchs were simply in no position to bring outlying kingdoms and provinces under tight royal control. At the same time it guaranteed to provincial elites continued enjoyment of their existing privileges combined with the potential benefits to be derived from participation in a wider association.

The extent to which such benefits actually materialised varied from union to union and from one period to another. In terms of military security and economic advantage, the benefits to Portugal of union with Castile looked much greater to the generation of 1580 than to that of 1640. The hopes of provincial elites for increased economic opportunities, and a steady flow of offices and honours, were all too often disappointed, but the seductions of the court and of a dominant rival culture could make them willing accomplices in the perpetuation of a union from which they still hoped for better things. The pressures for perpetuation, indeed, might come as much, or more, from provincial elites as from the central government. Even if disillusionment came, as it often did, where else were they to turn? As the provinces of the northern Netherlands found during the early years of their struggle against Spain, secessionist movements culminating in some form of republic were looked at askance in the monarchical world of early modern Europe. One reason for the success of the Portuguese revolt was that, in the Duke of Braganza, Portugal had a potentially legitimate king in waiting.

In so far as the perpetuation of these unions also depended on the deterrent of coercion, the rulers of multiple kingdoms possessed an advantage over those of single kingdoms in the additional resources on which they could draw in emergencies. The forces of one kingdom could be used to put down trouble in another. The financial and military reserves of Castile helped Philip II to keep control over Naples and Aragon; those of England enabled the Tudors to persist in their expensive attempts to tighten their hold on Ireland; the Austrian Habsburgs could draw on the resources of their patrimonial lands to keep up the pressure on the Magyars. Multiple monarchies presented multiple opportunities as well as multiple constraints.

The test of statesmanship for early modern rulers was whether they could realise the opportunities while remaining aware of the constraints. Forms of union that in the sixteenth century seemed adequate enough were beginning by the early seventeenth century to seem inadequate. But the pressures exerted by the state apparatus to achieve a more perfect union—conventionally conceived in terms of closer legal, institutional and cultural conformity to the model provided by the dominant partner in the association—only served to reinforce the sense of separate identity among populations threatened with absorption. This in turn raised the possibility of recourse to more drastic measures, including outright conquest and the large-scale transfer of peoples. Sir William Petty, Surveyor-General of Ireland, proposed a massive exchange of populations between England and Ireland; Leopold I's commissioners in the government of Hungary recommended preferential treatment for Germans in the resettlement of lands taken from the Turks, in order to temper unruly Hungarian blood with the loyal Germanic strain.[64]

The eighteenth-century fiscal-military state, with more power at its disposal than its seventeenth-century predecessor, also had more to offer in terms of employment and economic opportunities. Yet the 'enlightened' monarchies of the eighteenth century remained essentially composite; and closer integration, where sought, remained difficult to achieve, as the Emperor Joseph II discovered to his cost. The sudden upsurge of nationalism at the turn of the eighteenth and nineteenth centuries would give a greater impetus to the creation of a unitary nation state than royal decrees and the actions of bureaucrats had given it over many decades. Yet ironically, at this same moment, the beginnings of the Romantic movement were endowing national and ethnic diversity with a fresh aura of legitimacy by providing it with stronger literary, linguistic and historical

---

[64] M. Perceval-Maxwell, 'Ireland and the Monarchy in the Early Stuart Multiple Kingdom', *Historical Journal*, xxxiv (1991), p. 295; Spielman, *Leopold I*, pp. 139–40.

foundations. In consequence, in the unitary state as much as in its predecessor, the relationship of component regions and provinces both to each other and to the state itself would involve complex and constantly changing shifts in the balance of loyalties—shifts based on political calculation, economic realities and changing cultural attitudes.

Now that the inadequacies of that creation of the nineteenth century, the integrated nation state, are themselves in turn being painfully exposed, and union *aeque principaliter* again becomes the order of the day, the composite monarchy of the sixteenth and seventeenth centuries can begin to be seen for what it was—not simply as an unsatisfactory prelude to the construction of a more effective and permanent form of political association, but as one among several attempts to reconcile, in terms of contemporary needs and possibilities, the competing aspirations towards unity and diversity that have remained a constant of European history. As such, the composite monarchy had its successes as well as its failures. More perfect union, after all, is likely to have its imperfections in a world in which, to quote Bishop Palafox in the aftermath of the catastrophe of Olivares's plans for the union of Spain, Valencia grows oranges but not chestnuts, and Vizcaya grows chestnuts but not oranges, and that is how God made them.[65]

---

[65] Palafox y Mendoza, 'Juicio interior', pp. 145–6.

CHAPTER II

LEARNING FROM THE ENEMY: EARLY MODERN BRITAIN AND SPAIN

On 29 December 1956, Hugh Trevor-Roper wrote to tell me that he had cancelled a proposed visit to Spain. 'I had intended to go', he wrote, 'in connexion with the subject which I had chosen for the Ford Lectures, which I had confidently supposed that I would be asked to give.' But the Board of Electors, which moved, and still no doubt moves, in mysterious ways, decided otherwise. 'So now', wrote Trevor-Roper, 'instead of pursuing my thus frustrated studies, I am scheming revenge.' If his appointment to Oxford's Regius Chair of Modern History six months later gave him his revenge against the medievalists who blocked his selection as Ford's Lecturer, his lectures, sadly, remained unwritten and undelivered. The world was thus deprived of what would surely have been a scintillating survey of Anglo-Spanish relations between 1604 and 1660. Although the loss can never be made good, it none the less seemed to me appropriate, when I was honoured by the Trustees of the Dacre Trust with the invitation to inaugurate the annual series of Dacre Lectures, that I should choose a topic related to the theme of those undelivered lectures. I do so as a tribute not only to the greatest historical essayist of my lifetime, but also to a man to whom I remain for ever grateful for the kindness and generosity shown to a young historian at the start of his professional career.

Hugh Trevor-Roper first went to Spain in 1951—five years before his letter to me—and he wrote to Bernard Berenson that his visit had '*almost*—but not quite' seduced his affections away from Italy. He was deeply impressed by 'the wonderful, high, endless, golden emptiness of the Castilian plateau', and by 'the ancient *gravitas* of even the poorest Spanish peasant.'[1] The country, as he wrote, fascinated him, and, as a historian, he was fascinated, too, by the Spanish past. Preparing for a visit to the great national archive of Simancas in the province of Valladolid in the summer of 1953, he wrote to Berenson: 'What wonderful subjects of history there are in Spain, if only there were historians to exploit them . . .'[2] Always alert to the similarities and differences between Spain and other contemporaneous societies, he was convinced that a knowledge of the history of Spain was essential for understanding developments in early modern Europe as a whole—a conviction reinforced by his admiration for Fernand Braudel and his *The Mediterranean and the Mediterranean World in the Age of Philip II*. It is not surprising, then, that he regularly gave an undergraduate lecture course on sixteenth-century Spain and Europe; and his Ford Lectures, devoted to the seventeenth century, would have been a logical extension of some of the themes developed in that course. If they had ever been given, they would, I suspect, have dwelt heavily on the activities of Spain's famous ambassador to the court of James I, the Count of Gondomar. Trevor-Roper once asked me to try and find for him a rare Gondomar publication, and he read the four volumes of Gondomar's published correspondence closely enough to produce a typescript of corrections, in which he identified Spanish pensioners in James I's court who appeared only under pseudonyms, while also pointing out that Julius Caesar was not a pseudonym, as the Spanish editor not unreasonably supposed, but none other than Sir Julius Caesar, master of the rolls.

This essay says less about Gondomar than Trevor-Roper would have said, and it largely bypasses the diplomatic relationship between Habsburg Spain and Stuart England that would presumably have been at the heart of his lectures. We still do not have a full picture of this troubled relationship in the first half of the seventeenth century—a relationship that is only understandable in the context of the confrontation between the Spain of Philip II and the England of Elizabeth I in the last decades of the sixteenth century.[3] In one of his letters, Gondomar recalled that the Emperor Charles V liked to say: '*Guerra con toda la tierra y paz con Inglaterra*' ('War with the whole world and

---

[1] *Letters from Oxford: Hugh Trevor-Roper to Bernard Berenson*, ed. Richard Davenport-Hines (London, 2006), pp. 72–3 (25 Sept. 1951).
[2] *Ibid.*, p. 122 (9 Aug. 1953).
[3] I have given a summary account of this relationship, under the title of 'A Troubled Relationship: Spain and Great Britain, 1604–1655', in Jonathan Brown and John Elliott, eds, *The Sale of the Century: Artistic Relations between Spain and Great Britain, 1604–1655* (New Haven, Conn. and London/Prado Museum, Madrid, 2002), pp. 17–38.

peace with England').[4] In the years immediately following the death of Mary Tudor in 1558, the traditional Anglo-Spanish amity was visibly crumbling, and, by the 1580s, in spite of the natural caution of the two monarchs, the breach that had opened between their countries had widened into a chasm. The failure of Philip's 'Enterprise of England' in 1588 was followed by sixteen years of open war, which would only end in 1604, after the deaths of both Philip and Elizabeth.

The events of the reigns of Mary and Elizabeth were to colour everything that followed. They were to create mutual perceptions that lingered on into the twentieth century and have perhaps not quite been dispelled, even today. In both countries, the religious conflict sharpened the sense of national identity, and helped shape images of the other which hardened into stereotypes. England now proudly identified itself with the Protestant cause. Simultaneously it entered the collective Spanish consciousness as a nation of heretics. This negative image of the English was nurtured by reports of persecution spread by Catholic exiles who had taken refuge in Spain.[5] In 1588 the Jesuit Pedro de Ribadaneyra, who had been in London at the time of Mary Tudor's death, offered Spanish readers a graphic account of the origins and development of the Protestant Reformation in England in his *Historia eclesiástica del Cisma del reino de Inglaterra*. 'A kingdom', he wrote, 'which was formerly a delightful paradise, a garden of the sweetest and most beautiful flowers', had been transformed into 'a cave of wild beasts, a refuge of traitors, a harbour of corsairs, a nest of serpents.'[6]

The English, for their part, responded in kind. It was in the second half of the sixteenth century that the Black Legend of Spanish fanaticism and cruelty etched itself into the English national consciousness. This dark image of Spain was compounded of a number of elements: unhappy memories of the reign of Mary Tudor; reports of atrocities committed by the Duke of Alba and his army in the Netherlands; tales of the Spanish Inquisition that circulated endlessly around Protestant Europe; accounts of the extinction of the indigenous peoples of America, given additional credibility by the publication in 1583 of the first English version of Bartolomé de Las Casas's *Short Account of the Destruction of the Indies*; and lurid stories of Philip II and his court, attributed

---

[4] *Correspondencia oficial de Don Diego Sarmiento de Acuña, Conde de Gondomar*, in *Documentos inéditos para la historia de España*, 4 vols (Madrid, 1936–45), ii, pp. 102–3.

[5] See Albert J. Loomie, *The Spanish Elizabethans: The English Exiles at the Court of Philip II* (New York, 1963).

[6] Pedro de Ribadaneyra, S.I., *Historias de la Contrarreforma* (*Biblioteca de Autores Cristianos*, Madrid, 1945), 196, p. 1.

to the king's former secretary, Antonio Pérez, who found temporary refuge in England in 1593.[7]

These negative perceptions in both England and Spain created a climate of public opinion in the two countries that complicated and hampered every official attempt at rapprochement in the decades following the Anglo-Spanish peace treaty of 1604. The Count of Gondomar, using all his remarkable diplomatic skills to promote a dynastic alliance, was the most hated man in Jacobean London, as the spectacular dramatic success of Thomas Middleton's *A Game at Chess* (1624) reminds us. The prospect of a marriage between Charles, Prince of Wales, and Philip IV's sister, the Infanta María, was contemplated with deep mistrust in Spain; and when Charles returned home in the autumn of 1623 from his disastrous trip to Madrid without a bride, his homecoming was a cause for wild celebrations among his future subjects, and provoked a fresh wave of anti-Spanish sentiment that propelled England into five years of war with Spain in 1625.[8] During the 1630s Charles I's fresh attempts to strengthen his ties with Spain contributed to the widening of the rift between him and his subjects. Twenty years later, when Cromwell, in Elizabethan mode, launched his Western Design of 1655 for an attack on the Spanish Caribbean, he drew on a deep reservoir of hostility to a country that was still perceived as aspiring to universal monarchy.[9] 'Why, truly', said Cromwell in his famous speech at the opening of Parliament in September 1656, 'your great enemy is the Spaniard . . . He is a natural enemy, he is naturally so.'[10]

Yet there is another, and less well known, side to the story of the Anglo-Spanish relationship in the early modern period. As the dominant European power, Spain was a source of hypnotic fascination for other European states; and while its political hegemony was not accompanied by cultural hegemony,

---

[7] See William S. Maltby, *The Black Legend in England: The Development of Anti-Spanish Sentiment, 1558–1660* (Durham, N.C., 1971). For a comprehensive study of the image of early modern Spain among non-Spaniards, see J. N. Hillgarth, *The Mirror of Spain, 1500–1700* (Ann Arbor, Mich., 2000).

[8] For the Spanish Match and its consequences, see Thomas Cogswell, *The Blessed Revolution: English Politics and the Coming of War, 1621–1624* (Cambridge, 1989); Brown and Elliott, eds, *The Sale of the Century*; Glyn Redworth, *The Prince and the Infanta: The Cultural Politics of the Spanish Match* (New Haven, Conn. and London, 2003); Alexander Samson, ed., *The Spanish Match: Prince Charles's Journey to Madrid, 1623* (Aldershot, 2006).

[9] See, for instance, Benjamin Worsley, *The Advocate* (1652), cited in Steven C. A. Pincus, *Protestantism and Patriotism: Ideologies and the Making of English Foreign Policy, 1650–1668* (Cambridge, 1996), p. 48: 'The design of Spain is, to get the universal monarchy of Christendom.'

[10] *The Writings and Speeches of Oliver Cromwell*, ed. Wilbur Cortez Abbott, 4 vols (Cambridge, Mass., 1947; repr. Oxford, 1988), iv, p. 261.

which rested firmly with Italy, Spain's cultural influence—expressed in language, fashion, literature, the theatre and devotional writings—extended widely, and sometimes ran deep. Elizabeth I, Lord Burghley and Sir Robert Cecil were all proficient in Spanish, and Burghley, who was fascinated by Spain and its literature, may have owned the largest private collection of Spanish books—fifty-six titles—in Elizabethan England.[11] From the 1590s Spanish became a fashionable language to learn,[12] and useful aides began to be published, like John Minsheu's *A Dictionarie in Spanish and English* of 1599, and his *A Spanish Grammar*, and *Pleasant and Delightful Dialogues* in Spanish and English.[13]

For those who lacked the inclination or the ability to read works in the original, a spate of translations from the Spanish appeared in the opening decades of the seventeenth century, headed by Thomas Shelton's 1612 version of the first part of *Don Quijote*, seven years after the book's publication in Spain. In spite of the religious divide, Spanish devotional literature found English readers, and John Donne and Richard Crashaw were among those who turned for inspiration to the Spanish mystics. Donne wrote of his library that he met there 'more Authors of that nation than of any other.'[14] As for dress, Spanish black came to be regarded as the height of elegance. 'I have heard', wrote Francis Bacon in 1616, 'that in Spain (a grave nation, whom in this I wish we might imitate) they do allow the players and courtesans the vanity of rich and costly cloaths, but to sober men and matrons they permit it not, upon pain of infamy.'[15] But since his words were addressed to the future Duke of Buckingham, they were no doubt wasted.

English interest in Spain was not in general reinforced by first-hand acquaintance with the country. Few English, other than Catholic exiles, made their way to the peninsula during the years of open war under Elizabeth, but with the return of peace in 1604 the situation changed. A large number of

---

[11] Gustav Ungerer, 'The Printing of Spanish Books in Elizabethan England', *The Library*, 5th series, 20 (1965), pp. 177–229. See Appendix II for a list of Spanish titles in Burghley's collection.

[12] Gustav Ungerer, *Anglo-Spanish Relations in Tudor Literature* (Bern, 1956), pp. 168–71.

[13] Hillgarth, *Mirror of Spain*, pp. 449–51. A facsimile edition of John Minsheu, *A Dictionarie in Spanish and English*, with a short preliminary study, was published by the University of Málaga in 2000.

[14] Cited by Ungerer, 'The Printing of Spanish Books', p. 182 n. 2; and see Peter Russell, 'English Seventeenth-Century Interpretations of Spanish Literature', *Atlante*, 1 (1953), pp. 65–77; R. V. Young, *Richard Crashaw and the Spanish Golden Age* (New Haven, Conn. and London, 1982).

[15] *The Works of Francis Bacon*, ed. James Spedding, 14 vols (London, 1858–74), xiii, p. 23 (Letter of Advice to George Villiers).

courtiers had their first, not always welcome, exposure to the sights and sounds of Spain in 1605 when the Earl of Nottingham travelled to Valladolid for the ratification of the peace treaty with an entourage five hundred strong, and in the succeeding years the resumption of trading relations brought English merchants back to the peninsula. Yet Spain, with its difficult travelling conditions, its atrocious inns, and above all its religious hazards, never became part of the English Grand Tour.[16]

However, the unexpected arrival in Madrid of Charles, Prince of Wales, in the spring of 1623, added a whole new dimension to the cultural as well as to the political relationship of Spain and England. His nearly six months in Madrid introduced the prince to a court, and a court culture, very different from the disorderly court of his father James I. On his accession to the throne in 1625 Charles I's attempts to introduce a greater degree of gravity and decorum into English court ritual and etiquette would seem to reflect the strength of the impression made on him by his exposure to the elaborate rituals of the court of Philip IV, so carefully designed to keep the monarch at a distance.[17] Charles's exposure, too, to the extraordinary Spanish royal collection of paintings, with its superb Titians and other Venetian masters, sharpened his own collecting instincts and helped turn him into one of the greatest princely art collectors of the seventeenth century.[18] He was also able to see with his own eyes the Escorial, which he toured with Philip on the first stage of his journey home. The Escorial had long been a subject of fascination in the capitals of Europe. Lord Burghley owned a remarkable drawing of the building in the process of construction in the 1570s, endorsed in his own hand as 'The King of Spaine's house' (Fig. 1).[19] When Charles's thoughts turned to the rebuilding of the palace of Whitehall, the Escorial seems to have been very much on his mind; and in the days of his captivity in Carisbrook Castle in 1647–8 he was to be found poring over the pages of Juan Bautista Villalpando's three-volume commentary on the prophet Ezekiel, with its

---

[16] See John Stoye, *English Travellers Abroad, 1604–1667* (1952; revised edn, New Haven, Conn. and London, 1989), chs 10 and 11. The visit of Nottingham's deputation is described on pp. 233–40.

[17] Kevin Sharpe, *The Personal Rule of Charles I* (New Haven, Conn. and London, 1992), pp. 216–19. For Spanish court culture, see J. H. Elliott, *Spain and its World, 1500–1700* (New Haven, Conn. and London, 1989), ch. 7.

[18] See Brown and Elliott, eds, *The Sale of the Century*; Jonathan Brown, *Kings and Connoisseurs: Collecting Art in Seventeenth-Century Europe* (New Haven, Conn. and London, 1995), ch. 1.

[19] George Kubler, *Building the Escorial* (Princeton, N. J., 1982), p. 21. For a discussion of the drawing and its authorship, see Pedro Navascués Palacio, 'La obra como espectáculo: el dibujo Hatfield', in *Las Casas Reales. El Palacio* (IV Centenario del Monasterio de El Escorial, Madrid, 1986), pp. 55–67.

Figure 1 Anon., *The Escorial During Construction* (Hatfield House, Hertfordshire).

illustrations for the reconstruction of the Temple of Solomon in Jerusalem, which was seen as the model for Philip II's monastery-palace (Fig. 2).[20]

Spanish influence on the behaviour and attitudes of Charles I is one example, if at an elevated level, of a cultural relationship between England and Spain whose variety and richness have yet to be fully explored. But the story of the relationship, cultural as well as political, deserves to be set in the wider context, as relevant today as it was in the sixteenth and seventeenth centuries, of the inevitably ambivalent responses of lesser states to a hegemonic power. Between the 1550s and the 1650s Spain, with overwhelming military and financial resources at its command, exercised a hegemony, if at times a precarious one, over the western world. The response of those who feel themselves threatened by, or under pressure from, a state that possesses overwhelming

---

[20] See Roy Strong, *Britannia Triumphans: Inigo Jones, Rubens and Whitehall Palace* (London, 1980), pp. 56–63. Although the idea for a palace on the Solomonic model may already have been mooted in the reign of James I and taken up by Inigo Jones, it would seem natural to expect that the impression made on Charles by his visit to the Escorial would have given a new impetus to the project.

Figure 2 Elevation of the Temple of Solomon.

power and is assumed to be motivated by aspirations to global domination, is one that shades from distrust and suspicion into outright hostility. But at the same time the hostility is liable to be accompanied by a degree of admiration, tinged with envy. What, if anything, can be learned from the enemy?

Britain, like Spain, was one of Europe's composite monarchies, and was made still more composite by the dynastic union with Scotland in 1603.[21] In the debate about the form that the union should take following the accession of James VI and I, it was natural that participants should turn to the Spanish example. In 'A Brief Discourse Touching the Happy Union of the Kingdoms of England and Scotland', Sir Francis Bacon observed that 'The lot of Spain was to have several kingdoms of the continent (Portugal only except) to be united, in an age not long past; and now in our age that of Portugal also, which was the last that held out, to be incorporate with the rest.'[22] He saw forms of union as including 'union in name', language, laws, manners and employments, and noted, under 'union in name' that 'the common name of Spain (no doubt) hath been a special means of the better union and conglutination of the several kingdoms of Castile, Arragon, Granada, Navarra, Valentia, Catalonia, and the rest, comprehending now lately Portugal.'[23] Sir Henry Savile, for his part, singled out the union between Castile and Portugal in 1580 as 'in mine opinion the likest to ours'.[24]

In the event, both the Anglo-Scottish union and that of Portugal with Castile proved, as seen from London and Madrid, to be far from perfect unions. In 1625 the Count-Duke of Olivares launched his grand scheme for a closer union of the various kingdoms and provinces of the composite Spanish Monarchy with a call for a military union, a Union of Arms, designed to ensure that all of them came to the help of any part of the Monarchy subjected to attack. Two years later Secretary Coke took a leaf out of the Spanish book. Remarking on similar developments in the Holy Roman Empire and France, he noted that 'the Spaniards by a late union or association have joined all their remote provinces for mutual defence, and [are enabled] to raise thereby great forces for the enlarging of their monarchy both by land and sea. My proposition therefore is to learn wisdom from our enemies . . . .' After commenting on the desirability of a closer association of the Protestant powers of Europe, he continued: 'But our union at home is that which most importeth us, and therefore His Majesty may be pleased to consider whether it be not necessary

---

[21] See above, ch. 1.

[22] Spedding, ed., *Works of Francis Bacon*, x, pp. 90–9, at p. 92.

[23] *Ibid.*, p. 97.

[24] 'Historicall Collections', reprinted in *The Jacobean Union: Six Tracts of 1604*, ed. Bruce R. Galloway and Brian P. Levack (Edinburgh, 1985), p. 229. Cited above, ch. 1, n. 38.

upon the same grounds of State as the Spaniards have built to unite his three kingdoms in a strict union and obligation each to other for their mutual defence when any of them shall be assailed, every one with such a proportion of horse, foot, or shipping as may be rateably thought fit.'[25]

In the Spanish Monarchy the plans for a Union of Arms led to the formation of a joint Castilian–Portuguese expeditionary force for the recovery of Brazil from the Dutch, and in Britain to the creation of the Earl of Morton's Scottish regiment. They also led to the unsuccessful negotiation over the Graces or royal concessions to Catholic Old English landowners in Ireland in return for subsidies and to the similarly unsuccessful attempts of Olivares to secure the military cooperation of the Crown of Aragon. In both monarchies, efforts by the Crown to move towards a more perfect union were in the end to prove dangerously counter-productive. Neither Charles I nor Olivares took to heart Bacon's sagacious counsel that 'unnatural hasting thereof doth disturb the work, and not dispatch it.'[26]

Preoccupation with the strength of the ties that bound disparate kingdoms and provinces together was a natural feature of life in the composite monarchies of early modern Europe. But this preoccupation, which was to become intense in the first half of the seventeenth century, needs to be related to the wider early modern European debate about the greatness and durability of states, and the sources of their power. The terms of this debate, which is associated in particular with the names of Giovanni Botero and Tommaso Campanella, both of them writing at the turn of the sixteenth and seventeenth centuries, had been shaped, and to some extent set, by the rise of Spain to its position of dominance, and its alleged aspirations after universal monarchy. How had Spain attained to this position of overwhelming preeminence? How could its global ambitions be halted in their tracks? What could others learn from Spain's successes—and also from its failures? As England moved in the second half of the sixteenth century into confrontation with the Spain of Philip II, these were questions that became of pressing concern to the English political establishment.

---

[25] For the Union of Arms, see J. H. Elliott, *The Count-Duke of Olivares: The Statesman in an Age of Decline* (New Haven, Conn. and London, 1986), ch. 7. Sir John Coke's proposal is calendared in *State Papers Domestic*, vol. DXXVII, *Addenda, 1625–1649*, no. 44 (1627), pp. 241–2. See also Conrad S. R. Russell, 'Monarchies, Wars and Estates in England, France and Spain, c.1580–c.1640', *Legislative Studies Quarterly* 7 (1982), pp. 205–20, and his *The Fall of the British Monarchies, 1637–1642* (Oxford, 1991), pp. 27–8.
[26] Spedding, ed., *Works of Francis Bacon*, x, p. 98.

The possession of overseas empire—an empire rich in precious metals—set Spain apart from its European rivals. Already in the 1550s the marriage of Mary Tudor had awakened a new English interest in Spain, and prompted one or two of Philip and Mary's subjects to take a closer look at the Spanish transatlantic enterprise. In 1558, benefiting from the closeness of Anglo-Spanish relations at that moment, the chief pilot of the Muscovy Company, Stephen Borough, was allowed to tour the Casa de Contratación—the House of Trade—in Seville, and was much impressed by the systematic instruction given to Spanish pilots in seafaring skills. He wanted a similar tuition to be given to English mariners—a theme that would later be taken up by Richard Hakluyt—and in 1561, at Borough's instigation, Richard Eden translated for English readers *The Arte of Navigation*, the seafaring manual published by Martín Cortés in Seville ten years before.[27]

Through this and other translations Eden sought to provide information for his fellow-countrymen about Spain's overseas activities, and encourage them to follow in Spain's footsteps.[28] But it was only in the years around 1580, as Spain and England moved towards open conflict, that Eden's message about the desirability of English overseas expansion began to find an audience. During the 1580s, as privateering in the Caribbean was followed by the first transatlantic English colonising ventures in Newfoundland and off the Carolina coast, Richard Hakluyt the younger took up where Eden had left off, and embarked on his lifelong campaign to persuade England to follow the Spanish example and grasp its own imperial destiny.[29]

As a result of the efforts of Hakluyt and others, by 1607, the year of the foundation at Jamestown of England's first successful settlement on the North American mainland, a considerable amount of information was available to interested English readers about Spain's conquering and colonising enterprises in the New World. When Bartolomé de Las Casas' *Short Account of the Destruction of the Indies* appeared in English in 1583, it was significantly re-titled *The Spanish Colonie*. In that same year, Sir George Peckham, a leading

---

[27] David W. Waters, *The Art of Navigation in England in Elizabethan and Early Stuart Times* (London, 1958), pp. 103–6; and see Appendix 16 for Hakluyt's efforts to establish a navigational lectureship in London.

[28] See John Parker, *Books to Build an Empire* (Amsterdam, 1965), ch. 4.

[29] For a recent comprehensive survey of Hakluyt's writings and career, see Peter C. Mancall, *Hakluyt's Promise: An Elizabethan's Obsession for an English America* (New Haven, Conn. and London, 2007). Jonathan Hart, *Representing the New World: The English and French Uses of the Example of Spain* (New York and Basingstoke, 2000), is a useful compendium of English and French references to the Spanish example in overseas colonisation.

promoter of Sir Humphrey Gilbert's voyages, could list Peter Martyr's *Decades*, and Gómara's and Zárate's accounts of the conquest of Mexico and Peru respectively, as being 'extant to be had in the English tongue'. 'I do therefore heartily wish', he continued, 'that seeing it hath pleased almightie God of his infinite mercy at the length, to awake some of our worthy Countrey men, out of that drowsie dreame, wherein we all have so long slumbered: that wee may nowe not suffer it to quaile for want of maintenance.'[30] Persistence and determination were required if England was to emulate Spain in founding a colonial empire.

It was above all in the circle of Sir Walter Raleigh that the dream of an English empire on the model of the Spanish was most enthusiastically embraced. Raleigh himself might fail in his quest for El Dorado, but his personal misfortunes did not dampen his enthusiasm for the cause. In his *History of the World*, written as the shadows were closing in around him, this arch-enemy of Spain penned a message for his countrymen that reads in retrospect as a last bequest: '. . . I cannot forbear to commend the patient virtue of the Spaniards; we seldom or never find that any nation hath endured so many misadventures and miseries as the Spaniards have done, in their Indian discoveries; yet persisting in their enterprises with an invincible constancy, they have annexed to their kingdom so many goodly provinces, as bury the remembrance of all dangers past.'[31]

Raleigh wrote these words around 1610 when the young Jamestown settlement was faltering and could well have gone the way of the Roanoke Island venture. Spanish constancy and persistence as models for the pioneers of English colonisation were in fact to be a continuing refrain of the early colonising enterprise. Although Hakluyt and others had injected a strong commercial element into their proposals for overseas expansion, the first settlers of Virginia, and most obviously Captain John Smith, tended to cast themselves in the role of Spanish *conquistadores*. The role was one that called for courage and resolution in the face of adversity. Following the 'Great Massacre' by the Indians in 1622 of some 400 of the 1,240 Virginia settlers, Edward Waterhouse, a Virginia Company official, published a treatise in which he used the Spanish example to rally colonists and investors at a moment of discouragement: 'Since the *Spaniard* (as we see) in his Plantations

---

[30] Richard Hakluyt, *The Principall Navigations Voyages and Discoveries of the English Nation* (facsimile of the 1589 edition, 2 vols, Cambridge, 1965), ii, p. 704.
[31] Sir Walter Raleigh, *History of the World*, in *The Works of Sir Walter Raleigh, Kt.*, ed. William Oldys and Thomas Birch, 8 vols (Oxford, 1829), vi, pp. 113–14.

hath gone [through] farre more hazards, and greater difficulties then ever wee have had, we therefore in looking to what is past, upon great reason ought likewise not to be deterred, but so much the rather invited to proceed with constancy and courage.'[32]

In the eyes of Company officials in London, the Virginia massacre of 1622 underlined the need to follow the Spanish example by concentrating colonists in cities and towns. In a letter to the colony's governor and council, the Company insisted that the settlers, instead of straggling along the shores of the Chesapeake, should stay close together in order to defend themselves against Indian attacks: '. . . that this is the most proper, and successful manner of proceeding in new plantations, beside those of former ages, the example of the Spaniards in the West Indies doth fully instance . . .'[33] But if the lesson was obvious to Company officials, it was less obvious to the Virginia settlers themselves. In their eyes there were better, if more brutal, ways of dealing with the threat of Indian attacks. 'Our first work', wrote the governor, Sir Francis Wyatt, 'is expulsion of the Salvages . . .'[34]

Expulsion—now known as ethnic cleansing—was a device that had already been employed in the Ulster Plantation. It was also a device adopted on a massive scale in the Iberian Peninsula, from where some 300,000 moriscos were deported between 1609 and 1614. Sir John Davies, advocating the removal of the 'ancient' Irish tenants in a letter of November 1610 to Sir Robert Cecil, alluded directly not only to past practice in the Roman empire and in Ireland itself, but also to recent or current events in Spain: 'the Spaniards lately removed all the Moors out of Grenada into Barbary, without providing them with any new seats there.'[35] But originally it had seemed that there were other, less drastic, ways of dealing with indigenous populations, including the native Irish. Sir Henry Sidney, lord deputy of Ireland in the 1560s, had spent three years in Spain as Mary Tudor's envoy, and may well have had the New World in mind as he laid his plans for the colonisation of Ulster. If the Spaniards could tame and civilise the barbarous Aztecs, could not the English do the

---

[32] Edward Waterhouse, *A Declaration of the State of the Colony in Virginia (1622)*, facsimile edn (Amsterdam and New York, 1970), p. 31. See also Sir William Alexander, *An Encouragement to Colonies* (London, 1624), p. 8, for words to a similar effect.

[33] Cited in J. H. Elliott, *Empires of the Atlantic World: Britain and Spain in America, 1492–1830* (New Haven, Conn. and London, 2006), p. 42.

[34] Cited in *ibid.*, p. 85.

[35] *Historical Tracts by Sir John Davies, Attorney General* (Dublin, 1787), pp. 283–4. See Jane H. Ohlmeyer, ' "Civilizing of those Rude Partes": Colonization within Britain and Ireland', in *The Oxford History of the British Empire*, ed. Wm. Roger Louis *et al.*, 5 vols (Oxford, 1998), i, pp. 135–7.

same with the barbarous Irish?[36] But the Irish, it transpired, proved less amenable than the Aztecs to the imposition of civilised graces.

Confronted first by the Irish, and then by native Americans, the English continued to express at least a grudging admiration for the success of the Spaniards in 'reducing' their Indian subjects to Christianity and civility,[37] even if the form of Christianity they introduced was full of popish superstitions. At the same time, the tales of atrocity reported by Las Casas and others had left them well aware of the brutality of Spanish methods. 'The Spaniard', wrote Richard Eburne in his *A Plain Pathway to Plantations* of 1624, 'hath reasonably *civilized*, and better might if he had not so much tyrannized, people far more savage and bestial' than any of those in the British settlements.[38]

Early advocates of English colonisation in the New World hoped to avoid Spanish-style brutality, to which they attributed the demographic disaster that had overtaken the indigenous peoples of Spanish America. Robert Johnson, remarking that 'the honor of a king consisteth in the multitude of subjects', urged the English in his *Nova Britannia* to convert '(not as the West Indies was converted) with rapiers point and musket shot, murdering so many millions of naked Indians, as their stories do relate, but by faire and loving meanes, suiting to our English natures . . .'[39] Unhappily, our English natures proved unequal to the task. At an early stage, both in Virginia and New England, relations with the indigenous population turned sour. The English, in spite of their initial optimism about the tractability of the indigenous population of North America, were to find it easier to expel or marginalise their Indians than to incorporate them, as the Spaniards sought to incorporate them, within the social and religious framework of colonial societies in process of construction.

The Spaniards, unlike the English settlers, managed to turn their Indians into a docile labour force. The proof of their success was to be seen in the

---

[36] See Nicholas Canny, *The Elizabethan Conquest of Ireland: A Pattern Established* (Hassocks, Sussex, 1976), pp. 66, 126 and 133–4 for the possible influence of Spanish colonisation on Sidney and others in their plans for the submission and colonisation of Ireland. Also David Beers Quinn, *The Elizabethans and the Irish* (Ithaca, N. Y., 1966), pp. 106–7.

[37] See Elliott, *Empires*, pp. 11 and 66, for Christopher Carleill in 1583 on 'reducing the savage people to Christianity and civility'. See also p. 72 for William Strachey's awkward question in his *The Historie of Travell into Virginia Britania* (1612) as to whether the English had 'lesser meanes, fainter spiritts, or a charity more cold, or a Religion more shamefull' that prevented them from imitating Spanish successes in converting the Indians.

[38] Richard Eburne, *A Plain Pathway to Plantations (1624)*, ed. Louis B. Wright (Ithaca, N.Y., 1962), p. 56.

[39] Robert Johnson, *Nova Britannia* (1609), in Peter Force, *Tracts and other papers relating principally to the origin, settlement and progress of the colonies in North America*, 4 vols (Washington, DC, 1836–46), i, no. 6, p. 14.

steady stream of silver that flowed into Seville from the mines of Mexico and Peru and was conventionally regarded as the source of Spain's imperial power. Sir Benjamin Rudyard took his place in a long line of commentators when he observed in the House of Commons in 1624: '. . . they are his mines in the West Indies, which minister fuell to feed his vast ambitious desire of universall monarchy.'[40] The awareness of Spanish dependence on American silver had inspired in the reign of Elizabeth the various projects for attacks on the West Indies and on the Spanish treasure fleets, but it also raised questions about the depth and extent of Spain's power if it were once deprived of the silver of the Indies. Hakluyt, although an early advocate of commercial coloni-sation, to which the English would turn by default once they had failed to find precious metals in North America,[41] also favoured an assault on Spain's American possessions. In his *Discourse of Western Planting* of 1584, he asserted that 'any reasonable man that knoweth the barrenness, desolation and want of men in Spain . . . must needs confess that they have very simple forces there. The provinces which he holdeth are indeed many, yet more denuded than ever was any Empire since the creation of the world. . . . His might and greatness is not such as *prima facie* it may seem to be . . .'[42]

In fact, Spain's military power remained formidable, as English soldiers serving in the Netherlands could confirm. Belatedly, in the last decade of the sixteenth century, Spanish treatises on warfare, either in the original or in trans-lation, began to attract serious attention in England. Sir George Carey would bequeath four such treatises, all in Spanish, to the Bodleian Library in Oxford.[43] Yet at the same time the optimism generated by the defeat of the Armada in 1588, and the setbacks suffered by Spain in the final years of Philip II, helped to reinforce the sense of Spanish vulnerability, and inspire the hope that the days of Spanish hegemony were drawing to a close. Sir Henry Wotton, in his *The State of Christendom*, written in 1594, gave reasons for believing that 'neither is his power greatly to be feared, nor his wealth far exceeding her Majesties and

---

[40] L. F. Stock, *Proceedings of the British Parliaments Respecting North America*, 2 vols (Washington, 1924–7), i, p. 62 (19 May 1624).

[41] For the commercialising of English colonisation, see Carole Shammas, 'English Commercial Development and American Colonization, 1560–1620', in *The Westward Enterprise: English Activities in Ireland, the Atlantic and America 1480–1650*, ed. K. R. Andrews, N. P. Canny and P. E. Hair (Liverpool, 1978), ch. 8.

[42] *The Original Writings and Correspondence of the Two Richard Hakluyts*, ed. E. G. R. Taylor, 2nd series, 2 vols (Hakluyt Society, London, 1935), vol. 77, p. 251 (*The Discourse of Western Planting*, ch. 8).

[43] Ungerer, *Anglo-Spanish Relations*, pp. 60–7.

other Princes substance.'[44] Those like Sir Walter Raleigh who were opposed to any peace negotiations with Spain, naturally tended to emphasise, and indeed overemphasise, Spanish weakness, in the hope of being able to deliver a decisive strike against a power described by Wotton as 'our mortal and professed enemy'.[45] 'The Spanish empire', wrote Raleigh in the early years of the reign of James I, 'hath been greatly shaken, and hath begun in late years to decline. . . . And commonly, when great monarchies begin once in the least to decline, their dissipation will soon follow after.'[46]

In speaking of 'decline'—a word that Spanish commentators were themselves beginning to use at this same moment as they analysed the problems confronting their homeland [47]—Raleigh, encouraged by the lessons of history, was situating Spain in the standard narrative of imperial trajectory. Empires rose and fell, and what was to prevent the English nation, if it acted with resolution, picking up the baton now falling from the faltering grasp of Spain, and striking out courageously on the road that led to worldwide empire?

Although the terms of the narrative were shaped by reference to the fate of imperial Rome, Spain's weakness would also come to be analysed in relation to a developing international discourse about the true sources of national power and prosperity. The Dutch, in successfully defying the overwhelming might of Spain, had also defied the conventional wisdom. Without any obvious natural resources other than the industry and enterprise of its people, a small state, it seemed, could not only hold its own against the greatest power on earth, but had also found the keys that would unlock new and unsuspected sources of wealth.

The success of the Dutch played into a widening debate about bullion and the balance of trade, overseas empire and size of population. Giovanni Botero, in his highly influential *The Reason of State* of 1589, had helped popularise the notion that underpopulation was a source of Spanish weakness. But he also argued, somewhat improbably, that a scattered empire was as secure and lasting as a compact one, and that Spain's empire, 'which might otherwise appear scattered and unwieldy', should be accounted 'united and compact' because it was held together by Spain's power at sea.[48] Naval power was coming to be seen as the key to survival and success. Francis Bacon, in reviewing the

---

[44] Sir Henry Wotton, *The State of Christendom* (London, 1657), p. 110.
[45] *Ibid.*, p. 2.
[46] 'A Discourse Touching a War with Spain', in Raleigh, *Works*, viii, 8, p. 309.
[47] See Elliott, *Spain and its World*, p. 248.
[48] Giovanni Botero, *The Reason of State*, trans. P. J. and D. P. Waley (London, 1956), pp. 143–6 and 11–12.

case for war with Spain in 1624, argued, as against Botero, that the dispersed character of Spain's empire made it vulnerable, and that it was the general opinion that the combined fleets of England and the United Provinces could beat the Spaniards at sea. 'If that be so', he wrote, 'the links of that chain whereby they hold their greatness are dissolved.'[49]

The humiliating failure of the English in the Anglo-Spanish war of 1625–30 makes it clear that Bacon, like others before him, had underestimated Spanish resilience, and overestimated English naval capacity and the possibility of joint action with the Dutch. In spite of the revolts of the 1640s which seemed to threaten the Spanish Monarchy with imminent collapse, policy discussions in London continued to be haunted by the spectre of Spain's ambitions for universal monarchy, and it is significant that Tommaso Campanella's *A Discourse Touching the Spanish Monarchy*, written in the belief that Spain was God's chosen instrument for worldwide empire, first appeared in English translation in 1653.[50] In fact, the disappointing outcome of Cromwell's Western Design in 1655 showed that Spain still retained the capacity to defend its empire of the Indies, but during the 1660s it became increasingly apparent that the days of its European hegemony were at an end. English fears over projects for universal monarchy would now shift from the Spain of Philip IV to the France of Louis XIV, and Sir Richard Fanshawe was instructed in 1663, when embarking on his mission to Lisbon and Madrid, to represent to the Spanish ministers that 'the Monarchy of Spain is fallen to a great declination, more especially in maritime strength. . . .'[51] For Algernon Sidney, writing at about the same moment, 'The vast power of Spain, that within these thirty years made the world tremble, is now like a carcass without blood or spirits, so that everyone expects the dissolution of it.'[52]

From now on, the image of Spain as a nation in terminal decline began to establish itself as firmly in the English imagination as the previous image of Spain as a mighty power on the way to universal monarchy. With the change of image came a change of attitude about the lessons to be learnt. For a century, Spain's achievements had been so impressive and its power so

---

[49] Spedding, ed., *Works of Francis Bacon*, 'Considerations Touching a War with Spain' (1624), xiv, pp. 498–9. For the political context in which Bacon turned to advocacy of war with Spain, see Noel Malcolm, *Reason of State, Propaganda and the Thirty Years' War* (Oxford, 2007), pp. 82–3.

[50] Pincus, *Protestantism and Patriotism*, pp. 184–5.

[51] *Original Letters of his Excellency Sir Richard Fanshaw during his Embassy in Spain and Portugal* (London, 1701), p. 5.

[52] Algernon Sidney, *Court Maxims*, ed. Hans W. Blom, Eco Haitsma Mulier and Ronald Janse (Cambridge, 1996), p. 78.

imposing that it provided a model for at least selective imitation, most notably when it came to the construction of England's overseas empire. Even at the end of the seventeenth century, when the Spain of Carlos II had become a byword for misgovernment, Charles Davenant was proposing an equivalent body to Spain's Council of the Indies for the administration of Britain's American colonies, although he found it necessary to explain and defend his choice of the model to be followed. 'Here it may be objected', he wrote, 'that the Spaniards are not very good patterns to follow in any model or scheme of government; to which it may be answered, that whoever considers the laws, and politic institutions of Spain, will find them as well formed, and contrived with as much skill and wisdom, as in any country perhaps in the world: so that the errors that people is observed to commit from time to time, do not proceed from wrong and ill projection, but from the negligent, loose, and unsteady executions of their councils.'[53]

In general, however, the English perception of Spain from the later seventeenth century onwards was profoundly negative. For Slingsby Bethel, writing in 1680, 'Spain . . . is a clear demonstration that misgovernment, suffering all manner of Frauds, and neglecting the interest of a nation, will soon bring the mightiest Kingdoms low, and lay their honour in the dust.'[54] Spain in its current condition became a dreadful warning, providing a useful counter-example for those with their own agenda to promote. The resort to foreign examples, after all, was a useful device for criticising perceived or imagined failings in one's own society. For Algernon Sidney, Spain furnished evidence of the nefarious consequences of unrestrained monarchical government. England, he argued, could equally be laid low by 'weak, tyrannous princes and their wicked ministers'.[55] For William Petyt, the author of *Britannia Languens*, a discourse on trade published in 1680, Spanish experience confirmed the importance of religious toleration for the achievement of national prosperity: 'We have the example of Spain, whose execrable and inexorable Cruelties towards dissenters hath mainly Assisted in the present poverty and weakness of that Nation.'[56]

As Petyt's words suggest, the example of Spain provided a particularly useful battery of arguments for participants in the great national discussion

---

[53] 'On the Plantation Trade', in *The Political and Commercial Works of Charles D'Avenant*, ed. Sir Charles Whitworth, 5 vols (London, 1771), ii, Discourse 3, pp. 30–1.
[54] Slingsby Bethel, *The Interest of Princes and States* (London, 1680), p. 75.
[55] Sidney, *Court Maxims*, p. 79.
[56] William Petyt, *Britannia Languens or a Discourse of Trade* (London, 1680), in *A Select Collection of Early English Tracts on Commerce*, ed. J. R. McCullough (London, 1856), p. 365.

of the later seventeenth and early eighteenth centuries about the role of commerce and colonies in promoting prosperity and power.[57] Colonial expansion, whether in Ireland or America, still had strong critics like Petyt himself, or Roger Coke, who, in 1670, warned of the dangers of depopulating the mother country: 'Let us compare the state of England with that of Spain, and see if from not unlike causes it does not necessarily degenerate into the condition of it. First, Ireland and our Plantations, do in proportion to England more exhaust it of men, than the West-Indies do Spain.'[58] Such criticism made it imperative for the advocates of American colonisation, like Sir Josiah Child or John Locke,[59] not only to rebut the charges, but also to identify the faults in Spain's treatment of its American possessions and indicate the alternative route that Britain should follow at a time when the air was filled with new colonising projects. Locke's constitutions for the new colony of South Carolina envisaged a form of colonisation that would avoid the mistakes made by the Spaniards, like exploiting the Indians or placing excessive reliance on mining, and would instead create a well-governed and industrious settler society that would cultivate and improve the land.[60]

It had long been a source of wonder to the English that Spain, with all the wealth of the Indies at its disposal, should have remained a barren and impoverished country. The bullionists may have been in retreat, but it was easy for the English, having signally failed to find silver mines of their own, to expatiate on the disastrous obsession of Spaniards with silver. As Sir Josiah Child wrote: 'The Spaniards Intense and Singular Industry in the Mines for Gold and Silver ... doth cause them to neglect in great measure cultivating the earth, and producing commodities from the growth thereof.'[61] The assumption, which hardened into gospel in the course of the eighteenth century, that Spain had placed conquest before commerce, and silver before the cultivation of the soil and the promotion of industry, made clear to Britain that it must at all costs avoid the trap into which the Spaniards had fallen.

Spain's fatal example therefore served to reinforce the lesson already inculcated by the Dutch that commerce, industry and enterprise were essential

---

[57] For the seventeenth- and eighteenth-century debate on trade and economic growth, see in particular Joyce Oldham Appleby, *Economic Thought and Ideology in Seventeenth-Century England* (Princeton, N.J., 1978), and Istvan Hont, *Jealousy of Trade: International Competition in Historical Perspective* (Cambridge, Mass., 2005).

[58] Roger Coke, *A Discourse of Trade* (London, 1670), p. 12.

[59] See Barbara Arneil, *John Locke on America: The Defence of English Colonialism* (Oxford, 1996).

[60] *Ibid.*, p. 122.

[61] Sir Josiah Child, *A New Discourse of Trade* (London, 1693), p. 192.

constituents of national prosperity and power. It underlined the need for an enterprise culture both at home and in the colonies, and helped popularise the notion of 'improvement' as the key to national success.[62] Daniel Defoe, one of the most forceful advocates of an enterprise culture, took delight in his *A Plan of the English Commerce* of 1728 in pointing out the contrasts between the English and the Spaniards. 'Had the *Spaniards*', he wrote, 'been an industrious, improving Nation, like the *English*, the Islands of *Cuba* and *Hispaniola* alone, having been planted and improved, as our small Island of *Barbadoes* is improved, would have produc'd more Sugar, Cotton, Indigo, Cocoa, Piemento, and other valuable things, than all *Europe* could have consumed. . . .'[63] Enterprise and improvement were to be integral components of a developing British ideology of empire, distinguished by its insistence on exactly those elements that had been so conspicuously absent from Spanish imperial practice: a faith in productivity rather than precious metals as the source of true wealth; an open-door policy to immigrants, both at home and in the colonies, as potential contributors to national prosperity;[64] the concomitant of this, a degree of religious toleration; and, above all, the absence of arbitrary power. Britain's empire, unlike Spain's, was to be an empire of the free.[65]

There were enemies, or potential enemies, on every side in the ruthless environment of early modern European international rivalries, and for the English there were lessons, both positive and negative, to be learnt not only from Spain but also from France and the Dutch Republic. The long period of Spanish hegemony, however, had kept Spain for over a century as the focus of world attention, while Spain's pioneering role in the acquisition of overseas empire suggested that the British could learn much, both by way of example and of warning, from the colonising efforts of the Spaniards. But it may reasonably be asked whether learning from the enemy was a purely one-way

---

[62] For the notion of 'improvement' see especially David Hancock, *Citizens of the World: London Merchants and the Integration of the British Atlantic Community, 1735–1785* (Cambridge, 1995), ch. 9.

[63] Daniel Defoe, *A Plan of the English Commerce* (1728), facsimile edn (Oxford, 1928), p. 231. For Defoe and the enterprise culture see Peter Mathias, 'Economic Growth and Robinson Crusoe', *European Review*, 15 (2007), pp. 17–31; and Laurence Dickey, 'Power, Commerce and Natural Law in Daniel Defoe's Political Writings, 1698–1707', in *A Union for Empire: Political Thought and the British Union of 1707*, ed. John Robertson (Cambridge, 1995), ch. 3.

[64] Cf. Coke, *A Discourse of Trade*, p. 12; John Locke, *Locke on Money*, ed. Patrick Hyde Kelly, 2 vols (Oxford, 1991), ii, pp. 487–92 ('For a General Naturalization').

[65] For the eighteenth-century ideology of empire see David Armitage, *The Ideological Origins of the British Empire* (Cambridge, 2000), and especially pp. 166–7; and Linda Colley, *Britons: Forging the Nation 1707–1837* (New Haven, Conn. and London, 1992).

process. Did the Spanish learn from the English, as the English learned from the Spanish?

One deterrent was sheer ignorance. In 1619 the Count of Gondomar complained bitterly that, in his six years of service in the London embassy, 'nobody in Spain cared to know where England is, unless they were angling for special missions, gifts, or personal favours'.[66] Since the reign of Mary Tudor, few Spaniards had come to the country except on official business or as prisoners of war, and the Spanish court relied heavily on ambassadors and envoys, and on the testimony of English exiles, for essential information. Few personal impressions are known. The Count of Villamediana, who arrived in England in 1604 to open negotiations for the peace settlement, wrote privately from Richmond in a letter to the future Count of Gondomar that London was 'a large place with a great deal of trade. It is not very refined or clean, but has a pleasant riverside where ships abound. They are the castles and walls of this kingdom, and the only ones it has. . . . Outside London, there are no cities or towns of any great consideration, and what this kingdom used to have, its abbeys and monasteries, have mostly been pulled down and fallen into ruin, and are uninhabited.'[67]

But ignorance is unlikely to be the whole story where Spanish responses to England are concerned. How far is any superpower interested in learning from its enemies when its power is at its height? It is tempting to recall the reply of a White House aide in 2004 when a commentator rather mildly suggested that solutions to political problems emerge from a 'judicious study of discernible reality'. 'That's not the way that the world really works anymore', the official remarked. 'We're an empire now, and when we act we create our own reality.'[68] In spite of recent setbacks, the rulers of Spain in the years around 1600 still assumed that they were creating their own reality. As a result, they were not in listening mode.

There was, however, at least one Spaniard capable of making a judicious study of discernible reality. This was the Count of Gondomar, whose natural acumen together with his many years in England, from 1613 to 1618 and again from 1620 to 1623, made him a well-informed judge of the English

---

[66] *Correspondencia de Gondomar*, ii, p. 132. I am grateful to Dr Sylvia Hilton for her help in translating this somewhat enigmatically expressed passage.
[67] Biblioteca Nacional, Madrid, Ms. 13141 (Gondomar Correspondence), fo. 149, the Count of Villamediana to Don Diego Sarmiento de Acuña, 4 February 1604. I am grateful to Professor Fernando Bouza for bringing this letter to my attention and providing a transcript.
[68] Ron Suskind, 'Without a Doubt', *New York Times Magazine*, 17 Oct. 2004.

scene. From his observation post in London he realised that the world around him was changing. Warfare, for instance, was no longer what it used to be: 'Today it is not a question simply of natural strength, as with bulls, nor even of battles, but of losing or gaining friends and trade. . . .'[69] He noted the great increase in London's wealth since the peace settlement of 1604. With England and the United Provinces building up their commercial and maritime strength, it was essential that his own country should follow suit, 'for the greatness and survival of Spain depends on the increase of ships and mariners, because in today's world he who is lord of the sea is also lord of the earth, and everyone can see that Spain is losing out . . . .'[70]

Gondomar's comments echoed those of the growing number of critics of the policies of Philip III and the Duke of Lerma in Spain itself,[71] but it was only after the accession of Philip IV in 1621 that a new administration, dominated by the Count of Olivares, embarked on a serious programme of economic reform. Although Olivares believed, with some justice, that Gondomar tended to exaggerate English power,[72] he was well aware of the widening economic and technological gap between Spain and northern Europe, and put forward plans for the promotion of industry and trade that, if implemented, would have brought Spain closer to the Anglo-Dutch model for economic growth. But his reform programme foundered in the face of domestic opposition and the turmoil of war,[73] and in the aftermath of Olivares the imperial mind-set proved largely impervious to change. Even as late as 1699, Alexander Stanhope, the English ambassador to the court of Madrid, noted that however wretched the state of Spain might seem to others, 'they are in their own conceit very happy, believing themselves still the greatest nation in the world; and are now as proud and haughty as in the days of Charles the Fifth.'[74]

---

[69] *Correspondencia de Gondomar*, ii, p. 140 (to Philip III, 28 March 1619).

[70] *Cinco cartas político-literarias de Don Diego Sarmiento de Acuña, primer conde de Gondomar. . .*, ed. Pascual de Gayangos (Madrid, 1869), pp. 53 and 59 (letter of 1 Nov. 1616).

[71] See Elliott, *Spain and its World*, ch. 11 ('Self-Perception and Decline in Early Seventeenth-Century Spain').

[72] *Memoriales y cartas del Conde Duque de Olivares*, ed. J. H. Elliott and José F. de la Peña, 2 vols (Madrid, 1978–81), ii, p. 114.

[73] See Elliott, *Count-Duke of Olivares*, especially ch. 4, for the reform programme and the resistance it met.

[74] Alexander Stanhope, *Spain under Charles the Second (or, Extracts from the Correspondence of the Hon. Alexander Stanhope, British Minister at Madrid 1690–1699)* 2nd edn (London, 1844), p. 152 (letter to Marquis of Normanby, 6 Jan. 1699).

It was not until the eighteenth century, when the advent of a new dynasty and the loss of Spain's European possessions at the Treaty of Utrecht in 1713 brought a sharpened awareness of how far Spain had fallen in the international league table, that Spaniards began to take a close look at the methods and practices of their European rivals. France, the Dutch Republic and England all engaged the attention of Gerónymo de Uztáriz, who published in 1724 the first edition of a treatise that was to be widely read and admired in Europe, and would be published in English in 1751 under the title *The Theory and Practice of Commerce and Maritime Affairs*.[75] As a Colbertian mercantilist, Uztáriz looked more to the French than to the English for economic remedies, but he had visited England as well as Holland and France,[76] and he was impressed by the long-term impact of England's Navigation Acts.[77]

Uztáriz was writing a decade after the end of the War of the Spanish Succession, when Britain and Spain were again, at least temporarily, at peace. But, like the ministers he served as a royal official, he was preoccupied with the need to rebuild Spanish power. Now that Spain had been stripped of its possessions in the Netherlands and Italy, its future lay in a more effective administration of its empire of the Indies. British power was visibly in the ascendant, and there was a growing realisation in Madrid that there was much to be learnt from the policies pursued by the British in the development and exploitation of their American territories.

The lesson was spelled out in 1743, at a time of renewed Anglo-Spanish conflict, by another bureaucrat, José del Campillo y Cosío, whose 'New System of Economic Government for America', although not published until 1789, circulated widely in government circles, and was to have a profound impact on policy-making in the second half of the century.[78] His treatise was suffused with the awareness that Britain, even more than France, was benefiting from trade with its American colonies in ways that Spain was not. 'In the beginning', he wrote, '[England and France] followed the example of Spain, and established more or less the same restrictions, and high duties, as us. But in time reality

---

[75] Geronymo de Uztáriz, *The Theory and Practice of Commerce and Maritime Affairs*, trans. John Kippax, 2 vols (London, 1751). For the author, see Reyes Fernández Durán, *Gerónimo de Uztáriz (1670–1732). Una política económica para Felipe V* (Madrid, 1999). See also Stanley J. Stein and Barbara H. Stein, *Silver, Trade and War: Spain and America in the Making of Early Modern Europe* (Baltimore, Md., and London, 2000), pp. 164–79.

[76] Fernández Durán, *Gerónimo de Uztáriz*, p. 257.

[77] Uztáriz, *Theory and Practice*, ch. 30.

[78] José del Campillo y Cosío, *Nuevo sistema de gobierno económico para América*, ed. Manuel Ballesteros Gaibrois (Madrid, 1993). For Campillo, see also Stein, *Silver, Trade and War*, pp. 204–15.

broke through. . . .' England and France came to realise that it was necessary to give their colonies 'liberty and space, removing the shackles and restrictions that oppressed their industry, and giving them the means to enrich themselves first, before enriching their mother country.'[79] All this suggested that Spain needed to adopt a new policy towards exploiting the resources of its American possessions, a policy in which 'the advantages and usefulness of trade' would replace the 'spirit of conquest' that had hitherto prevailed.[80]

The distinction between an empire of conquest and an empire of commerce made in later seventeenth-century England by John Locke, Josiah Child and others[81] now entered Spanish discourse, and the ministers of Charles III would seek to redirect Spanish policy in ways that would maximise the commercial benefits which could be derived from the possession of a transatlantic empire. This meant following, as far as circumstances allowed, the English model for the organisation of the transatlantic relationship, although ironically at the very moment when that relationship was running into trouble. Spanish ministers adopted the English practice, at least among themselves, of referring to the American possessions as 'colonies' rather than as 'kingdoms', as they had traditionally been styled.[82] Economic development and colonial exploitation were now the order of the day, and the kind of liberal mercantilism espoused by one of Charles III's principal policy-makers, the Count of Campomanes, owed an acknowledged debt to English economic thinking of the later seventeenth century.

Making use of a French translation of Child's *A New Discourse of Trade*, Campomanes wrote in 1762 what he called an 'Examination of the Reflections of Josiah Child on the Progress of the Spanish colonies in the West Indies'. Deeply impressed by England's commercial and maritime successes, he pointed out that while seventeenth-century Spain had been distracted by its wars, England had 'laid the foundations of the mercantile revolution that inclined the balance to its side . . .. From this it can be inferred how backward was Spain in the true principles of commerce.'[83] But in examining Child's analysis of the failings of Spanish policy, Campomanes ran into the problem, common to all imitators, of the degree to which foreign models lend

---

[79] Campillo, *Nuevo sistema*, pp. 79–80.

[80] *Ibid.*, p. 72.

[81] Arneil, *John Locke in America*, p. 106.

[82] Guillermo Céspedes del Castillo, *Ensayos sobre los reinos castellanos de Indias* (Madrid, 1999), p. 300.

[83] Pedro Rodríguez Campomanes, Conde de Campomanes, *Reflexiones sobre el comercio español en Indias (1762)*, ed. Vicente Llombart Rosa (Madrid, 1988), p. 242; and see also the editor's introduction.

themselves to imitation when translated to a different environment. Religion was a particular stumbling block, and Campomanes decided to leave out of his summary of Child's proposals the passages on freedom of conscience in the English colonies—what Child called 'an Amsterdam liberty in our planta-tions'[84]—as 'not compatible with our religion. I therefore omit it as being irrelevant.'[85] This inevitably complicated the task of Campomanes when he came to deal with the demographic impact of colonisation on the mother country. He proposed that Spain should follow the English example of reducing the impact of emigration on the home country by allowing foreigners to settle in its colonies. But for religious reasons the foreigners would have to be German or Irish Catholics. If only they had been allowed to settle in the previous century, 'our colonies would now be as active as those of the English'.[86] But freedom of conscience would have been a step too far.

Campomanes's engagement with the work of Josiah Child, even if across a seventy years' divide, suggests how the example of the enemy—as England had again become at the time of his writing—could encourage new approaches and sometimes new behaviour. Campomanes was in fact to be one of the leading promoters of the 'free trade' policy that his government would pursue. But it was, and remained, 'free trade' within the framework of the later seventeenth-century neo-mercantilist thinking from which it drew its inspiration, and which continued to dominate eighteenth-century international practice. Spain, in partially liberalising its traditional commercial policies while continuing to protect national shipping and production, was simply catching up.

But catching up was essentially what learning from the enemy was all about. It was what the English sought to do when Spanish power was at its height, and what Spaniards were trying to do as the English moved into the position once occupied by themselves. It depended on a willingness to imitate, at least selectively, and such willingness comes more easily when one finds oneself in second rather than in first place. It requires, too, a certain degree of humility, although not perhaps for long. Robert Johnson, in the second part of his *Nova Britannia*, published in 1612, saw short-term humility as a cause for long-term pride. After urging that England should look to the Spanish example of overseas colonisation in order to 'stirre us up', he continued: '. . . English men are best at imitation, and doe soon excell their teachers.'[87]

---

[84] Child, *A New Discourse*, p. 191.
[85] Campomanes, *Reflexiones*, p. 238.
[86] *Ibid.*, p. 241.
[87] Robert Johnson, *The New Life of Virginea* (1612), in Force, *Tracts*, i, p. 19.

A readiness to imitate naturally posits the existence of something or someone worthy of imitation. Here, various possibilities were open to early modern Europeans. One possibility was to look to the past—to the early Christian past for the reform of religion, and to ancient Greece and Rome for models of political and social organisation and cultural achievement. Classical republicanism would provide a model for seventeenth-century political theorists; Roman military organisation would provide a model for military theorists and commanders; and the Roman imperial example would provide a model for Spanish conquistadores and officials as they set out to build an empire in America.[88]

Another possibility was to look not to the past but the present for models. The Ottomans offered an obvious point of reference, but the transposition of some of the more admired features of the Ottoman empire, like its military discipline, into a Christian environment presented obvious problems. European princes would have had some difficulty in putting teetotal armies in the field on the Islamic model. Contemporary Europe itself had much more to offer, not least because of its enormous diversity. Beneath the superficial unity of Christendom lay a divided continent, fragmented into rival polities, torn between competing faiths, and shot through with ethnic, national and social diversity. This diversity offered scope for comparison, and thus for imitation.

One of Hugh Trevor-Roper's preoccupations was the question of how and why societies become dynamic at certain moments in their history. This was a concern that he addressed directly in one of his most brilliant essays, 'Religion, the Reformation and Social Change', first published in 1963.[89] That essay starts with the assertion that 'if we look at the 300 years of European history from 1500 to 1800, we can describe it, in general, as a period of progress'. The progress, as he argues, was neither smooth nor uniform, and in this essay he was primarily concerned to search for an explanation of the reasons why economic and intellectual leadership should have passed from the Mediterranean countries in the age of the Renaissance to the northern nations in the age of the Enlightenment. 'Just as the northern nations, in the first period', he writes, 'looked for ideas to the Mediterranean, so the Mediterranean nations, in the second period, looked north.'[90] The history of the Anglo-Spanish relationship

---

[88] David A. Lupher, *Romans in a New World: Classical Models in Sixteenth-Century Spanish America* (Ann Arbor, Mich., 2003).
[89] Reprinted in H. R. Trevor-Roper, *Religion, the Reformation and Social Change, and Other Essays* (London, 1967), ch. 1.
[90] *Ibid.*, p. 2.

provides a good example of this process. In the sixteenth century England looked to Spain for ideas. By the later eighteenth, Spain looked to England.

I believe that this willingness to look elsewhere provides a key to the progress that Trevor-Roper sees as a general characteristic of early modern Europe. In the highly competitive international environment of those critical early modern centuries, no state could afford for long to ignore the achievements of successful rivals. As new and more sophisticated criteria were developed for assessing national power and wealth, it became increasingly important to scrutinise the behaviour and resources of other states and societies, to avoid being left behind. As a result, societies still congenitally imbued with a deep distrust of novelty were forced to contemplate the need for change.

Awareness of others—and these would overwhelmingly be European others until the expansion of Europe's world brought other others into play—was therefore an essential element in the process by which European civilisation, rather than remaining static, changed and evolved. As a history of the uneasy relationship between early modern England and Spain demonstrates, awareness of the other may well be tempered by a heavy dose of ignorance, and distorted by negative images and the crudest of stereotypes. But the example, both of how to do things, and of how not to do them, was there at hand for those with eyes to see. Whether observation is followed by action is, of course, another matter. But past experience suggests that even a superpower can learn something from its enemies.

CHAPTER III

THE GENERAL CRISIS IN RETROSPECT: A DEBATE WITHOUT END

Some fifty years ago, Eric Hobsbawm published in *Past and Present* (1954) an article that was to spark one of the great historical debates of the second half of the twentieth century: the debate on the 'General Crisis of the Seventeenth Century'. It was a debate that shaped the approach of a whole generation of historians to seventeenth-century Europe, and indeed to the development of early modern Europe as a whole. It was critically reviewed as long ago as 1975 by Theodore K. Rabb in the opening chapter of his *Struggle for Stability in Early Modern Europe*, and more recently by Francesco Benigno in his comprehensive historiographical survey, *Specchi della rivoluzione* (1999). It has been anthologised in selections of articles, notably in Trevor Aston's *Crisis in Europe, 1560–1660* (1965), and later in Geoffrey Parker and Leslie Smith, *The General Crisis of the Seventeenth Century*, first published in 1978, and republished in a new edition, with additional contributions, as recently as 1997.

The world has clearly moved on since those dramatic days in the 1950s and 1960s when historians of the calibre of Hobsbawm, Hugh Trevor-Roper, Lawrence Stone and Roland Mousnier shed their ink, and sometimes their blood, in a series of encounters not unworthy, in their passion and duration, of the Thirty Years War itself. A survivor of those now distant battles may perhaps be permitted a preliminary observation about their character, which may come as something of a surprise to later generations of historians who subject them to solemn retrospective analysis. The debate, although hard fought, was highly enjoyable.

The distant origins of the general-crisis theory have to be sought in the temper and climate of the immediate postwar world of the later 1940s—a world in which many of the old certainties had collapsed, and in which there were high hopes, all too soon to be disappointed, that a new and better age was dawning. Historiographically, this was the period of the rise, particularly in continental Europe, of Marxist or *marxisant* history, and of the establishment of the *Annales* as the dominant school of historical writing. The first edition of Fernand Braudel's *La Méditerranée et le monde méditerranéen à l'époque de Philippe II* was published in 1949. The continent, as always, was cut off from Britain by fog, but, at the time when I was a student in Cambridge at the beginning of the 1950s, British history, traditionally pragmatic and highly sceptical of grand theory, had areas of considerable strength and vitality, one of the strongest being economic history. Insularity, however, remained its besetting sin, and one of the purposes of the group of Marxist historians who founded the journal *Past and Present* in 1952 was to shake up British historiography by introducing into contemporary British debate some of the engagement with major historical problems, and the aspirations after *l'histoire totale*, which had made the *Annales* such a lively and influential journal.

It was two years later, in 1954, that Eric Hobsbawm published the famous article, originally entitled 'The General Crisis of the European Economy in the Seventeenth Century'—a title changed in Trevor Aston's anthology to 'The Crisis of the Seventeenth Century'—that was to initiate the general crisis debate. Hobsbawm's article was in fact primarily an important contribution to an internal and ongoing Marxist debate about the process and timing of the transition from feudalism to capitalism, a debate that had been reopened by the publication in 1946 of Maurice Dobb's *Studies in the Development of Capitalism*, and by Christopher Hill's publications depicting 'The English Revolution' of 1640 as a bourgeois revolution that opened the way to the development of England as a capitalist society.[1] In addressing his central question of 'Why did the expansion of the later fifteenth and sixteenth centuries not lead straight into the epoch of the eighteenth- and nineteenth-century Industrial Revolution?' Hobsbawm extended the discussion to embrace Europe as a whole.[2] His answer pointed to internal contradictions in the European economy and to the 'failure to surmount certain general obstacles

---

[1] For a useful summary, see Francesco Benigno, *Specchi della rivoluzione. Conflitto e identità politica nell'Europa moderna* (Rome, 1999), pp. 64–72. A full bibliography of the debate, listed by date of publication, can be found in Philip Benedict and Myron P. Gutmann, eds, *Early Modern Europe. From Crisis to Stability* (Newark, Del., 2005), pp. 25–30, the volume for which this essay was originally written.

[2] E. J. Hobsbawm, 'The Crisis of the Seventeenth Century', in Trevor Aston, ed., *Crisis in Europe, 1560–1660* (London, 1965), p. 14.

which still stood in the way of the full development of capitalism'.[3] At the heart of this failure was the failure to revolutionise the 'social framework' of a still feudal and agrarian society, which succeeded in holding the emerging forces of capitalism in check.[4] The seventeenth century thus becomes a century of 'general crisis' in which the crisis of the economy builds up tensions and frustrations that provide the impetus for social revolt. 'This clustering of revolutions', writes Hobsbawm, 'has led some historians to see something like a general social-revolutionary crisis in the middle of the century.'[5] The footnote reference here is to a survey of European history 1640–1789 published in 1951 by the Russian historian Boris Porshnev, with the further comment that 'this follows a suggestion of Marx in 1850. . . . The coincidence has often been noted, e.g. Merriman, *Six Contemporaneous Revolutions* (Oxford, 1938).'[6]

This allusion to the contemporaneous revolutions of the 1640s was no more than a glancing reference in an article that was essentially concerned with providing evidence and explanations for the existence of a general European economic crisis, and was primarily inspired by the internal Marxist debate on the development of capitalism. But Hobsbawm's article was to have a wide resonance in a British historical world that was in the process of renewal and transition. The article's comparative and European approach appealed to younger historians, like myself, who were reacting against the parochialism of the British historical profession, while its socio-economic approach was in tune with the changing historical climate of the British Isles in the early 1950s, where the great Tawney/Stone/Trevor-Roper debate on the rise or fall of the gentry was in full swing. It was a moment, too, of impending crisis in the world of international Marxism, which was to be split by the Hungarian uprising of 1956 and its brutal repression by Russian tanks. *Past and Present* was a Marxist journal—a 'journal of scientific history' as its subtitle proudly proclaimed—and its editorial board was much preoccupied by these international and internal developments. But at a more mundane level it was exercised, too, by the limited circulation and readership of a journal that, however lively, was fatally compromised in the eyes of many by its affiliations with the Communist Party. The Institute of Historical Research in London refused to subscribe to it, even as late as 1961, if I remember correctly.

---

[3] Hobsbawm, 'The Crisis of the Seventeenth Century' in Aston, ed., *Crisis in Europe*, p. 29.
[4] *Ibid.*, p. 27.
[5] *Ibid.*, p. 12.
[6] *Ibid.*, note 17.

In the summer of 1957, in a bid to capitalise on the interest provoked by Hobsbawm's article and to open the discussion to a wider group of historians, the editorial board organised a one-day conference in London on the theme of the 'contemporaneous revolutions' of the seventeenth century. The conference, whose proceedings as summarised in *Past and Present*, 13 (1958) still make for lively reading, drew some thirty historians. In the absence of Hugh Trevor-Roper, who was to have opened the discussion, it was initiated by Eric Hobsbawm with the assertion that 'the abnormal "clustering of revolutions" between 1640 and 1660 could best be discussed as part of that period of difficulties, both economic and political, which most historians now recognised in the seventeenth century'.[7]

Hobsbawm's conceptualisation of the seventeenth century as a century of crisis seems to have been accepted by the participants as the natural starting-point for the subsequent discussion. Only Peter Laslett, very characteristically, took a contrary line, as we can see from the following summary of his intervention: 'T.P.R. Laslett (Cambridge) doubted whether a real problem was being discussed. Both the Liberal and Marxist interpretations reserved—from different points of view—a special place of importance for the seventeenth century, but need we do so? If there was any unity in "Europe" at this period it was intellectual. Revolutionary ideas were omnipresent in Natural Law, which was universally accepted at the time, and this was the revolutionizing agent.'[8]

My recollections of the events of that day are now very dim, but as far as I can remember, Laslett's scepticism was neither supported nor shared. The concept of crisis, the history of which would later be traced by Randolph Starn in a valuable article on 'Historians and "Crisis" ', published in *Past and Present*, 52 (1971), had entrenched itself in western historiography as long ago as the nineteenth century, although it was used in different contexts and about different topics by Karl Marx and Jacob Burckhardt.[9] As Starn demonstrates, the notion of crisis was extensively appropriated by economists and economic historians in the period after the First World War, and became a standard theme of the *Annales* in the 1930s. But it was by no means the monopoly of Marxist or *marxisant* historians, and it provided the central organising principle for Roland Mousnier's influential survey, *Les XVIe et XVIIe Siècles* (1953), where all the major aspects of seventeenth-century life were depicted in terms of crisis and the struggle to contain it.[10]

---

[7] 'Seventeenth-Century Revolutions', *Past and Present*, 13 (1958), p. 63.
[8] *Ibid.*, p. 65.
[9] Randolph Starn, 'Historians and "Crisis" ', *Past and Present*, 52 (1971), pp. 3–22.
[10] Roland Mousnier, *Les XVIe et XVIIe Siècles* (Paris, 1954).

We were therefore well attuned to an approach to seventeenth-century history conceived in terms of crisis, although Hobsbawm's formulation gave it a new specificity. As a result, most of us were inclined to take his general approach for granted, although I notice that in a contribution to *Past and Present* only six years after the London conference, in 1963, I would be remarking that 'perhaps the time has come to place a moratorium on the word [crisis] before it becomes yet one more piece of debased historical currency'.[11] On the whole, however, the notion of the seventeenth century as a century of crisis swept everything before it, although Maurice Ashley was still able in 1969 to publish a resolutely upbeat survey, *The Golden Century*, which T. K. Rabb would review in the *Journal of Modern History* in 1973 alongside Henry Kamen's recently published *The Iron Century*. 'It would be difficult', the review began, in what can only be regarded as the understatement of the year, 'to imagine two surveys of the same approximate century of European history, published within three years of one another, which could be more different.'[12]

It fell to me to open the afternoon session of the 1957 *Past and Present* conference in London with a brief account of the general conclusions of my research into the causes of the revolt of Catalonia in 1640, which was only to appear in book form in 1963. My talk was followed by a paper by Brian Manning on the outbreak of the English Civil War, which laid stress on 'the role of the urban and peasant mass movements in crystallising the political situation and precipitating critical events'.[13] Although the inclusion of Manning's paper by the organisers of the conference represents a clear attempt to incorporate events in the British Isles into the comparative European framework that Hobsbawm was proposing, it is noticeable that all the recorded comments on the paper were confined exclusively to English domestic developments, with the 'general consensus of opinion being unfavourable to Prof. Trevor-Roper's views that [the gentry] represented a declining class'.[14] England, it appears, was still a historical island unto itself. Now, some forty years later, we find Jonathan Scott in his *England's Troubles* pressing for the recovery of the European context for English political developments of the seventeenth century.[15] Clio, it seems, is a leisurely muse.

---

[11] John H. Elliott, 'Notes and Comments', *Past and Present*, 25 (1963), p. 96.

[12] Maurice Ashley, *The Golden Century* (London, 1969); Henry Kamen, *The Iron Century* (London, 1971); Theodore K. Rabb, 'Early Modern Europe from Above and Below', *Journal of Modern History*, 45 (1973), pp. 456–62.

[13] 'Seventeenth-Century Revolutions', pp. 69–70.

[14] *Ibid.*, p. 71.

[15] Jonathan Scott, *England's Troubles: Seventeenth-century English Political Instability in European Context* (Cambridge, 2000).

One historian, however, was very conscious of the need to set the British upheavals of the mid-seventeenth century within the wider, European context of revolutionary ferment. This was Hugh Trevor-Roper, the great absentee from the 1957 conference. It was two years later that *Past and Present*—which had now taken Lawrence Stone, Trevor Aston and myself on board, abandoning in the process its claims to be a journal of scientific history—published the dazzling Trevor-Roper article that, by providing an alternative thesis, was to give a new impulse to the debate. In this article, he famously argued that the general crisis was 'a crisis not of the constitution nor of the system of production, but of the State, or rather, of the relation of the State to society'.[16] Central to this crisis was the growth of the top-heavy and overblown princely court.

One of the weaknesses of the Hobsbawm thesis as applied to the mid-century revolutions was that, even accepting the existence of a generalised economic crisis, there was no explanation of the mechanism by which economic crisis was translated into revolutionary action. By shifting attention to the structure of the state and its relationship to society, Trevor-Roper in fact offered such an explanation, in ways that preserved important elements of the theory of a general economic crisis. 'The depression of the 1620s', he argued, 'is perhaps no less important, as a historical turning-point, than the depression of 1929: though a temporary economic failure, it marked a lasting political change.'[17] Faced with the rising costs of the apparatus of the state, governments responded—some more successfully than others—by turning to reform. In England, Stuart incompetence meant that there was 'no such previous revolution, no such partial reform'. As a result, the 'country', defined as all those who opposed the 'vast, oppressive, ever-extending apparatus of parasitic bureaucracy', rose in their exasperation against 'the most rigid court of all and brought it violently down'.[18]

This was heady stuff. Trevor-Roper had produced an extremely ingenious thesis, argued with characteristic verve and with a wealth of illustrative detail. But was the thesis right? Half a dozen historians, British, European and one American, Jack Hexter, were invited by *Past and Present* to pass judgement on it, and their comments, published in 1960, did much to broaden and internationalise the debate.[19] I remember Trevor-Roper remarking to me later that we

---

[16] H. R. Trevor-Roper, 'The General Crisis of the Seventeenth Century', in Aston, ed., *Crisis in Europe*, p. 95.
[17] *Ibid.*
[18] *Ibid.*, pp. 94–5.
[19] Roland Mousnier; J. H. Elliott; Lawrence Stone; H. R. Trevor-Roper; E. H. Kossmann; E. J. Hobsbawm; and J. H. Hexter, 'Discussion of H. R. Trevor-Roper, "The General Crisis of the Seventeenth Century" ', *Past and Present*, 18 (1960), pp. 8–42. Unfortunately, and I think mistakenly, only Mousnier's and my own comments were included in Trevor Aston's *Crisis in Europe*.

had let him off pretty lightly. My own view, on the other hand, is that we holed his ship beneath the waterline. What in effect he had done was to transpose to continental Europe a court–country explanation of the conflict that he had originally propounded as an explanation of the English Civil War. For E. H. Kossmann, Roland Mousnier and myself, the English analogy, even if it were correct for England, simply did not work for our own European regions, the Netherlands, France and Spain respectively. Trevor-Roper's definition of the court, for example, raised serious difficulties. If office-holders were part of the court, how does one explain their participation in the Fronde? Nor were we persuaded that the costs of the court amounted to anything comparable to the burden imposed on seventeenth-century societies by the costs of war.

I believe we proved our case. I also believe, as I believed at the time, that Trevor-Roper, even if taking issue with Hobsbawm, was in fact arguing within the same terms of reference. For both of them, in their different ways, the mid-century upheavals were essentially 'social' revolts, somehow more profound than other kinds of revolt, and their causes and explanation were to be found deep down in the structure of society. My own view, as developed in *The Revolt of the Catalans*, published in 1963, and then in an inaugural lecture delivered at King's College, London, in 1968 on 'Revolution and Continuity in Early Modern Europe', was that such assumptions should not be taken for granted, and that there might perhaps be a case for beginning not with society but the state.[20] This does not of course preclude the need for the analysis of societies in revolt, of the kind that I tried to undertake in my study of the relations between the principality of Catalonia and Madrid. But it does suggest the importance of scrutinising the aims and aspirations of central governments, which might well prove to be more genuinely 'revolutionary' than the forces of revolution thrown up by social and economic pressures emanating from below.

I came to this conclusion as a result of my study of the policies of the Count-Duke of Olivares in the 1620s and 1630s and the explosive response they evoked in Catalonia. In *The Revolt of the Catalans* I attempted to show how the pressures and costs of war forced Olivares and his government in Madrid to devise policies that would mobilise the resources of a Spanish Monarchy and empire

---

[20] J. H. Elliott, *The Revolt of the Catalans. A Study in the Decline of Spain 1598–1640* (Cambridge, 1963, repr. 1984); J. H. Elliott, 'Revolution and Continuity in Early Modern Europe,' *Past and Present*, 42 (1969), pp. 35–56; reprinted in J. H. Elliott, *Spain and its World, 1500–1700* (New Haven Conn. and London, 1989), ch. 5, and in Geoffrey Parker and Lesley M. Smith, eds, *The General Crisis of the Seventeenth Century*, 2nd edn (London, 1997), ch. 5.

made up of widely dispersed territories, each with its own laws, institutions and distinctive constitutional arrangements—what we have since learned to call a 'composite monarchy'. Catalonia, or for that matter Portugal, so far from being burdened by Trevor-Roper's top-heavy court, was, relative to Castile, an under-taxed society with a very small bureaucracy of royal officials. But it was in Catalonia, not Castile, that revolt broke out. In looking for possible explanations, I became impressed with the important part played in the mentality of seventeenth-century Catalans by the idea of the *patria*, as a community founded on shared space, shared memories, shared historical experiences, shared laws and institutions, and shared patterns of life and behaviour.

In retrospect, I think that this insight into the importance of the *patria*, on which I elaborated in my 1968 lecture, and of the way in which the *patria* became the rallying-point for resistance to the demands of central governments bent on introducing fiscal, administrative and constitutional change, was my most useful contribution to the general-crisis debate. It suggested the need to look more closely not only at the seventeenth-century state as an innovating entity, but also at resistance to innovations by the state from communities under pressure. This resistance, reaching far back into the past for its arguments, is likely to be cast in a conservative mould, although counter-revolutions in the name of historic laws and liberties may well have revolutionary and innovating consequences, as indeed the sixteenth-century revolt of the Netherlands made clear.

I think this formulation helped to focus attention where it needed to be focused at this stage of the discussion—on the intentions of the state and resistance to the state. This in turn suggested the need for case studies of individual revolts and their origins, of the kind attempted by me in *The Revolt of the Catalans*, or by Rosario Villari, in his book published four years later, in 1967, on the origins of the Neapolitan revolt of 1647 to 1648.[21] The climate was propitious for this. The 1960s, themselves a decade of protest and revolt, were a time when, especially in the Anglo-American world, social scientists such as Chalmers Johnson were exercised by the typology of revolution, and historians were quick to pick up their concerns.[22] At the Johns Hopkins University in 1967 and 1968, Robert Forster and Jack P. Greene organised a cycle of lectures on *Preconditions of Revolution in Early Modern Europe*.[23] The revolts chosen,

---

[21] Rosario Villari, *La rivolta antispagnola a Napoli. Le origini, 1585–1647* (Bari, 1967).
[22] Chalmers A. Johnson, *Revolution and the Social System* (Stanford, Calif., 1964).
[23] Robert Forster and Jack P. Greene, eds, *Preconditions of Revolution in Early Modern Europe* (Baltimore, Md., 1970).

which included the revolt of the Netherlands and Pugachev's revolt, were not confined to the 1640s, but three of the five lecturers—Mousnier, Stone and myself—were all participants in the general-crisis debate. Lawrence Stone in his contribution on the English Revolution sought to harness Chalmers Johnson to his analysis of its origins, by identifying in turn long-term preconditions, medium-turn precipitants and short-term triggers for revolt.[24]

In the resulting volume the editors fought valiantly to produce a system of classification for our various revolts and revolutions, but the attempt, I fear, was doomed to failure. For all the efforts to produce a comprehensive framework, it was the diversity rather than the similarity of the different revolts that most impressed. Models had, and have, a tiresome way of collapsing under scrutiny. Is it really possible, for instance, to draw a clear distinction between preconditions and precipitants? The models were also essentially static, as H. G. Koenigsberger was later to point out in one of the shrewdest assessments of the general-crisis debate, his 1986 essay rather optimistically entitled 'The Crisis of the Seventeenth Century: A Farewell?'[25] Static models presuppose societies whose normal state is one of equilibrium—an equilibrium that under the pressure of circumstances may occasionally be fatally disturbed. But this approach, as he points out, is to miss the inherently unstable character of early modern European societies, endlessly prone to riots and revolts. This misreading, as I suggested in my 1968 lecture on 'Revolution and Continuity', is part and parcel of an approach to revolution that takes the French Revolution, or rather one particular reading of it, as the paradigm for revolutionary movements in earlier centuries. But early modern societies were not so much horizontally as vertically structured. As I wrote: 'A society grouped into corporations, divided into orders, and linked vertically by powerful ties of kinship and clientage cannot be expected to behave in the same way as a society divided into classes.'[26]

In view of this inherent instability of early modern societies, frequent revolts can scarcely be seen as a cause for surprise. Given this, one has to question the uniqueness of the clustering of revolutions in the 1640s, and with it the whole notion of a general crisis of the seventeenth century. At the time when I gave my inaugural lecture of 1968 I had just finished writing a survey of European history in the second half of the sixteenth century, *Europe*

---

[24] Lawrence Stone, 'The English Revolution', in Forster and Greene, eds, *Preconditions of Revolution*, p. 65.

[25] H. G. Koenigsberger, 'The Crisis of the Seventeenth Century: A Farewell?', in *Politicians and Virtuosi* (London, 1986), ch. 7.

[26] J. H. Elliott, 'Revolution and Continuity in Early Modern Europe', in Elliott, *Spain and its World*, p. 99.

Divided, 1559–1598, and I was struck as I wrote it by the number of revolts that occurred in the opening decade of my period. I counted seven in all. This inspired me to include a teasing footnote that we seemed here to be faced by 'a general crisis of the 1560s',[27] and I played around a little more with this idea in my lecture. Nobody, I am sorry to say, has taken up my challenge to study the revolts of the 1560s as a group, but by insisting on underlying continuities in early modern Europe I did, I hope, raise some doubts as to the significance, and perhaps even the existence, of a general crisis of the seventeenth century.

I was not alone in this. Just at this time a powerful attack on the whole enterprise was launched from Leningrad by Madam Lublinskaya. In the opening chapters of her *French Absolutism: The Crucial Phase, 1620–1629*, to which the Cambridge University Press asked me to contribute a foreword, she turned her fire on each of us in turn. The effect was to produce widespread devastation. 'To enumerate', she wrote, 'under the single heading of "revolution" such essentially different phenomena as the English bourgeois Revolution, the restoration of Portuguese independence, the rising in Naples against Spanish rule, and, finally, the complex web of different movements which is called the Fronde, testifies first and foremost to the fact that the very concept of "revolution" is being used in an unscientific spirit.'[28] As for economic crisis, 'The difficulties encountered were of a special kind, and supply no basis for discussion of a "crisis of capitalism" in the seventeenth century.'[29] So much for Hobsbawm. His quest for that elusive crisis had dissolved into thin air.

Or had it? It is true that the case of the Dutch Republic in particular had always been difficult to fit into the picture of a general crisis, whether economic or political. Kossmann had pointed to the problems in his contribution to the Trevor-Roper debate (which I think was unwisely not included in the Trevor Aston anthology); and as early as 1964 Ivo Schöffer had posed the question: 'Did Holland's Golden Age Coincide with a Period of Crisis?'[30] In what to my mind remains one of the most intelligent treatments of the evidence for the alleged economic crisis of the seventeenth century, Niels Steensgaard argued persuasively in an article published in 1970 that the 'seventeenth-century crisis was not a universal retrogression, but ... hit

---

[27] J. H. Elliott, *Europe Divided, 1559–1598* (London, 1968), p. 107.
[28] A. D. Lublinskaya, *French Absolutism: The Crucial Phase, 1620–1629* (Cambridge, 1997), p. 101.
[29] *Ibid.*, p. 329.
[30] Mousnier *et al.*, 'Discussion of H. R. Trevor-Roper', pp. 8–11; Ivo Schöffer, 'Did Holland's Golden Age Coincide with a Period of Crisis?', in Parker and Smith, *General Crisis*, pp. 87–107.

various sectors at different times and to a different extent'.[31] I think that this
formulation would still, thirty years later, be widely accepted. Even the Dutch
economy had its troubles, as Jonathan Israel has reminded us in his monumental study of the Dutch Republic: 'Dutch overseas trade had lapsed into
recession (1621–32). ... Overall, the period 1621–47 was one of hesitant
growth, the setbacks in European trade being compensated for, on the one
hand, by the demand for Dutch-supplied provisions of all kinds in Germany
and the south Netherlands, and, on the other, by the gains in colonial
commerce.'[32]

But, after reviewing the evidence, Steensgaard took the argument one stage
further, by suggesting that, with the rise in protection costs as a consequence
of the Thirty Years War, the seventeenth-century crisis was 'a distribution
crisis, not a production crisis'. 'Every attempt', he wrote, 'to understand the
seventeenth-century economic crisis without taking account of the distribution of income that took place through the public sector is doomed to
failure.'[33] One of the great strengths of this argument, at least from the point
of view of historians of the mid-century revolutions, is that it again gave the
state centre stage, and, in the process, pointed to the mechanism that related
economic to political crisis. What we find in this period, in Steensgaard's
formulation, is a 'dynamic absolutism' (a word perhaps less acceptable today
than it was thirty years ago), a 'dynamic absolutism which, with its taxation
policy, violated the customary laws and threatened to disrupt the social
balance or deprive parts of the population of their livelihood'. His conclusion
was the one that I had been seeking to advance since the beginning of the
debate, though I might not have expressed it quite so starkly: 'The six contemporaneous revolutions can only be seen as one if we rechristen them "the six
contemporaneous reactions".'[34]

Whether the individual revolts of the 1640s were reactions or revolutions or
something in between, it was quite clear by the beginning of the 1970s that, if
we were to get much further, they required closer study, and that ideally this
study should take place within a comparative framework. This was a point
made by Lloyd Moote in a valuable critical assessment of the debate, published
in 1973, where he also sought to relate it to modern theories of revolution, and

---

[31] Niels Steensgaard, 'The Seventeenth-Century Crisis', in Parker and Smith, eds, *General
Crisis*, p. 44.
[32] Jonathan Israel, *The Dutch Republic: Its Rise, Greatness and Fall, 1477–1806* (Oxford,
1995), p. 610.
[33] Steensgaard, 'Seventeenth-Century Crisis', pp. 44–5.
[34] *Ibid.*, p. 47.

to set the upheavals of the 1640s in the wider context of European uprisings from the revolt of the Netherlands to the French Revolution.[35] Perez Zagorin would attempt something along these lines in his *Rebels and Rulers, 1500–1660* (1982), in which he bravely tried to classify the various upheavals of the sixteenth and seventeenth centuries into general categories such as revolutions, rebellions and revolutionary civil wars, but the scale was perhaps too vast, the categories too general, and the accounts of the revolts too summary, to allow the close comparison for which Lloyd Moote and others had called.[36]

It is, I suppose, all too true that every debate tends to peter out into a plaintive cry for more work, and in this respect the debate on the general crisis has been no exception. By the early 1970s a debate that had begun in the 1950s was, not surprisingly, running out of steam. But it is also fair to say that, in addition to exposing some significant areas of ignorance in our knowledge of both the economic and the political history of the seventeenth century, it also brought into sharper focus some major historical problems that refused to go away. These were elegantly identified and explored by T. K. Rabb in his *The Struggle for Stability* of 1975. After summarising the general-crisis debate, Rabb remarked—and I find myself in agreement in spite of any observations I may have made on the underlying continuities of the period—that 'one cannot escape the impression that something of great importance did in fact take place roughly in the middle third of the seventeenth century'.[37] The particular value of his contribution, as I see it, lay in his determination to set this 'something of great importance' into both a longer and a wider historical perspective.

His longer historical perspective was the perspective of a *before* and an *after*, with particular emphasis on the *after*. The great *before* is the age of the Reformation, in particular the first three decades of the sixteenth century, a period of seismic upheavals that permanently transformed the European landscape. The *after* was located in the years post-1660, a period that J.H. Plumb had recently identified as marking the gradual achievement of political stability in England.[38] In a rather undifferentiated way Roland Mousnier had depicted the entire seventeenth century as an age of crisis, parallel to which ran the

[35] A. Lloyd Moote, 'The Preconditions of Revolution in Early Modern Europe: Did They Really Exist?', *Canadian Journal of History*, 8 (1973), pp. 207–34.

[36] Perez Zagorin, *Rebels and Rulers, 1500–1660*, 2 vols (Cambridge, 1982).

[37] Theodore K. Rabb, *The Struggle for Stability in Early Modern Europe* (New York, 1975), pp. 27–8.

[38] J. H. Plumb, *The Growth of Political Stability in England, 1675–1725* (London, 1967).

'lutte contre la crise', equally undifferentiated chronologically, but ending with a kind of equilibrium achieved in 1715.[39] Rabb's chronology is more precise, with the tensions mounting to crisis point in the middle third of the seventeenth century, and the crisis being successfully resolved in the following decades. This seems to me a more satisfying and useable chronological framework than that provided by Mousnier, and it properly draws attention to the need to examine closely both consequences and causes of the upheavals of the 1640s. Something about historians seems to make them more inclined to study causes than consequences, and Rabb's call is salutary.

If Rabb lengthens the perspective on the mid-century revolutions, he also widens it, again in ways reminiscent of Mousnier, by insisting on the cultural characteristics and manifestations of the crisis and its resolution. This was both bold and brave, and inevitably it gives many hostages to fortune. 'The quest for authority and certainty', which he sees as central to the seventeenth-century enterprise, was itself ambiguous and uncertain, and the evidence provided by the arts can point in many directions, as Rabb himself is aware.[40] His interpretation of individual paintings may be open to question, but one can only admire his determination to relate the arguments over economic and political crisis to the intellectual and aesthetic concerns of the Europe of the baroque. We shall never fully understand the mid-century upheavals without making a serious attempt to enter the mind-sets both of the upholders of established authority and of those who challenged it.

At the same time, *The Struggle for Stability* can be seen as presaging a movement away from the relatively precise discussion of the economic and political crisis of the mid-seventeenth century that had characterised most of the general-crisis debate. This may in part have reflected a sense that the debate, as formulated until then, was leading nowhere rather slowly, but it also reflected the changing historiographical climate of the 1970s. The reaction against Fernand Braudel was gathering strength; the balance of the *Annales* was shifting away from economic and social history to the history of *mentalités;* and historical determinism was in retreat, as the contingent and the individual were rediscovered, political history was reinvented, the art of narrative (to Lawrence Stone's astonishment) was revived, and the revisionists settled down to the systematic deconstruction of everything we thought we knew and understood before their demolition squads moved onto the scene.

---

[39] Mousnier, *Les XVIe et XVIIe Siècles*, 2nd edn (Paris, 1967), pp. 208, 276.
[40] Rabb, *The Struggle for Stability*, pp. 107, 123.

Such a climate was hardly propitious to the general-crisis theory, or indeed to any other theory. The links, or presumed links, between the economy and politics had been snapped, and what had once been seen as great revolutions were all too easily reduced to the contingency of day-to-day events. Yet even in this bleak era, not everything was lost. In particular, as I was happy to observe, my *Revolt of the Catalans* had not after all been written in vain. Conrad Russell, in his explorations of the English Civil War, had picked up from it the idea of the composite monarchy, even if the term itself came later, and was, I believe, invented by Koenigsberger, although he seems to think that it was invented by me.[41] I had tried to demonstrate the impact on Catalan society of the royal absenteeism that necessarily arose from the King of Spain's sovereignty over many different kingdoms and provinces, all with their own laws and institutions. This proved to be critical for Russell's discussion of the origins of the English Civil War in terms of the problem of the multiple kingdoms of England, Ireland and Scotland, all owing allegiance to Charles I. In his *The Causes of the English Civil War* Russell writes, 'The hypothesis that the problem of multiple kingdoms was a major cause of instability in Britain looks perfectly plausible when considered in a European context.'[42]

Even if Russell's *The Fall of the British Monarchies, 1637–1642* is only tenuously connected with contemporaneous events on the continent of Europe, the setting of the English rebellion in a wider, British, context— the three-kingdoms context—has helped, I believe, to maintain a possibly uneasy awareness in the Anglo-American historical world that the questions of simultaneity raised by Merriman's *Six Contemporaneous Revolutions* and by the general-crisis debate cannot be totally ignored, or summarily dismissed as the construct of crisis-minded historians reflecting the preoccupations of their own times.[43] Such preoccupations certainly influenced Merriman when he published his book in 1938. As he himself explains, in writing it he had in mind not only the simultaneous revolutions of 1848, but also the Bolshevik revolution and its contemporary impact. This helps to explain both his choice of topic, and his general focus. Much of Merriman's space is devoted to what he calls the 'Cross-Currents', the transnational links between the rebels and the

---

[41] See the published version of Koenigsberger's Inaugural Lecture at King's College, London, in 1975, 'Dominium regale or Dominium politicum et regale', in *Politicians and Virtuosi*, p. 12, where he writes that 'most states in the early modern period were composite states'; J. H. Elliott, 'A Europe of Composite Monarchies', *Past and Present*, 137 (1992), pp. 48–71, and above, ch. 1.

[42] Conrad Russell, *The Causes of the English Civil War* (Oxford, 1990), p. 29.

[43] Conrad Russell, *The Fall of the British Monarchies, 1637–1642* (Oxford, 1991).

attempts at intervention by one state in the domestic upheavals of another—something that seems to have been inspired in particular by the intervention of foreign powers in the Spanish Civil War.[44] But his book also brought out the fact that contemporaries themselves were very conscious of living in a period of unusual commotion and upheaval. In other words, the problem of the contemporaneous revolutions was a problem for contemporaries long before it became a problem for historians.

This contemporary awareness had also been remarked upon from the earliest stages of the general-crisis debate. Trevor-Roper quoted the words of an English preacher in 1643 that 'these days are days of shaking', and in the 1957 London symposium I quoted Olivares's observation that 'if kings look not to themselves, there will be but few kings left in few years'.[45] Since the 1950s we have learned a great deal more about newsgathering and newspapers in early modern Europe, and about the networks through which information was disseminated.[46] The hunger for information was enormous. Jonathan Scott writes of England that 600,000 corantos were published in the decade 1622 to 1632 alone.[47] Sufficient information about corantos and newsletters should now be available to make possible a systematic survey of the spread of information about the revolts through Europe, and of the speed with which the latest news arrived, whether carried in prints or forwarded in private correspondence, like the letters from René Augier in Paris informing Giles Greene, a member of the English parliamentary committee on foreign affairs, of the latest developments in Naples in 1647.[48]

The Europe-wide dissemination of information about the Catalan insurrection, or the meteoric rise and fall of Masaniello in Naples in 1647, or the execution of Charles I, brings us back again to Merriman's questions about the spread of the revolutionary virus and the impact of the news of revolts on the decisions of governments. Reports of internal unrest were a standing invitation to statesmen to fish in a neighbour's troubled waters, as Richelieu's

---

[44] See the conclusion to R. B. Merriman, *Six Contemporaneous Revolutions* (Oxford, 1938), especially pp. 215–16.
[45] H. R. Trevor-Roper, 'General Crisis', p. 59; 'Seventeenth-Century Revolutions,' *Past and Present*, 13 (1958), p. 65.
[46] See, for instance, Paul Arblaster, 'Current-Affairs Publishing in the Habsburg Netherlands, 1620–1660, in Comparative European Perspective' (Ph.D diss., Oxford University, 1999); Brendan Dooley and Sabrina A. Baron, eds, *The Politics of Information in Early Modern Europe* (London, 2001).
[47] Scott, *England's Troubles*, p. 100.
[48] Rosario Villari, *Elogio della dissimulazione. la lotta politica del seicento* (Rome, 1987), pp. 66–8.

reaction to the 1640 revolts in Portugal and Catalonia indicates. As I suggested in my lecture on 'Revolution and Continuity', and as Koenigsberger reiterated in his 'Farewell' to the crisis of the seventeenth century, the mid-century revolutions cannot simply be treated as self-contained phenomena, particularly where their development and outcome are concerned.[49] At this point, social analysis falls silent, and a knowledge of internal politics is no longer sufficient. Just as the study of international relations is essential to an understanding of the impetus to the new royal fiscalism of the 1620s and 1630s, it is also essential to an understanding of the *dénouement* of the revolutions that the new fiscalism unleashed.

It follows from this that the general-crisis debate is, or at least should be, a standing reproach to the insular treatment of national histories. It is a debate that indicates, however imperfectly, the enriching possibilities of a pan-European approach—an approach that demands the making both of connections and comparisons. The comparisons, as I see them, should not only be between the revolutionary societies themselves, but also between the revolutionary societies and those societies in which revolutions did not occur. As long ago as 1957 at the *Past and Present* conference, Lawrence Stone raised the question of non-revolution in societies where all the necessary preconditions would appear to exist.[50] As far as I know, his appeal has had little echo, although I made an attempt to analyse the reasons for non-revolution in one of the most striking examples of a non-revolutionary society, the Castile of the 1640s, in an essay in a volume presented to one of the leading typologists of seventeenth-century revolts, René Pillorget, in 1990, and here reprinted as Chapter 4.[51]

Where, then, are we, and where do we go from here? As I have suggested, many of the challenges raised by the debate, like the comparison between revolutionary and non-revolutionary societies, still remain to be taken up, and individual case histories deserve more intensive study. But what have now become old historical problems cannot, or should not be, treated in old ways. The *mentalités* of historians have changed since the 1950s and 1960s, for good and ill, and the new approaches and new information that have emerged since those exciting decades have somehow to be incorporated within the terms of discussion.

---

[49] Elliott, *Spain and its World*, p. 111; Koenigsberger, *Politicians and Virtuosi*, p. 167.

[50] Lawrence Stone, 'Seventeenth-Century Revolutions', *Past and Present*, 13 (1958), p. 65.

[51] J. H. Elliott, 'A Non-Revolutionary Society: Castile in the 1640s', in Jean de Vigerie, ed., *Etudes d'histoire européenne. Mélanges offerts à René et Suzanne Pillorget* (Angers, 1990), pp. 253–67.

As far as Hobsbawm's economic crisis is concerned, the days when historians would talk of a 'European' economy are now surely past. It was already apparent from the very early stages of the debate that there were enormous varieties in the timing and extent of depression, even where depression can be proved, and that one region's depression could well be another region's growth. The best documented and most convincing account of economic crisis on a European scale remains that of the late Ruggiero Romano on the crisis of 1619 to 1622, but that crisis is two decades away from the revolutions of the 1640s, and in any event the nature of the link between economic depression and political and social upheaval remains as uncertain as ever.[52] Following the publication of his article in 1962, Romano, while holding to the thesis of a decrease in productive activity in seventeenth-century Europe— with the qualitative and quantitative exception of England and the quantitative exception of the Low Countries—changed his views about economic development in Spanish America, whose precious metals were so closely related to the economic and fiscal fortunes of European states. The thesis of Romano's book, *Conjonctures opposées*, published in 1992, is that, if the seventeenth century was a century of economic crisis for Europe, it was, as colonial specialists now tend to argue, a century of growth for Iberian America, in spite of evidence of temporary dislocations and setbacks.[53]

At a time when the dominant trend has been towards the deconstruction of the economic and political crises of the seventeenth century, it is ironical that in one area at least the trend has been in the opposite direction. Meteorological historians have for some time been informing those who wish to listen of a general deterioration of climate in the seventeenth century, with a drop in temperatures which they relate to fluctuations in sunspots and to a dramatic increase in volcanic activity.[54] So there looms ahead of us the possibility of another debate, this time on the global crisis of the seventeenth century. We await with interest Geoffrey Parker's findings as he continues on his indefatigable pursuit of political and social unrest in farthest Asia, but I have an

---

[52] Ruggiero Romano, 'Between the Sixteenth and Seventeenth Centuries: The Economic Crisis of 1619–22' (1962), in Parker and Smith, eds, *General Crisis*, pp. 153–205.

[53] Ruggiero Romano, *Conjonctures opposées. La 'crise' du XVIIe siècle en Europe et en Amérique ibérique* (Paris, 1992). For the English and Dutch exceptions to the crisis, see p. 91.

[54] See Geoffrey Parker and Lesley M. Smith, 'Introduction', in Parker and Smith, eds, *General Crisis*, pp. 1–31; William S. Atwell, 'A Seventeenth-Century "General Crisis" in East Asia?' in Parker and Smith, eds, *General Crisis*, pp. 235–54; John A. Eddy, 'The "Maunder Minimum": Sunspots and Climate in the Reign of Louis XIV', in Parker and Smith, eds, *General Crisis*, pp. 264–98.

uneasy suspicion that, if climate and revolution are brought into close conjunction, temperatures may rise without an equivalent increase in the richness of the harvest.

But let us for the time being leave the fate of the world to others, and return to Europe, specifically to the 1640s and the challenges that, as I see it, currently face us in relating the upheavals of that decade to contemporary historiographical interests and concerns. By way of conclusion, I will try to indicate very briefly two or three areas in which the developments of the last few years would seem to me to suggest the need for a reappraisal and a deepening of the themes that have conventionally featured in the debate.

In the first place we have learned a good deal more about kingship and the projection of kingship in early modern Europe than we knew when the debate was launched in the 1950s. Political historians today are probably more inclined now than they were half a century ago to dwell on the sacred character of seventeenth-century kingship; and indeed the princely court, as depicted by the contributors to a recent volume on European courts, bears all the hallmarks of a quasi-religious institution, in which the liturgies of the royal chapel and of court etiquette are complementary and mutually reinforcing.[55] The conscious exaltation of sacred kingship in the opening decades of the seventeenth century may be seen as a reassertion of traditional assumptions about the need for human society to pattern the divine. But that reassertion itself requires explanation. If in part it reflects the perceived importance of enhancing the Crown's authority in reaction to the civil and religious disorders of the sixteenth century, it would also seem to respond to the need felt by seventeenth-century governments to deploy the full panoply of royal power in order to mobilise the resources of their societies more effectively at a time when they were being sucked into the international conflicts of the Thirty Years War.

The panoply of power included the imagery of kingship, and we are all now alive to the extensive recourse made by the early modern monarch to ceremony, visual representation and court theatre in order to project the glory and triumphs of the dynasty. No doubt such devices could help to mitigate the baleful consequences of absentee kingship, even as far away as Spain's viceroyalties in Mexico and Peru.[56] Yet at the same time it is easy to be overimpressed,

---

[55] Paul Kléber Monod, *The Power of Kings: Monarchy and Religion in Europe, 1598–1715* (New Haven, Conn. and London, 1999); John Adamson, ed., *The Princely Courts of Europe, 1500–1700* (London, 1999).
[56] See Víctor Mínguez Cornelles, *Los reyes distantes. Imágenes del poder en el México virreinal* (Castelló de la Plana, 1995). See below, p. 182.

as I think José Antonio Maravall in his *Culture of the Baroque* was over-impressed, by their effectiveness.[57] In his elegant little book *Elogio della dissimulazione* (1987), Rosario Villari has drawn attention to the role of dissimulation in seventeenth-century life and thought, and the way in which it helped to create space for movement and innovation in societies that found themselves constricted by the heavy apparatus of state power.[58] For their part, literary historians and historians of the theatre have uncovered ambiguities and subversive intent in the works of authors like Calderón who initially give the appearance of being totally identified with court policy and the preservation of the status quo.[59]

There can be no doubt that a strong vein of criticism and dissent ran through these monarchical societies—criticism and dissent that subverted accepted views and helped prepare the ground for the open protests of the 1640s. In spite of Olivares's belief that 'if kings look not to themselves there will be but few kings left in few years', however, the degree to which this dissent was turning people against the institution of monarchy itself remains uncertain. In recent years historians of political theory have given new impetus to the study of the republican tradition in early modern Europe, and their findings need to be incorporated into the history of the mid-century revolutions.[60] It is certainly possible that we have underestimated the part played by republican thinking in the revolutions, perhaps because it was only in England and Naples that it appears to have had any significant impact. But we may ourselves have been deceived by seventeenth-century dissimulation into undervaluing the strength of republican ideals. The survival of republics in a predominantly monarchical Europe and the successful incorporation of the rebellious provinces of the northern Netherlands into their ranks certainly provided a living and working model of an alternative and apparently viable system of political organisation. But the transfer of that model from smaller to larger states raised problems, in particular about popular participation in

---

[57] José Antonio Maravall, *Culture of the Baroque: Analysis of a Historical Structure* (Minneapolis, Minn. 1986), and J. H. Elliott, 'Concerto Barocco', in the *New York Review of Books*, 34: 6 (9 April 1987).

[58] Villari, *Elogio della dissimulazione*, p. 17.

[59] Margaret Rich Greer, *The Play of Power: Mythological Court Dramas of Calderón de la Barca* (Princeton, N. J., 1991).

[60] J. G. A. Pocock, *The Machiavellian Moment: Florentine Political Thought and the Atlantic Republican Tradition* (Princeton, N. J. 1975); Quentin Skinner, *The Foundations of Modern Political Thought*, 2 vols (Cambridge, 1978); David Wootton, ed., *Republicanism, Liberty and Commercial Society, 1649–1776* (Stanford, Calif., 1994); Martin van Gelderen and Quentin Skinner, eds, *Republicanism: A Shared European Heritage*, 2 vols (Cambridge, 2002).

the exercise of power, which tended to unleash the deep-seated fears of the political nation about the rule of the mob.[61]

Loyalty to the monarch remained deeply ingrained in these societies, and it would take a powerful combination of circumstances, whether in Catalonia, England or Naples, to uproot it. But at a time when public opinion was finding a voice and had increasingly to be taken into account by kings and their ministers, the very enhancement of majesty in an attempt to maximise power played its part both in isolating the court and in alienating significant elements of the political nation from the Crown. In this sense at least, Trevor-Roper's court–country dichotomy still needs to be taken into account, whether in England or on the continent. Charles I's court masques, or the festivities in Philip IV's palace of the Buen Retiro, created, at least among the rulers themselves, illusions of power and of harmony resulting from their own benevolent rule—illusions that shielded them from the unpleasant realities of the unruly world outside the palace walls.[62] Inevitably, these celebrations of majesty provoked widespread complaints about royal extravagance in times of hardship and war. Even for the select audiences for whom they were intended, extravagant representations of triumphant kingship, whether in the theatre or in visual imagery, were all too likely to provoke scepticism rather than awe among those who knew the real score.[63]

A widening credibility gap in the 1620s and 1630s can only have under-mined the capacity of the Crown to rally support when the crisis came. But the long-term impact on monarchy itself would seem to have been mitigated by the existence of another institution whose importance has been brought into sharper focus in recent years. This was the institution of the favourite, or minister-favourite, the study of which, as a European phenomenon, was the theme of a 1999 conference at Oxford whose proceedings were subsequently published under the title *The World of the Favourite*.[64] Although favourites came in many shapes and sizes in the Europe of the first half of the seven-teenth century, their impact on politics and society was profound.

---

[61] H. G. Koenigsberger, 'Republicanism, Monarchism and Liberty', in G. C. Gibbs, Robert Oresko and H. M. Scott, eds, *Royal and Republican Sovereignty in Early Modern Europe* (Cambridge, 1997), ch. 1.

[62] Kevin Sharpe, *The Personal Rule of Charles I* (New Haven, Conn. and London, 1992); Jonathan Brown and John H. Elliott, *A Palace for a King: The Buen Retiro and the Court of Philip IV* (New Haven, Conn. and London, 1980, revised and expanded edn, 2003).

[63] J. H. Elliott, 'Power and Propaganda in the Spain of Philip IV', in *Spain and its World*, ch. 8.

[64] J. H. Elliott and Lawrence Brockliss, eds, *The World of the Favourite* (New Haven, Conn. and London, 1999).

Ruthless minister-favourites—a Richelieu, an Olivares—pushed ahead with fiscal and military projects that built up widespread and deep-seated resentment, and fanned the flames of rebellion. Their ruthlessness derived from an exalted sense of the majesty of kingship and their duty to their monarchs, and seems to have been informed by a neo-Stoic philosophy insistent on discipline, order and authority, whose importance in shaping the attitudes of the European elites of the early seventeenth century has become increasingly apparent in recent years.[65]

At the same time, in order to achieve their objectives, minister-favourites were forced to use the family networks and clientage systems that have been the subject of such intensive study over the last few decades.[66] This in turn alienated members of the political nation who found themselves excluded from the magic circle of office and influence, and gave rise to dark mutterings about over-mighty subjects and the corruption that accompanied the unfettered exercise of personal power. Yet, paradoxically, even as they aroused widespread opposition, minister-favourites performed a valuable service to their royal masters by acting as lightning rods, diverting wrath that would otherwise have fallen on the person of the king.

In the longer perspective of the seventeenth century, the mid-century revolutions can therefore be seen, at least in part, as a reaction to the policies, the comportment and the very existence of favourites and minister-favourites who seemed to have usurped the functions of the sovereign. Their removal from office, and the expressed determination of a number of monarchs—Philip IV, Louis XIV, the Emperor Leopold I—to govern in future by themselves, helped to reduce the tensions and create those conditions conducive to the achievement of stability in later seventeenth-century Europe which constitute the theme of Theodore Rabb's *The Struggle for Stability in Early Modern Europe*.

These summary points may provide a few hints and suggestions about possible directions that fresh approaches to the seventeenth-century 'general crisis' might take. That new approaches are both desirable and necessary I have no doubt. Whatever the defects in the original formulation of the general crisis debate, the participants in the debate identified a series of questions about the interaction of politics, the economy, society and culture that are

---

[65] See, for example, Gerhard Oestreich, *Neostoicism and the Early Modern State* (Cambridge, 1982), and Peter N. Miller, *Peiresc's Europe: Learning and Virtue in the Seventeenth Century* (New Haven, Conn. and London, 2000).

[66] Sharon Kettering, *Patrons, Brokers and Clients in Seventeenth-Century France* (Oxford, 1986); Antonio Feros, *Kingship and Favoritism in the Spain of Philip III, 1598–1621* (Cambridge, 2000).

fundamental to our understanding not only of the seventeenth century but of early modern Europe as a whole. There is still, as always, scope for a closer investigation of the causes and consequences of individual revolts and revolutions. But I would hope that, if nothing else, the historians engaged in that debate succeeded in demonstrating the possibilities, as well as the difficulties, of engaging with the subject on a Europe-wide basis, and approaching national events within a wider framework of international comparison. For all their failings, historians of that generation, unlike some of their successors, were not afraid to ask big questions, or paint with a broad brush on a large canvas. This, more than anything else, is what we need today.[67]

---

[67] Further evidence that this is indeed a debate without end is provided by the most recent assessment, published three years after my own: 'The General Crisis of the Seventeenth Century Revisited', *AHR* Forum, *American Historical Review*, 113 (2008), pp. 1,029–99. The Forum indicates that historians are beginning to reconsider the theory of seventeenth-century crisis from the perspective of global as well as European comparison. The broad brush is perhaps returning.

CHAPTER IV

A NON-REVOLUTIONARY SOCIETY: CASTILE IN THE 1640s

The great historical debate of the 1950s and 1960s over the so-called 'General Crisis of the Seventeenth Century' led to some important and interesting attempts to compare the various revolutionary movements that occurred in Europe during the middle years of the century, and to produce a typology of revolution.[1] It is, however, a striking feature of the debate that the comparisons have always been revolutionary comparisons, in the sense that one movement of protest is compared with another, across either time or space. What has so far been largely missing from the discussion is an attempt to compare societies that did not revolt with those that did.[2] A comparison between revolutionary and non-revolutionary societies which appear on the surface to be subjected to similar 'revolutionary' pressures might perhaps enable us to identify with more precision some of the essential conditions for revolt. Against this it can reasonably be argued that it is hard enough to draw any valid comparisons between revolutionary societies without embarking on a comparison of the revolutionary and the non-revolutionary. But obvious differences can sometimes be more revealing than superficial similarities. Nor should it be forgotten by those sceptical about the study of non-revolution that Sherlock Holmes did not entirely waste his time by paying attention to the dog that did not bark in the night.

---

[1] See above, ch. III.
[2] For one such attempt, however, see J. G. Casey, *The Kingdom of Valencia in the Seventeenth Century* (Cambridge, 1979) which seeks to explain the absence in 1640 of a 'revolt of the Valencians' comparable to the revolt of their neighbours, the Catalans.

During that revolutionary decade of the 1640s, there was revolt and revolution in all three great western monarchies, the British, the French and the Spanish. But while the revolutionary movements in the British Isles and France struck at the very heart of the monarchy, including the capital cities themselves, those in the Iberian Peninsula were confined to the peripheral regions—Catalonia, Portugal and, in a very modified form, Andalusia[3]—and left its heartland, Castile, virtually unscathed. Why should Castile have remained exempt from this Europe-wide epidemic? Looking back at the England or France of the early 1640s from a vantage point at the end of the decade, we naturally tend to say, with our knowledge of what happened afterwards, that these societies were already in a pre-revolutionary situation. We would certainly be saying the same of Castile at the same moment if in fact it had subsequently succumbed to its own version of the Fronde or the English Civil War. Similarly, with the benefit of hindsight, it would not be difficult to draw up an impressive list of Castilian social and political discontents, and neatly package them as 'preconditions of revolution'. The only problem in this instance is that no revolution actually occurred. Against all 'rational' expectation, the dog failed to bark in the night.

There is evidence of such expectation in a dispatch written in cipher to the Venetian senate by Venice's ambassador to Madrid in April 1642. Describing the misery and poverty of the country, the disastrous state of the debased copper coinage (*vellón*) and the open denunciation of the government from the pulpits, he noted that, 'not unreasonably', some *sollevazione*, or uprising, was feared.[4] Yet none materialised. In other words, if the Venetian ambassador is to be trusted, we have what contemporaries regarded as preconditions for revolution, but without a subsequent revolt. Possible reasons for the absence of the expected *sollevazione* provide the subject of this essay. Unfortunately, so little is known about Castile in the 1640s, particularly in the years following the fall from power of the Count-Duke of Olivares in January 1643, that a close analysis of the political, social and economic conjuncture is at present out of the question. Any conclusions are therefore likely to remain highly speculative. But extrapolation from contemporary developments in France and England may itself help to identify certain features in the Castilian political and social

---

[3] For Catalonia, see J. H. Elliott, *The Revolt of the Catalans: a Study in the Decline of Spain, 1598–1640* (Cambridge, 1963; reprinted 1984); for the background to the Portuguese revolution see António M. Hespanha, *Vísperas del Leviatán* (Madrid, 1989), and Jean-Frédéric Schaub, *Le Portugal au temps du comte-duc d'Olivares, 1621–1640* (Madrid, 2001); for Andalusia, see A. Domínguez Ortiz, *Alteraciones Andaluzas* (Madrid, 1973).

[4] Archivio di Stato, Venezia, Spagna, filza 77, letter from Niccolò Sagrado, 16 April 1642.

order deserving investigation as possible explanations for its political quiescence. By way of corollary, Castile's non-revolution may in turn help to highlight particular aspects of the French and English scenes.

A comparison of the condition of France and Spain at the beginning of the 1640s finds them in a broadly similar situation.[5] The two countries were heavily engaged in a long and exhausting war—a war in which, from 1639 to 1640, the French were gradually gaining the upper hand. Both countries had been subject, for the better part of two decades, to authoritarian regimes tightly controlled by a principal minister in whom their monarchs appeared to place unswerving confidence. These regimes had been driven by the demands of war to engage in an almost obsessive fiscalism. On both sides of the Pyrenees, state expenditure had risen spectacularly since the 1620s; and in order to meet the increased expenditure, the Crown had been driven to impose new taxes and resort to a host of fiscal expedients which had infringed or removed the traditional rights and exemptions of privileged regions and sections of society. For England, unlike France and Spain, much of the 1630s had been a time of peace. But the costs of war during the 1620s and of maintaining the fleet in the 1630s had driven the English government into new financial expedients which, as in France and Spain, were bitterly resented; and the military confrontation between the government of Charles I and the Scots at the end of the decade involved the Crown in the same kind of financial crisis that threatened to overwhelm the governments of Louis XIII and Philip IV.

The collapse of the personal government of Charles I and the execution of the Earl of Strafford—the iron man who, with a less distrustful monarch, might have been his Cardinal Richelieu or Count-Duke of Olivares—showed vividly what could happen to a regime that had become so alienated from broad sections of the political nation that the latter was unwilling to rally to its support when it was struck by an emergency. A comparable problem of alienation faced the regimes of Richelieu and Olivares at the beginning of the decade. Both ministers were the object of intense hatred and vilification as the visible incarnations of what were widely perceived as tyrannical governments. For the best part of twenty years, with the assistance of a loyal group of confidants and henchmen, they had used the authority of their respective royal masters to drive their countries down the road to total war. In the process, they had trampled on personal and corporate rights and sensibilities, and, not surprisingly, found themselves surrounded by enemies. The populace was

---

[5] See J. H. Elliott, *Richelieu and Olivares* (Cambridge, 1984), pp. 144–5.

either sullen, or openly hostile; the traditional elites and the ranks of the bureaucracy had been alienated by the erosion of their privileges and the intrusion into their spheres of influence of the dependants and instruments of the two ministers, their *créatures* or *hechuras*; and the high aristocracy, in both France and Spain, had been deeply antagonised by the contemptuous treatment meted out to them by an all-powerful minister, and by his obvious determination to exclude them from what they regarded as their natural prerogative of offering counsel to the king.

In such a situation, both Richelieu and Olivares were, and knew themselves to be, highly vulnerable. Each was faced in effect with an incipient counter-revolutionary movement from within the political nation against the revolutionary changes in the fields of administration, finance and politics, with which his regime had come to be identified. Both were utterly dependent for survival on the continuing support of their king, and there are some indications in 1642, during the Cinq-Mars conspiracy, that the support of Louis XIII for Richelieu was wavering.[6] But in other respects the Cardinal's underlying position in 1642 looks considerably more favourable than that of his Spanish rival. France might be weary of the war, but at least the tide of war had turned in its favour. The prestige associated with victory gave Richelieu a strength in defying his domestic enemies that his Spanish rival could no longer command. He had also succeeded, where Olivares had failed, in crushing potentially dangerous provincial revolts before they could take hold and spread. By 1642 dissent in both Normandy and Périgord had been silenced, whereas in the Iberian Peninsula the revolutions in Catalonia and Portugal had taken root and flourished.

While Richelieu's aristocratic enemies remained a constant threat, he seems to have succeeded in containing the opposition of the *officiers* through his political skills and capacity for compromise.[7] He had also succeeded where Olivares had failed, in stabilising the currency. The Count-Duke's last months in power were passed in a climate of profound economic depression and widespread fears of social unrest following the drastic deflation to which his government resorted in September 1642 in an effort to check the inflation of *vellón* prices.[8] In France, on the other hand, the great currency operation of 1640–1 stabilised the *livre tournois*; and the underlying strength and soundness of the French currency were to provide an important element of stability

---

[6] *Ibid.*, pp. 147–8.
[7] A. Lloyd Moote, *The Revolt of the Judges* (Princeton, N.J., 1971) p. 63.
[8] Antonio Domínguez Ortiz, *Política y hacienda de Felipe IV* (Madrid, 1960), pp. 262–3.

in the otherwise volatile situation created by the death of Richelieu in December 1642 and of Louis XIII in the following spring.[9]

Through a combination of skill and luck Richelieu had held the dike against the forces of counter-revolution. His death brought an immediate lessening of pressures before they would begin to build up again in a new reign and trouble the regime of a new first minister. On the other hand, in Spain, during the winter of 1642–3, the waters were to engulf Olivares, who left the palace for domestic exile on 23 January 1643 after being given formal permission by Philip IV to retire from office. Given Olivares's record of failure and defeat over the last three years, we may well wonder how it was that he had not fallen earlier, and, since the king seemed so unwilling to dispense with his services, in more violent circumstances.

In the British Isles the downfall of the personal government of Charles I had been brought about by a conjunction of the forces of opposition at the centre and the periphery. The Scottish rebellion allowed the English enemies of the regime to seize the political initiative, and, by their collusion with the leaders of that rebellion, to extract from the king the concessions that they demanded.[10] Could the rebellion of Catalonia have been used by the Count-Duke's enemies in Madrid to similar effect? There is evidence of some sympathy in Castile for the Catalan uprising against the Olivares government, and there is also evidence in the initial stages of the revolt of contacts between certain disgruntled Castilian aristocrats and the rebels.[11] But the kind of co-ordination to be found in the British Isles between the peripheral and central forces of opposition was out of the question in the Spain of the early 1640s. In proclaiming the Duke of Braganza as their king, the Portuguese had in effect ruled themselves out by replacing Philip IV with a monarch of their own. Although this provided some encouragement for that misguided Andalusian noble, the Duke of Medina Sidonia, to indulge in a wild conspiracy in 1641, there could be no question of association between the court opposition to Olivares and a 'tyrant'[12] who had usurped the throne of Portugal. The Catalans, for their part, promptly threw themselves into the arms of the French, and from that moment any serious collusion between the Madrid dissidents and the leaders of the Catalan revolt would smack of treason. In

---

[9] See Richard Bonney, *The King's Debts* (Oxford, 1981), p. 170, and René Pillorget, *Les Mouvements insurrectionnels de Provence entre 1596 et 1715* (Paris, 1975), pp. 486–7.

[10] Conrad Russell, *The Crisis of Parliaments* (Oxford, 1971) pp. 329–30.

[11] Elliott, *The Revolt*, pp. 453 and 490.

[12] John H. Elliott and José F. de la Peña, *Memoriales y cartas del conde duque de Olivares*, 2 vols (Madrid, 1978–80), ii, p. 236 ('Cargos contra el Conde Duque').

addition to this, the religious question, so critical for the development of events in England, was entirely absent in Spain. By attempting religious innovations which affronted significant sectors of opinion among his English and Scottish subjects alike, Charles I succeeded in consolidating the forces of opposition around an issue that crossed the boundary lines of kingdoms and transcended local and sectional grievances.

The enemies of Olivares were deeply frustrated by the king's reluctance to dismiss him, but the problem that confronted them was how to force Philip IV's hand. Of the possibilities open to them, armed insurrection was the least attractive, and the most unthinkable. In France, the use of violence to achieve political ends was a continuing feature of national life; between 1602 and 1674 there were to be more than twenty aristocratic conspiracies and insurrections.[13] In Castile, on the other hand, which had been spared the religious wars of the sixteenth century, the Crown had succeeded in domesticating its nobility. During the 1630s Olivares's enemies in the ranks of the aristocracy sulked, or indulged in harmless clandestine discussions, like those held in the Madrid town house of the Duke of Medinaceli.[14] Among these nobles, the sense of loyalty to the monarch was deeply ingrained, and their principal aim was to open his eyes to what was going on around him. This had to be done without antagonising him, and thus running the risk of mortgaging their own future.

A possible setting for the overthrow of the Olivares regime might have been the application of intense aristocratic pressure on the king in conjunction with a popular insurrection in Madrid. But no such insurrection occurred, either then or later in the 1640s at moments of serious stress. In this respect, Madrid presents a striking contrast to Paris. The fact that it was a relatively new and artificial capital city of courtiers and bureaucrats, with a significant part of its population engaged in ministering to the needs of the court, may go a long way towards explaining its apparent passivity. It was also a well-policed city, with its hundred court bailiffs, *alguaciles de corte*, under the supervision of the Sala de Alcaldes de Casa y Corte.[15] But, in the absence of an urban study which will take into account the policing, provisioning and

---

[13] Roland Mousnier, 'La Francia da Richelieu a Mazzarino', in *La Storia*, 5 vols (Turin, 1987), v, p. 274.

[14] J. H. Elliott, *The Count-Duke of Olivares: The Statesman in an Age of Decline* (New Haven, Conn. and London, 1986), p. 557.

[15] Jose Deleito y Piñuela, *Sólo Madrid es corte* (Madrid, 1942), pp. 142–5; Enrique Villaba Pérez, *La administración de la justicia penal en Castilla y en la corte a comienzos del siglo XVII* (Madrid, 1993), pt 2.

occupational and social structure of Madrid, there can be no satisfactory explanation of why it escaped the turbulence of Paris and London in the 1640s.[16]

Without resort to violence, either aristocratic or popular, the only way to secure the downfall of Olivares was to engineer a palace coup. This in fact is what occurred in the winter of 1642–3, when the combination of concerted protest by the grandees and the defection of key members of the Olivares family connection, concerned for their own future in a post-Olivares era, left the king with no choice but to dispense with his minister's services.[17] It was hardly surprising that in Spain, as in France, the disappearance of the author-itarian first minister should have led to an immediate slackening of tension. Since it had become a habit to attribute to his evil advice and tyrannical government all the ills that afflicted the body politic, it was natural to assume that, once he was gone, the ills themselves would also disappear. Seventeenth-century Spain was a society conditioned by its political and religious litera-ture, and not least by its theatre, to look to its monarch for the solution to its problems. When, therefore, Philip announced to the delight of his subjects that he would take the reins of government into his own hands and be his own first minister,[18] he naturally raised high expectations of a new and happier age.

A revolutionary change, or so it seemed, had been achieved without recourse to revolution. The grievances and the aspirations that had conspired to bring about that change found expression in a printed pamphlet containing a series of charges against the fallen minister, which was circulating in the court within a few weeks of the Count-Duke's fall.[19] This pamphlet, written by Andrés de Mena, a former royal official with close links to one of the nobles disaffected to Olivares, the Duke of Béjar, was in large part a catalogue of the Count-Duke's sins of omission and commission, but the catalogue itself was informed by an underlying political philosophy, which may be described as profoundly tradi-tionalist. At its heart lay the demand that Philip IV should be a real king, on the

---

[16] David E. Ringrose, *Madrid and the Spanish Economy 1560–1850* (Berkeley/Los Angeles, Calif. and London, 1983), p. 89, offers a few figures for Madrid's seventeenth-century occu-pational structure, but is more concerned with the subsequent centuries. The study of Madrid's municipal oligarchy by Mauro Hernández, *A la sombra de la corona. Poder local y oligarquía urbana, Madrid, 1606–1808* (Madrid, 1995) indicates some of the ways in which proximity to, and dependence on, the court restricted the town's ability to develop its own social space, and constrained its capacity for independent action.

[17] For Olivares's fall, see Elliott, *The Count-Duke*, pp. 640–51, but many mysteries remain.

[18] *Ibid.*, p. 651.

[19] Elliott and de la Peña, *Memoriales y cartas*, ii, doc. XX a.

model of his grandfather, Philip II, rather than of his father, Philip III, who 'placed the burden of the monarchy on other shoulders'. The grandees, in other words, were demanding the abolition of government by royal favourite.

As the grandees saw it, a return to personal kinghip, in the manner of Philip II, entailed a return to a style of kingship that followed the proper forms. These had been violated by the Count-Duke's arbitrary behaviour, to the detriment in particular of the old nobility. The nobles had seen their status devalued by arbitrary fiscal demands, unjust imprisonments, the sale of titles and privileges, and the acquisition of intolerable power and riches by ministers and officials, who had come to resemble fifteenth-century grandees, while modern grandees for their part were treated like fifteenth-century officials. This was an old aristocratic complaint in Castile, as elsewhere, but the pamphlet does not betray the deep divisions between *noblesse d'épée* and *noblesse de robe* to be found in the France of Richelieu and Mazarin. The real targets of the grandees' attack were the new ministers, the Count-Duke's confidants and henchmen, and the counter-revolution advocated in Mena's pamphlet was a counter-revolution against recent administrative practices, rather than against the whole bureaucratic order. Indeed, it was this order that the Count-Duke's opponents wanted to see restored. Their demand was for a return to the old and idealised days, when business was conducted by qualified ministers operating through the proper bureaucratic channels. This meant the restitution of effective conciliar government, in place of arbitrary government by specially created juntas, the hated hallmark of the Olivares regime. Nor should ministers be foreigners—another bitterly resented characteristic of the Olivares years.

The nobles, in effect, were fighting the battles of the bureaucrats for them, since the university-trained *letrado* hierarchy, with its carefully graded *cursus honorum*, had been as outraged as the grandees by the Count-Duke's practice of diverting important business away from the councils and into the new juntas. These were packed with his own creatures, some of whom, like the Bolognese historian Virgilio Malvezzi, were not even Castilians. This *letrado* hierarchy would have had no difficulty in subscribing to the form of government in the post-Olivares era advocated by Mena and his friends. Nobles and *letrados* alike were reacting to the practices of the Olivares years by demanding the restoration of an essentially consultative monarchy, conducted by a king who worked hard at his papers, chose as his ministers 'men well regarded and liked by the people',[20] and took his own decisions in the light of the *consultas*,

---

[20] *Ibid.*, p. 244.

or state papers, forwarded to him by his councils. This was a constitutionalist programme within the Castilian constitutionalist tradition, which placed few institutional restraints on the conduct of kingship, but expected it to be highly responsive to divine and human law and to the legitimate claims of loyal subjects to have their grievances heard and be taken seriously when they proffered advice to their monarch.

This joint aristocratic-*letrado* programme for counter-revolution in 1643 was intended to put the clock back to an idealised pre-Olivares era. But how successful was it? The king showed every sign of wanting to govern by himself; and there was an immediate dismantling of that most obnoxious feature of the Olivares regime, government by junta.[21] In addition, one or two of the figures most closely associated with the fallen minister were pushed out of office; but, on the surface at least, it is the continuity rather than the change that impresses most in these post-Olivares years. The Modenese ambassador said as much when he observed in September 1643 that 'the new government follows the same maxims as the Count-Duke but without his rigour'.[22] The continuity was most striking in the field of foreign policy. In spite of the immense war-weariness of Castile, it would take another five years to conclude peace with the Dutch, while the war with France would continue for another sixteen. But there was also an impressive continuity of men as well as of measures. Although some of the nobles most opposed to the Count-Duke returned to court, and one or two of his relatives suffered at least a temporary eclipse, it became apparent when the smoke of battle cleared that the commanding heights of power were still in the hands of members of that same Guzmán-Haro-Zúñiga family connection which had first occupied them in 1621 with the advent of Olivares. Nothing underlined this continuity more than the growing dependence of the king, for all his good resolutions, on the Count-Duke's nephew, Don Luis de Haro, who was to inherit (but would be careful not to flaunt) his uncle's title of Count-Duke of Olivares. If a modified form of government by royal favourite finally returned to Madrid in the post-Olivares period, so also did several of the more unpopular features of the Olivares regime. Gradually, juntas began to creep back into existence, and foreigners began to make their reappearance.[23]

---

[21] Elliott, *The Count-Duke*, p. 653.

[22] *Ibid.*, pp. 664–6.

[23] I. A. A. Thompson, 'The government of Spain in the Reign of Philip IV', in his *Crown and Cortes: Government, Institutions and Representation in Early-Modern Castile* (Aldershot, 1993), ch. 4, p. 59.

Change, and yet no change, therefore seemed to be the order of the day in post-Olivares Spain. The sense of disillusionment was profound, but the regime in Madrid, although confronted by numerous crises—disturbances in the city of Valencia in 1646–7, a new royal bankruptcy in 1647, revolts in Naples and Sicily in 1647–8, a conspiracy by the Duke of Híjar in Aragon in 1648, and a series of urban uprisings in Andalusia between 1647 and 1652—did not have to face the kind of generalised challenge to its authority that plunged France into chaos between 1648 and 1652.

A prime reason for this may lie in an area of collective psychology which historians have not yet begun to penetrate. They have not yet devised ways of measuring loyalty, and the loyalty of a 'faithful and domesticated Castile, full of a religious respect for royal authority' contrasts strikingly with the rebelliousness of Catalonia, Portugal and Vizcaya.[24] If Castile was indeed unusually loyal, it would still be necessary to explain why this should have been. Loyalty, after all, can be enthusiastic or grudging, and it may simply be ingrained by force of habit. It can also be reinforced by circumstances, and it is very possible that the sheer fact of revolt in so many of the territories owing allegiance to their king helped to reinforce among Castilians, by way of reaction, their own self-image as a people of unswerving fidelity. Loyalty can also be maintained by fear and force, but one of the most striking features of seventeenth-century Castile, when compared with France, is the absence of powerful instruments of repression. The government in Madrid had no effective forces at hand to deal with emergencies, since the two or three thousand men constituting the Guardas de Castilla, a militia confined to Old Castile, seem to have been largely inoperative.[25] It took time to assemble an army in the peninsula to put down a rebellion, as Olivares found to his cost when confronted in 1640 with the revolt in Catalonia. The absence of any emergency force would seem to have left Madrid very vulnerable, yet events themselves were to prove that no such emergency force was necessary. The urban revolts in Andalusia in the late 1640s simply died away without the need to resort to repression; and it may well be that the very absence of repressive forces helped to keep down the level of violence in seventeenth-century Castilian society, since violence feeds on violence.

---

[24] Domínguez Ortiz, *Alteraciones*, p. 20. Since the original publication of this essay in 1990, Ruth Mackay has usefully explored the question of popular loyalty and obedience in *The Limits of Royal Authority: Resistance and Obedience in Seventeenth-Century Castile* (Cambridge, 1999).

[25] Domínguez Ortiz, *Alteraciones*, pp. 21–2.

Even at the local level the degree of disorder was limited. Throughout the seventeenth century, in Castile and Andalusia, there was a marked absence of serious agitation in the countryside. Although there was a steady alienation of land and rights of lordship by a financially hard-pressed crown, it was difficult for the purchasers to impose heavy new demands on peasants when these could always take advantage of the prevailing scarcity of rural population by voting with their feet and moving elsewhere. Occasionally, as in the Valle de Lozoya in 1646, a *señor* who attempted strong-arm methods paid for his intransigence with his life, but such violent outbursts were rare.[26] The urban uprisings in Andalusia, although preoccupying, were spontaneous but brief upsurges of popular anger against the agents of the central government, tax-collectors, town governors (*corregidores*) and special commissioners of one kind and another.[27] The uprisings had no coherent programme; they received little support from the middle ranks of urban society; and, for reasons that still have to be explored, they did not spread in the 1640s to the cities of Castile, where fiscal demands remained heavy, but where population pressure on food supplies seems to have been less acute, and harvest fluctuations less brusque, than in Andalusia.[28] Although no new taxes had been imposed since Olivares's fall,[29] the burden of taxation was deeply resented, in part at least because it was so inequitably distributed, both between social classes and between one locality and another; but any major challenge to the regime of Don Luis de Haro, who manoeuvred his way into the space left vacant by the fall of Olivares, would have to come from the ranks of the upper classes, and, in sharp contrast to France, no such challenge materialised.

Why this should have been so is partly suggested by the character of the Fronde. Against a general background of rural and urban unrest, the upper classes in France seized the opportunity presented by a crisis of authority in the central government to satisfy a series of individual and corporate demands. The crisis of authority was precipitated by the acute financial problems beset-ting the French Crown in 1647–8, and the attempts of the ministry to redress them. But it originated in the constitutional and political problems attendant on the royal minority of Louis XIV, at a time when pressures of war were unre-lenting, and power was exercised for the queen regent Anne of Austria by a

---

[26] Angel García Sanz, *Desarrollo y crisis del antiguo régimen en Castilla la Vieja* (Madrid, 1977), pp. 270–1; Domínguez Ortiz, *Alteraciones*, pp. 137–8.
[27] Domínguez Ortiz, *Alteraciones*, p. 155.
[28] *Ibid.*, p. 32.
[29] Thompson, 'Government of Spain', p. 60.

bitterly hated foreign favourite, Cardinal Mazarin, who still had the Richelieu administrative machine at his disposal.

Against the major disruption of the French political system caused by the death of Louis XIII in 1643 must be set the continuity of kingship in Spain during the 1640s. By surviving, unlike his French brother-in-law, Philip IV offered in his person a vital element both of continuity and of stability in potentially turbulent times. There was no royal minority to provoke awkward questions about the distribution of power, and the death in 1646 of the heir to the throne, prince Baltasar Carlos, presented a long-term threat to the survival of the dynasty, rather than any immediate crisis. As a result, there was no constitutional pretext for mounting a challenge to the system. The key to power lay, as always, in gaining the ear of the king. Here, the growing influence of Don Luis de Haro represented a potential obstacle. But Haro was no Olivares. The new situation was well described by the courtier Matías de Novoa in his journal, when he wrote that 'there was no true intermediary or favourite, or figure of power between the prince and petitioners. Only Don Luis de Haro ... had a modified and restricted position as favourite, and a limited power.'[30] Don Luis was suave in his treatment of the aristocracy whereas Olivares had been abrasive, and aristocratic discontent was channelled back into palace faction feuds.

In the vacuum created by the weakening of royal authority in France, the *parlements*, and especially the *parlement* of Paris, were able to stake out a position for themselves which, in the circumstances of 1648, created the potential for revolutionary change. If the potential was not finally realised, this was in part because the *parlement* of Paris, unlike the English House of Commons, was unable to present itself convincingly as an alternative focus of loyalty that transcended sectional interests. The Cortes of Castile, although nominally in a position to speak at a national level in a way that the *parlement* of Paris was not, suffered from other limitations, which seriously diminished its effectiveness as an organ of protest. In the early years of the seventeenth century the Cortes of Castile had managed to secure sufficient financial leverage over the Crown through its control over the new tax of the *millones* to be able to act as the focus of a constitutionalist opposition.[31] But even then its scope for action was

---

[30] Matías de Novoa, 'Historia de Felipe IV', *Colección de documentos inéditos para la historia de España*, vol. 86, p. 391. Don Luis de Haro and his methods of government are the subject of an as yet unpublished Oxford D. Phil. thesis by Alistair Malcolm, 'Don Luis de Haro and the Political Elite of the Spanish Monarchy in the Mid-Seventeenth Century' (1999).

[31] For the seventeenth-century Castilian Cortes, see Charles Jago, 'Habsburg Absolutism and the Cortes of Castile', *American Historical Review*, 86 (1981), pp. 307–26, and I. A. A. Thompson, 'Crown and Cortes in Castile, 1590–1665', *Parliaments, Estates and Representation*, 2 (1982), pp. 29–45, reprinted in his *Crown and Cortes*, ch. 6.

limited by its small size and the narrowness of its representation, confined as it was to the *procuradores*, or deputies, of eighteen cities, who themselves tended to act primarily as the spokesmen for their respective municipal oligarchies. Their wings had been further clipped by Olivares, who managed to insist on the *procuradores* being sent to Madrid with full powers by their city councils.

The battle, however, was not permanently won by the Crown, and the opening of the first post-Olivares Cortes in 1646 was delayed by disputes between the Crown and the cities over the conferment of full powers.[32] These disputes reflected the mounting anger and frustration of the municipal oligarchies at the Crown's tax demands and fiscal expedients, like the withholding of interest payments on government bonds, which directly affected the well-being of the urban elites. The Crown, therefore, in 1646–7 was faced with the possibility of a major confrontation with the urban patriciates at a time when it was sliding into bankruptcy and the Cortes was in session. But again the Cortes revealed its fundamental weakness when confronted by a determined ministry with all the resources of Crown patronage at its disposal. The year 1647, with its combination of high grain prices, urban unrest in Andalusia and the suspension of payments to the royal bankers in October, was an exceptionally difficult one for the government in Madrid. But, with the session of the Cortes behind it, it was able to manoeuvre its way to an accommodation with the cities, at one and the same time containing popular unrest in the Andalusian towns by timely concessions on taxes on basic foodstuffs, and addressing the grievances of the urban patriciates by restoring interest payments on bonds and rescinding the unpopular 1642 tax on property.[33]

The Cortes of Castile, therefore, in failing to broaden the specific concerns and discontents of the urban oligarchies into a reformist programme that would involve it in a direct confrontation with the regime, followed a very different course from that pursued by the *parlement* of Paris in 1647–8. In France, the impetus behind such a programme came from the accumulated grievances of a class of *officiers* which had seen its influence and authority steadily undermined by the activities of an alternative administrative class of *intendants*, and which then found its hereditary hold on offices jeopardised by the financier Particelli d'Hémery's heavy-handed interference with the workings of the *droit annuel*.[34] The Castilian situation was simply not comparable.

---

[32] Jago, 'Habsburg Absolutism', p. 323.

[33] *Ibid.*

[34] The degree to which the *parlement*'s programme was genuinely reformist as opposed to a defence of corporate interests remains a matter of debate. See Moote, *The Revolt of the Judges*, and Richard Bonney, 'La Fronde des officiers. Mouvement réformiste ou Rébellion corporatiste?', *XVIIe Siècle*, 145 (1984), pp. 323–40.

The Cortes, unlike the *parlement* of Paris, was not a forum for the office-holding class; and while Castilian office-holders had their own grievances, like the tax of the *media anata* on salaries, they had not been challenged by the emergence of a new administrative bureaucracy. Equally, they had never enjoyed a right to hereditary transmission of office, although this had not prevented the establishment of *letrado* dynasties with inside advantages when judicial and administrative appointments were made.[35]

Whatever the extent of the reformist aspirations of the *parlement* of Paris, its demands precipitated what was in effect a struggle for power in a kingdom where the accident of a royal minority had opened up unexpected opportunities for all kinds of sectional and corporate interests to roll back the frontiers of royal authority that had been so forcefully extended under the Richelieu administration. There were sufficient constitutional ambiguities about the location of power during a royal minority in France to provide these sectional interests with at least a specious legitimacy for their assault on the regency government. No such legitimising philosophy would have been available to an opposition movement in the Castile of the 1640s, where the prime demand remained, as always, that the king should govern personally.

Potentially the best justification available for opposition in Castile was to be found in the theory of contract. While this had enjoyed something of a resurgence in early seventeenth-century Castile, and had found expression in the constitutionalist opposition led by Mateo de Lisón y Biedma and his friends in the Cortes of the early 1620s,[36] it was not effectively institutionalised, as it was in Catalonia. There, rebellion was justified in 1640 by the elected representatives of the people on the grounds that the king had broken the terms of his contractual relationship with his Catalan vassals, and that the contract was thereby terminated.[37] In the early years of opposition to Olivares, the Cortes of Castile had proved insufficiently strong and resolute to succeed in establishing on a solid basis the idea of a firm contractual relationship between king and kingdom. There was even less chance of achieving this by the 1640s, after the Cortes had been weakened by Olivares's measures against it, and the Crown had made the useful discovery that it could bypass the Cortes entirely by engaging in direct negotiations with individual city councils.[38] As a result of this discovery, the Cortes as an institution was becoming marginal to

---

[35] See Janine Fayard, *Les Membres du Conseil de Castille à l'époque moderne, 1621–1746* (Geneva/Paris, 1979), part 2.

[36] Elliott, *The Count-Duke*, pp. 109–10.

[37] Elliott, *The Revolt*, p. 549.

[38] Thompson, *Crown and Cortes*, pp. 41–2.

Castilian life, and even if its demise was not yet assured, it was now firmly pointed down the path that would lead to its disappearance from the scene after 1665.

The occasion, the justification and an adequate institutional forum for revolutionary protest—all these, then, were missing in post-Olivares Castile. This is not to say that some great upheaval, on the scale of the Fronde, was beyond the bounds of possibility. Ultimately it is no more conclusive to provide, with hindsight, a more or less plausible list of reasons for the impossibility of revolution than reasons for its inevitability once it has occurred. Revolution or no revolution, room should always be left in any explanatory interpretation for the role of personality, collective psychology, political management and the sheer conjunction of events. But, given the survival of Philip IV, the balance of probability seems heavily tilted against a revolution in the Castile of the 1640s after the downfall of Olivares; and perhaps the best argument of all in favour of this assumption is that a revolution of the kind most likely to occur in mid-seventeenth century Castile had in fact *already occurred*.

This assertion is best understood if we look again at the Fronde, and see it as the confused reaction of a confused society to a period in which the state apparatus had arrogated to itself extraordinary powers, and made unprecedented demands on the population, in the pursuit of victory in war. At its deepest level it was an anti-Richelieu reaction, but one that was deferred until six years after Richelieu himself was dead and buried. The death of the cardinal, the uncertainties following the change of monarchs and the imminent expectation of a victorious peace had all helped to put off the eventual day of reckoning, which may have been all the more explosive for having been so long deferred. Fragmented as it was by sharp sectional divisions, as different groups competed in defence of their corporate interests, the opposition was at least agreed in demanding a return to the 'ordinary' order of things, however variously that word might be interpreted by different sections of society, against the 'extraordinary' assertion of power by the state.[39]

This same return to the ordinary, or customary, form of government had been demanded in Spain in 1642–3 by the opponents of Olivares. They achieved their immediate end by securing his dismissal. But they also achieved,

---

[39] For the distinction between ordinary and extraordinary government, see Robert Descimon and Christian Jouhaud, 'La Fronde en Mouvement: le Développement de la Crise politique entre 1648 et 1652', *XVII Siècle*, 145 (1984), pp. 304–22, esp. p. 308.

with setbacks and modifications, their much more important long-term goal of halting in its tracks the movement towards the concentration of extraordinary powers in the hands of the Crown that was identified with the Count-Duke and his regime. The Count-Duke had always seen himself as locked in a life-or-death struggle with the 'powerful ones'—the *poderosos*—the oligarchical forces in Castilian society that were gradually eroding the Crown's authority.[40] The *poderosos* were the high nobility and the local *señores*, the municipal oligarchs, and the *letrado* bureaucrats—members of a constantly ramifying network of family interests and clientage systems which was progressively consolidating its power and influence at both the local and national levels. The events of 1642–3 proved in retrospect to be a decisive moment for their fortunes. Olivares had not only fallen, but was discredited, and the revolution from above that he had sought to introduce was discredited with him. It was true that certain features of the Olivares regime, like the juntas, survived or returned. But the political atmosphere was profoundly different in the post-Olivares era. The reformist drive had gone from government, and power was shared between competing aristocratic groups and a *letrado* hierarchy governing through the traditional conciliar institutions. The whole character of this system of power-sharing was such as to favour the interests of the *poderosos*. Essentially, 1643 had given them what they wanted, and the forces of counter-revolution had won.

There was no need, therefore, for the Castilian elite to mount a further challenge to the government in the immediate post-Olivares years. There were other, less confrontational, ways of securing what they wanted, and in a time of potentially dangerous social unrest they had more to gain than to lose by putting the weight of their support behind the regime of Don Luis de Haro. In France, on the other hand, Richelieu had died, but he had not fallen, and the rule of his chosen successor, Mazarin, was a perpetual reminder of this fact.

In 1648 the forces of opposition in the French political elite staged their own equivalent of the 1643 Spanish challenge to the system of 'extraordinary' government. The outcome of the challenge, however, was profoundly different. The Richelieu system, although unpopular, was not discredited, thanks in particular to its continuing capacity to bring military successes in the war with Spain. These in turn enhanced the possibility of successful resistance by the Crown. As the opposition challenge encountered resistance it took a violent turn, only to become caught up in the cross-currents of social antagonisms and competing sectional interests that were inevitably brought

[40] Elliott, *The Count-Duke*, pp. 410, 514–16.

into play as the forces of opposition failed to establish on an agreed basis an overriding legitimacy for their actions. With the formal ending of the royal minority all claim to legitimacy was removed, and the challenge collapsed in defeat. It would then fall to the monarchy of Louis XIV to construct a new balance of forces on the basis of a system of order that transcended and abolished the distinction between ordinary and extraordinary systems of government.[41]

It may, then, have been the very completeness of the failure of Olivares that prevented a violent upheaval in the Castile of the 1640s. There was such a broad unanimity about the undesirability of repeating the experiences of the Olivares years that no serious divisions opened up in the political nation to provoke a violent conflict. Instead, it was able to rally round the Crown on the basis of the restored status quo. In this respect, Spain differed from England, where the innovations introduced in religion and politics by the government of Charles I were so closely associated with the monarch himself that the role of the Crown was brought into question. It was the resulting disagreements about the proper extent and limits of royal power that finally brought the political nation to blows and helped precipitate a civil war.

Yet ironically, in the long run, Castile may have lost rather than gained from the passivity with which it responded to the challenges of the 1640s. In France, as a result of the collapse of the Fronde, the political initiative passed to the Crown, and Louis XIV was in a position to carry over what he wanted from the administrative and political revolution introduced by Richelieu. In England, as a result of the execution of Charles I, the initiative passed to the political nation, which from 1660 was once again broadly reunited around a restored, but limited, monarchy. The very limitations on that restored monarchy helped create a climate in which the executive power could be expanded and used in the later years of the seventeenth century for what was widely perceived as the national interest. In Spain, on the other hand, monarchical power remained institutionally unrestricted, but the political initiative had passed to the forces within society that had defeated Olivares. Crown and *poderosos* therefore coexisted on the basis of a mutual dependence which precluded innovating change. The Crown, as a potential force for change, was immobilised by the dead weight of the *poderosos*. They, in turn, were so dependent on the Crown for offices, favours and concessions to cushion them against hard economic times, that they had neither the desire nor the ability

---

[41] Descimon and Jouhaud, 'La Fronde en Mouvement', p. 320.

to strike out in new directions.[42] The result was half a century of stagnation and inertia, which contrasted sharply with the dynamism of contemporary France and England. The price of revolution may well have been high, but the price of non-revolution was perhaps even higher.

---

[42] For the mutual dependence of Crown and nobility, as it was already developing in the first half of the seventeenth century, see Charles Jago, 'The Influence of Debt on the Relations between Crown and Aristocracy in Seventeenth-Century Castile', *Economic History Review*, 26 (1973), pp. 218–36; I. A. A. Thompson, *War and Government in Habsburg Spain, 1560–1620* (London, 1976), ch. 5; Ignacio Atienza Hernández, *Aristocracia, poder y riqueza en la España moderna. La Casa de Osuna siglos XV–X1X* (Madrid, 1987), pp. 53–4. The continuing dependence of the nobility on the Crown suggests the weaknesses of the term 'refeudalisation', as applied to seventeenth-century Spain. See A. Domínguez Ortiz, 'Algunas consideraciones sobre la refeudalización del siglo XVII', in María Carmen Iglesias, Carlos Moya, Luis Rodríguez Zúñiga, eds, *Homenaje a José Antonio Maravall*, 3 vols (Madrid, 1985), i, pp. 499–507.

CHAPTER V

EUROPE AFTER THE PEACE OF
WESTPHALIA

The Peace of Westphalia of 1648 has impressed itself on the collective memory of Europe as bringing to an end a European conflict more devastating than any before the twentieth century. Voltaire, in *Le Siècle de Louis XIV*, describes the 'celebrated peace of Westphalia' which ended the Thirty Years War as having become 'the basis for all future treaties'. In other words, it marked the beginning of a new international order in which the European state system was henceforth to be regulated on the basis of a set of political arrangements made in the middle years of the seventeenth century and agreed by the leading European powers. These arrangements included international acceptance of the sovereignty of the Dutch Republic and the Swiss Confederation, and, most importantly, the establishment of a settled constitution for the Holy Roman Empire. In effect, the peace settlement banished the spectre of a Habsburg universal monarchy that had long haunted Europe, and confirmed the character of the Empire as a loose confederation of independent units, which would seek to resolve their differences through a set of elaborate constitutional procedures without resorting to war.[1]

---

[1] Voltaire, *Le Siècle de Louis XIV*, ed. René Groos (Paris, 1947), i, p. 66 (ch. 6). In recent years there has been much discussion, especially among legal scholars and historians of international relations, about the Peace of Westphalia as marking the emergence of a new international order, in which states were accepted as sovereign and state relations came to be regularised by a nascent international law. In reality, Westphalia can be seen as further codifying a process, both in the areas of state sovereignty and of the development of rules for the regulation of inter-state relations, that had been going on for many centuries, and was far from completed in 1648. For a succinct refutation of the alleged 'paradigm shift' of 1648, see Stéphane Beaulac, 'The Westphalian Orthodoxy—Myth or Reality?', *Journal of the History of International Law*, 2 (2000), pp. 148–77.

This generally benign view of the effects of the Peace of Westphalia was first questioned by Friedrich Rühs in 1815, but was only to be seriously challenged in the period between the later nineteenth century and 1945, when German nationalists argued that the peace settlement had prevented the establishment of German unity, and had condemned Germany to two centuries of impotence, to the benefit of France.[2] But the creation of the Federal Republic of Germany after the end of the Second World War represented a reversion to the principles of 1648, and this in turn helped revive the reputation of the Westphalian settlement. Today it tends to be seen much as it was seen in the days of Voltaire and of Rousseau—as marking the beginnings of a new and more rational reordering of the European state system.

At the heart of this reordering was the recognition of certain religious as well as political realities. With varying degrees of reluctance, the confessional diversity of Germany and of Christendom was accepted at Westphalia as a fact of life. Innocent X, whom Velázquez would depict in all his restless obstinacy in the year following the peace conference, was reduced to impotent protests against a settlement that the Emperor and the leading European powers had negotiated without recourse to papal mediation, and that was bound to diminish papal influence in the lands of central Europe. The peace settlement against which Innocent raged in vain reaffirmed the religious freedom granted to the Lutherans in 1555, while also allowing the enjoyment of the same rights to the Calvinists, and to those religious minorities that had enjoyed them at least until 1 January 1624 (a base-date agreed after protracted negotiations).

Not surprisingly, Protestants gradually came to include the anniversary of the peace settlement in their list of annual celebrations.[3] In September 1748 the city of Hamburg, in common with other Protestant states and cities, decided to commemorate the first centenary of Westphalia. Special services were held in all the churches; an oratorio by Georg Philipp Telemann was performed at the city church of St Peter's; and a suitably restrained prayer was composed which asked God to have mercy not just on Protestants but on all

---

[2] Martin Heckel, *Deutschland im konfessionellen Zeitalter* (Göttingen, 1983), pp. 208–9; Geoffrey Parker, ed., *The Thirty Years' War*, 2nd edn (London and New York, 1997), pp. 192–4. For Rühs, and for the plans being made under the Third Reich for reversing three centuries of European history in the projected commemoration in 1948 of the third centenary of the Treaty of Westphalia, see Klaus Bussmann and Heinz Schilling, eds, *1648: War and Peace in Europe* (Exhibition Catalogue, Münster/Osnabrück, 1998), nos 1253–6, and Heinz Duchhardt, 'The Peace of Westphalia as *Lieu de mémoire* in Gemany and Europe', in Klaus Bussmann and Heinz Schilling, eds, *1648: War and Peace in Europe: Essays*, 2 vols (Münster/Osnabrück, 1998), i, pp. 41–7.

[3] Étienne François, 'De l'Uniformité à la tolérance. Confession et société urbaine en Allemagne, 1650–1800', *Annales*, 37 (1982), pp. 783–800, at p. 789.

Christians, and celebrated the Peace of Westphalia as marking the end of religious conflict and the beginning of Hamburg's peace and prosperity.[4]

In the worlds of politics and religion alike, therefore, the Westphalian settlement was being seen, within a hundred years of the signing of the treaties, as a turning point for Germany and Europe. To eighteenth-century eyes the problem of the Holy Roman Empire had been solved. The rule of law, and a carefully negotiated system of checks and balances, had replaced the anarchy and violence of a barbarous age, while guarantees of freedom for religious minorities, and a degree of toleration, had brought to an end the bitter sectarian conflicts of the past. The Europe of the Enlightenment looked back on these achievements with satisfaction, as clear signs of the progress of European civilisation over the course of a century. Later generations, for their part, have tended to ratify this verdict.

But how far, we may ask, did the verdict respond to historical realities? The Holy Roman Empire itself was dissolved in 1806, and the twentieth century was to witness wars far more devastating than those that ravaged the continent between the 1620s and the 1640s. Moreover, these wars, like the Thirty Years War, originated in those very same parts of Europe whose problems the negotiators at Münster and Osnabrück had sought to resolve. It is true that no treaty arrangements, however intelligently conceived, can be expected to last for ever. But, even if we take a more limited view, and do not move beyond the celebrations of its first centenary, it is hard not to question some of the more easy assumptions about the benign effects of the Westphalian settlement.

In the first place, the settlement did not extend to the war (in itself a Thirty Years War) between Spain and France, which would continue until 1659; and it did not bring an end to hostilities between the Baltic powers. Although the spectre of a Habsburg universal monarchy might have been banished, it was promptly to be replaced by that of a Europe dominated by the France of an ambitious Louis XIV. Between 1600 and 1650 there was only one calendar year without war between European states: 1610. In the second half of the seventeenth century, there were six—1669–71 and 1680–2—but European civilisation was, and remained, a military civilisation, whose normal state was war.[5] The size of armies was appreciably larger in the second half of the century than

---

[4] Joachim Whaley, *Religious Toleration and Social Change in Hamburg, 1529–1819* (Cambridge, 1985), p. 194.
[5] George N. Clark, *The Seventeenth Century*, 2nd edn (Oxford, 1950), p. 98; and see George N. Clark, *War and Society in the Seventeenth Century* (Oxford, 1958), for Europe as a 'military civilisation'.

in the first; wars proliferated until they escalated into the comprehensive European War of the Spanish Succession between 1701 and 1713; and it is perhaps symptomatic of the bellicose character of European civilisation that a number of later seventeenth-century princes took to dressing, and having their portraits painted, in military uniform.[6] War itself continued to be depicted in the two modes, allegorical and documentary, in which it had been depicted in the earlier part of the century.

If Westphalia failed to bring lasting peace to Europe, it was also less successful than is sometimes alleged in healing the religious divisions of the age. Louis XIV's Revocation of the Edict of Nantes in 1685 is evidence that the age of religious persecution was still far from over, although the inclusion of Alsace in the Westphalian settlement meant that Alsatian Protestants at least were spared the fate of their French brethren.[7] But it has been persuasively argued that even in the Empire the outcome of the peace settlement was in many ways to harden rather than weaken religious divisions.[8] The effect of the Westphalian settlement was to sanction the territorialisation of creeds, although the settlement did ensure the survival of a Protestant Saxony when the ruling house converted to Catholicism at the end of the seventeenth century. Ecumenical experiments, like those of the Elector Palatine Charles Louis, proved an abject failure, but in a few states and towns, notably in southern Germany, religious coexistence was achieved on the basis of a genuine parity, with offices shared equally between Protestants and Catholics. But real religious toleration would not make much of an appearance in the German lands before the late eighteenth century, and religious exclusiveness continued to characterise the confessional life of the majority of the cities of the Empire. Similarly, the Jews remained, as they had always been, the objects of harsh discrimination.

Yet if the religious, as well as the international, picture remains bleak after 1648, this does not mean that there were no important changes in the wake of the Westphalian settlement. One of the most important of these changes was the emergence of a new collective sense of Europe itself. The development of newsletters and gazettes during the course of the Thirty Years War had helped to develop a pan-European vision of contemporary events. Abraham Verhoeven's *Nieuwe Tijdinghen,* the various Dutch and Italian gazettes and the

---

[6] Michael Roberts, *Essays in Swedish History* (London, 1967), ch. 10; Geoffrey Parker, *The Military Revolution* (Cambridge, 1988), pp. 43–4. For monarchs in uniform, see Roberts, *Essays in Swedish History,* p. 206.

[7] Warren Candler Scoville, *The Persecution of Huguenots and French Economic Development, 1680–1720* (Berkeley/Los Angeles, Calif., 1960), p. 5 note 11.

[8] See François, 'De l'Uniformité à la tolérance'.

French *Gazette* of Théophraste Renaudot, all depended on a network of contacts and informants across the continent, and their efforts created the beginnings of an informed European public and public opinion. It was to this public opinion that Cardinal Richelieu was appealing in his unfortunate allegorical drama, significantly entitled *Europe*, in which Francion comes to the rescue of a Europe on the point of being ravished by Ibère.[9] This new Europe of sovereign states did not at once banish the old Christendom, which enjoyed moments of resurgence, especially at times of external threat, as during the Turkish siege of Vienna in 1683. Indeed, the very absence of that threat, during the 1620s and 1630s, when the Turks were preoccupied with their frontier with Persia, played an important part in shaping the character and course of Europe's civil war during those same decades, and thus of strengthening the secular vision of a Europe of sovereign states. But if the idea of Europe coexisted with that of Christendom, as it did in the mind of Richelieu, it was Europe that was gaining the upper hand in the later seventeenth century.[10]

There is a strong case for arguing that the Europe that emerged from the middle decades of the seventeenth century was a Europe transformed, but we need to look further than the peace settlement itself if we are to understand what was happening. It would seem that the transformation resulted less from the peace settlement than from the character and intensity of the conflict that made it necessary.

For two decades or more, large parts of continental Europe had been subjected to massive strains imposed by more or less continuous warfare. Even those populations not directly affected by the marching of armies and the physical destruction provoked by conflict had felt the impact of war in their homes, as tax collectors beat on their doors, and recruiting sergeants carried off fathers and sons. Simultaneously these same demands of war tested the administrative and political capacity of the early seventeenth-century state to its limits. Everywhere, governments struggled to mobilise the resources required for the financing of armies and fleets. This frequently required the concentration of power for the more effective prosecution of the war in the hands of a few chosen individuals—notably minister-favourites like Richelieu and Olivares—who in turn relied on the loyalty of a small group of officials to see that the Crown's demands were obeyed. The efforts of these officials

[9] *Europe: Comédie héroique* (Paris, 1643); and see Léopold Lacour, *Richelieu dramaturge et ses collaborateurs* (Paris, 1925), pt 3, ch. 4.

[10] For the emergence of the idea of Europe see Denys Hay, *Europe: The Emergence of an Idea* (Edinburgh, 1957), which, however, has little to say about the seventeenth century.

involved the infringement on a large scale of corporate rights and privileges as they demanded fiscal and military assistance from institutions, social groups, and regions and provinces which had hitherto enjoyed a relative degree of exemption from the demands of the state.

The social and political strains imposed by these enhanced demands of the state were compounded by the emergence of a class of *nouveaux riches* who had made money out of the war—financiers, military entrepreneurs, army commanders, and ministers and officials with privileged access to royal patronage. Many of these people in turn used part of their new-found wealth to promote a lifestyle that had significant consequences for the arts. For example, financiers like Barthélemy Herwarth made an important contribution to the urban development of mid-seventeenth-century Paris.[11] Army commanders like the Marqués de Leganés in Spain and the Maréchal de Créquy in France assembled impressive collections of paintings.[12]

Such manifestations of wealth only served to aggravate existing social tensions. Urban populations, squeezed by the tax collectors, saw the war profiteers and newly enriched royal officials as legitimate targets for their hatred. Members of the old nobility and of the traditional ruling elites resented being pushed aside by newly promoted ministers of low social rank. All these political and social resentments came to a head in the revolutionary upheavals that swept continental Europe during the course of the 1640s.

The causes of these upheavals have long been a source of historical debate, but they cannot be understood without taking into account the strains imposed on society and the structure of the state by a period of intense and prolonged warfare.[13] The continental revolts and disturbances may in large part be seen as a response to the pressures generated by the increased interventionism of the early modern state as it struggled to meet the challenges presented by the demands of war. In this sense, the revolts and disturbances can be regarded as counter-revolutionary movements against the innovating activities of the state. The counter-revolution, however, was intended to restore an imagined political and social harmony, rather than one that had actually existed, since the societies of early modern Europe can hardly be said

---

[11] G. Depping, 'Barthélemy Herwarth. Un banquier protestant en France au dix-septième siècle', *Revue historique*, x (1879), pp. 285–338, and xi (1880), pp. 63–80; Pierre Francastel, 'Versailles et l'architecture urbaine au XVIIe siècle', *Annales*, 10 (1955), pp. 465–79.

[12] Mary Crawford Volk, 'New Light on a Seventeenth-Century Collector: The Marquis of Leganés', *Art Bulletin*, 62 (1980), pp. 256–68; Jean-Claude Boyer and Isabelle Volf, 'Rome à Paris. Les tableaux du maréchal de Créquy (1638)', *Revue de l'Art*, 79 (1988), pp. 22–41.

[13] For the historical debate on the mid-century upheavals, see above, ch. III.

to have lived before the Thirty Years War in a state of equilibrium.[14] But these upheavals, while temporarily pushing the interventionist state onto the defensive, also released social and political forces which frightened the propertied classes, and in due course, whether in Catalonia, or Naples, or the France of the Fronde, drove them back to their traditional loyalty to the Crown, which seemed to offer the best guarantee of stability and order.

As if by reaction, therefore, to the conditions of anarchy or near anarchy that for a moment threatened to engulf large areas of mid-seventeenth century Europe, the psychological climate of the post-Westphalia period was characterised by a yearning for a new stability.[15] Although a growing war-weariness may have played its part in encouraging artists—a Rubens or a Callot—to emphasise the horrors of war and by contrast the blessings of peace,[16] it does not seem to have had much impact on the actual behaviour of later seventeenth-century states, which proved just as ready to take up arms as their early seventeenth-century predecessors in the pursuit of territorial and dynastic ambitions. But it may well have helped to bring about one of the fundamental political developments of later seventeenth-century Europe— the growing tendency of the state to acquire a monopoly of force.

'To the king alone belongs the right of the sword'—*Le roi seul a droit de glaive.* This was to become a central theme of the later seventeenth century, as monarchs sought to curb those elements in their states that possessed the potential to unleash the forces of anarchy, and at the same time to obtain closer personal control over their armies—those great military machines that, as the career of Albrecht von Wallenstein had shown, had become too formidable to be left in the hands of the *condottieri.* In attempting to assert their monopoly of force, the princes of the later seventeenth century benefited from the desire of the propertied classes for the restoration of order and good government. But the princes also had to make concessions to those same classes in order to reach a mutually satisfactory accommodation.

One of the most significant of these concessions was the abandonment by many rulers of the earlier seventeenth-century practice of government by minister-favourite. A striking characteristic of the Europe of the Thirty Years War had been the dominance of apparently all-powerful ministers whose

---

[14] See Helmut G. Koenigsberger, *Politicians and Virtuosi: Essays in Early Modern History* (London, 1986), p. 165.
[15] For the theme of stability in later seventeenth-century Europe, see Theodore K. Rabb, *The Struggle for Stability in Early Modern Europe* (Oxford, 1975).
[16] See *ibid.*, pp. 123–5. See below, Fig. 17.

power was based on winning and retaining the favour of the prince—a dominance vividly suggested by the looming presence of the Count-Duke of
Olivares just behind Philip IV in Juan Bautista Maino's great painting of the
Recapture of Bahía for the Hall of Realms in the new palace of the Buen Retiro
in Madrid (Fig. 3).[17] The revolutionary movements of the 1640s had been, at
least in part, a reaction to this dominance. When Olivares fell from power in
1643, Philip IV announced that in future he would govern by himself.[18]
Although Philip never really managed this, Don Luis de Haro, who negotiated
the Peace of the Pyrenees with Cardinal Mazarin, never enjoyed as much
power as his uncle, the Count-Duke. In 1661, on the death of Mazarin, the
young Louis XIV surprised the world by refusing to replace him, as had been
expected, by Nicholas Foucquet, and announcing that he, too, intended in
future to govern by himself.[19] Four years later, on the death of his principal
minister Prince Ferdinand Portia, the Emperor Leopold I made a similar
pronouncement. The age of the minister-favourite was officially at an end.[20]

This had important implications, not only for the world of politics, but also
for that of the arts. Richelieu, Mazarin, Foucquet himself, had used their influence and riches to exercise cultural patronage on a lavish scale. Their disappearance reinforced the role of the monarch as the supreme patron of the arts,
and consolidated the position of the royal court as an exemplary centre and as
the arbiter of taste. The later seventeenth century was to be preeminently the
age of court society—a court society that Norbert Elias has taught us to see as
a powerful driving force of the civilising process.[21] Elias took as his model the
court of Louis XIV, and presented the royal court as an instrument for that
domestication of the nobility that contributed to the gradual reduction of
violence in post-Westphalian Europe. Court culture and ceremonial no doubt
played their part in restraining the passions. *Politesse* became the preeminent
ideal, covering with a veneer of civility the power struggles and the play of
interests that characterised life both within, and beyond, the court. This was a

---

[17] For seventeenth-century favourites see John H. Elliott and Laurence Brockliss, eds, *The World of the Favourite* (New Haven, Conn. and London, 1999), and J. H. Elliott, *Richelieu and Olivares* (Cambridge, 1984). See also above pp. 71–2 and 76–7.

[18] John H. Elliott, *The Count-Duke of Olivares: The Statesman in an Age of Decline* (New Haven, Conn. and London, 1986), p. 651.

[19] For the Foucquet affair, see Marc Fumaroli, *Le Poète et le roi. Jean de la Fontaine en son siècle* (Paris, 1997), ch. 4.

[20] For developments in the empire, see Jean Bérenger, 'The Demise of the Minister-Favourite, or a Political Model at Dusk: the Austrian Case', in Elliott and Brockliss, eds, *The World of the Favourite*, ch. 16.

[21] Norbert Elias, *Die Höfische Gesellschaft* (Darmstadt-Neuwied, 1969); trans. in English as *The Court Society* (Oxford, 1983).

Figure 3 Juan Bautista Maino, *The Recapture of Bahía.*

world in which Baltasar Gracián's *Oráculo*, first published in 1653, became a necessary handbook, a survival kit for the courtier in the essential court arts of dissimulation and deceit.[22]

But courts, although obviously providing opportunities for monarchs to impose themselves on their nobilities, are best seen as places within which the interests of Crown and aristocracies were mediated to mutual benefit.[23] Even the so-called 'absolutist' states of the later seventeenth century, starting with the France of Louis XIV itself, depended on a close working relationship between the monarch and the traditional ruling elites—a relationship that was reordered and revitalised in the wake of the political upheavals of the middle years of the century. Crown and nobilities remained mutually dependent, but inevitably the balance between them varied from state to state,

---

[22] For the influence of Gracián in later seventeenth-century Europe, see Otto Brunner, *Adeliges Landleben und Europäischer Geist* (Salzburg, 1949), pp. 130–3.

[23] See the Introduction to Ronald G. Asch and Adolf M. Birke, eds, *Princes, Patronage and the Nobility: The Court at the Beginning of the Modern Age, c. 1450–1650* (Oxford, 1991); Jeroen Duindam, *Myths of Power: Norbert Elias and the Early Modern Court* (Amsterdam, 1995), ch. 4.

reflecting national traditions and the success of individual monarchs in combining their functions as administrators, ceremonial rulers and dispensers of patronage. Among later seventeenth-century rulers, Louis XIV proved to be particularly skilful in combining these three functions, just as he also proved particularly skilful in using artists and men of letters to project his royal image.[24]

The projection of the grandeur and glory of the *roi soleil* across Europe was a reflection of the changed balance of European power brought about by the Westphalian settlement, but cultural hegemony did not automatically accompany political and military hegemony, and in this instance lagged behind it. The image of the sun had previously been applied to Louis' uncle, the 'planet king', Philip IV of Spain,[25] and at the meeting of uncle and nephew on the Isle of Pheasants in 1660 to ratify the Peace of the Pyrenees, the ceremonial grandeur of the Spanish court put that of Louis in the shade.[26] Nor did the French have the benefit of a Velázquez to plan the decoration of their island pavilion. After 1665 the puny figure of Carlos II was no match, either in symbolic or political terms, for the vigorous young Louis XIV, but Louis' style of kingship owed more to Spanish ceremonial than he may have been prepared to admit.[27]

The traditionally close ties between Madrid and Vienna meant that Spanish influences were also strong at the court of another beneficiary of the peace settlement, the Austrian Habsburgs, who shared the inclination of their Spanish cousins for a style of rulership whose principal characteristics were *gravitas* and *pietas*. Since the Westphalian settlement deprived both Ferdinand III and Leopold I of any further possibility of imposing their will on the Empire, they devoted themselves to consolidating their authority in their patrimonial lands and the conquered kingdom of Bohemia. It was an authority that rested heavily on divine sanction, and its projection was intimately linked to the projection of the doctrines and values of the Counter-Reformation.

---

[24] For Louis XIV and his relationship with traditional ruling elites, see especially William Beik, *Absolutism and Society in Seventeenth-Century France* (Cambridge, 1985). For developments in other European states, see the survey in John Miller, ed., *Absolutism in Seventeenth-Century Europe* (London, 1990). For the projection of Louis XIV's image, see Peter Burke, *The Fabrication of Louis XIV* (New Haven, Conn. and London, 1992).

[25] Jonathan Brown and John H. Elliott, *A Palace for a King: The Buen Retiro and the Court of Philip IV* (New Haven, Conn. and London, 1980), rev. and expanded edn, 2003, p. 40.

[26] Jonathan Brown, *Velázquez* (New Haven, Conn. and London, 1986), p. 249.

[27] Burke, *Fabrication of Louis XIV*, pp. 183-4. For the ambivalent Franco-Spanish relationship in the period, see Jean-Frédéric Schaub, *La France espagnole. Les racines hispaniques de l'absolutisme français* (Paris, 2003).

In the hands of Ferdinand, and particularly of Leopold, the Imperial court became a vital instrument in the creation of a political and religious culture which transcended national boundaries and did much to inculcate a sense of loyalty to the dynasty among multiethnic populations. In the absence of an Austrian 'state' comparable to the French state, this common court culture became even more crucial as a unifying element than it was in the France of Louis XIV. As the centre of an international nobility the court of Vienna, even more than the court of Versailles, linked ruler and aristocracy in a relationship based on shared allegiance to a set of political, religious and cultural ideals. The nobility in turn transmitted those ideals to their homelands. Through art and architecture, literature and music—and notably opera—the court of Vienna promoted the diffusion of a shared baroque civilisation through the lands of central and eastern Europe, making it a pole of counter-attraction to the court at Versailles.[28]

For all its Catholic characteristics, this baroque culture spilled over into Protestant societies. It has been suggested, for example, that the Lutherans of Augsburg, who in the later seventeenth century were in the majority, appropriated some of the motifs and methods of their Roman Catholic rivals, precisely in order to affirm more strongly their Protestant identity. Their churches took on something of the exuberant splendour of contemporary Catholic churches, while their commemorative festivities acquired a flamboyance more commonly associated with Catholic feast days.[29] But in general we still have too little precise information about the degree to which religious affiliation influenced aesthetic sensibilities, for instance as reflected in the acquisition or commissioning of works of art. In an article on the ownership of paintings in seventeenth-century Metz, Philip Benedict used the evidence provided by inventories compiled in 1645–7 and 1667–72 to show that there were significant contrasts, as well as similarities, between Catholic and Protestant taste. The number of paintings owned by Protestants and Catholics of the same social class was roughly the same, but, as might have been expected, religious paintings were much rarer in Protestant than Catholic households, forming 27 per cent as compared with 61 per cent of the works of art they contained. By way of compensation, the Huguenots owned more genre paintings and historical and mythological works than their Catholic

[28] Robert J. W. Evans, *The Making of the Habsburg Monarchy, 1550–1700* (Oxford, 1979), especially pp. 152–4, and Victor L. Tapié, *Baroque et classicisme* (Paris, 1957), bk 3, ch. 1, for the Baroque in Central and Eastern Europe. See also Duindam, *Myths of Power*, pp. 126–33, for a comparison of Vienna and Versailles.
[29] François, 'De l'Uniformité à la tolérance', p. 789.

counterparts. Not surprisingly, Catholic households were crowded with devotional images, among which representations of the Virgin, the saints, the
crucifixion and deposition, and the Magdalen enjoyed the greatest popularity.
By contrast, the religious paintings in Huguenot households mostly depicted
biblical episodes, with 37 per cent devoted to Old Testament subjects as
against only 6 per cent in the houses of Catholics.[30]

The evidence of inventories in one religiously mixed city can hardly be
regarded as providing a very solid basis for sweeping generalisations about the
character of European civilisation in the later seventeenth century. But, in its
largest sense, it seems reasonable to see the Westphalian settlement as hard-
ening and perpetuating the division between Protestant and Catholic Europe
that had emerged during the course of the sixteenth century. In one of his
essays, Hugh Trevor-Roper writes of 'the fatal union of Counter-Reformation
Church and princely state'.[31] In post-Westphalian Europe there seems to be a
significant accentuation of the differences between those societies that
submitted to this 'fatal union' and those that tentatively embarked on the
alternative route pioneered by the Dutch. The growing prosperity of the
Dutch Republic, together with that of England in the aftermath of the Civil
War, offered striking evidence that a degree of political and religious liberty
was not necessarily inimical to success—even to success as defined by princely
states obsessed by the need to maximise power. In the Europe of the era before
the Thirty Years War, it had generally been assumed that religious disunity
meant the downfall of the state. But the survival of the Dutch in their
prolonged confrontation with the greatest power in Europe had shown, not
only that this assumption was far from axiomatic, but that a relatively open
society, which was prepared to accept a diversity of creeds and which reached
its political decisions through discussion in representative assemblies, might
actually possess a greater degree of political and economic resilience than a
closed society characterised by uniformity in religion, and the monopolisa-
tion of power by the prince.

This was not a lesson that many princes of later seventeenth-century Europe
were prepared to learn, although the successes of the Dutch could hardly fail to
sharpen their awareness of the close correlation between prosperity and power.
But the placing near the top of state agendas of long-term measures for the

---

[30] Philip Benedict, 'Towards the Comparative Study of the Popular Market in Art:
The Ownership of Paintings in Seventeenth-Century Metz', *Past and Present*, 109 (1985),
pp. 100–17.
[31] H. R. Trevor-Roper, *Religion, the Reformation and Social Change, and Other Essays*
(London, 1967), p. 40.

creation of prosperity required a sometimes painful readjustment of traditional priorities, pushing the claims of fiscalism and confessionalism into
second place. For this reason the advocates of economic reform often found it
difficult to get their message accepted. In Germany, for example, the cameral-
ists, arguing for populationist and other policies that would promote recovery
and economic growth, found themselves engaged in an uphill struggle with
the fiscalists, whose concerns were limited to the raising of revenue.[32] In many
societies, too, confessional considerations and age-old prejudices were an
obvious impediment to economic advance. The continuing strength of such
prejudices was revealed in the anti-Jewish legislation that swept central Europe
after 1648 and reached a climax in 1669–70 when Leopold I expelled the Jews
from Vienna and Lower Austria.

But the Emperor, under pressure simultaneously from the Ottoman Empire
and the France of Louis XIV, was soon to find that he could not dispense with
the services of the Jews, and was forced to make concessions that would gradually bring them back. Other rulers were quicker than Leopold to read the
economic signs. In their determination to repair the ravages of war in their
lands, the Elector Palatine Charles Louis and the Great Elector Frederick
William of Brandenburg-Prussia set their faces against the anti-Semitism of
their populations, and actively encouraged the readmission of Jewish communities.[33] Frederick William followed a similar policy when a flood of Huguenot
refugees was unleashed on Europe by the Revocation of the Edict of Nantes.[34]
In some states at least, economic advantage was coming to be seen as more
important than uniformity of belief.

Although economic imperatives may to some extent have begun to temper the
winds of religious passion in post-Westphalian Europe, they also helped to
sharpen international rivalries, as states struggled for commercial advantage over
their neighbours in a world in which wealth was still regarded as severely limited.
With commercial considerations increasingly important in the European wars of
the later seventeenth century, the ultimate goal of states was the maximisation of
their power. To achieve this they looked to a more rational organisation of their
resources, a process that involved building up their bureaucracies and bringing a
new precision to the activities of government, for example by seeking recourse to
statistics, or what Sir William Petty called 'political arithmetic'.

---

[32] Ingomar Bog, 'Mercantilism in Germany', in Donald C. Coleman, ed., *Revisions in
Mercantilism* (London, 1969), p. 176.
[33] See Jonathan Israel, *European Jewry in the Age of Mercantilism, 1550–1750*, 2nd edn
(Oxford, 1989), pp. 146–52.
[34] Scoville, *Persecution of Huguenots*, p. 125.

This new enthusiasm for the application of mathematics and reason to the organisation of the state[35] reflected the most profound of all the changes occurring in Europe in the middle and later decades of the seventeenth century—the great intellectual transformation that we can describe as the triumph of the system-builders. A Europe that had experienced the trauma of national and international breakdown on a massive scale was a Europe yearning for new certainties. The rising tide of scepticism in later sixteenth- and early seventeenth-century Europe had called forth a variety of responses from those who had sought to curb its destructive effects,[36] and the philosopher and mathematician Marin Mersenne in particular had sought to demonstrate the existence of a type of knowledge that was not open to question. But Mersenne's brand of constructive scepticism was insufficient to meet the needs of his age.[37] This was, after all, an age that had become accustomed to the precise and orderly movement of clocks and watches. Timepieces, conveying a sense of motion regulated by exact and knowable law, epitomised the precision, balance and control that the seventeenth century craved. Unlike Mersenne's scepticism, Cartesian mechanism, beginning with doubt but ending in certainty, responded perfectly to the aspirations of those who sought to bring order out of chaos. The notion of a universe constructed and kept in motion by a Great Watchmaker and based on mathematically knowable laws—the notion that was to find its fullest formulation in Isaac Newton's *Principia* (1686–7)—offered a new confidence that every problem could ultimately be solved by an effort of the will and the application of reason to human affairs. The results of this approach were to be seen not only in the new scientific and astronomical discoveries of the age of Boyle and Huygens, but also in the great philosophical systems of Spinoza, Hobbes and Leibnitz.[38]

With the advent of the system-builders, Europe entered the age of the pre-Enlightenment, an age in which traditional discourses—for instance the discourse of witchcraft—coexisted uneasily, at the individual as well as at the collective level, with the new discourse of reason.[39] But in these

---

[35] For a not always persuasive exposition of this in the France of Louis XIV, see J. E. King, *Science and Rationalism in the Government of Louis XIV, 1661–1683* (Baltimore, Md., 1949).

[36] See especially Richard H. Popkin, *The History of Scepticism from Erasmus to Descartes* (Assen, 1960).

[37] Robert Lenoble, *Mersenne ou la naissance du mécanisme* (Paris, 1943).

[38] See Rudolf W. Meyer, *Leibnitz and the Seventeenth-Century Revolution* (Cambridge, 1952), for an attempt to relate the philosophical system-building of the later seventeenth century to the problems of the age.

[39] For a useful survey of recent work on the history of witchcraft, see Jonathan Barry, Marianne Hester and Gareth Roberts, eds, *Witchcraft in Early Modern Europe* (Cambridge, 1996).

post-Westphalian decades there are enough indications of change to suggest that a new Europe was in process of construction. It was a Europe characterised by a greater degree of order and stability. Domestically, states succeeded in asserting their monopoly of power over those elements of society whose disaffection had provoked the revolts and disturbances of the 1640s. As a result, violence was tamed, and a certain calm descended on political life at the national level. Internationally, the European state-system was as competitive and bellicose as ever, but certain restraints were being introduced in the age of Louis XIV into the conduct of war which tended to moderate its violence,[40] while the mechanistic principles that were assumed to govern the workings of the universe were transposed to the diplomatic scene to produce the adjustments necessary to secure and maintain a balance of power between competing states. Above all, across the confessional frontiers, encouraged by the academies and by the circulation of journals, a comprehensive European republic of letters was in process of formation, and with it the creation of a new community of the spirit and the arts.

How far the Peace of Westphalia itself was responsible for the psychological, political and social changes of the later seventeenth century is open to question. But the vast diplomatic effort that finally brought forth the peace settlement of 1648 can properly be regarded as a response to a general European breakdown, which provoked terrible sufferings and acute war-weariness among the masses and left political elites searching for a formula that would prevent a recurrence of the disasters of the Thirty Years War. Their search was hesitant, tentative and attended by numerous reverses. But at least they had taken the first faltering steps on the long and tortuous road that might one day lead to a Europe united by commerce and manners.

---

[40] John U. Nef, *War and Human Progress* (Cambridge, Mass., 1950), pp. 155–7.

PART II

A WIDER WORLD

CHAPTER VI

THE SEIZURE OF OVERSEAS TERRITORIES BY THE EUROPEAN POWERS

Preconditions

'The establishment of the European colonies in America and the West Indies', wrote Adam Smith in a famous phrase, 'arose from no necessity.'[1] A vast literature has accumulated around the fifteenth-century European background to the overseas voyages of discovery—the motivations, the technology, the methods that made it possible for Europeans to break through the confines of their traditional space and, in due course, to encompass the globe. Much of this literature, however, has tended to ignore the distinction made by Smith between the 'project of commerce' which, as he saw it, took Europeans to the East Indies, and the 'project of conquest' which occasioned the establishment of the Spaniards, and in due course other European nationals, in the Americas.[2] Instead, the tendency has been to subsume into a single process, conceptualised as 'overseas expansion' or 'imperialism', a whole range of early modern European activities, running all the way from commerce to conquest, which were not always, or necessarily, mutually supportive or even mutually compatible.

There are solid reasons for this tendency to merge activities which Adam Smith found it convenient to separate. It is enough to look at the Hernán Cortés expedition of 1519 to the coast of Mexico, which was authorised as an expedition for *rescate* (trade and barter) and was transformed by its commander into an expedition of conquest, to appreciate the fineness of the line

---

[1] Adam Smith, *The Wealth of Nations*, ed. Edwin Cannan, 2 vols (repr. London, 1961), ii, p. 68 (bk iv, ch. 7, pt 1).
[2] *Ibid.*, p. 75.

dividing one form of activity from another. Attempts at classification therefore tend to look artificial, and would have appeared largely meaningless to many of the sixteenth-century Europeans who ventured overseas in pursuit of profit. But in spite of this, it is not immediately apparent why so much European activity in the non-European world should have taken the particular form of the seizure and settlement of other peoples' territories. Adam Smith himself seems to have been rather puzzled: it 'arose from no necessity'. As they developed the skills, the experience and the daring to make long-distance oceanic voyages, fifteenth- and sixteenth-century Europeans were faced with a range of possibilities in their approach to the non-European civilisations with which they came into contact. These possibilities might be crudely summarised as trading, raiding, or conquest and settlement, or some combination of the three. Of these options, conquest and settlement beyond the confines of Europe itself was the one least pursued by medieval Europeans. The Middle Eastern Crusader states, along with Iceland and Greenland, represented the extent of medieval European overseas expansion before the fifteenth-century settlement of Madeira and the Azores, and the conquest of the Canaries. In this respect, the large-scale European seizure of overseas territories from the sixteenth-century onwards constituted a new and distinctive phase in the continent's relationship with the outside world.[3]

Medieval precedents for overseas conquest and settlement were therefore limited, although there were some important internal precedents within Europe itself—the colonisation movement into central and eastern Europe, the activities of the Catalan Grand Company in fourteenth-century Greece, and, above all, the prolonged process, part conquest, part colonisation, of the *reconquista* of the Iberian Peninsula from Islam. But, while precedents existed, they hardly seem sufficient of themselves to have ensured that the conjunction of conquest with economic enterprise would become so dominant a feature of Europe's relations with non-Europeans. Nor is it clear, as the discussion of protection costs in European overseas commercial enterprise has indicated,[4] that this conjunction was the most economically beneficial method of operation for those who adopted it. The Portuguese empire in India was hardly a shining example of the advantages of the use of force over peaceful commercial competition.[5]

---

[3] For this point, see J. R. S. Phillips, *The Medieval Expansion of Europe* (Oxford, 1988), pp. 254–5.

[4] See the essays by Frederic C. Lane collected in pt iii of his *Venice and History* (Baltimore, Md., 1966), and the comments of Niels Steensgaard, *The Asian Trade Revolution of the Seventeenth Century* (Chicago, Ill. and London, 1973), pp. 16–21.

[5] M. N. Pearson, 'The Portuguese in India', *The New Cambridge History of India* (Cambridge, 1987), 1, 1, pp. 74–5.

To what impulses, then, were early modern Europeans responding when, in the words of that sensitive sixteenth-century French observer Lancelot de La Popelinière, they chose to hazard 'their lives, their possessions, their honour and their conscience to trouble the ease of those who, as brethren living with us in this great house of the world, asked only to live the rest of their days in peace and contentment?'[6] For Adam Smith, comparing the first modern European colonies with those established by Greece and Rome, the former, unlike the latter, derived from no 'irresistible necessity, or from clear and evident utility'.[7] 'Irresistible necessity' for him seems to have been defined by excess of population and, in this respect, although there may have been local situations—as in the lands of the Order of Santiago in fifteenth-century Extremadura[8]—where restricted opportunities at home encouraged dreams about seizing and settling new territories abroad, a Europe slowly recovering from the demographic catastrophe of the fourteenth century had no great compulsion to export its people. The position slowly changed as the demographic losses were made good, and Europe's population once again began to press hard on resources. Late sixteenth- and early seventeenth-century England seems to have been the first society in which the promotion of overseas settlement was linked with assertions of overpopulation at home;[9] but only in the decades after 1760, when the whole scale of European migration to America is transformed,[10] does the occupation of overseas lands begin to look like an 'irresistible necessity' deriving from the vast upsurge of Europe's population.

It seems, therefore, that we should look elsewhere than to population pressure as an explanation for the move by early modern European states to seize overseas territories. Nor should we necessarily expect to find that 'clear and evident utility' for which Adam Smith looked in vain as a motive for the initial establishment of European colonies, although there may well have been more of this than he was prepared to allow. The occupation by the Portuguese of the Atlantic islands in the fifteenth century was in large part prompted by their desire to increase the area available to them for the growing of cereals and

---

[6] Lancelot Voisin, sieur de La Popelinière, *Les Trois Mondes* (Paris, 1582), p. 38.

[7] Smith, *Wealth of Nations*, ii, p. 68.

[8] Mario Góngora, 'Regimen señorial y rural en la Extremadura de la Orden de Santiago en el momento de la emigración a Indias', *Jahrbuch für Geschichte von Staat, Wirtschaft und Gesellschaft Lateinamerikas*, 2 (1965), pp. 1–29.

[9] Cf. Richard Hakluyt, 'Discourse of Western Planting' (1584), in E. G. R. Taylor, ed., *The Original Writings and Correspondence of the Two Richard Hakluyts* (Hakluyt Society, 2nd series, vol. 77), p. 234: 'wee are growen more populous than ever heretofore: So that nowe there are of every arte and science so many, that they can hardly lyve one by another, nay rather they are readie to eate upp one another.'

[10] Bernard Bailyn, *Voyagers to the West* (New York, 1986), p. 24.

sugar-cane.[11] But in general the seizure of territories resulted from a complicated variety of motives, springing partly from aspirations and predisposi-
tions that had developed in Europe, and especially Mediterranean Europe,
during the Middle Ages, and partly from local circumstances in the overseas
territories themselves.

A glance at a map of the world in 1800 suggests that the largest share of overseas territories in European hands had fallen to what might be called the three
'conquest societies' of late medieval or sixteenth-century Europe: Portugal,
Spain and England. Portugal and Spain had forged many of their social aspirations and characteristics in their long holy war with Islam. This war had given
them a traditional, hereditary enemy, the Moslem world, against which they
measured themselves, and in response to which they had developed a militant,
crusading tradition that was kept alive by the proximity of the Moors of North
Africa, even as the Moslem danger within the Iberian Peninsula itself receded.
The continuation of the *reconquista* across the Straits of Gibraltar in the
fifteenth and early sixteenth centuries was therefore a natural prolongation of
a well-proven process—a prolongation that seemed all the more necessary in
view of the resurgence of the Moslem world as the Ottoman Turks continued
their inexorable advance. The extension of Europe's room for manoeuvre
through the development of its navigational skills created for the first time, at
the end of the fifteenth century, the possibility of waging the holy war on a
global scale, and of outflanking Islam by way of the Indian Ocean and Asia.

The *reconquista* had also instilled in the Castilians and Portuguese certain
assumptions about the character and proper treatment of wealth, land and
alien peoples. As might have been expected of societies engaged for centuries
in warfare along a moving frontier, wealth was conceived in the essentially
portable terms of gold and booty. Land was seen in terms of lordship, and
alien peoples in terms of vassals, slaves and converts.[12] These attitudes, which
were not confined to nobles and *hidalgos,* coexisted with more calculating
attitudes towards commerce, profit and improvement—attitudes to be found
in the commercial and seafaring centres of Portugal, Andalusia and northern
and Mediterranean Spain, and reinforced in the later Middle Ages by the
influx into the Iberian Peninsula of Italian, and more especially Genoese,
merchants and capital.[13] At times, the tension between the two sets of

---

[11] V. De Maghalães Godinho, *A economia dos descobrimentos henriquinos* (Lisbon, 1962),
p. 81.
[12] See Pedro Corominas, *El sentimiento de la riqueza en Castilla* (Madrid, 1917).
[13] See Charles Verlinden, *The Beginnings of Modern Colonisation* (Ithaca, N.Y. and
London, 1970).

attitudes reached breaking point, as in the expostulation of a Venetian factor on Pedro Álvares Cabral's voyage of 1500, destined for India: 'If you wish to trade, you do not rob competitors' ships.'[14] But the particular commercial aspirations of late fifteenth-century Europe—the pressing need for bullion, the hunger for spices, the desire to acquire new land for the development of sugar plantations—created at least a temporary union of interest which enabled the merchant and the military man to cooperate in their enterprises and talk the same aggressive language.

Conditions, however, first in North Africa and then in the lands bordering the Indian Ocean, did not prove conducive to large-scale territorial conquest. The Portuguese and the Spaniards in turn were to discover that the Moslem societies of North Africa were too rich, sophisticated and populous to lend themselves to easy conquest; all they could secure was a series of footholds, beginning with Ceuta in Morocco in 1415 and gradually extending around the African coastline during the following decades. These consisted of forts, factories and *presidios*, or frontier posts, that could be used for raiding and trading, and for tapping into the traffic in gold and slaves of the African interior.[15] This pattern was to repeat itself when the Portuguese moved into Asia. Deflected eastwards by the new and glittering possibilities of the Indian and Asian trades, they could make use of their superior naval technology and gunnery to seize an initial advantage and string together an empire of scattered bases running from the west coast of Africa to the Moluccas. But they failed at critical points, as at Aden; and India was to prove as unfavourable as North Africa to inland penetration and large-scale conquest. La Popelinière, attempting in 1582 to analyse their failure, ascribed it not to lack of will, *volonté*, but of *puissance*. The Portuguese found themselves confronting old-established and powerful states, and highly civilised societies which soon learnt to imitate their methods of warfare; and the Portuguese came to conclude, in La Popelinière's words, that the game was not worth the candle— 'le jeu ne valait pas la chandelle'.[16] Modern analyses have added little to this sixteenth-century diagnosis.

---

[14] Cited by Steensgaard, *The Asian Trade Revolution*, p. 84.

[15] Andrew C. Hess, *The Forgotten Frontier* (Chicago, Ill., 1978), esp. ch. 3; Fernand Braudel, 'Les espagnols en l'Afrique du nord de 1492 à 1577', *Revue africaine*, 69 (1928), pp. 184–233 and 351–428; E. W. Bovill, *The Golden Trade of the Moors* (Oxford, 1958).

[16] La Popelinière, *Les Trois Mondes*, pp. 51–3. For a valuable and up-to-date survey of Portuguese overseas activities, see Francisco Bethencourt and Diogo Ramada Curto, eds, *Portuguese Oceanic Expansion, 1400–1800* (Cambridge, 2007).

The Spaniards, too, were deflected from North Africa, but by the very different world of America. Here, as reported by Christopher Columbus in his account of his first voyage in 1492, was the prospect of incalculable gold (*oro sin cuento*), rhubarb and cinnamon, spices and cotton, and slaves 'from among the idolators'.[17] It was a list of desiderata well calculated to appeal to mercantile and military elements alike in the Spain of the late *reconquista*. Columbus held out the prospect of wealth as booty, and of wealth through trade and development; and this, as it soon became apparent, in a world that, unlike the Moslem world, had apparently never heard of the Christian gospel, and was therefore ripe for evangelisation. This itself was not only an important incentive to intervention by the Castilian Crown and Church, but also made it possible to secure the requisite papal authorisation for the conquest (under certain specified conditions) of infidel societies which the medieval canon law tradition had come to recognise as viable entities with their own legitimate rights to dominion and property.[18] In the Christendom of the late fifteenth century there was no more essential precondition than this for the seizure of overseas territory.

By the time Hernán Cortés landed on the east coast of Mexico in 1519, many of the characteristic features of Castilian *reconquista* society had reproduced themselves on the far side of the Atlantic: raiding, plunder, enslavement and exploitation under the sign of the cross, in a new, Caribbean, world with a moving frontier. But there was another element of the *reconquista* in Spain that was less in evidence in the Antilles: settlement and colonisation. In spite of the efforts of the Spanish Crown through its governor, Nicolás de Ovando, to stabilise the society of Hispaniola through the founding of cities and the *repartimiento* of the indigenous inhabitants to settlers in return for their instruction and conversion,[19] the catastrophic decline of the native population and the reports of gold and booty to be won further to the west left Antillean society in flux, as adventurers moved from island to island, and on to the mainland, in the pursuit of easy riches. This was less the seizure of territory than its laying waste by bands of marauders.

'Without settlement there is no good conquest, and if the land is not conquered, the people will not be converted. Therefore the maxim of the conqueror must be to settle.'[20] This maxim expressed the philosophy of

---

[17] Cristóbal Colón, *Textos y documentos completos*, ed. Consuelo Varela, 2nd, expanded, edn (Madrid, 1992), 'Carta a Luis de Santángel' (15 Feb. 1493), p. 225.
[18] Cf. James Muldoon, *Popes, Lawyers and Infidels* (Philadelphia, Pa., 1979).
[19] Ursula Lamb, *Frey Nicolás de Ovando, gobernador de las Indias (1501–1509)* (Madrid, 1956).
[20] Francisco López de Gómara, *Historia general de las Indias* (Madrid, 1852), p. 181.

Cortés, whose first-hand knowledge of the destruction of the Antilles left him determined to avoid a repeat performance as Montezuma's Mexican empire fell into his hands. The dispersal of the *conquistadores* through the continent continued, especially as reports began to percolate back of the fabulous riches of Peru—already a myth in the 1520s before its conquest by Francisco Pizarro in the 1530s made them a reality.[21] But two features of Spain's expanding world in mainland America helped to ensure that the Spaniards would subject substantial parts of it to a 'good conquest', in Cortés's understanding of those words. The first of these was the presence, especially in the central Mexican plateau and the Andean highlands, of large, sedentary populations. The second was the appearance of substantial quantities of gold and silver arte-facts, followed by the discovery in both regions, in the 1540s and 1550s, of exceptionally rich silver deposits.

To Castilians and Andalusians living in the world of the *reconquista*, seden-tary infidel populations who were capable of being subjugated, implied simul-taneously souls for salvation and bodies to provide tribute and labour. For their part, gold and silver hinted at the presence of mines capable of yielding a steady flow of bullion for the Spanish Crown and unparalleled wealth for private individuals. Consequently, the seizure of the American mainland—the acquisition of an 'empire of the Indies'—came to be seen as justifying an investment of men, money and national energy on a scale that would have been unthinkable without the prospect not only of instant bonanzas but also of continuing long-term yields. This investment, like the reconquest of southern Spain from the Moors, proved attractive for differing reasons to the various sectors of Castilian society—Crown, Church, *hidalgos,* merchants, peasants and artisans. The seizure of central and southern America could therefore assume the form of a collective enterprise, conducted, as the *recon-quista* had been conducted, under the supervisory regulation of a king to whom belonged the ultimate lordship (*señorío*) of the newly conquered lands.

The Spanish Crown, however, was operating within the framework of a competitive European state-system, in which any accretion of wealth and power by one state had immediate repercussions on its rivals. For this reason, its new-found wealth of the Indies was bound to spark off a fresh round of competition, together with attempts at imitation. In promoting voyages of exploration, Ferdinand and Isabella had themselves been responding in part to the overseas successes of their Portuguese fellow monarch, Manuel I, the self-proclaimed 'Lord over conquests, navigation and trade with Ethiopia,

---

[21] Antonello Gerbi, *Il mito del Perù* (Milan, 1988), pp. 24–6.

Arabia, Persia and India'.[22] As Spain tightened its grasp on the Indies, Portugal countered by moving in the 1530s to take possession of Brazil, where the indigenous population proved less amenable to subjugation and exploitation than that of Mexico and the Andes. Through the device of parcelling out the land into fourteen captaincies (in fifteen lots) held by twelve *donatários*, who were to settle and develop the land at their own expense under the system of obligatory cultivation (*sesmaria*) already employed in the Atlantic islands,[23] the Portuguese Crown hoped to save the actual or potential resources of Brazil from falling into the hands of its European rivals.

National and dynastic rivalries in Europe, therefore, were already operating by the middle decades of the sixteenth century to encourage the occupation of fresh chunks of overseas territory, either to provide additional protection for those areas already seized or to serve as a form of reinsurance against the loss of future potential assets. Where Brazil was concerned, brazilwood might be the immediate attraction to other European predators, especially the French,[24] but there was always the hope that gold would be discovered; and although it was to be almost two hundred years before this particular dream was realised, the highly profitable development of large sugar plantations on the fertile Atlantic littoral of Brazil was to make it a particularly valuable prize by the early seventeenth century. From the first stages of their movement overseas, Portuguese and Spaniards had taken formal possession of foreign soil in the name of their respective monarchs.[25] Now, as European rivalries were carried over into the non-European world, and other European rulers, beginning with Francis I, refused to acknowledge the validity of the papal arbitration of newfound lands to the Iberian monarchs, the convention was gradually developed that right to exclusive possession was to be based on fixed and permanent establishment.[26] In this way, the seizure and occupation of territory became a *sine qua non* of the overseas activity of European societies, informed by their highly developed territorial consciousness.

For all the activity of the French in Brazil and, later, in the West Indies and Canada, they were to be late and—before the nineteenth century—not

---

[22] Steensgaard, *The Asian Trade Revolution*, p. 84.

[23] Verlinden, *Beginnings of Modern Colonisation*, p. 220.

[24] C. A. Julien, *Les Débuts de l'expansion et de la colonisation françaises (XVe–XVIe siècles)* (Paris, 1947), chs 2 and 4.

[25] Cf. Cortés at Vera Cruz, who 'took possession of the country, and of all the land as yet unexplored, in the name of the Emperor Don Carlos, King of Spain', in Francisco López de Gómara, *Cortés: The Life of the Conqueror by his Secretary*, Engl. trans. ed. L. B. Simpson (Berkeley and Los Angeles, Calif., 1964, p. 66).

[26] Julien, *Les Débuts*, p. 114.

spectacularly successful players in the process of carving up and occupying large areas of the non-European world. The religious divisions and civil upheavals of sixteenth-century France were no doubt an impediment to sustained and effective overseas enterprise in the important initial stages of the game, and the English, although beginning later, were to prove themselves more adept. One important reason for this may be that, unlike the French, but like the Spaniards and Portuguese, the English too were a 'conquest society' when they launched out on overseas enterprise. Their chosen land of conquest—unlike the southern half of the Iberian Peninsula—was to be an adjoining island, rather than part of the mainland; and the people to be subjugated and converted were not Moors but Gaelic Catholics. But there are indications that the sixteenth-century conquest of Ireland, like the medieval Iberian conquest of Islamic Spain, was a useful prelude to, and perhaps even an essential precondition for, the subsequent successful occupation of overseas territory.[27]

The English Crown considered that it had established its title to most of Ireland as a consequence of the Norman offensive of the twelfth and thirteenth centuries. Although the native Irish had subsequently repossessed much of the land, it was therefore taken for granted in the sixteenth century, when schemes were put forward for the establishment of 'plantations' or 'colonies' of English and Scottish settlers, that they were occupying land that was already the rightful property of the Crown. Justification for settlement in areas previously unconquered was found in the argument of land utility, since it seemed wrong that good Irish soil should go uncultivated.[28] Add to this the assumption that the native Irish were to all intents and purposes pagans, and that—in the words of Queen Elizabeth—it was necessary to 'bring in that rude and barbarous nation to civility',[29] and it is clear that a battery of arguments was already in place for subsequent justification of the seizure and settlement of land in North America. Nor is it a coincidence that several of the pioneers of the first projects for British settlement in America—Sir Humphrey Gilbert, Sir Walter Raleigh, Ralph Lane—were closely associated with schemes for Irish plantations. Ireland for the English, like Andalusia for the Spaniards, served as a useful

---

[27] The theme of the conquest and colonisation of Ireland as a prelude to the colonisation of America, which was argued by David Beers Quinn in *The Elizabethans and the Irish* (Ithaca, N.Y., 1966), esp. ch. 9, has been developed by Nicholas Canny, notably in *The Elizabethan Conquest of Ireland: A Pattern Established, 1565–1576* (New York, 1976), and *Kingdom and Colony: Ireland in the Atlantic World, 1560–1800* (Baltimore, Md. and London, 1988).

[28] Canny, *The Elizabethan Conquest*, pp. 118–19.

[29] *Ibid.*, p. 121.

laboratory for developing the ideas and techniques that would make possible the subsequent establishment of overseas empire.

Although the first successful British settlement in mainland America, that of Jamestown in 1607, was to be conducted under the auspices of a joint-stock company, it would be a mistake to read into this an exclusively commercial orientation to the new enterprise. As with the attempts directed by the German banking firm of the Welsers to conquer and exploit Venezuela in the 1530s and 1540s,[30] the efforts of the Virginia Company were characterised by a mixture of motives and interests: a hunger for precious metals; desire for trade with the natives; hopes of plunder; vague schemes for colonisation.[31] In both instances the desire was for quick profits, and in both instances the companies failed. As in Ireland, there was a strong *conquistador* element in the Jamestown settlement. Like the *conquistadores*, many of the first Jamestown settlers were adventurers who dreamt of finding gold and silver, had no taste for routine work and looked forward to living on the tribute and the labour of a servile Indian population. But the Indians of Virginia, unlike those of Central Mexico and the Andes, did not prove a useful workforce. The Virginia settlement was to be saved by the development of a crop, tobacco, which was to be cultivated not by the Indians but, in the first instance, by indentured servants from England, and subsequently by African slaves.

This transformation of the colony's prospects inevitably transformed also the settlers' attitude to the land and its indigenous inhabitants. Now that land had become desirable, its acquisition along the banks of the River James became a principal objective of the colonists. This meant, as in Ireland, the development of a 'pale', which by 1633 consisted of 300,000 acres of land cleared of Indian title.[32] In effect, an Indian frontier had been established; and in spite of sporadic attempts to maintain it, and to guarantee the rights of Indians to the lands beyond it, it was constantly being pushed back under the pressure of population growth in the settler community, and of insatiable hunger for more land for the planting and cultivation of tobacco.

The experience of Virginia suggests, and that of British settlements in New England confirms, that there were important distinctions between the British and Spanish approaches to the seizure of territory in the Americas. The

---

[30] Juan Friede, *Los Welser en la conquista de América* (Caracas, 1961).

[31] Wesley Frank Craven, *Dissolution of the Virginia Company: The Failure of a Colonial Experiment* (New York, 1932), p. 29. For recent work on the early years of Virginia, see Peter C. Mancall, ed., *The Atlantic World and Virginia, 1550–1624* (Chapel Hill, N.C., 2007).

[32] Wesley Frank Craven, 'Indian Policy in Early Virginia', *William and Mary Quarterly*, 3rd series, 1 (1944), pp. 65–82.

Spaniards, on arrival, would find a pretext for 'conquering' large areas of terri-tory deep into the interior, and then would subsequently, and slowly, fill in the conquered areas by founding cities and settlements. The British, on the other hand, were more likely to establish a base, settle a relatively narrow coastal or riverine strip, and then, by degrees, push back the boundaries and, with the boundaries, the Indians. This process, as in New England and the Middle Colonies, might often be very slow. For generations, the settlers clung close to the Atlantic seaboard, held back partly by geography and fear of the Indians, and partly, at least in the Puritan colonies of New England, by a strict social discipline which for a surprisingly long time managed to contain the pressures generated both by immigration and by natural, and exceptionally vigorous, population growth.[33] It was only with the late eighteenth century and the coming of independence that the boundaries were finally breached, and tidal waves of migrants moved westwards across the Appalachian Mountains to seize and settle the lands of the interior.

This difference between the British and the Spanish approach to the seizure of Indian territory may in part derive from differences, at least in emphasis, in their attitudes to the land. In spite of high-sounding claims, both countries displayed initial uncertainties about their titles to land in the Americas. Cortés engineered a 'voluntary' transfer of Montezuma's imperial title to the Emperor Charles V; and, in apparent imitation of the Spanish precedent, Captain Christopher Newport, on the instructions of the Virginia Company, 'crowned' a reluctant 'Emperor' Powhatan in 1608, as a vassal of James I.[34] But the Spaniards, setting aside legal niceties and papal authorisation, soon came to regard the Indies as a 'conquest' of the Crown of Castile, entitling the Crown, in theory at least, to free disposal of the land. For its part, the English Crown, in blithe disregard for any prior Indian rights, gave the Massachusetts Bay Company the right to 'have and to hold, possess and enjoy all and singular the aforesaid continent, lands, territo-ries, islands, hereditaments, and precincts, seas, waters, fishings. . . .'[35]

---

[33] See, for example, Philip J. Greven, *Four Generations: Population, Land and Family in Colonial Andover, Massachusetts* (Ithaca, N.Y. and London, 1970). For further comparisons between English and Spanish colonisation of America, see below, ch. 8, and J. H. Elliott, *Empires of the Atlantic World: Britain and Spain in America, 1492–1830* (New Haven, Conn. and London, 2006), pt 1.

[34] For Cortés, see J. H. Elliott, 'Cortés, Velázquez and Charles V' in *Hernán Cortés: Letters from Mexico*, trans. and ed. Anthony Pagden (1971; rev. repr., New Haven, Conn. and London, 1986), pp. xxvii–xxviii; for Newport, see Philip L. Barbour, ed., *The Complete Works of Captain John Smith*, 3 vols (Chapel Hill, N.C., 1986), i, p. 237.

[35] Cited by William Cronon, *Changes in the Land: Indians, Colonists and the Ecology of New England* (New York, 1983), p. 71.

Yet, for both colonising powers, a nagging question remained. This was well put by Robert Gray in his *A Good Speed to Virginia* (1609): 'The first objection is by what right or warrant we can enter into the land of these Savages, take away their rightfull inheritance from them, and plant ourselves in their places, being unwronged or unprovoked by them.'[36] The Spanish Crown, although anxious to prevent the development of a feudal aristocracy in the Indies, had no compunction about exercising its rights as a conqueror to reward *conquistadores* for their services with grants of land; but it also recognised prior Indian titles. Influenced, however, by Roman Law conceptions of land ownership, it drew a distinction between those lands actually used by Indian communities for production and those that stood vacant, and it was these latter that it distributed to Spaniards.[37] Once the vacant land was distributed, however—and large quantities became available as the indigenous population shrank and Indian communities were regrouped at the command of their European rulers—the distinction between ownership and use tended to be forgotten, in spite of viceregal efforts to ensure that land allocated to settlers should be forfeited if it were not promptly exploited.[38]

In British America, a similar distinction was drawn between land ownership and use, with consequences that—given the pattern of Indian life over large parts of North America—were even more detrimental to Indian rights than in Mexico and Peru. English settlers failed to realise that Indian concepts of property related not to the land but to what was on the land at different seasons of the year. As a result, they occupied land that in their eyes, but not in Indian eyes, was being left shamefully unused; and when they purchased Indian land, as distinct from seizing it, the mutual misunderstanding as to what in fact was being bought and sold led to countless incidents.[39] The general tendency, however, was for the Crown simply to grant large tracts of land to the colonists, on the basis both of its own presumed rights of sovereignty and the assumption that land that was unfenced and uncultivated was not being properly used. The seizure of Indian land therefore came to be justified in terms of a doctrine of 'improvement'—a word that was to be widely used in British settlements in mainland America and the West Indies in the seventeenth and eighteenth centuries.[40] The contrast was with the 'wilderness'

---

[36] Cited by Craven, 'Indian Policy in Early Virginia', p. 65.

[37] Woodrow Borah, *Justice by Insurance* (Berkeley and Los Angeles, Calif., 1983), pp. 38–9.

[38] François Chevalier, *La Formation des grands domaines au Mexique* (Paris, 1952), p. 178.

[39] Cronon, *Changes in the Land*, pp. 65–9.

[40] *Ibid.*, pp. 77–8; Jack P. Greene, *Pursuits of Happiness* (Chapel Hill, N.C. and London, 1988), pp. 197–8.

which the colonists had found on their arrival. They 'came to a wilderness', wrote William Penn, but 'it was not meet that [they] should continue it so'.[41]

In speaking the language of improvement, British settlers—whether they were New England farmers, Virginian tobacco growers or Caribbean sugar planters—were in effect using as justification for their occupation of American Indian territory a term expressive of the accumulative and developmental approach to resources that was steadily gaining ground in pre-industrial England. The extent to which the Spaniards in America shared the same approach remains unclear. As Hernán Cortés showed with his Cuernavaca sugar plantation and his plans for Pacific trade, there was a strong entrepreneurial element among some at least of the *conquistadores* and early settlers.[42] López de Gómara wrote approvingly in 1552 of the extent to which Spanish settlers had 'improved' Hispaniola and New Spain, while Gonzalo Fernández de Oviedo recounted with pride how 'we found no sugar mills when we arrived in these Indies, and all these we have built with our own hands and industry in so short a time'.[43] But it is uncertain whether Spaniards shared the English conception of America as a 'wilderness' waiting to be developed; and, if they did not, whether the difference derived from different attitudes to wealth in the two metropolitan societies, or from the fact that they had come to a different America.

For Spanish America, with its silver mines and its large, sedentary Indian populations, *was* a different America, and this undoubtedly helps to explain the contrasting approaches to the occupation of Indian land. Whereas the English, if they were to justify the retention of their American settlements as valuable long-term investments (the short-term rewards being so disappointing), had no option but to develop with their own labour, or with that of imported African slaves, the resources of an apparently virgin continent, the prime concern of the Spaniards was to extract its rich mineral deposits and the labour and tribute of its indigenous peoples. This made the physical occupation of the land, once it had been formally conquered, a lesser priority for Spanish settlers and the Spanish Crown. For the Spanish Crown and settlers alike the essential requirement was not so much the domination of the soil as the domination of its inhabitants. This requirement implied for the whole process of conquest

---

[41] Quoted by Michael Zuckerman, 'Identity in British America: Unease in Eden', in Nicholas Canny and Anthony Pagden, eds, *Colonial Identity in the Atlantic World, 1500–1800* (Princeton, N.J., 1987), p. 133.

[42] See France V. Scholes, 'The Spanish Conqueror as Businessman: A Chapter in the History of Fernando Cortés', *New Mexico Quarterly*, 28 (1958), pp. 1–29; Ward Barrett, *The Sugar Hacienda of the Marqueses del Valle* (Minneapolis, Minn., 1970).

[43] Cited in J. H. Elliott, *The Old World and the New, 1492–1650* (Cambridge, 1970), p. 78.

different methods, and a different rhythm, from those that would characterise the later English conquest of North America. But at the same time the two societies would be faced by many of the same problems, and would adopt many of the same techniques for their solution—techniques that would also be used, with greater or lesser success, by Europeans attempting to seize territory in other parts of the non-European world.

Execution

By 1800, Europeans had secured control over 35 per cent of the total land area of the globe.[44] The development by Renaissance Europe of the gun-carrying sailing ship clearly played a crucial part in the establishment of European domination, especially in the initial stages of this process when Europeans still enjoyed the advantage of surprise.[45] Sea power not only facilitated the first establishment of Portuguese bases in Asia; it also allowed the Spaniards to secure a stranglehold over the Aztec capital of Tenochtitlán by dominating Lake Texcoco with their brigantines, and to destroy the highland empire of Atahualpa by bringing in their men and supplies over an ocean that the Incas regarded as an impassable barrier.[46] Similarly, it would be their command of the sea that would enable Europeans in the seventeenth and eighteenth centuries to maintain and extend their Asian bridgeheads, and dominate local trade through the use of terror and force.

On land, too, superior military technology gave Europeans important initial advantages, especially when combined with the use of the horse.[47] The use of cavalry had all the advantages of surprise in the Americas, where the horse was unknown; but it also enabled the Portuguese to make conquests in India, and to recapture Goa, benefiting from the local shortage of horses in

---

[44] Geoffrey Parker, *The Military Revolution: Military Innovation and the Rise of the West, 1500–1800* (Cambridge, 1988), p. 117, citing D. R. Headrick, *The Tools of Empire: Technology and European Imperialism in the Nineteenth Century* (Oxford, 1981).

[45] See Carlo M. Cipolla, *Guns and Sails in the Early Phase of European Expansion, 1400–1700* (London, 1965). For the careful weighing by Europeans of cost and operational factors in opting for wrought-iron, bronze or cast-iron cannon, see especially John F. Guilmartin Jr, 'The cannon of the *Batavia* and the *Sacramento*: Early modern cannon founding reconsidered', *International Journal of Nautical Archaeology and Underwater Exploration*, 11 (1982), pp. 133–44.

[46] C. Harvey Gardiner, *Naval Power in the Conquest of Mexico* (Austin, Tex., 1956); George Kubler, 'The Quechua in the Colonial World', in Julian H. Seward, ed., *Handbook of South American Indians* (Washington, D.C., 1946), ii, pp. 380–1.

[47] See Parker, *The Military Revolution*, ch. 4, for an excellent survey of European military power and the non-European world; for European and indigenous arms in America, see Alberto María Salas, *Las armas de la conquista* (Buenos Aires, 1950).

regions that depended on Persia and Arabia for their supply.[48] Yet European superiority in military, and equine, technology soon proved to be a diminishing asset in Asia, and even in the Americas. In Asia, itself already part of the gunpowder culture, sheer numbers were bound to tell after the first shock of the advent of the Portuguese. Portugal had a population of barely a million. In late sixteenth-century India, the Mughals had at least that number of men under arms, many of them equipped with muskets.[49] The Indians were quick to acquire European weaponry, and it was not until the middle of the eighteenth century, when a second military revolution gave Europeans a light, and relatively cheap, field artillery, that the latter were again able to seize the initiative, and move effectively into the interior of the subcontinent.[50] Further east, the Chinese, with their own indigenous firearms, and the Japanese, who both imported and copied European cannon in the sixteenth century, possessed military cultures and war machines that made them formidable potential adversaries for Europeans, most of whom were in any event more interested in trade than in conquest in regions so remote from Europe.[51]

Although the technological gap between Europeans and non-Europeans was much wider in the Americas than in Asia, a grand total of fewer than seven hundred Spaniards, with a combined strength of eighteen cannons and eighty-three horses, could hardly have toppled the Aztec and Inca empires, with their many millions of inhabitants, if they had not been able to draw on many other assets besides sheer technological superiority. The shock effect of horses and guns, although initially powerful, tended to wear off, and it was probably less difficult for Aztecs and Incas to adjust to such innovations than to a European style of warfare with objectives very different from those of the warfare to which they were accustomed. Where Europeans fought to conquer and kill, Aztecs fought to take captives, and the precise rituals that governed Aztec and Inca forms of combat placed them at a grave disadvantage in their first, critical, encounters with European warriors.[52]

---

[48] G.V. Scammell, 'Indigenous Assistance in the Establishment of Portuguese Power in the Indian Ocean', in John Correia-Afonso S. J., ed., *Indo-Portuguese History: Sources and Problems* (Bombay, 1981), pp. 166–7.

[49] Parker, *The Military Revolution*, p. 129.

[50] Philip D. Curtin, *Cross-cultural Trade in World History* (Cambridge, 1984), pp. 230–1.

[51] For the European, and non-European, origin of Asian artillery, see C. R. Boxer, 'Asian Potentates and European Artillery in the 16th–18th Centuries', in his *Portuguese Conquest and Commerce in Southern Asia, 1500–1750* (London, 1985), ch. 7.

[52] For Aztec warfare see Inga Clendinnen, 'The Cost of Courage in Aztec Society', *Past and Present*, 107 (1985), pp. 44–89; for the Incas see Kubler, 'The Quechua', in *Handbook of South American Indians*, ed. Seward, ii, p. 380.

The two great empires fell too rapidly for them to have time to adapt themselves to an unfamiliar style of warfare and unfamiliar technology, but it was a different story for the Indians on the fringes of Spain's American empire, and for those in North America. Decades of uneasy coexistence and of continued exposure to European influences enabled some tribes at least to acquaint themselves closely with European military methods and acquire European weapons through trade, just as the peoples of Asia acquired them. The Araucanian Indians of Chile, for instance, became formidable opponents of the Spaniards, incorporating the horse into their armies from the late 1560s, adapting the Spanish saddle to their own needs and lengthening their pikes to counter the attacks of Spaniards on horseback.[53] The Chichimec Indians on Spain's northern frontier in Mexico showed a similar capacity for adaptation; the Great Plains Indians acquired European war accoutrements and transformed themselves into a horse culture; and northern tribes like the Pequots and the Iroquois assimilated European firearms, and took to forms of guerrilla warfare which in turn forced military acculturation upon their European enemies.[54]

In both North and South America, therefore, the European seizure of land was slowed down, or stopped, by the resistance of scattered peoples, who made use of the time-lag before Europeans encroached seriously on their territory to familiarise themselves with European methods of warfare and devise appropriate responses. No comparable time had been afforded to the great settled empires of the Aztecs and the Incas; and here the very fact of their high degree of organisation worked to their disadvantage. As centralised empires, they were peculiarly vulnerable to the strategy employed successively by Cortés and Pizarro of seizing the emperor, and leaving the imperial structure effectively headless. They were also made vulnerable by the accumulated resentments of the peoples they had subjugated in the process of extending their domination. Consequently, the conquest of Mexico and Peru was a testimonial at least as much to Spanish political, as to Spanish military, skills. By exploiting the internal divisions of the two empires, Cortés and Pizarro turned small-scale European invasions into large-scale native uprisings which

---

[53] Álvaro Jara, *Guerre et société au Chili. Essai de sociologie coloniale* (Paris, 1961), ch. 3.
[54] Philip Wayne Powell, *Soldiers, Indians and Silver: The Northwest Advance of New Spain, 1550–1600* (Berkeley, Calif., 1952); Edward H. Spicer, *Cycles of Conquest* (Tucson, Ariz., 1962); David J. Weber, *Bárbaros: Spaniards and their Savages in the Age of the Enlightenment* (New Haven, Conn., and London, 2005); Francis Jennings, *The Invasion of America* (Chapel Hill, N.C., 1975), pp. 165–70; Jill Lepore, *The Name of War: King Philip's War and the Origins of American Identity* (New York, 1998).

they orchestrated to their own advantage, and conquered vast areas of territory in what were effectively combined European and indigenous operations.
The Portuguese in Asia made comparable use of indigenous collaboration,
although with less spectacular results.[55] This kind of political machination
was at its most effective in places where, as in Mexico and Peru, Europeans
were confronted by large and inflexible state structures. It proved much more
difficult to employ, and much less far-reaching in its results, when they were
faced by clusters of small states, or tribal groupings, as in Yucatán, with no
formal centre of domination commanding a reluctant loyalty.[56]

Biology, however, played a larger part than any conscious effort by
European intruders and invaders in undermining the resistance of the indigenous peoples of America, and clearing the land for occupation. The impact of
European-borne diseases was devastating on peoples who had lived isolated
from the plagues and ailments that had become endemic in the Eurasian
landmass. Smallpox sapped the strength of the Aztec warriors defending
Tenochtitlán against the forces of Cortés; and the Spanish conquest of Central
and South America was accompanied, and followed, by demographic catastrophe. The English arrived in a North America to which European diseases
had already preceded them, with the result that many of the areas into which
they moved were already sparsely settled; and epidemics continued to reduce
the numbers of North American Indians well into the eighteenth century. If,
on the basis of an extrapolation from the figures for Central Mexico, the
Indian population of the Americas as a whole can be regarded as having
suffered a decline of the order of 90 per cent in the century following its first
contact with Europeans, the relative ease with which Europeans were able to
seize such vast areas of territory becomes far more comprehensible.[57]

The biological benefits enjoyed by Europeans in America, however, were
replaced by a net biological loss in their dealings with Asia. Sharing the same
pandemic diseases, the Asians were exposed to no mass biological effects from
contact with Europeans who, for their part, were all too likely to succumb to the

---

[55] Scammell, 'Indigenous Assistance', in Correia-Afonso, ed., *Indo-Portuguese History,* ch. 11.
[56] Ralph L. Roys, *The Indian Background of Colonial Yucatan* (Washington, D.C., 1943); Inga
Clendinnen, *Ambivalent Conquests: Maya and Spaniard in Yucatan* (Cambridge, 1987).
[57] The pioneer work of statistical analysis for Spanish America by Sherburne F. Cook and
Woodrow Borah has been conveniently assembled in the three volumes of their *Essays in
Population History* (Berkeley/Los Angeles, Calif. and London, 1971–9). For the polemic
sparked by their methods and findings, see below, ch. 8, note 61. There is no work of
comparable sophistication for North America, where the available evidence for the size of
the indigenous population at the time of the European intrusion is scanty. See Jennings,
The Invasion of America, ch. 2.

deleterious effects of climate and conditions in regions unfamiliar to them. A high rate of mortality was endemic to European enterprises in Africa and Asia, and the drain on human resources, especially for a country with a population as small as that of Portugal, must in time have come to operate as an inhibiting factor in the seizure of yet more territory. For the seizure and holding of territory carried costs that could at least be roughly appreciated, even when they did not necessarily lend themselves to precise calculation; and—as the anxious discussion by seventeenth-century Spanish *arbitristas* of the impact of emigration to the Indies indicates[58]—a moment was liable to come when the demographic costs to the metropolitan centre of overseas enterprise could not be entirely ignored in drawing up the balance sheet of empire.

Some such balance sheet, however rough and ready, was being drawn up from the very beginnings of European overseas enterprise. Expeditions of discovery and conquest required significant initial investment, either by the state, or private individuals, or both. The hope, and the intention, was that conquest and empire could soon be made to pay for themselves; and it was on the basis of this hope that the ruling houses of Portugal and Spain were prepared to raise loans and play some direct part in the financing of the early stages of overseas enterprise, before having any clear idea of what return could be expected for their investment. As soon as it became apparent that rich pickings were to be anticipated in Asia and America, local and international merchants and financiers—Genoese, Florentines and Germans—moved in and assumed the bulk of the financial responsibility. Then, as the first overseas settlements took root, it became possible, as in Spanish America, to mobilise an increasing proportion of resources locally for further expeditions of conquest. Here, investors in expeditions formed their own private partnerships, or *compañías*, like that between Pizarro and Almagro preceding the conquest of Peru.[59]

Private investment, however, required relatively quick returns, and this requirement had a major impact on the character of European overseas enterprise, going far to determine both the character of colonisation and the limits

---

[58] See, for example, Pedro Fernández Navarrete, *Conservación de monarquías* (Madrid, 1626), *discurso* viii. For Spanish perceptions of the consequences for Spain of the acquisition of its American empire, see below, ch. 7.

[59] For the Portuguese see G. V. Scammell, *The World Encompassed* (Berkeley and Los Angeles, Calif., 1981), p. 264; for Spaniards in the Indies see Mario Góngora, *Studies in the Colonial History of Spanish America* (Cambridge, 1975), pp. 5–16; Hermann Kellenbenz, 'Die Finanzierung der spanischen Entdeckungen', *Vierteljahrschrift für Sozial- und Wirtschaftsgeschichte*, 69 (1982), pp. 153–81. The Pizarro–Almagro partnership, and the controversial role of Hernando de Luque, an entrepreneurially minded priest, is discussed in James Lockhart, *The Men of Cajamarca* (Austin, Tex., and London, 1972), pp. 70–3.

of territorial expansion.[60] Along the northern frontier of the sixteenth-century viceroyalty of New Spain, for example, it proved virtually impossible to mobilise adequate funds for war against the Chichimecs—a war in which further territorial expansion offered scant hope of reward. Such frontier areas, which required the establishment of defensive settlements and garrisons, imposed heavy financial burdens, which had to be set against the profits secured from the more lucrative regions of the viceroyalty.[61] This was to prove a common pattern in the overseas enterprises of early modern Europe whenever they involved the acquisition of territory. Yet the benefits of forcible acquisition were by no means necessarily short-term, as can be seen from Portuguese South Asia. Estimates prepared in the 1630s for the Estado da India indicate that the Crown was then drawing at least 31 per cent of its revenues from its land possessions, as against 47 per cent from seaborne commercial activities. Moreover, in comparison with fluctuating customs dues, these land-derived revenues possessed a welcome stability.[62] Here, as elsewhere, however, the costs of defence were not only heavy but tended to rise, as local forces regrouped themselves and European rivals appeared on the scene.

Although Iberian adventurers and clerics might continue to propose ambitious expeditions of conquest in Southeast Asia at the end of the sixteenth century,[63] an increasingly sombre awareness of the costs to the Crown of empire helped to stifle such proposals at birth. Perhaps coercion was not after all the most cost-effective approach to the conduct of foreign trade. As George Cokayne put it after a visit to the Moluccas: 'The trade that comes by compulsion is not profitable.'[64] It was easier, however, for purely commercial corporations to act on this maxim than governments subjected to a multiplicity of pressures from ecclesiastics and military men, bureaucrats and merchants, all lobbying for their particular projects and for state protection and special privileges. By inserting themselves into existing trading relationships, and taking profitability, rather than 'victory or conquest',[65] as their yardstick, such corporations, with their

---

[60] Cf. D. W. Meinig, *The Shaping of America* (New Haven, Conn. and London, 1986), i, pp. 7 and 55.
[61] Powell, *Soldiers, Indians and Silver*, esp. ch. 7.
[62] See Anthony Disney, 'The Portuguese Empire in India, c. 1550–1650', in Correia-Afonso, ed., *Indo-Portuguese History*, ch. 10, pp. 150–1.
[63] Boxer, 'Portuguese and Spanish Projects for the Conquest of Southeast Asia, 1580–1600', in his *Portuguese Conquest and Commerce*, ch. 3.
[64] Cited in Steensgaard, *The Asian Trade Revolution*, p. 123.
[65] *Ibid.*, p. 137. For discussions from a variety of angles of European long-distance trade and trading companies in the early modern period, see the two volumes ed. by James D. Tracy, *The Rise of Merchant Empires* (Cambridge, 1990) and *The Political Economy of Merchant Empires* (Cambridge, 1991), which contain much useful material.

restricted economic goals, were better placed to break free of the kinds of shackles that crippled the freedom of manoeuvre of territorially-conscious nation states.

This at least would seem to be true in theory, and the activities of the Dutch and British East India Companies would suggest that, to some extent at least, it was also true in practice. But just as questions of profitability had a way of inserting themselves into the approach of the state to overseas enterprise, so too the chartered companies proved unable to rid themselves of the territorial preoccupations normally associated with states. This was particularly apparent in the experience of the Dutch, those latecomers to the practice of empire. In the Americas the West India Company was conceived from the beginning as an instrument for breaking the Iberian monopoly, and was soon involved in a long and ultimately abortive effort to conquer and colonise Brazil.[66] In Asia, the principal theatre of Dutch overseas interests, the Dutch East India Company, the VOC, quickly discovered that, like the Portuguese, it needed entrepots, factories and bases to protect its sea lanes; this in turn involved securing voluntary or involuntary concessions from rulers, and in some instances, as in the Moluccas, open conquest, whether from the Portuguese or from weak local potentates. 'Trade', argued Jan Pieterszoon Coen in 1614, 'cannot be maintained without war, nor war without trade.'[67] The directors at home might attempt to rein him in, but neither then, nor later in the century, was the VOC immune to the temptations of conquest and colonisation that afflicted other European peoples engaged in overseas enterprise.

It could, of course, be argued that the VOC from its early years was in some ways contaminated by its close association with the rulers of the Dutch Republic, and that the English East India Company, with its independence from existing political institutions,[68] provides a fairer test. But although many of that company's directors fought hard to save their company from incurring the kind of military protection costs that weighed so heavily on the Portuguese and the Dutch, they, too, proved in the end to be fighting a losing battle. The experiences of the East India Company, indeed, provide a paradigm of the dilemmas involved in attempting to isolate commerce from conquest.[69]

---

[66] C. R. Boxer, *The Dutch in Brazil, 1624–1654* (Oxford, 1957).

[67] Cited in Parker, *The Military Revolution*, p. 132.

[68] Steensgaard, *The Asian Trade Revolution*, p. 120.

[69] See particularly K. N. Chaudhuri, *The Trading World of Asia and the English East India Company, 1660–1760* (Cambridge, 1978), ch. 6, and I. Bruce Watson, 'Fortification and the "Idea" of Force in Early English East India Company Relations with India', *Past and Present*, 88 (1980), pp. 70–87.

The seventeenth-century directors of the company clearly hoped to ensure themselves a relatively trouble-free existence by concentrating trading activities in areas like the Carnatic and Bengal where European rivals offered no strong competition and the native Indian states themselves were weak.[70] But, like the Portuguese and the Dutch before them, they came to depend for their trade on the presence of fortified settlements defensible from the sea. These settlements, like those of the Portuguese and the Dutch, proved to be both assets and liabilities—assets in that, in the event of local disorders and attack, they offered protection to English nationals and the Indian merchants with whom they traded, and liabilities in that they were capable of absorbing and diverting into local defence costs a sometimes substantial portion of the profits arising from commercial operations. This in turn intensified the search for alternative sources of income, with the result that local revenue-raising became an increasingly important part of the activities of the English East India Company.

However hard the company's directors in London might work to steer their agents in India clear of local involvements, changes in the subcontinent itself had come to make this a totally unrealistic policy by the mid-eighteenth century.[71] The establishment of French settlements in the area of the company's activities meant that it could not escape being embroiled in an increasingly global Anglo-French conflict; the northward drive of the Marathas sent shock waves through the entire region, and inflicted grave damage on the rich and productive areas of western Bengal; and deteriorating political and economic conditions compelled the company's agents to intervene increasingly at the local level, whether to protect, or intimidate, local clients, and to salvage company interests. With a large army to be paid for, the English East India company needed still larger resources, which could only be obtained by securing the cession of more territory. The 1765 treaty with the Mughal emperor, which in effect gave the company control of the rich province of Bengal, was no more than the logical outcome of the process by which the East India Company had been progressively sucked into an Indian quagmire from which it must have seemed to the directors that there was no way of escape. By the 1780s the company was described as possessing a 'voracious desire' for lands and territory, and at the end of the 1790s the governor-general, Richard Wellesley, was asserting Britain's right to India by conquest.[72]

---

[70] Parker, *The Military Revolution*, p. 133.

[71] See P. J. Marshall, *Bengal: The British Bridgehead*, in *The New Cambridge History of India*, ii, 2 (Cambridge, 1987), ch. 3.

[72] C. A. Bayly, *Indian Society and the Making of the British Empire*, in *The New Cambridge History of India*, ii, 1 (Cambridge, 1988), pp. 79 and 81.

This process seems characteristic of the entire European overseas enterprise in the early modern period: every forward step created a fresh disturbance which weakened the ground beneath the feet and made it harder to draw back. But the image, while telling some of the story, does not tell it all. These Europeans who, in the words of La Popelinière, were prepared to hazard 'their lives, their possessions, their honour, and their conscience' to disturb the peace of the world, were no passive victims of a natural phenomenon. Nor were their failings simply those of execution. Rather, they were implicit in the very preconditions and preconceptions that sent them overseas. Consumed by the lust for profit; driven forward by a strong territorial imperative which made concepts of empire and sovereignty as natural to them in their dealings with non-Europeans as in their dealings with themselves; and arrogant, and increasingly self-confident, in their attitude to the non-Christian peoples of the world, they proved incapable of observing or preserving a distinction between the pursuit of trading relationships and the exercise of power. If, in consequence, they were sucked into a quagmire, they went into it with their eyes half open, and they made it for themselves.

CHAPTER VII

ILLUSION AND DISILLUSIONMENT: SPAIN AND THE INDIES

In his *History of the Discovery of the Indies*, written at some moment in the 1520s, the Spanish humanist Hernán Pérez de Oliva tells us that Columbus 'sailed from Spain ... to mix the world together and give to those strange lands the form of our own'.[1] In these few vivid words we can see unfolding before us the story of five centuries of European overseas expansion and imperialism, which was indeed successful in 'mixing the world together', although ultimately rather less successful in 'giving those strange lands the form of our own'. Pérez de Oliva's story, the story of European imperialism, has long been a favourite historical topic, but in general historians have been more interested in the impact of empire on subject peoples, and the outcome of the attempts by the imperial power to mould them to their image, than in the impact of the imperial experience on the metropolitan centres of empire themselves. The impact of empire—the empire of the Indies—on metropolitan Spain is the theme of this essay.

The subject is certainly not a new one. In particular we are well informed on many of the material and economic consequences of empire for Spain, as the names of Earl J. Hamilton and Pierre Chaunu at once remind us.[2] But it is not easy to get a sense of the ideological and psychological consequences of empire—of what the possession of overseas empire meant to Spaniards of the

---

[1] Hernán Pérez de Oliva, *Historia de la invención de las Indias*, ed. José Juan Arrom (Bogotá, 1965), pp. 53–4.
[2] Earl J. Hamilton, *American Treasure and the Price Revolution in Spain, 1501–1650* (Cambridge, Mass, 1934); Pierre and Huguette Chaunu, *Séville et l'atlantique, 1504–1650*, 8 vols (Paris, 1955–9).

sixteenth and seventeenth centuries, and of how it shaped their responses to the world around them. The subject, by its very nature, is elusive, and no doubt future historians of nineteenth- and twentieth-century Britain will find themselves facing the same difficulties as those that now confront historians of Habsburg Spain. The major problem lies in determining how far the attitudes of mind that we can discern among Castilians and Andalusians in what might loosely be described as the age of the Baroque are indeed attributable to the experience of empire, and how far they are totally independent of it. We may on occasion suspect that the connection is close, but our suspicions in general are unlikely to lend themselves to verification. Yet if we refuse to postulate any direct causal connection, on the grounds of the lack of firm documentary proof, we may well be guilty of a failure of the imagination, which itself leads to historical distortion no less serious than if we were to assume that the possession of empire was the critical element in the shaping of a Baroque mentality.

The popular image of the viceroyalties of Mexico and Peru was that of lands of boundless wealth and unlimited opportunity. It was an image purveyed by the regular annual arrival of the silver fleets in Seville, by the cash remittances from the New World for the construction of family chapels with their ornate silver altar-frontals, and by the ostentatious lifestyle of the so-called *indianos* or *peruleros*—emigrants who had made their fortunes in the Indies and came back to flaunt their wealth in the cities of southern Spain. The image was disseminated, too, by the letters that the colonists sent back to their relatives at home. For example, a settler called Antonio Pérez writes from Puebla in Mexico to his brother in Alburquerque, back in Spain, in 1559: 'Here, unlike with you, as I can see from your letter, there is no shortage of money. . . . If (God willing) you come to these parts and live with us, you would lack for nothing.'[3] 'After we came to this land', writes Diego de Pastrana to his uncle in 1571, 'things have gone, and are going, very well, thanks be to God, and since coming here we have had lots to eat.'[4] 'Take courage', writes Sebastián Pliego to his brother, 'you are coming to a good land, the best in the world.'[5] This vision of an alternative society, remote but not entirely impossible of attainment, must have implanted itself in the mind of every sixteenth-century Spaniard, holding out the prospect, however distant, of a better life in a new world beyond the seas.

---

[3] Enrique Otte, *Cartas privadas de emigrantes a Indias, 1540–1616* (Seville, 1988), letter 153.
[4] *Ibid.*, letter 160.
[5] *Ibid.*, letter 173.

In *Exit, Voice and Loyalty* Albert Hirschman outlined for the modern consumer-citizen three options which are equally applicable to the subjects of early modern European monarchs.[6] Castilians had, and exercised in growing numbers, the option of exit, or emigration—perhaps 2,500 a year took passage for the Indies in the sixteenth century, and 4,000 a year in the first half of the seventeenth.[7] The very existence of this option must have helped to reduce the dangers of voice, of social and political protest, and so have contributed to the high degree of political quiescence and conformity which seem such pronounced characteristics of early modern Castile following the collapse of the Comunero revolt in 1521. Exit was easy—as easy, wrote the great Jesuit historian José de Acosta in 1590, 'as for a labourer to travel from his village to the town'.[8] One could buy a passage to the Indies without a licence, a contemporary tells us, 'just as if one were buying and selling bread and meat', for a mere twenty or twenty-five ducats, 'and as many as want to come over, do so'.[9] By way of comparison, a skilled building labourer in seventeenth-century Madrid would earn a little under a ducat a day.[10] But if we have a reasonable idea of the popular image of the Indies, and can see how the New World represented at least a window of opportunity for the population of Castile and Andalusia, the impact of the possession of the Indies on educated opinion, and the way in which that opinion affected government policy and action, need closer analysis than they have so far received. Here it will be necessary to trace how attitudes and perceptions changed over time, and how, too, they varied with the standpoint of the viewer. In the current state of knowledge it is not possible to do more than advance one or two general hypotheses.

Educated Spanish opinion of the sixteenth century was faced with the double challenge of situating Spain's empire of the Indies both in space and in time—in other words, seeing it both geographically and historically. The way in which this was done would help to determine responses and reactions as its relationship with the Indies fluctuated under the pressure of events. As far as

---

[6] Albert Hirschman, *Exit, Voice and Loyalty* (Princeton, N.J., 1970).

[7] For emigration statistics see Woodrow Borah, 'The Mixing of Populations', and Magnus Mörner, 'Spanish Migration to the New World prior to 1800' in Fredi Chiappelli, ed., *First Images of America*, 2 vols (Berkeley and Los Angeles, Calif., 1976), ii, pp. 707–22 and 737–82; also Nicolás Sánchez-Albornoz, 'The Population of Spanish Colonial America', in *The Cambridge History of Latin America* (Cambridge, 1984), ii, ch. 1.

[8] José de Acosta, *Historia natural y moral de las Indias*, ed. Edmundo O'Gorman (Mexico City, 1962), p. 49.

[9] Rodrigo de Vivero, *Du Japon et du bon gouvernement de l'Espagne et des Indes*, ed. Juliette Monbeig (Paris, 1972), p. 93.

[10] Jonathan Brown and John H. Elliott, *A Palace for a King: The Buen Retiro and the Court of Philip IV* (rev. and expanded edn, New Haven, Conn., and London, 2003), p. 97.

questions of space are concerned, the humanist circle around Charles V would appear to have developed an enormously potent image in the Emperor's device of the pillars of Hercules framing a globe, an image that stamped itself indelibly on the minds of generations of Spaniards. Let us first of all take the globe, surmounted either by a single-headed Roman eagle, or by the double-headed eagle of the Habsburgs, a device repeated in the Emperor's living quarters in the Alhambra and then in his new Granada palace.[11] The world seen as a globe, with the continents, including the newly discovered continent of America, bound so closely together in a narrow compass, must have done a great deal to reduce previously inconceivable distances to a human scale. In 1566 Carlos de Borja, the son of San Francisco de Borja, wrote to thank his father for the gift of a sphere. 'Before seeing it,' he wrote, 'I had not realised how small the world is.'[12] The image of the globe was a constant, if misleading, temptation to think of the world as small rather than vast, and as united rather than divided. As the Inca Garcilaso de la Vega wrote, 'there is only one world, and although we speak of the Old World and the New, this is because the latter was lately discovered by us, and not because there are two.'[13]

If the world was small, and potentially one, it was clearly amenable to conquest and control, as Bernardo de Vargas Machuca implied when he illustrated his *Milicia y descripción de las Indias* of 1599 with an engraving of himself holding a pair of compasses over the globe, while the motto beneath the engraving ran: *A la espada y el compás / Más y más y más y más* (Fig. 4). Man, and more specifically Castilian man, was in a position to dominate the globe. It was hardly surprising if Gonzalo Fernández de Oviedo, sitting writing his *General History of the Indies* in Santo Domingo, in Hispaniola, in the 1520s and 1530s, should have proudly described Charles V as 'Emperor of the universe'.[14] The Habsburg eagle, with its wings outstretched over the sphere of the world, vividly symbolised Spanish and imperial power conceived in global terms, creating expectations of unlimited dominance. The same image was conveyed, too, by the pillars of Hercules, their antique message of limitation and constraint now transformed into a message of unlimited

[11] Earl E. Rosenthal, *The Palace of Charles V in Granada* (Princeton, N.J., 1985), pp. 252, 257–8.
[12] François de Dainville, *La Géographie des humanistes* (Paris, 1946), p. 92 n. 3.
[13] Garcilaso de la Vega, *Primera parte de los comentarios reales de los incas*, lib. 1, cap. 1, in *Obras completas del Inca Garcilaso de la Vega* (*Biblioteca de Autores Españole*, 132–5, Madrid, 1960), 133, p. 7.
[14] Gonzalo Fernández de Oviedo, *Historia general y natural de las Indias*, lib. 5. cap. 8. (*Biblioteca de Autores Españoles*, 117), p. 135.

Figure 4 Frontispiece to Bernardo de Vargas Machuca, *Milicia y descripción de las Indias* (Madrid, 1599).

possibilities by the proud device, *Plus Ultra*. This message conveyed a new, more expansive, and far more hopeful vision of the world.[15]

The novelty of this vision extended beyond space to time. In penetrating far beyond the pillars of Hercules and establishing their dominion over the

---

[15] Earl Rosenthal, 'Plus Ultra, Non Plus Ultra and the Columnar Device of Emperor Charles V', *Journal of the Warburg and Courtauld Institutes*, 34 (1971), pp. 204–28.

unknown peoples of hitherto unknown lands, Castilians and Andalusians had far exceeded the achievements of all who came before them, as Hernán Pérez de Oliva proudly explained: 'Hercules, wishing to travel the world, came to a halt in Gibraltar, which was also the halting-place of all our ancestors, because of their fear of the ocean sea. . . . But now the great power of our princes has passed through these columns, and has revealed endless lands and peoples, who will take from us their religion, laws and language, and will be forever obedient to Spain, and will look upon it as the mother of all the good that comes to them. And thus the weight of the world, and the preservation of its peoples, settles upon this land of ours.'[16] This shift in the world's centre of gravity—and Pérez de Oliva leaves his readers in no doubt that he saw his native city of Córdoba as the new centre of a world that had been enlarged by its expanding transatlantic dimension—was a phenomenon that had to be set into the framework of the general historical process. For this, a convenient concept lay ready to hand, in the form of the *translatio imperii.*

The *translatio imperii* was an idea that had first appeared in the historiography of Imperial Rome, as an explanation of the process by which supremacy passed from one people to another, and had been incorporated into medieval western historiography through St Jerome's commentary on the Book of Daniel. In the twelfth century, Otto of Freising had linked it to another popular medieval idea, the movement of history from east to west,[17] and it was in this form that Pérez de Oliva appropriated it to make sense of the dramatic events of his own lifetime. 'At the beginning of the world, hegemony dwelt in the east, and then lower down, in Asia. Afterwards it passed to the Persians and Chaldeans; from there it moved to Egypt, then Greece, then Italy and afterwards to France. Now, little by little as it moves westwards, it has arrived in Spain, and has grown so great in so short a time that we expect to see its culmination, without its ever leaving here, where it is held in by the sea, and so well protected that it cannot escape.'[18] How wrong he was! There were others waiting to take up the theme, and the baton, as Bishop Berkeley reminds us: 'Westward the Course of Empire takes its way'—until, of course, it came to a final halt in California.

Spain therefore assumed its place in a divine and historical process, the westward movement of empire, that now reached its appointed end in Castile's conquest and settlement of the new lands beyond the seas. From the

---

[16] Hernán Pérez de Oliva, *Las obras* (Córdoba, 1586), fos 133v–134.
[17] John M. Headley, *Luther's View of Church History* (New Haven, Conn. and London, 1963), pp. 240–2.
[18] Pérez de Oliva, *Las obras*, fo. 135v.

moment when Columbus first set foot in the Antilles and took possession in the names of King Ferdinand and Queen Isabella, the enterprise of the Indies had been interpreted as part of God's providential design. Contributing to the belief that Spain and its monarchs were uniquely favoured by the Lord were the triumphalist atmosphere at the court of the Catholic monarchs as the *reconquista* approached its victorious end and the unity of Visigothic Spain was once again restored; the messianic expectations centred on the figure of Ferdinand the Catholic; and the Franciscan millenarianism which looked forward to the conversion of the world as a prelude to its end.[19]

Not only the apparently miraculous acquisition of an empire in the Indies, but the very character of the newly conquered lands, confirmed the providentialist interpretation of Spanish history and became important elements in the development of Castilian national consciousness in the sixteenth century. These new lands offered, or appeared to offer, untold riches in the form of gold and silver, and millions of souls to be brought to the faith. 'Gold', wrote Columbus in a famous passage in the account of his fourth and final voyage, 1502–4, 'is most excellent; from gold one makes treasure, and he who has treasure can do whatever he wants in the world. . . .'[20] 'Those lands', wrote Pérez de Oliva, 'do not yield bread, or wine, but they do yield much gold, and lordship consists in gold.'[21]

The providential process was made apparent, too, in the alleged coincidence in the dates of birth of Martin Luther and Hernán Cortés. Just at the moment when millions of souls were being lost in the east to the Lutherans and Turks, many more benighted beings, hitherto deprived of the light of the gospel, had been brought under Spanish rule in the west.[22] At this climactic moment of world history, Castile had been entrusted with a sacred mission, the conversion and civilisation of the peoples of the Indies. It was God's providential design that the Indies should be conquered by Spain, wrote Juan de Matienzo in his *Gobierno del Perú* of 1567, 'so that the barbarous peoples should not remain in perpetual oblivion, but rather should be instructed in human civility and have the holy gospel preached them . . .'[23]

---

[19] For these various traditions and their fusion in the mind of Columbus, see Alain Milhou, *Colón y su mentalidad mesiánica en el ambiente franciscanista español* (Valladolid, 1983).

[20] Cristóbal Colón, *Textos y documentos completos*, ed. Consuelo Varela, 2nd, expanded edn (Madrid, 1992), p. 497. For the interpretation of this passage and its enigmatic continuation about gold bringing souls to paradise, see Milhou, *Colón*, ch. 4.

[21] Pérez de Oliva, *Las obras*, fo. 135v.

[22] See John Leddy Phelan, *The Millennial Kingdom of the Franciscans*, 2nd edn (Berkeley and Los Angeles, Calif., 1970), p. 32, citing Gerónimo de Mendieta.

[23] Juan de Matienzo, *Gobierno del Perú (1567)*, ed. Guillermo Lohmann Villena (Paris/Lima, 1967), p. 13.

Every empire needs an ideology and a *raison d'être*, and the empire of Castile was no exception. The messianic, or providentialist, vision of Spain's imperial mission was a source of pride and solace, and a legitimation of Castilian rule. For Fray Juan de Salazar, a Benedictine whose highly providentialist *Política española* was published in 1619, 'the Spanish people is similar to the Hebrew, as God's people', and—following in the tradition of Pérez de Oliva almost a century earlier—he had no doubt that 'the Spanish Monarchy will endure for many centuries and will be the last one.'[24]

In retrospect, with our own acute awareness of Spain's accumulating problems in the late sixteenth and early seventeenth centuries, it is easy to dismiss this type of providentialist thinking as of little importance. But it would be a mistake to neglect it. It had been deeply instilled into the Castilian ruling class over several generations, giving them that sense of natural superiority that seems to be an enduring characteristic of the rulers of the empire. It created an attitude of mind that may have subtly influenced the dealings of Castilian officials with the non-Castilian peoples of Spain and the subject populations of Spanish Italy,[25] and aroused complaints that Castilians behaved 'as if they alone are descended from heaven, and the rest of mankind are mud'.[26]

It is against this inherited tradition of confidence in Castile's God-appointed imperial mission that we have to set an alternative tradition of disillusionment with empire which begins at a relatively early stage of Spain's imperial experience, but only acquires real momentum in the early seventeenth century. *El villano del Danubio*, published in 1529 by the famous court humanist and preacher, the Franciscan Antonio de Guevara, reminds us that from the early years of the conquest of America there had been a persistent current of criticism of the behaviour and the motives of the conquerors. In this story, which passed into the mainstream of European literature and resurfaced in its most famous form in the *Fables* of La Fontaine, Guevara is clearly using the speech of the Danubian peasant before the Roman Senate to send a message to his compatriots. Although in the printed version the peasant has a long beard and a venerable appearance, whereas in the manuscript versions he is beardless like an Indian, his readers can hardly have failed to see the parallels between the Romans and themselves: 'I cannot think what madness overtook Rome when it set out to conquer Germany. For if it acted out of greed for its treasures, it

---

[24] Fray Juan de Salazar, *Política española (1619)*, ed. Miguel Herrero García (Madrid, 1945), pp. 88 and 199.
[25] For the equation made by one official between Italians and Indians, see H. G. Koenigsberger, 'El arte de gobierno de Felipe II', *Revista de Occidente*, 107 (1972), p. 138.
[26] See J .H. Elliott, *The Revolt of the Catalans* (Cambridge, 1963), p. 13.

spent incomparably more on conquering it, and now on keeping it, than all that Germany yields, or is likely to yield for many years to come.'[27] If the sudden cascade of gold and silver from the Indies temporarily silenced those who tended to doubt the practical advantages of empire, it only added to the concern of those who were preoccupied by its adverse moral consequences. In the greed—the *codicia*—that characterised the conquest and exploitation of the Indies, and was roundly condemned by Columbus himself,[28] the strong moralist tradition in sixteenth-century Castile found a central target for attack. This greed, Guevara prophesied, would be the destruction of Spain.

The argument of the moralists against the greed encouraged by Spain's domination of the Indies was all the more telling when it was set, like the providentialist vision of empire, in a historical frame of reference. There was a longstanding equation in western thought between riches and moral decline, and a tradition in western historiography, reaching back to the Roman historians themselves (especially Sallust, who was frequently quoted by Spanish writers), that specifically related the decline and fall of the Roman empire to the softness and corruption induced by excessive riches. With all the Roman parallels that had accompanied the rise of Spain's sixteenth-century empire, it was inevitable that its present and future trajectory should also be the subject of similar attempts at comparison. In the preface to his *Memorial* of 1558, Luis Ortiz, a financial official of the Spanish Crown, wrote of how the 'Roman people and other empires' in due course abandoned themselves to 'pleasures and idleness, greed (*codicia*) and other vices which brought about its destruction, as the ancient histories tell us at length. These gave birth to the calamities which overtook them, as they will overtake any other kingdoms which indulge in these evils.'[29] The treatise that followed was an admonition to Spaniards to avoid the temptation of succumbing to that fatal cycle of riches–idleness–vice–decadence that had destroyed the Roman empire.[30]

The warnings to Castilians implicit in this moralist tradition, and exemplified by the fate of Rome, were reinforced in the second half of the sixteenth century by the reflections of those, like Tomás de Mercado, who had watched and studied the workings of the American market and the impact of

---

[27] Antonio de Guevara, *El villano del Danubio y otros fragmentos (1529)*, ed. Americo Castro (Princeton, N. J., 1945), p. 8; Augustin Redondo, *Antonio de Guevara (1480?–1545) et l'Espagne de son temps* (Geneva, 1976), pp. 661–90.

[28] See, for example, the *Libro Copiador de Cristóbal Colón*, ed. Antonio Rumeu de Armas, 2 vols (Madrid, 1989), ii, pp. 478 and 535

[29] *Memorial del Contador Luis Ortiz* (Madrid, 1970) p. 25.

[30] Pierre Vilar, *Crecimiento y desarrollo* (Barcelona, 1964), p. 198.

American silver on the level of prices in Castile and Andalusia. Those who operated the system, he wrote, 'destroy both republics, Spain and the Indies'.[31] The sophistication of the monetary theories of the school of Salamanca, with its discovery of the correlation between abundant precious metals and inflation, gave to the generalised moralising of the puritanical element in Castilian society a degree of scientific precision which made the prognosis for the future of Spain all the more alarming. By the late sixteenth century it was becoming painfully clear that, for moral and practical reasons alike, the possession of riches was the quickest road to poverty. Justus Lipsius, observing from the Netherlands, expressed in a letter of 1603 to a Spanish friend the irony that was now beginning to be seen as implicit in Spain's imperial inheritance: 'Conquered by you, the New World in its turn has conquered you, and has exhausted and debilitated your former vigour. These are the fruits that riches always bring.'[32]

It was left to the generation of the early seventeenth century to explore this irony to the full. This was the generation that had lived through the defeats and disappointments of the last years of Philip II, that had witnessed the royal bankruptcy of 1597, and had experienced the hunger and plague to which the new reign of Philip III had opened in 1598. It was the generation of the so-called *arbitristas*, the economic projectors and moralists who sought to diagnose and produce remedies for the many ills of the Castilian body politic. All the paradoxes of this terrible moment were caught in the famous *Treatise on the Restoration of Spain* written in 1600 by perhaps the most intelligent of all the economic writers of seventeenth-century Spain, Martín González de Cellorigo, who, in the section entitled 'How the republic of Spain out of its great wealth has extracted utter poverty', pronounces the following judgement on the consequences for Spain of its American empire: 'Our Spain has had its eyes so fixed on trade with the Indies, from which it gets its gold and silver, that it has given up trading with its neighbours; and if all the gold and silver that the natives of the New World have found, and go on finding, were to come to it, they would not make it as rich or as powerful as it would be without them.'[33]

This paradoxical theme of poverty in spite of riches, of weakness in spite of power, was echoed by one after another of the theorists preoccupied by the future of imperial Spain, and anxious to prevent it from succumbing to the

---

[31] Tomás de Mercado, *Suma de tratos y contratos*, ed. Nicolás Sánchez Albornoz, 2 vols (Madrid, 1977), i, p. 208; and see Vilar, *Crecimiento y desarrollo*, pp. 189–90.
[32] Alejandro Ramirez, *Epistolario de Justo Lipsio y los españoles (1577–1606)* (Madrid, 1966).
[33] Martín González de Cellorigo, *Memorial de la política necesaria y útil restauración a la república de España* (Valladolid, 1600), fo. 15v.

same process of decay as had previously destroyed imperial Rome. Castilian society, as depicted by that famous Spanish historian Juan de Mariana and by other contemporaries, was one that had become fatally addicted to the regular injection of silver from the Indies, and had, in the process, lost the will to work; and 'idleness', as the Jesuit Pedro de Guzmán reminded his readers in 1614, 'is the cause of the vice of luxury, and the destroyer of empires'.[34]

The paradoxes were everywhere. The wealth of the Indies, which should have enriched Spain, had merely enriched its enemies. Spain, as the saying went, had become 'the Indies of Europe'.[35] Instead of being retained in the peninsula for the benefit of the economy, silver had simply drained out of it through the conduits provided by the Genoese and other foreign merchants. It was to stop the haemorrhage that Luis Valle de la Cerda put forward his famous scheme for a national banking system. 'Indies without deposit banks, and with usury', he wrote in 1600, 'are nothing but the ruin of our greatness and of the ancient majesty of Spain, since the disembowelling of the earth and the transformation of the ocean into ships laden with gold and silver serve no purpose but to strengthen and sustain our enemies.'[36]

It was not only the loss of silver to its enemies that was weakening Spain. The writings of Giovanni Botero had given wide currency to the notion that a large population was the key to national power, and there was a growing sense from the end of the sixteenth century that Spain, relative to other European states, was underpopulated. At the same moment, therefore, as English projectors, following in the wake of Richard Hakluyt,[37] were representing colonial ventures in America as the answer to the problem of overpopulation, Spaniards were coming to regard the Indies as responsible for depriving Castile of its most valuable asset, people.[38]

In a fascinating passage of his *General History of Spain*, Juan de Mariana sums up the ambivalent feelings of his generation—the generation of the early seventeenth century, of the Spain of Philip III—towards the experience of the Indies: 'From the conquest of the Indies have come advantages and disadvantages. Among the latter, our strength has been weakened by the multitude of people who have emigrated and are scattered abroad; the sustenance we used

---

[34] Pedro de Guzmán, *Bienes de el honesto trabajo y daños de la ociosidad* (Madrid, 1614), fo. 69.
[35] Vilar, *Crecimiento y desarrollo*, p. 192.
[36] Luis Valle de la Cerda, *Desempeño del patrimonio de Su Magestad* (Madrid, 1600), fo. 157v.
[37] Richard Hakluyt, 'Discourse of Western Planting' in E. G. R. Taylor, *The Original Writings and Correspondence of the Two Richard Hakluyts* (Hakluyt Society, 77, London, 1935), p. 234.
[38] Pedro Fernández Navarrete, *Conservación de monarquías* (Madrid, 1626), discurso viii ('La segunda causa de la despoblación de Castilla ha sido la muchedumbre de colonias que de allá salen para poblar el nuevo mundo hallado y conquistado por los españoles.').

to get from our soil, which was by no means bad, we now expect in large measure from the winds and waves that bring home our fleets; the prince is in greater necessity than he was before, because he has to go to the defence of so many regions; and the people are made soft by the luxury of their food and dress.'[39]

A variety of responses was possible to the dilemmas expressed in this judgement by Mariana. The simplest, and most negative, was xenophobia. It was easy—too easy—to blame others, and in particular the Genoese and the Dutch, for the misfortunes of Spain. There was a strong element of hostility in Spain to foreigners throughout the seventeenth century. The mid-century memorialist, Francisco Martínez de Mata, was only summarising a long-established and widely held opinion when he wrote, 'The trade that Spain established with the Indies was the happiest that has ever been seen', and then went on to argue that this happiness was 'destroyed and usurped' by Genoa when it secured from Charles V the right to trade freely with Castile, and subsequently proceeded to show its gratitude by exploiting its privileged position for its own selfish purposes.[40]

This kind of xenophobia would give vigour to the Castilian protectionist movement of the 1620s, and find a destructive outlet in the campaign that came to a head in the late 1630s to exclude Portuguese merchants from the commanding positions they had won for themselves in the economic life of Spanish America and the Iberian Peninsula.[41] But while the paradox of America tended to reinforce the prejudices of Castilians against the outer world, it also had the more salutary effect of persuading a few of them at least to question traditional assumptions about the relationship of precious metals to national prosperity.

The anti-bullionist sentiments already apparent in Luis Ortiz's *Memorial* of 1558[42] become much more pervasive in the early seventeenth century as González de Cellorigo and his contemporaries wrestled with the problem of the nature of true riches. The burden of Cellorigo's treatise was captured in his chapter heading: 'Much money does not sustain states, nor is their wealth to be found in it.'[43] Where, then, was true wealth to be found? Essentially in the hard

---

[39] Juan de Mariana, *Historia general de España,* lib. 26, cap. 3 (*Biblioteca de Autores Espanoles,* 30–1, Madrid, 1864–72), 31, p. 245.

[40] *Memoriales y discursos de Francisco Martínez de Mata,* ed. Gonzalo Anes (Madrid, 1971), p. 147.

[41] Cf. Jose Pellicer, *El comercio impedido* (Madrid, 1640).

[42] Vilar, *Crecimiento y desarrollo,* p. 195.

[43] González de Cellorigo, *Memorial,* fo. 22. For further discussion of this debate about the nature of riches, see Michel Cavillac, *Gueux et marchands dans le Guzmán de Alfarache, 1599–1604* (Bordeaux, 1983), pp. 263–8.

work and productivity of a country's inhabitants, who would dedicate themselves to manufactures, trade and agriculture. This theme was to be echoed
over and over again during the next three decades, as projectors and memori-
alists expatiated on the need to develop Spain's natural resources rather than
succumb to the glitter of the gold and silver of the Indies, which one of them,
Miguel Caxa de Leruela, described as 'elfin treasure, blown in, and then out
again, by the same wind'.[44] For some, like Caxa de Leruela himself, priority
should be given to sheep farming. The gold and silver mines of the Indies were
quickly exhausted, wrote a contemporary historian of Segovia, but the golden
fleece of the Spanish sheep was not consumed.[45] Others demanded urgent help
for the peasant farmer. But although they spoke for different interests and
pressure groups, they were united in their concern for what they called the
'restoration of Spain' by taking measures to increase its productivity.

This meant, in effect, changing the ways of Spaniards, for in the final analysis,
the fault lay not in the Indies but in the Spaniards themselves. Although he entitled one of his chapters 'The poverty of Spain has arisen from the discovery of
the West Indies', Sancho de Moncada went on in the text to qualify this
resounding assertion by explaining that 'the damage cannot be attributed to the
discovery, because the Indies have been very useful' (in providing gold, silver,
merchandise and natural products, and in serving as an outlet for those of
Spain). 'But it is clear that it has arisen from them, because people in Spain have
not made use of the prosperity.'[46] It was, in other words, a false sense of values
that needed changing, and the desire of economic reformers for a transformation of Castile's national psychology turned them into moralists, denouncing
the sin of idleness and preaching the value of hard work and sobriety.

But this was a lesson not easily taken to heart. The revulsion against the
false values allegedly inculcated by the possession of the Indies slid easily into
a revulsion against the Indies themselves. Not everyone would have concurred
with the sentiments of the doctor in *El passagero* of Cristóbal Suárez de
Figueroa when he remarked that 'the Indies for me have something so awful
about them, that I abhor even the name of them';[47] but it is hard to escape the
feeling that the Indies, as the principal purveyor of what Luis de Góngora, in

---

[44] Miguel Caxa de Leruela, *Restauración de la abundancia de España,* ed. Jean Paul Le Flem
(Madrid, 1975), p. 32.
[45] Diego de Colmenares, *Historia de la insigne ciudad de Segovia,* 3 vols, (Segovia, 1974–84),
i., p. 316.
[46] Sancho de Moncada, *Restauración política de España,* ed. Jean Vilar (Madrid, 1974), p. 142.
[47] Cristóbal Suárez de Figueroa, *El passagero,* ed. Francisco Rodríguez Marín (Madrid,
1913), p. 147.

his poem 'Las Soledades', called 'the homicidal metals',[48] had become for many educated Castilians a source of profound disenchantment. This disenchantment found one of its most authoritative and surprising expressions in a remark made by the Count-Duke of Olivares in a discussion of German affairs in the Council of State in September 1631: 'its great conquests have put this monarchy in such a miserable state that one can truly say that it would have been more powerful without that new world.'[49]

It is hard to believe that the Count-Duke would have made this remark if it had not reflected a widespread and fashionable opinion. A well-qualified body, the Almirantazgo, or merchant corporation, for trade with northern Europe, had recently expressed similarly trenchant views in a letter of 1627 to the king in which it contrasted the present misery of Spain with its felicity and prosperity before the discovery of the Indies.[50] While the Flanders merchants had their own special concerns to advance, the language of disillusionment clearly had its resonance at the court of Philip IV.

Although the sense of disenchantment arising from the contrast between appearances and reality was inherent in the culture of the Baroque, it is difficult to avoid the impression that for seventeenth-century Spaniards it was powerfully reinforced by the experience of the Indies. Formerly the symbol of unlimited riches, they now offered a potent image—indeed, perhaps the most potent of all available contemporary images, other than death itself—of the *vanitas* of human hopes and the ultimate futility of the search for gold and silver. Francisco de Quevedo, for one, drew the appropriate conclusion when he wrote in his life of Marcus Brutus (1631), 'it is better, and nearer, to be your own Indies than to search for them'.[51]

It would, however, be a serious oversimplification to suggest that, at a given moment, located somewhere in the opening decades of the seventeenth century, we are faced with the transition from a positive to a negative assessment by educated Spaniards of the consequences of empire. On the contrary, the fascination of Baroque Spain lies in the very coexistence of the two contrasting standpoints, one resolutely hopeful and the other pessimistic. Sancho de Moncada pointed to this coexistence in his *Political Restoration of*

---

[48] 'Soledad primera', line 419, in *The Solitudes of Don Luis de Gongora*, trans. and ed. Edward M. Wilson (Cambridge, 1965), p. 30.

[49] Archivo General de Simancas, Estado, legajo. 2332, consulta, 7 September l631.

[50] Antonio Domínguez Ortiz, 'El Almirantazgo de los países septentrionales y la política económica de Felipe IV', *Hispania*, 7 (1947), pp. 272–90.

[51] Francisco de Quevedo, *Obras completas. Prosa*, ed. Felicidad Buendía (Madrid, 1966), p. 825.

Spain of 1619, when he wrote that 'to many the Spanish Monarchy seems so great as to be eternal. But there is much talk of the dangers that threaten it on every side.'[52] While Quevedo might lament the effects of the discovery of the Indies, Lope de Vega would continue to represent them in the old simplistic terms as the land of gold and silver, and portray a victorious Spain uniquely blessed by God.[53] While González de Cellorigo or Sancho de Moncada might seek to educate their contemporaries with respect to the false system of values that the treasures of the Indies introduced into Spain, Fray Juan de Salazar was congratulating his compatriots on having an empire with such an 'abundance of mines of silver and gold . . . that like perennial fountains constantly bathing Spain, they maintain and preserve it with all its possessions'.[54] This image of a perpetual fountain was fatally persistent and fatally seductive. In 1636, the British ambassador in Madrid gave his opinion that Spain's rulers, assessing their war prospects, believed that 'their golden spring, which like Martial's *aqua perennis* runs from the Indies, will keep them fresh here when France will have spent itself dry'.[55]

It would seem, therefore, that we find in the Spain of the early seventeenth century two contrasting attitudes to Spanish power and the empire of the Indies, representing the extreme boundaries between which informed opinion moved. At one extreme is the continuing belief in the providential mission of the Spanish Monarchy and empire which looked forward to eventual triumph in spite of temporary adversity. At the other is a deepening pessimism about Spain's long-term prospects, a pessimism sharpened by the parallels with the rise and decline of Rome, and—as a result—liable at any moment to lapse into fatalism. If it is reasonable to assume there was a continuing tension between triumphalism and fatalism, this hypothesis may help us to understand better the group mentality of the men who ruled Spain under Philip III and Philip IV, and the kind of thought processes that determined their priorities and resulted in the decisions they took.

This is not, of course, to suggest that members of the Council of State can be neatly divided into *triumphalists* and *fatalists*, although certain individual councillors may well deserve these labels. In the early years of Philip IV, for example, Don Pedro de Toledo, who possessed an exalted view of Spain's military capacity, was something of a triumphalist, while Don Baltasar de Zúñiga, a diplomat who

---

[52] Moncada, *Restauración política*, p. 96.
[53] See Marcos A. Morínigo, *América en el teatro de Lope de Vega* (Buenos Aires, 1946).
[54] Salazar, *Política española*, p. 183.
[55] J. H. Elliott, *The Count-Duke of Olivares: The Statesman in an Age of Decline* (New Haven, Conn. and London, 1986), pp. 520–1.

admired Montaigne and Justus Lipsius, inclined towards fatalism. His nephew, the Count-Duke of Olivares, might perhaps be described as a fatalist with triumphalist moments. Out of this clash of conflicting attitudes a kind of consensus was fashioned, which took as its point of departure the idea of *conservation*, but conservation with *reputation*. If Castile's imperial inheritance was divinely ordained, then it was incumbent upon each generation to maintain that inheritance and transmit it to the next, accepting that the final disposition of events lay in the hands of God and not of man. This meant that there could be no retreat from empire, and no formal abandonment of its more vulnerable outposts. As a consequence of this line of thinking, what we now know as the domino theory became an article of faith. The Count-Duke spelled it out in 1635, just before the outbreak of the war with France: 'The most serious dangers threaten Milan, Flanders and Germany. A blow against any of these would be fatal for this Monarchy, since in each case the rest of the Monarchy would follow. Germany would be followed by Italy and Flanders, and Flanders by the Indies.'[56]

The debate therefore became one about methods rather than ends. There were hardliners, who advocated preemptive strikes against Spain's enemies, even at the risk of extending the international conflict, and softliners, who were anxious not to weaken Spain by overcommitting its resources, and preferred to wait upon events. But whatever the disagreement about methods, the universally agreed aim was the *conservation* of the Spanish Monarchy. This placed a heavy burden on Spain's ruling elite, fostering a defensive and conservative mentality which seems to be a characteristic of ruling elites in the centres of empire. The possession of empire is, after all, likely to be viewed as a sacred mission and, therefore, as an awesome and unique responsibility. This attitude is liable to lead to mental rigidity and a fear of innovation, and in this respect the ruling class of seventeenth-century Spain was no exception. Legalistic and precedent-bound, the hierarchy of councillors and officials who governed the empire was unlikely to take initiatives that would place it at risk. If, even by seventeenth-century standards, Spain seems unusual in its distrust of novelty, this may not be unrelated to its possession of overseas empire, with all the weight of ideological baggage that empire carries in its train.

Yet the sheer logic of events in the opening decades of the seventeenth century was itself conspiring to force some degree of change and innovation on a reluctant ruling elite, if only because without them the task of *conservation* threatened to become unmanageable. It was becoming clear that the growing

---

[56] Cited in John H. Elliott, *El Conde-Duque de Olivares y la herencia de Felipe II* (Valladolid, 1977), p. 91.

costs of imperial defence, in both the Old World and the New, were placing intolerable burdens on an impoverished royal treasury, and this was happening just when the most tangible benefits of empire, in the form of the remittances from the Indies, were beginning to decline dramatically. A drop in Indies revenues from two million ducats a year at the start of the reign of Philip III to under one million in its final years provided eloquent confirmation of the argument that was now being heard on every side—from the Cortes, the *arbitristas* and sections of the royal administration itself—that something must be done. It was this conviction, increasingly widespread among informed elements of Castilian society, that helped bring a reforming regime to power in 1621.

The two central planks in the programme of this reformist regime of Zúñiga and Olivares were the restoration of Castile's shattered economy and a more rational organisation of the programme of imperial defence, designed to share the defence burden more equitably among the different kingdoms and provinces of the Monarchy. In this, as in many other features of the programme, the new regime was drawing heavily on the *arbitrista* writings of the reign of Philip III. But behind the programme for fiscal and economic reform, designed to conserve the Monarchy and empire, lay a puritanical philosophy, also shared by many of the *arbitristas,* which might almost be described as anti-imperialist, in that it was inspired, at least in part, by the prevailing sense of disillusionment with the consequences of empire.

The regime of Olivares was asking for a profound moral regeneration of Castile as an essential accompaniment to the economic regeneration to which it was committed. The programme of moral regeneration was prompted by a mood of revulsion against the general laxity of government and society during the reign that had recently drawn to a close. By means of a kind of spiritual house-cleansing, which would lead the Olivares regime to impose new sumptuary legislation, close the brothels, and tighten the censorship on books and plays, it was hoped to oblige God to look with favour once again on His chosen people of Castile. For how else were the present calamities to be explained except by the sins of a nation which, like the children of Israel, had gone astray?

The laxity to which Castile had succumbed could be directly attributed to the corrupting effects of empire. Garcilaso de la Vega had written in his *Conquest of Peru:* 'Those who look with other than common eyes on the riches that Peru has sent to the old world and dispersed through it, say that they have been of more harm than value. For they claim that riches are normally a source of vice rather than virtue, because those who possess them are inclined to pride, ambition, gluttony and luxury, and men brought up on so many delicacies like those that abound today turn out effeminate, useless for government in times of peace, and still less in times of war. . . .'[57] In the eyes of its new rulers, the Castile they had inherited from Philip III was a living witness to the truth of this diagnosis. There was no doubt that it had fallen victim to the disease that had killed the Roman empire.

To reverse this process and check the disease, it was essential to return to the morals and the values of a pre-imperial age. Some years earlier, Quevedo had provided a text for the men of the new regime when he wrote in *La España defendida*: 'If we look back to the customs of the good men of Castile of four or five hundred years ago, what holiness, what virtue and what truth do we see! None of this have we imitated or inherited, but remain content only with the name. . . . Poor, we conquered foreign riches; rich, those same riches conquer us.'[58] Austerity; hard work; the military virtues of loyalty, integrity and courage—these were what were needed to make Castile great again. We might almost say that it was a kind of Castilian fundamentalism that provided the driving force for the reform programme of the Olivares regime, a nostalgia for an idealised medieval Castile before victory had brought riches, and riches corruption.

The reforming ideas developed by the writers of the reign of Philip III, and adopted as official government policy in the reign of Philip IV—reforms to increase productivity and restore morality—may therefore be seen, from the perspective taken here, as an attempt to find a middle way between the extremes of unthinking triumphalism and unthinking disillusionment, each of which, in their different ways, threatened Spain with disaster. Both triumphalism and disillusionment would seem to have been encouraged by Spain's experience of empire. That experience was so dramatic, and so overwhelming in its consequences, that it is not surprising if the mood of Castilian society in the age of the Baroque oscillated violently between moments of exaltation and profound despair. Nor is it surprising that the kind of reformist movement that evolved in response to these swings of mood was itself heavily influenced by the experience of empire, seeking as it did to return to a pre-imperial age in order to revive the virtues that had originally given Castile its empire and marked it out as the chosen of the Lord. But the nostalgia for a pre-imperial past was itself a kind of illusion. In the circumstances of the seventeenth century there could be no going back. No doubt, as Quevedo said, 'it is better, and nearer, to be your own Indies than to search for them'. But perhaps to be your own Indies while possessing the Indies was to ask for the impossible.

---

[57] Garcilaso de la Vega, *Segunda parte de los comentarios reales de los incas*, lib. 1. cap, 7, in his *Obras completas* (*Biblioteca de Autores Españoles*, 132–5, Madrid, 1960–5) 134, p. 26.
[58] Quevedo, *Obras completas. Prosa*, pp. 523–4.

CHAPTER VIII

BRITAIN AND SPAIN IN AMERICA: COLONISTS AND COLONISED

One of the pleasures of historical research lies in the finding of improbable connections. At first sight it would seem that no one could be more remote from Spanish America than the great chronicler of Anglo-Saxon England, the Venerable Bede. But it so happens that Bede crossed the Atlantic in the sixteenth century, although travelling in a Spanish rather than an English ship. At least in spirit he was the travelling companion of Bartolomé de las Casas, the 'Apostle of the Indians', who tells the readers of his *Apologetic History* that, according to Bede, Pope Gregory the Great did not despise the English and Scots in spite of their vicious and bestial customs, but sent St Augustine to convert them. Las Casas explained that Bede himself 'translated the liberal arts into the English language' in order to remove from his compatriots the stigma of barbarism.'[1] Las Casas's message was clear. The indigenous inhabitants of America, once their long night of darkness was brought to an end, were no less capable than the ancient Britons of taking their rightful place among the civilised peoples of the world.

The allusions to Bede in the writings of Las Casas, or in those of José de Acosta, another Spaniard concerned with the evangelisation of America,[2] suggest something of the intricate interplay between Britain and Spain as they embarked on the conquest and colonisation of the New World. Although their

---

[1] Bartolomé de Las Casas, *Apologética historia sumaria*, ed. Edmundo O'Gorman, 2 vols (Mexico City, 1967), ii, pp. 633 and 638.
[2] See José de Acosta, *Historia natural y moral de las Indias*, ed. Edmundo O'Gorman, 2nd edn (Mexico City, 1962), p. 228.

American empires were developed in very different conditions and possessed distinctive characters, they faced certain common problems, and in dealing with these problems there were moments when the present or past experience of one society became a significant point of reference for the other.[3]

There were points both of similarity and contrast in the ways in which the Spaniards and the English responded to some of the challenges that confronted them, and in particular to the challenge presented by the encounter with the indigenous inhabitants of the lands on which they had intruded. Shortly after the British colonies secured their independence, Henry Knox, the American Secretary of War, remarked on the contrast between the British and Spanish treatment of the Indians. 'It is a melancholy reflection', he wrote to President Washington in 1794, 'that our modes of population have been more destructive to the Indian natives than the conduct of the conquerors of Mexico and Peru. The evidence is the utter extirpation of nearly all the Indians in most populous parts of the Union. A future historian may mark the causes of this destruction of the human race in sable colors.'[4]

Knox was making this comparative observation on the consequences of British and Spanish colonisation of the Americas at a time when the indigenous population of Hispanic America, which had been devastated in the sixteenth century by European diseases and by the trauma of conquest and colonisation, was showing unmistakable signs of demographic recovery. In 1789, five years before Knox's comment on the 'utter extirpation' of the Indians of British America, Spain's American colonies contained eight million Indians and one million mestizos in an estimated total population of fourteen million.[5] The total population of British North America in 1770 was 2,283,000, of whom 1,816,000 were whites and 467,000 blacks. Significantly, contemporary statistics included no separate figures for native Americans, but it is thought that the number of those east of the Mississippi was around 150,000.[6]

The contrast between a 56 per cent and a 6 per cent Indian population underlines the profoundly different character of the colonial societies that had emerged in Spanish and British America by the eve of independence. In their

---

[3] For an extended comparative study of the British and Spanish empires in America, for which this essay was a preliminary exploration, see J. H. Elliott, *Empires of the Atlantic World: Britain and Spain in America, 1492–1830* (New Haven, Conn. and London, 2006).

[4] Quoted in Richard White, *The Middle Ground* (Cambridge, 1991), p. 469.

[5] See Table 1 in Richard Morse, 'The Urban Development of Colonial Spanish America', in *The Cambridge History of Latin America*, ed. Leslie Bethell (Cambridge, 1984), ii, p. 89.

[6] John J. McCusker and Russell R. Menard, *The Economy of British America* (Chapel Hill, N.C., 1985), p. 54; James H. Merrell,' "The Customes of Our Countrey" ', in Bernard Bailyn and Philip D. Morgan, eds, *Strangers within the Realm* (Chapel Hill, N.C., 1991), p. 124.

racial composition, as in so much else, these were very different worlds. But how they came to be so different deserves analysis. In his essay, *Of National Characters,* David Hume wrote: 'The same set of manners will follow a nation, and adhere to them over the whole globe, as well as the same laws and language. The Spanish, English, French and Dutch colonies, are all distinguishable even between the tropics.'[7] Henry Knox, in distinguishing between the fate of the North American Indians and those of Spanish America, found his explanation in the contrast between what he called the 'modes of population' of the Spanish and the English. This essay seeks to explore the difference in these 'modes of population' in so far as it affected relationships with the indigenous peoples of America, and to consider the extent to which the cultural inheritance of the colonists may have been responsible for it.

When the Spaniards, and subsequently the English, moved across the Atlantic to settle in America, their new colonial societies were not established in a void. On the contrary, they were founded on soil that was used, or settled—and sometimes densely settled—by peoples who had often been there for many centuries. This immediately raised an awkward question, succinctly formulated by Robert Gray when he wrote in his *A Good Speed to Virginia* (1609): 'The first objection is by what right or warrant we can enter into the land of these Savages, take away their rightful inheritance from them, and plant ourselves in their places, being unwronged or unprovoked by them.'[8]

It was the Spaniards who first had to grapple with the delicate problem of the legitimacy of their title to American land. Initially they rested it on papal donation; and although the critical scrutiny of the theologian Francisco de Vitoria and his fellow scholastics was in course of time to raise grave questions about the right of the papacy to dispose of non-Christian lands, the papal charge to the rulers of Spain to bring the blessings of Christianity to the benighted peoples of America was always to remain fundamental to Spain's enterprise of the Indies. Conquest, or so it was assumed, was a prerequisite for conversion, and effective conquest was dependent on settlement of the land.[9]

Obviously papal authorisation was not an option for the English when they found themselves faced with identical problems of conscience, although the

---

[7] David Hume, 'Of National Characters', in his *Essays: Moral, Political and Literary* (Oxford, 1963), p. 210.
[8] Above, p. 120. Cited in Wesley Frank Craven, 'Indian Policy in Early Virginia', *William and Mary Quarterly*, 3rd series, 1 (1944), pp. 65–82, at p. 65.
[9] Cf. the words of Francisco López de Gómara: 'Without settlement there is no good conquest, and if the land is not conquered the people will not be converted. Therefore the maxim of the conqueror must be to settle', cited above, p. 114.

general tenor of the argument based on papal donation could easily be
adapted to English circumstances, as it was by Richard Hakluyt: 'Nowe the
Kinges and Queenes of England have the name of Defendors of the Faithe; By
which title I thinke they are not onely chardged to mayneteyne and patronize
the faithe of Christe, but also to inlarge and advaunce the same.'[10] England,
therefore, like Spain, acquired a providential mission in America, a mission
conceived, as by Christopher Carleill in 1583, in terms of 'reducing the savage
people to Christianitie and civilitie . . .'.[11]

The promoters of overseas enterprises in Elizabethan England had read
their Peter Martyr, their López de Gómara and their Agustín de Zárate,[12] and
they had the model of Spanish colonisation before their eyes as they embarked
on their own attempt to establish an empire of the Indies. Emigration and
systematic settlement, as they were soon to appreciate, were integral to the
success of expeditions to the Americas. 'The Spanyards', ran the preface to
John Florio's 1580 translation of Jacques Cartier's *Voyages to Canada*, 'never
prospered or prevailed, but where they planted'.[13]

While the English settlers, in their confrontations with the Indians, never
went so far as to produce an anglicised equivalent of that notorious summons
for securing their submission, the *requerimiento*, which left Las Casas not
knowing whether to laugh or to cry, Robert Johnson in his 1609 sermon for
the Virginia Company, entitled *Nova Britannia*, seems to have envisaged a
comparable, if more benign, document for use by the colonists of Jamestown.
'And as for supplanting the savages', he told his congregation, 'we have no such
intent: Our intrusion into their possessions shall tend to their great good, and
no way to their hurt, unlesse as unbridled beastes, they procure it to themselves: Wee purpose to proclaime and make it knowne to them all, by some
publike interpretation that our comming thither is to plant our selves in their
countrie: yet not to supplant and roote them oute, but to bring them from
their base condition to a farre better: First, in regard of God the Creator, and
of Jesus Christ their Redeemer, if they will beleeve in him. And secondly, in
respect of earthly blessings, whereof they have now no comfortable use, but in

[10] Richard Hakluyt, 'Discourse of the Western Planting' (1584), in E. G. R. Taylor, *The
Original Writings and Correspondence of the Two Richard Hakluyts* (Hakluyt Society, 2nd
series, vols 76–7, London, 1935), ii, p. 215.
[11] *The Voyages and Colonizing Enterprises of Sir Humphrey Gilbert*, ed. D. B. Quinn (Hakluyt
Society, 2nd series, vols 83–4, London, 1940), ii, p. 361.
[12] See Sir George Peckham's account of his sources in Quinn, *Voyages of Sir Humphrey
Gilbert*, ii, pp. 448–9.
[13] Cited in John Parker, *Books to Build an Empire: A Bibliographical History of English
Overseas Interests to 1620* (Amsterdam, 1965), p. 105.

beastly brutish manner, with promise to defend them against all publike and private enemies.'[14]

Yet if the English, when contemplating the settlement of the land and the conversion of the native population to Christianity and civility, had before their eyes the model—both positive and negative—of the Spaniards, they themselves were by no means novices in the arts of colonisation. Tudor England, after all, was planting settlements and holding in subjugation an alien population in its kingdom and colony of Ireland, just as Castile, before embarking on the conquest of the Indies, had been settling newly conquered lands, and acquiring dominion over an alien population, in the Moorish kingdom of Granada. Both Spain and England, in other words, have a claim to be regarded as proto-colonial powers even before they sent settlers to the Indies. In both instances one would expect their earlier, European, experience to have coloured their responses to the peoples of the Americas, but so far we lack a systematic and comprehensive analysis of the ways in which institutions and attitudes that had been shaped respectively in the conquest and colonisation of Andalusia and Ireland influenced the process of colonisation in America.[15]

It is enough, however, to look at the *Letters from Mexico* of Hernán Cortés to see how the conquistadores instinctively tended to equate the Mexica with the Moors. Aztec temples are described as mosques;[16] comparisons are drawn between Tlaxcala and Granada, to the advantage of the former;[17] and when the Mexica are fighting they are described, as the Moors used to be described, as 'mad dogs' (*perros rabiosos*).[18] Similarly, the English have a way of equating the Indians and the Irish. 'The Natives of New England', wrote Thomas Morton, 'are accustomed to build their houses, much like the wild Irish. . . .'[19] As Hugh Peter remarked in 1646, 'the wild Irish and the Indian do not much differ'.[20]

---

[14] Peter Force, *Tracts and Other Papers relating principally to the origin, settlement and progress of the Colonies in North America*, 4 vols (Washington, D.C., 1836–46), i, no. 6, p. 13.

[15] Though see Antonio Garrido Aranda, *Moriscos e Indios* (Mexico, 1980), and Mercedes García-Arenal, 'Moriscos e indios. Para un estudio comparado de métodos de conquista y evangelización', *Chronica Nova*, 20 (1992), pp. 153–75. For Ireland, see James Muldoon, 'The Indian as Irishman', *Essex Institute Historical Collections*, 111 (1975), pp. 267–89. By contrast, Alden T. Vaughan, 'Early English Paradigms for New World Natives', *Proceedings of the American Antiquarian Society*, 102 (1992), pp. 33–67, is sceptical about the role of Ireland as a formative model in the British colonisation of America.

[16] Hernán Cortés, *Cartas y documentos*, ed. Mario Hernández Sánchez-Barba (Mexico City, 1963), p. 25.

[17] *Ibid.*, p. 45.

[18] *Ibid.*, p. 159.

[19] Thomas Morton, *New English Canaan* (1632), in Force, *Tracts*, ii, no. 5, p. 19.

[20] Cited in H. C. Porter, *The Inconstant Savage* (London, 1979), p. 203.

How did these parallels influence colonial practice? An alien population, whether Irish, Morisco or Indian, was perceived as essentially inferior, in that it lacked certain essential aspects of civility, as revealed by such tell-tale signs as its state of dress or of undress, or the length of its hair—always a sensitive issue. In the mid-sixteenth century a Spanish official in Peru, Juan de Matienzo, showed himself more tolerant than many of his compatriots of the Andean custom of wearing the hair long. 'Some regard long hair as bad. But personally I see no objection, except perhaps on grounds of cleanliness.'[21] The case against long hair in the Anglo-American world was put more forcefully by John Bulwer in the mid-seventeenth century, when he criticised the practice among both the Irish and the Indians, whom he condemned for 'never cutting nor regulating their hair, as suffering themselves to enter into a neerer alliance with beasts than Nature ever intended'.[22]

Civility was first required if these people were to be brought to Christianity, for the Gaelic Catholics were considered quite as pagan as the American Indians.[23] The extirpation of barbarism therefore became a justification for domination, prompting the English and the Spaniards to see themselves as the heirs and successors of the imperial Romans, and bringing comparable benefits to their subject peoples.[24] Bishop Diego de Landa, in his *Account of the Affairs of Yucatán,* writes how the Indians now have Spanish money, and tools, and have been taught mechanical skills, enabling them to live 'incomparably more like men'.[25] In expatiating on the benefits that the Indians could expect from the coming of the English, Robert Johnson, in his *Nova Britannia,* drew an analogy, similar to that drawn by Las Casas from his reading of Bede, between the condition of the Britons before and after the coming of the Romans, 'comparing our present happinesse with our former ancient miseries, wherein wee had continued brutish, poore and naked Britanes to this day, if *Iulius Caesar* with his Romane Legions (or some other) had not laid the ground

---

[21] Juan de Matienzo, *Gobierno del Perú (1567),* ed. Guillermo Lohmann Villena (Paris/Lima, 1967), p. 80.

[22] See James Axtell, *The Invasion Within* (New York and Oxford, 1985), p. 175.

[23] Nicholas Canny, *The Elizabethan Conquest of Ireland: A Pattern Established, 1565–1576* (New York, 1976), p. 125.

[24] For the English and the Romans see Muldoon, 'The Indian as Irishman', p. 279, and Karen Ordahl Kupperman, *Settling with the Indians* (Totowa, N.J., 1980), p. 113. For Spanish America and the Roman model, see the admirable study by David A. Lupher, *Romans in a New World: Classical Models in Sixteenth-Century Spanish America* (Ann Arbor, Mich., 2003). The Roman imperial theme in Spanish America as expressed in architectural terms is discussed by Valerie Fraser, *The Architecture of Conquest* (Cambridge, 1990).

[25] *The Maya: Diego de Landa's Account of the Affairs of Yucatán,* trans. and ed. A. R. Pagden (Chicago, Ill., 1975), p. 163.

to make us tame and civill'.[26] But there were important differences in the British and Spanish approaches to these indigenous peoples, and it is not clear to what extent these should be attributed to colonial precedents in Europe.

In particular, there is a critical distinction between Spanish and English attitudes to intermarriage and cohabitation. King Ferdinand and Queen Isabella, in their instructions of 1503 to the new governor of Hispaniola, Nicolás de Ovando, ordered him to 'try to get some Christian men to marry Indian women, and Christian women to marry Indian men, so that they can communicate with and teach each other, and the Indians can be indoctrinated in our Holy Catholic Faith, and learn how to work their lands and manage their property, and be turned into rational men and women'.[27] In 1526 the Franciscans in Mexico wrote to the Emperor Charles V in a similar vein, urging that for the sake of conversion 'the two peoples, Christian and pagan, should unite, and join together in marriage, as is already beginning to happen'.[28]

Although racial intermarriage was officially sanctioned in the Spanish Indies, and at moments, as these citations suggest, positively encouraged, the extent to which it was practised remains unclear. Initially, a number of conquistadores and *encomenderos* married daughters of the Aztec and Inca high nobility, and in 1534 twenty of the eighty male settlers of Puebla had Indian wives.[29] But allegedly the concern of the colonists for the honour of their lineage soon came to inhibit all but the poorest from making Indian marriages.[30] On the other hand, in a letter of 1571 to his nephew in Spain, a merchant in Mexico City reports that he is happily married to an Indian wife, and adds: 'Although back in Spain it may seem that I was rash to marry an Indian woman, here this involves no loss of honour, for the nation of the Indians is held in high esteem.'[31] This may be no more than one individual seeking to place his own behaviour in the best possible light; but if not all Spanish colonists were so enthusiastic about taking Indians as wives, they had no scruples about taking them as mistresses. Moreover, in the first stages of

---

[26] Force, *Tracts*, i, no. 6, p. 14.

[27] Richard Konetzke, *Colección de documentos para la historia de la formación social de Hispanoamérica 1493–1810*, 5 vols (Madrid, 1953), i. doc. 9, pp. 12–13; and see Magnus Mörner, *Race Mixture in the History of Latin America* (Boston, Mass., 1967), p. 26.

[28] 'Carta colectiva de los franciscanos de México al Emperador', 1 Sept. 1526, in Fray Toribio de Benavente o Motolinía, *Memoriales o libro de las cosas de la Nueva España y de los naturales de ella*, ed. Edmundo O'Gorman (Mexico City, 1971), p. 429.

[29] Peggy K. Liss, *Mexico under Spain 1521–1556* (Chicago, Ill. and London, 1975), p. 136. *Encomenderos* were those Spaniards, or their descendants, who held grants of Indians from the Crown.

[30] Mörner, *Race Mixture*, pp. 37 and 26.

[31] Enrique Otte, *Cartas privadas de emigrantes a Indias 1540–1603* (Seville, 1988), p. 61.

colonisation at least, before their numbers proliferated, many of the mestizo children born of these unions were recognised by their Spanish fathers.

Despite the example of Pocahontas, daughter of the Indian chief Powhatan, marrying the English colonist John Rolfe, intermarriage in British America was almost nonexistent: there is no record of any legal marriages between English and Indians in Massachusetts between 1630 and 1676.[32] We find Robert Beverley lamenting this situation in his *History and Present State of Virginia* (1705), in words that recall those of the Mexican Franciscans in 1526: 'Intermarriage had been indeed the Method proposed very often by the Indians in the Beginning, urging it frequently as a certain Rule, that the English were not their Friends, if they refused it. And I can't but think it wou'd have been happy for that Country, had they embraced this Proposal: For, the Jealousie of the Indians, which I take to be the Cause of most of the Rapines and Murders they committed, wou'd by this Means have been altogether prevented, and consequently the Abundance of Blood that was shed on both sides wou'd have been saved; the Colony, instead of all these Losses of Men on both Sides, wou'd have been encreasing in Children to its Advantage; and, in all Likelihood, many, if not most, of the Indians would have been converted to Christianity by this kind Method. . . .'[33]

The colonisation of Ireland offered a precedent for the rejection of marriage with the native population. The Statutes of Kilkenny (1366) had forbidden marriage, or cohabitation, with the Irish, in the belief that mixed marriages would tempt the English partner to lapse into degenerate Irish ways.[34] In medieval Spain religion, rather than culture or ethnicity, was the dividing line between the Spanish and Moorish worlds, and technically the barrier to mixed marriage could be raised by conversion to Christianity.[35]

Although fifteenth-century Castilians might wage war against the Moors, their own lives were permeated by Moorish influences. Their houses, their

---

[32] Axtell, *The Invasion Within*, p. 304; Muldoon, 'The Indian as Irishman', p. 284; and see in particular the two surveys of attitudes to intermarriage, in Virginia and New England respectively, by David D. Smits: ' "Abominable Mixture": Toward the Repudiation of Anglo-Indian Intermarriage in Seventeenth-Century Virginia', *Virginia Magazine of History and Biography*, 95 (1987), pp. 157–92, and ' "We are not to Grow Wild": Seventeenth-Century New England's Repudiation of Anglo-Indian Intermarriage', *American Indian Culture and Research Journal*, 11 (1987), pp. 1–32. I am grateful to Dr Kenneth Mills for drawing these articles to my attention. I am also grateful to Clifford Potter for his kindness in assembling information for me on legislation and practice in British North America.

[33] Robert Beverley, *The History and the Present State of Virginia*, ed. Louis B. Wright (Chapel Hill, N.C., 1947), p. 38.

[34] Muldoon, 'The Indian as Irishman', p. 284; Smits, ' "We are not to Grow Wild" ', pp. 6–7.

[35] Thomas F. Glick, *Islamic and Christian Spain in the Early Middle Ages* (Princeton, N.J., 1979), p. 166.

furniture, their clothes, their taste in food, all bore the imprint of a life lived in close proximity to a Moorish population which possessed impressive technical and artistic skills.[36] Although in the sixteenth century Spaniards came to despise the Morisco population that remained in the peninsula after the completion of the *reconquista*, their long medieval experience of coexistence with a society that could only with difficulty be regarded as culturally inferior to their own may have made it easier for Spaniards in the Indies to contemplate ethnic intermarriage, at least where the social status of the Indian partner was sufficiently high. It may also have predisposed them to the kind of cultural *métissage* which would become such a striking feature of colonial society in Mexico and Peru.[37]

In spite of the Statutes of Kilkenny, many Anglo-Irish marriages did in fact occur,[38] and this makes it hard to know whether attitudes to intermarriage acquired in Ireland had any practical consequences for the social behaviour of the English in the colonisation of America. Yet, when it comes to cohabitation, there are indications of behaviour patterns among the English colonists that are difficult to explain if preexisting cultural attitudes are not taken into account.

Although there is bound to have been a good deal of clandestine cohabitation in British America, it was nothing like enough to produce the kind of mestizo society that was emerging in Spanish America by the seventeenth century. In British America there seems, almost from the start, to have been a sentiment against the taking of Indian mistresses. Sir Walter Raleigh reports proudly of one of his expeditions that, unlike the Spanish conquistadores, not one of his own men ever laid hands on an Indian woman.[39] If this is true, their behaviour was a world away from that of the Spaniards travelling up the River Paraguay in the 1530s, who, on being offered daughters by the Indians, called it a day, and settled down there to found what became the city of Asunción.[40] Given the shortage of English women in Virginia—men outnumbered women emigrants from London to the Chesapeake by six to one in the

---

[36] See García-Arenal, 'Moriscos e indios', pp. 155–6.

[37] See Carmen Bernand and Serge Gruzinski, *Les Métissages*, vol. ii of their *Histoire du Nouveau Monde* (Paris, 1993).

[38] Art Cosgrove, 'Marriage in Medieval Ireland', in *Marriage in Ireland*, ed. Art Cosgrove (Dublin, 1985), p. 35. I am grateful to Dr Toby Barnard for drawing this article to my attention. I am grateful also to Professor Nicholas Canny for his advice on the question of intermarriage in seventeenth-century Ireland.

[39] See Nicholas Canny and Anthony Pagden, *Colonial Identity in the Atlantic World, 1500–1800* (Princeton, N.J., 1987), pp. 145–6.

[40] See an anonymous Jesuit's report of 1620 cited in *The Cambridge History of Latin America* (Cambridge, 1984), ii, p. 76.

mid-1630s[41]—and the general imbalance of the sexes throughout the colonies, this reluctance to take Indian mistresses points to a more general distancing from the indigenous inhabitants which differentiates the English not only from the Spaniards but from all the other European colonists in the New World.

The reasons for the reluctance are not at all clear. In a world in which the shade of the skin was generally believed to be determined by the degree of exposure to the sun, the colour of the Indians—described by Juan López de Velasco in 1574 as 'cooked quince', and by William Strachey in the early seventeenth century as resembling 'a sodden quince'[42]—seems not to have been regarded as a serious impediment. Nor were Indian women regarded as physically unattractive, although social status was influential in determining reactions to feminine appearance.[43] The great divide was not ethnic but cultural. The English, unlike the Spanish, appear to have regarded cohabitation with the Indians as liable to plunge them back into a world of cultural degeneracy from which they had providentially managed to escape, and it would not be surprising if this were, at least in part, a legacy of their experiences in Ireland.

The fear of degeneration seems to have been deeply rooted among these English colonists.[44] In some respects it may be seen as part of a shared European tradition about the impact on temperament of climate and environment.[45] When Columbus told Queen Isabella that, because of the rainfall in the Indies the trees in Hispaniola had only shallow roots, her response, in line with current climatic theory, was that 'this land, where the trees are not firmly rooted, must produce men of little truthfulness and less constancy'.[46] In the circumstances, it was hardly surprising that metropolitan Spaniards should have considered that their creole cousins had run to seed in their lax

---

[41] Thad W. Tate and David L. Ammerman, eds, *The Chesapeake in the Seventeenth Century* (New York, 1979), p. 209. Nearly half of New England immigrants in the 1630s, however, were female. Cf. Virginia DeJohn Anderson, *New England's Generation* (Cambridge, 1991), p. 21.

[42] Juan López de Velasco, *Geografía y descripción de las Indias*, ed. Justo Zaragoza (Madrid, 1894), p. 27; Wesley Frank Craven, *White, Red, and Black: The Seventeenth-Century Virginian* (Charlottesville, Va., 1971), p. 39.

[43] Smits, ' "We are not to Grow Wild" ', pp. 5–6; Kupperman, *Settling with the Indians*, p. 37.

[44] For the theme of degeneration in colonial New England, see John Canup, *Out of the Wilderness: The Emergence of an American Identity in Colonial New England* (Middletown, Conn., 1990).

[45] See Marian J. Tooley, 'Bodin and the Medieval Theory of Climate', *Speculum*, 28 (1953), pp. 64–83; Canup, *Out of the Wilderness*, pp. 10–11; Karen Ordahl Kupperman, 'The Puzzle of the American Climate in the Early Colonial Period', *American Historical Review*, 87 (1982), pp. 1,262–89.

[46] Fernández de Oviedo cited in Antonello Gerbi, *The Dispute of the New World*, trans. Jeremy Moyle (Pittsburgh, Pa., 1973), p. 40.

American environment, or that the mestizos should have been seen as heirs to the worst characteristics of each of the races from which they sprang.

Reports of the effects of racial mixing in Spain's transatlantic colonies had reached the English before they began to emigrate to America,[47] and can only have reinforced their fears that those who chose to transplant themselves to the New World ran the same risks of cultural degeneration as had already over-taken all too many of their compatriots who had settled among the wild Irish. It is not therefore surprising to find that the sense of a providential mission in the promotion of the early colonial enterprises is accompanied by a rigorous insistence that those who followed Abraham's example in getting themselves out of their country 'unto the land that I will shew thee' should have been firmly enjoined to keep themselves apart. 'Then must Abrams posteritie', observed William Symonds in his sermon of 1609 to the adventurers and planters of Virginia, 'keepe them to themselves. They may not marry nor give in marriage to the heathen, that are uncircumcised. . . . The breaking of this rule, may breake the necke of all good successe of this Voyage. . . .'[48]

In New England the Puritans' sense of themselves as an elect people natu-rally reinforced the segregationist instincts of the settlers, and made them bitterly critical of deviants like Thomas Morton, whose settlement at Ma-re Mount was in their eyes scandalously hospitable to the Indians.[49] But the settlers of Virginia, even without the coherent philosophy of a 'New-England Israel' to justify their separation from the 'Canaanite' Indian tribes,[50] had already, in the wake of the 1622 Virginia massacre, begun to give physical expression to their segregationist instincts. By 1633 they had established a 'pale'—another inheritance from Ireland—six miles long, behind which they lived on 300,000 square acres cleared of Indian title.[51] In effect, the Virginians had drawn a frontier line[52] and the existence of this frontier points to perhaps the most important of all the distinctions between the approaches of British and Spanish settlers to the indigenous societies of America.

Frontiers existed, too, in Spanish America—along the Bío-Bío River in Chile, for example, and in northern Mexico. But these were frontiers drawn reluc-tantly, and, it was hoped, temporarily, in those regions where it had proved

---

[47] Smits, ' "Abominable Mixture" ', p. 162.
[48] See Alexander Brown, *The Genesis of the United States*, 2 vols (London, 1980), i, doc. lxxxvi, pp. 287 and 290.
[49] For reactions to Morton see Canup, *Out of the Wilderness*, pp. 105ff.
[50] For this analogy see Canup, *Out of the Wilderness*, pp. 79–80.
[51] See Craven, 'Indian Policy in Early Virginia'; and above, p. 118.
[52] Bailyn and Morgan, *Strangers within the Realm*, p. 118.

impossible to subjugate Indians who had shown themselves adept at resistance, like the Araucanians in Chile and the Chichimecs in Mexico. As colonisers, the Spaniards dispersed themselves through space, covering vast areas and here and there founding a city in order to establish their presence in an Indian world that surrounded and almost engulfed them. Their world was one in which the frontiers are best described as 'frontiers of inclusion', in the sense that the indigenous peoples who lived within their confines were in some way expected or invited to participate in the life of the society that was in process of creation.[53]

After initial and uneasy attempts at coexistence had failed, the frontier in British America, by contrast, became a frontier of exclusion, as British settlers cleared space for themselves at the expense of the Indians, whom they pushed to the edges. 'Our first worke', wrote the governor of Virginia, Sir Francis Wyatt, shortly after the 1622 massacre, 'is expulsion of the Salvages to gaine the free range of the countrey for encrease of cattle, swine &c which will more then restore us, for it is infinitely better to have no heathen among us, who at best were but as thornes in our sides, then to be be at peace and league with them.'[54] This was a far cry from the lofty ideal proclaimed for Virginia by William Crashaw in 1609: 'the high and principall end being plantation, of an English Church and Common-wealth, and consequently the Conversion of heathen.'[55]

What was coming into existence was a frontier on the model of the Irish pale, although in practice, like the pale, it would prove much more porous than is often allowed.[56] Was this frontier of exclusion one that the English wanted and expected to establish, or was it one that simply developed as a result of the character of the indigenous population and of local conditions? The evidence would seem to point in both directions.

In British America on the arrival of the Europeans there was no indigenous society—except perhaps, and to a limited extent, the 'empire' of Powhatan—comparable in the concentration of authority to the empires of the Aztecs and the Incas.[57] It has often been pointed out how much this very concentration of authority helped to facilitate conquest by the Spaniards. The seizure of Montezuma and Atahualpa left their empires deeply vulnerable. In those

---

[53] For the 'frontier of inclusion' see Magnus Mörner, 'The Colonization of Norrland by Settlers during the Nineteenth Century in a Broader Perspective', *Scandinavian Journal of History*, 7 (1982), pp. 315–37.

[54] 'Letter of Sir Francis Wyatt, Governor of Virginia, 1621–1626', *William and Mary Quarterly*, 2nd series, 6 (1926), pp. 114–21, at p. 118.

[55] Brown, *Genesis of the United States*, i, doc. cxx, p. 366.

[56] Cf. Francis Jennings, *The Ambiguous Iroquois Empire* (New York and London, 1984), pp. 58–60, who, while pointing out the differences between the various frontiers in North America, talks even in this context of an 'inclusive frontier'.

[57] Wilcomb E. Washburn, *The Indian in America* (New York, 1965), p. 46.

regions like Yucatán where authority was dispersed, the process of conquest was vastly more difficult and prolonged. By taking over from the Aztecs and the Incas large areas of territory containing settled and subjugated populations, together with an administrative apparatus still in reasonable working order for the collection of tribute and the organisation of public works, the Spaniards were well placed to recreate in the Indies the kind of hierarchical society based on lordship and vassalage that was familiar to them at home.

By contrast, the indigenous populations of the areas first settled by the English proved much less amenable to disciplined control. Early plans in Virginia for the collection of tribute from tribal chieftains, and for regular labour services, on the model of the Spanish Caribbean, Mexico and Peru,[58] quickly foundered on the resistance of Powhatan's Indians and on their apparent unsuitability for the kind of labour services that would allow the English to live the gentlemanly lives to which they felt themselves entitled. Providence, it seemed, was acting in mysterious ways. To the Spaniards it had assigned silver mines and Indians who could be domesticated, taxed and put to public use. To the English, on the other hand, it had allocated neither one nor the other.

Once the initial disappointment had passed, the English response was to make a virtue of necessity. Their Indians, unlike those of the Spaniards, might prove inadequate as a potential labour force, but they were also far fewer in number. The demographic catastrophe that followed on the heels of the Spaniards had reached North America before the arrival of English colonists in any significant numbers,[59] with the result that they found themselves coming to lands much less populous than a century earlier. The number of Indians to be found east of the Mississippi River on the eve of permanent British settlement has been estimated at about a million.[60] Against this must be set estimated figures of anything from five to fifteen or even twenty-five million for central Mexico and nine million for Peru on the eve of the Spanish conquest.[61]

[58] Craven, 'Indian Policy in Early Virginia', p. 70.

[59] Francis Jennings, *The Invasion of America* (Chapel Hill, N.C., 1975), p. 23.

[60] James Merrell, ' "The customs of our countrey" ', in Bailyn and Morgan, eds, *Strangers within the Realm*, p. 122.

[61] The high figures for the pre-Columbian populations of the Americas proposed by Sherburne F. Cook and Woodrow Borah in their various publications, and subsequently collected in their *Essays in Population History*, 3 vols (Berkeley/Los Angeles, Calif., and London, 1971–9), have been strongly contested and remain the subject of much debate. See J. N. Biraben, 'La population de l'Amérique pré-colombienne', in *Conferencia Internationale. El Poblamiento de las Américas*, Veracruz, 1992 (Institut National d'Etudes Démographiques, Paris); Hugh Thomas, *The Conquest of Mexico* (London, 1993), appendix 1; and Linda A. Newson, 'The Demographic Collapse of the Native Peoples of the Americas, 1492–1650', in Warwick Bray, ed., *The Meeting of Two Worlds: Europe and the Americas, 1492–1650* (Proceedings of the British Academy, 81, Oxford, 1993).

While in some regions like Tidewater Virginia, central and western New York and the South Carolina–Georgia frontier area, native Americans were still present in sufficient numbers to represent an obstacle to European settlement, in others they were no more than thinly scattered. Almost from the beginning in New England, for instance, settlers outnumbered native Americans, thousands of whom had been struck down by a smallpox epidemic on the eve of the Great Migration.[62] The resulting impression of an empty country was reinforced by Indian patterns of land use, so alien to European concepts of property and cultivation that it seemed natural to the first colonists that large tracts of what looked to them like virgin forest and wasteland were theirs for the taking.[63] The English therefore had the impression that they had arrived in a *wilderness*—a concept that does not seem to figure in the literature of Spanish colonisation.

The wilderness had its horrors, but it was there to be tamed.[64] Here was both an ordeal and an opportunity, and the promotional literature designed to attract colonists to English America made much of the abundance of land. For the Puritans, who came to accord the wilderness a redemptive significance,[65] the fact that this land had been cleared of its original occupants by the spread of disease was plain evidence of God's providential design. He 'hath hereby' claimed John Winthrop, 'cleared our title to this place'.[66]

Captain John Smith, in his *Advertisements for the Unexperienced Planters of New England or Any Where* (1631), drew a sharp contrast between the proportion of settlers to colonised in British and Spanish America. After observing that in the West Indies a handful of Spaniards had 'subdued millions of the inhabitants, so depopulating those countries they conquered, that they are glad to buy Negroes in Affrica . . .', he went on to say that, in spite of this, 'there is for every foure or five naturall Spaniards, two or three hundred Indians and Negros, and in Virginia and New-England more English than Salvages, that can assemble themselves to assault or hurt them.' As he saw it, there were clear advantages to the English in this state of affairs: 'it is much better to helpe to plant a country than unplant it and then replant it'. But, he continued, 'there

---

[62] T. H. Breen, 'Creative Adaptation', in Jack P. Greene and J. R. Pole, *Colonial British America* (Oxford, 1984), p. 212; T. H. Breen, *Puritans and Adventurers* (Oxford, 1980), pp. 75–6.

[63] William P. Cronon, *Changes in the Land* (New York, 1983), p. 56.

[64] Cf. William Penn's assertion that they 'came to a wilderness', but that 'it was not meet that [they] should continue it so', cited by Michael Zuckerman in Canny and Pagden, eds, *Colonial Identity*, p. 133.

[65] Avihu Zakai, *Exile and Kingdom: History and Apocalypse in the Puritan Migration to America* (Cambridge, 1992), p. 145.

[66] Cronon, *Changes in the Land*, p. 90.

[sic] Indians were in such multitudes, the Spaniards had no other remedy; and ours such a few, and so dispersed, it were nothing in a short time to bring them to labour and obedience'.[67]

It is one of the ironies of this passage from Smith that, within fifty years, his Virginians would be turning with enthusiasm to the Spanish device of importing African slaves in order to meet their labour shortfall. He was mistaken, too, in his belief that the English had the advantage when it came to the taming of the Indians. It was the Spaniards, not the English, who 'in short time' brought their Indians to 'labour and obedience', at least over large areas of Central America, New Granada and the Andes. Spain's Indian world, except at some of its edges like Guiana where the Orinoco Caribs could call on the Dutch for help,[68] was both figuratively and literally a world disarmed. In North America, on the other hand, any efforts made by the British settlers or authorities to deny arms to the Indians were largely doomed to failure since there were generally French and Dutch traders happy to supply them.

While the Indians of Spanish America had their own strategies of resistance, open rebellion was infrequent once the age of conquest was over, and was restricted in its range before the great Andean uprising led by Túpac Amaru II in 1780–1. In British America, by contrast, there was heavy slaughter of the Virginia colonists in 1622 and again in 1644, while the relative peace that descended on New England in the aftermath of the Pequot War of 1636–7 was bloodily ended in the 1670s by King Philip's War. These and lesser confrontations created among British settlers an image of the 'treacherous' Indian which left them deeply suspicious and mistrustful of their Indian neighbours, and aggravated still further a relationship that had been uncertain from the start.

Had there been in British America, as there was to the south, an initial and speedy conquest of the indigenous population, relations between the two communities would presumably have developed in ways closer to those to be found in Hispanic America. As it was, the English approach to colonisation—by way of the establishment of self-sufficient settler communities,[69] the clearing of Indians from the land and their expulsion to the farther side of perimeters defended by forts and blockhouses—tended to multiply the problems of security faced by the colonies. In particular this style of colonisation gave the Indian tribes beyond the perimeter time to make major political and

---

[67] *The Complete Works of Captain John Smith*, ed. Philip L. Barbour, 3 vols (Chapel Hill, N.C., 1986), iii, pp. 293–4.
[68] See Manuel Lucena Giraldo, *Laboratorio tropical* (Caracas, 1991), p. 45.
[69] George M. Frederickson, *White Supremacy: A Comparative Study in American and South African History* (Oxford, 1981), pp. 17 and 58.

economic readjustments to the presence of Europeans and, above all, to acculturate themselves to European styles of warfare in their 'forest' habitats so menacing and mysterious to the settlers.

A similar process of military acculturation occurred among the unsubdued Indian tribes like the Apaches on the fringes of Spain's American empire. There were times and places in which this posed acute problems for the Spanish authorities, and for generations the Araucanian war in Chile represented a major drain on Spanish manpower and resources. But the Spaniards succeeded in evolving responses to this problem of the frontier areas, which, although not uniformly successful, made the presence of unsubjugated Indian peoples beyond the limits of empire a less dominant concern for the American viceroyalties over much of the colonial period than it was for the British colonies. It was only with the eighteenth century, and the increasingly vigorous and organised response of the border Indians to the continuing expansion of the northern frontier of New Spain, that the defence of the border regions all the way from the Gulf of Mexico to Texas came to constitute a large-scale military problem for the Spanish authorities.[70]

By contrast, the English by the late seventeenth century had already created a new Indian problem for themselves by effectively encouraging the Indian peoples on the fringes of their colonies to reconstitute their polities in an effort to keep the intruders at bay. These polities in turn became a force to be reckoned with, especially as North America developed into a theatre of conflict between rival European powers. Indian cooperation was essential both for purposes of defence and for opening up the interior of the continent,[71] and this dependence of the English on Indians whom they at once needed and distrusted gave the Iroquois and the other peoples of eastern North America a formidable leverage over the colonists.

For all their dealings with the Indians along the borders of their colonies, the English had difficulty in developing and cultivating what Richard White has called 'the middle ground'—that world in which the ethnic boundaries between European and Indian melted and merged, a world in which the French in Canada had made themselves at home.[72] There were, of course, many instances

---

[70] See David J. Weber, *The Spanish Frontier in North America 1513–1821* (New Haven, Conn. and London, 1992), ch. 8, and his *Bárbaros: Spaniards and their Savages in the Age of Enlightenment* (New Haven, Conn. and London, 2005) for the range of eighteenth-century Spanish responses to the unsubjugated peoples.

[71] Jennings, *Ambiguous Iroquois*, p. 367; Richard R. Johnson, 'The Search for a Usable Indian: an Aspect of the Defense of Colonial New England', *Journal of American History*, 44 (1977), pp. 623–51.

[72] White, *The Middle Ground*. See the Introduction, p. x, for White's use of the expression.

of British settlers who had lived among the Indians, often as captives, and so had come to know their ways, and indeed there seems to be no real Spanish equivalent of the British captivity literature.[73] But in spite of the often intimate knowledge that captivity provided, and the many contacts between British traders and settlers and local Indians, the British village world that sprang up west of the Appalachian Mountains in the 1760s remained obstinately separate from, and disdainful of, its Algonquian neighbours.[74] The old segregationist attitudes remained as strong as ever.

The Spaniards along the borderlands of empire managed in the course of the sixteenth and seventeenth centuries to develop the kind of strategies for creating and expanding a middle ground that continued to elude the English. These borderlands, as everywhere, were rough and violent regions, where the normal rules were suspended or ignored. Indian slavery, for instance, which was prohibited in the New Laws of 1542, was permitted in frontier territories like Chile and New Mexico, where the Spaniards regarded themselves as waging a just war.[75] But the Spanish soldiers who manned the *presidios*, or frontier posts, and found some compensation in the taking of slaves for domestic service in these otherwise unrewarding outposts of empire, also took Indian mistresses and wives. In so doing, they propagated a biologically mixed population, natural occupants of the middle ground. The nominally Spanish inhabitants of the kingdom of New Mexico, founded in 1598, were described in the 1630s as '*mestizos*, mulattos and *zambohijos*' (the offspring of Africans and Indians), and since this was a region that received few Spanish immigrants, the description was no doubt correct.[76]

In seeking solutions to their border problems, the Spaniards resorted to both civil and religious agencies.[77] The mining camp and the *presidio* brought

---

[73] For British captives in North America see Linda Colley, *Captives: Britain, Empire and the World, 1600–1850* (London, 2002), pt 2. For Spanish captives, see Susan M. Socolow, 'Spanish Captives in Indian Societies: Cultural Contact along the Argentine Frontier, 1600–1835', *Hispanic American Historical Review*, 72 (1992), pp.73–99, and Fernando Operé, *Historias de la frontera. El cautiverio en la América hispánica* (Buenos Aires, 2001). For an isolated example of Spanish captivity literature, see Francisco Núñez de Pineda y Bascuñán, *Cautiverio Feliz* (Santiago de Chile, 1863), on his captivity among the Araucanian Indians of Chile in 1629 (abridged English trans. by William C. Atkinson, *The Happy Captive*, Chatham, 1979).

[74] White, *The Middle Ground*, pp. 315–17.

[75] Ramón A. Gutiérrez, *When Jesus Came, the Corn Mothers Went Away* (Stanford, Calif., 1991), p. 150. The same rules were applied to Indian prisoners of war by the British settlers of South Carolina in the eighteenth century; see Bailyn and Morgan, eds, *Strangers within the Realm*, p. 137.

[76] See Gutiérrez, *When Jesus Came*, p. 103.

[77] Edward H. Spicer, *Cycles of Conquest* (Tucson, Ariz., 1962), pt 2.

hispanicised Indians into the frontier areas,[78] and helped to spread Spanish cultural influences among Indian peoples not yet brought under Spanish control. At the same time, the missions established by the various religious orders, and especially by the Jesuits,[79] acted as important agencies of acculturation, although their degree of success depended on a whole variety of circumstances, related both to the character and quality of the missionaries themselves and to the character-istics of the particular Indian communities and tribal groupings they were attempting to convert.

Although inevitably there was friction between the civil authorities and the religious orders, the commitment of the Spanish Crown to the missionary enterprise over the course of three centuries underlines one of the sharpest points of difference between Spanish and British approaches to colonisation. English attempts at conversion of the Indians, although not as insignificant as is often suggested,[80] were from the beginning much less intensive and well organised than those of the Spaniards. The Virginia Company sent out no missionaries to America,[81] and in New England Protestant missions started late and were always short of ministers.[82] The fourteen so-called 'praying towns' of eastern Massachusetts[83]—which had some affinity to the settle-ments, known as *reducciones,* in which the Spaniards relocated the Indians in order to bring them under closer civil and ecclesiastical surveillance—had some success,[84] but both in Puritan New England and in Anglican Virginia educational experiments among the Indians proved disappointing. English ministers do not seem to have been as successful as their Spanish counterparts in mastering Indian languages, although to some extent this was compensated for in New England by the willingness to train and use native Indian minis-ters[85]—a clear point of contrast with the Spanish Church in America, which, after early embarrassments, set its face against ordaining Indians as priests.

In general, however, British America lacked the driving impetus to convert the indigenous population which informed so much of Spain's enterprise of the Indies. The reasons for this would seem to be both organisational and doctrinal. From the outset, the divisions within English Protestantism obviously inhibited

---

[78] Guillermo Céspedes del Castillo, *América hispánica (1492–1898)* (Barcelona, 1983), p. 125.
[79] Spicer, *Cycles of Conquest,* p. 298; Lucena Giraldo, *Laboratorio tropical,* pp. 46–58.
[80] Wesley Frank Craven, *The Colonies in Transition, 1660–1713* (New York/Evanston, Ill. and London, 1968), pp. 117–18.
[81] Jennings, *Invasion of America,* p. 55.
[82] James Axtell, *After Columbus* (New York and Oxford, 1988), p. 98.
[83] Bailyn and Morgan, eds, *Strangers within the Realm,* p. 150.
[84] Axtell, *After Columbus,* pp. 49–50.
[85] Axtell, *The Invasion Within,* p. 225.

a unified effort, and the institutional weaknesses of the Anglican Church, which failed to establish a single Anglican bishopric in America throughout the colonial period, made it difficult to mount and sustain an effective missionary policy. Protestant ministers, too, unlike Catholic missionaries in either Canada or Spanish America, were apparently unable or unwilling to adapt their doctrines and practices to the needs of the indigenous population.

Any attempt at adaptation was likely to be hampered by the close dependence of Protestantism on the printed word, and by the absence of the kind of ceremonial and ritual to be found in Spanish Christianity, a form of religion perhaps more easily appropriated by the Indians to their sense of the sacred. Moreover, in Puritan America, although some attempts were made to assimilate the Indians,[86] the doctrine of God's elect promoted an exclusivism which tended to leave the Indians on the outside. The Puritans, to use one of their own favourite words, chose to enclose themselves behind a 'hedge'.[87] Once again in British America frontiers and barriers—this time religious—stood in the way of mutual accommodation between the colonists and the colonised.

In the early years of New England, the settlers seem to have expected that the advantages of Christianity would be so blindingly obvious to the Indians that they would turn of their own accord to the light.[88] There was no parallel to the mass baptisms conducted by the friars in Mexico in the 1520s. It is true that in due course many of the friars themselves would come to question the sincerity of the converts and their degree of understanding of the religion that they had apparently adopted with such unfeigned enthusiasm at the moment of defeat. But for all the doubts surrounding the effectiveness of the evangelisation programme in New Spain and Peru, there can be none about the enthusiasm and commitment that drove it forward, at least in the initial stages of the colonial enterprise.

The dedication of the first generation of friars in the Indies inspired a remarkable attempt to understand the character and customs of the indigenous peoples they were seeking to convert. British colonial America has nothing to compare with the great ethnographical investigations of a Toribio Motolinía, a Bartolomé de Las Casas or a Bernardino de Sahagún. Although, like English observers of indigenous society, these Spanish observers were quick to attribute practices of which they disapproved to the machinations of

---

[86] See the introduction (pp. x–xi) to the rev. edn of Alden T. Vaughan, *New England Frontier, Puritans and Indians, 1620–1675* (New York, 1979; first published Boston, 1965).
[87] See Peter N. Carroll, *Puritanism and the Wilderness: The Intellectual Significance of the New England Frontier 1629–1700* (New York, 1969), pp. 17 and 87–90.
[88] Cf. Axtell, *The Invasion Within*, p. 219.

the devil, who stalked the New World whether Spanish or English,[89] they seem much more inclined than their English counterparts to get to grips with the character of Indian civilisation and make an effort to understand it on its own terms.

Fundamentally, this effort was motivated by their desire to bring the Indians into the Christian fold, but it may also reflect the insistence of sixteenth-century Spanish scholastic thought on the viability of non-Christian societies and the right of their people, in spite of grave deficiencies, to live their own lives. The result of this approach was the acceptance, at least in principle, of the continuing existence under Spanish rule of a *república de los indios*. Royal orders of 1530 for the guidance of provincial governors stipulated that the good usages and customs of the Indians should be preserved in so far as they were not contrary to the Christian religion.[90] In effect, the Indians were to be incorporated into, but not integrated with, the newly evolving colonial society.

This objective proved impossible to sustain. The ideal of Christianisation embraced so many social practices and customs, like those relating to marriage or conceptions of decency, that the conversion of the Indians to Christianity could not be separated from the ideal of reducing them to *policía* (civility), as defined by Spanish criteria. Inevitably, therefore, Christianisation involved hispanicisation, or the cultural assimilation of the conquered to the society of the conquerors.

Economic demands and demographic pressures also militated against the conservation of a relatively uncontaminated *república de los indios*. From the first years of conquest and settlement, the Indians were in demand as a potential labour force. As silver deposits were discovered and the mining economy developed, many more were drafted in to work in the mines of Mexico and Peru. Others were drawn into the rapidly growing world of the cities, as domestic servants or as artisans working for a creole elite. On top of all this, demographic catastrophe fundamentally transformed the character of Indian society. As the population succumbed to waves of European epidemics, old social structures were dissolved, and Crown and settlers found themselves competing for a shrinking labour supply. In the process, thousands of Indians were drawn inexorably into the world of the Europeans, and the *república de los indios* was still further eroded.

---

[89] For the devil in Spanish America see Fernando Cervantes, *The Devil in the New World: The Impact of Diabolism in New Spain* (New Haven, Conn. and London, 1994).

[90] Cited in Woodrow Borah, *Justice by Insurance* (Berkeley and Los Angeles, Calif., 1983), p. 34.

In comparison, the British colonies found it difficult, or impossible, to transform the indigenous population into a labour force for their growing economies. Some attempts were made to enslave Indians, and at one moment in the early eighteenth century they constituted around a third of all the slaves in South Carolina.[91] But from 1659 Virginia disallowed the use of Indians as slaves,[92] and the settlers either had to fall back on indentured servants from among the immigrants to meet their labour needs, or follow the path adopted by Spanish and British settlers in the Caribbean and purchase imported African slaves. As George Frederickson has suggested, this abandonment of the attempt to turn the Indians into a workforce may partly reflect the fact that the relatively thinly populated regions settled by the English could not provide a labour pool large enough for settler requirements, but it also reflects the whole pattern of English colonisation with its tendency to push Indians to the edges of the colonial settlements. It was easier to maintain control over an imported African population thousands of miles from home than over a native American population which possessed an intimate knowledge of the free world of the forests, still so dangerously close.[93]

Whereas, then, in spite of the existence of so-called 'settlement Indians',[94] the true 'republic of the Indians' in British America lay outside the areas of European settlement, in Spanish America it was located well and truly within the confines of colonial society. As such, it found itself exposed to innumerable pressures, economic, cultural and social, which posed a constant threat to its integrity and continuing survival. As the numbers of the indigenous population shrank, the settler community of the creoles was reinforced by the arrival of new immigrants from Spain. At the same time, a rapidly growing mestizo population was seeking to carve out space for itself in the evolving world of colonial society.

But the Indians, although battered and exploited, were by no means entirely defenceless in the face of oppression. In many parts of Spanish America they learnt the arts of what has been called 'resistant adaptation',[95] to often remarkable effect. But it must be recognised, too, that they were the beneficiaries of the Spanish political culture in which they now found themselves unwillingly

---

[91] Frederickson, *White Supremacy*, p. 56; Bailyn and Morgan, eds, *Strangers within the Realm*, p. 137.

[92] Craven, 'Indian Policy in Early Virginia', p. 79.

[93] Frederickson, *White Supremacy*, pp. 56–8.

[94] Bailyn and Morgan, eds, *Strangers within the Realm*, p. 119.

[95] Steve J. Stern, *Resistance, Rebellion, and Consciousness in the Andean Peasant World, 18th to 20th Centuries* (Madison, Wis., 1987), p. 9.

incorporated. From the beginnings of colonisation until the coming of independence for Spain's American possessions three centuries later, the Spanish
Crown consistently maintained that it had a special obligation to watch over
the interests of its Indian vassals. To meet this obligation, a large body of legislation was developed over the course of the years to protect the Indians.[96]
Inevitably there were wide divergencies between the intention and reality, but
the fact remains that the Indians of Spanish America continued to the end to
regard the Crown as their special protector; that large numbers of communities did succeed in clinging to their lands in spite of creole attempts to seize
them; and that the workings of the system gave them a latitude for manoeuvre
which enabled many of them to maintain their collective identity throughout
the colonial centuries.

It was, of course, a system in which their subordinate status was taken for
granted. Originally regarded as barbarians, they came to be viewed, in spite of
the efforts of Las Casas and his colleagues, as in some respects deficient in
rational capacity and therefore in need of close supervision. Juridically, they
were classified as *miserabiles,* and hence requiring special legal protection.[97] It
was a paternalistic approach, and in practice the consensus developed by both
civil and religious authorities over the course of the sixteenth century was that
their 'low and imperfect nature' justified their being treated as children, and
punished when they erred.[98]

English Americans also came to adopt this tutelary approach, and spoke of
the Indians, as Spaniards spoke of them, as 'our younger brethren'.[99] But in
British America the paternalism was not accompanied by the same degree of
protection for these wayward children. Even in New England, where relations
between the settlers and the native Americans were relatively harmonious for
four decades following the end of the Pequot War,[100] the legal rights initially
enjoyed by the native Americans were already being eroded before King
Philip's War of 1675–6 led to the dismantling of their courts and a sharp rise
in anti-Indian legislation.[101]

The British Crown was a much less effective presence in the New World
than the Spanish Crown. Such protection as was afforded therefore to native

---

[96] For this legislation in Mexico, see Borah's comprehensive study, *Justice by Insurance.*
[97] *Ibid.,* p. 80.
[98] José A. Llaguno, *La personalidad jurídica del indio y el III Concilio Provincial Mexicano
(1585)* (Mexico City, 1963), p. 195.
[99] Kupperman, *Settling with the Indians,* p. 170.
[100] Breen, *Puritans and Adventurers,* p. 76.
[101] Bailyn and Morgan, eds, *Strangers within the Realm,* pp. 144–6.

Americans had to come from the colonial governments themselves; and although efforts were made, as in Virginia in 1662,[102] to ensure an equitable land distribution and safeguard the Indian title, Nathaniel Bacon's rebellion of 1675–6 suggested how limited was their room for manoeuvre when settlers were hungry for land. It was not easy to persuade members of colonial assemblies to act against the wishes of their own kind, and when the Crown proclaimed its determination in 1763 to protect Indians in their territorial possessions,[103] it was already late in the day, and the commitment was far from wholehearted.[104]

Looking back over the panorama of two or more centuries of Spanish and British colonisation of the Americas, it is hard to dissent from Henry Knox's 'melancholy reflection' that British modes of population were 'more destructive to the Indian natives than the conduct of the conquerors of Mexico and Peru'. The tendency in the English colonies was persistently to regard the Indians as outsiders rather than insiders, and to treat them accordingly. William Penn seems to have been an exception in his desire to integrate the Indians into the life of his new colony, and it is significant that he was one of the rare English colonisers to make a serious effort to understand Indian manners and customs.[105]

The Spaniards, on the other hand, while no less assertive than the English of their own cultural superiority, found a place for the Indians, however lowly, in the new society they were creating. In a sense, the expansive style of their colonising process, and the large numbers of Indians that it brought under Spanish jurisdiction, left them with no alternative. The integration of the indigenous population into the Hispanic world was helped, too, by the speed with which many Indians, especially in the densely settled regions of central Mexico and Peru, accommodated themselves to the culture of the conquerors. But at the same time the stratified and strongly corporate character of Hispanic society as it reproduced itself overseas was itself an important enabling factor, since it allowed Indian communities to maintain some semblance of a collective identity while giving them certain rights within the structure of colonial society as a whole.

In David Hume's words, 'the same set of manners' followed the English and the Castilians across the Atlantic. If Spanish colonial America was to be inclusionist in its approach to the Indians, and British colonial America exclusionist, we must look to metropolitan as well as local American conditions for

---

[102] Craven, 'Indian Policy in Early Virginia', p. 80.
[103] Jennings, *Invasion of America*, p. 36.
[104] White, *The Middle Ground*, p. 308.
[105] Jennings, *Ambiguous Iroquois*, pp. 238 and 242.

the explanation. As we ponder, in the light of the comparison between them, the very different directions taken by these two colonial worlds, it is hard not to be struck by the almost obsessional fear among seventeenth-century English colonists of the dangers of cultural degeneration. Somehow, for all their brave words, they seem to have lacked the confidence displayed by the Spaniards in the superiority of their own religion and culture. If this diagnosis is correct, the reasons for their lack of confidence will need to be explored. But already there are sufficient hints to suggest that somewhere in the story, and not for the first time, the question of Ireland deserves to find a place.

CHAPTER IX

KING AND *PATRIA* IN THE HISPANIC WORLD

The Hispanic world of the sixteenth, seventeenth and eighteenth centuries was a world of multiple loyalties. Ties of kinship and obligation bound an individual and his immediate family to the larger, extended, family and its most prominent representatives. These family networks interlocked and overlapped with networks of patronage and clientage in which it was expected that loyalty would be rewarded with favours (*mercedes*). When the Duke and Duchess of Cardona, the patrons of the Catalan lawyer and diarist Jeroni Pujades, paid their first visit to their town of Castelló d'Empúries in July 1628, Pujades composed a poetic greeting for them: 'My desire was fulfilled/On seeing my lords./I see them with joy,/And wait for favours.'[1] These were the sentiments of a society that lived in a permanent state of expectation—the expectation, all too often defrauded, that loyalty would receive its just desserts.

Loyalty to a patron, real or putative, coexisted with loyalty to the corporate associations with which a person might be associated—guilds and confraternities, civic and ecclesiastical institutions—in a society that was structured into a multitude of corporations, all with their own statutes and privileges. Beyond these corporate loyalties there was loyalty, too, to the community, in the first instance the local community, but also to wider communities, with which it shared something of the same space, historical experience and points of reference.

---

[1] 'De ver mis señores/Cumplióse el deseo./Alegro los veo,/Y espero favores.' *Dietari de Jeroni Pujades*, ed. Josep Ma. Casas Homs, 4 vols (Barcelona, 1976), iv, pp. 143–4.

Embracing, at least in theory, all these multiple loyalties was the supreme loyalty, the loyalty owed by subjects to their monarch. As the highest representative of God on earth, the monarch was the guardian and guarantor of an ordered, hierarchical society which, as far as was humanly possible, was expected to pattern the divine. In sermons and on the stage, in treatises of political theory and in visual representation, the monarch was constantly presented as 'a likeness of God, who administers and governs all things', as Gregorio López Madera wrote, citing Plutarch.[2] The vision of kingship in these various forms of representation was essentially paternalist, with the king as a strict but loving father of his peoples, governing them and dispensing impartial justice in imitation of the divine Father who ruled heaven and earth. It was therefore entirely appropriate that Philip IV, in making an emotional appeal to the Catalans in the *Corts* of 1626, should address them as 'children'.[3]

Children, however, are inclined to disobedience, and one of the arts that every monarch had to learn was how to maintain loyalty to his royal person. In his *El príncipe en la guerra y en la paz*, published in that year of faltering loyalties, 1640, Vicente Mut observed that 'Loyalty is a delicate provision, and one that should not be allowed to slip from one's hands.'[4] In every monarchical society of early modern Europe there was always a delicate balance to be maintained between the need to uphold the royal authority and the dangers of adopting measures that would alienate the affections of subjects from their rulers. Every ruler therefore walked a tightrope between *rigor* and *blandura* (leniency) in a balancing act that was all the more precarious in an age when logistical difficulties and practical limitations on the exercise of royal power restricted the Crown's capacity to subdue resistance by force of arms.

If this was a perennial dilemma of early modern kingship, it was especially acute in Europe's first 'universal' monarchy, the *monarquía española*. Two to three weeks were required for messages to reach Madrid from Brussels; three to eight months for a royal decree signed by Philip II to reach his viceroy in New Spain; perhaps as much as two years for messages to make the round trip between Madrid and Lima, and back. Was not distance, as Geoffrey Parker asks about Philip II, his 'enemy number one'?[5] Over three centuries the rulers

[2] Gregorio López Madera, *Excelencias de la monarquía y reyno de España* (Madrid, 1625), p. 4v.
[3] Cited in J. H. Elliott, *The Revolt of the Catalans* (Cambridge, 1963; repr. 1984), p. 230.
[4] Cited in Juan E. Gelabert, '*Senza rumore*. El tránsito de Castilla por el tiempo de las seis revoluciones contemporáneas', in Ernesto García Fernández, ed., *El poder en Europa y América. Mitos, tópicos y realidades* (Bilbao, 2001), p. 119.
[5] Geoffrey Parker, *The Grand Strategy of Philip II* (New Haven, Conn., and London, 1998), ch. 2.

of the Spanish Monarchy were forced to work their way round, and through, these logistical difficulties, which inevitably hampered the effective implementation of royal policy. Yet the Monarchy survived, even if with casualties along the way: the northern provinces of the Netherlands in the later sixteenth century; Portugal, after sixty years of union, in 1640; and Flanders and Spanish Italy as a result of the international agreements flowing from the change of dynasty in 1700.

A number of explanations can be advanced for this ability of the Spanish Monarchy to avoid fragmentation and surmount so many of the external and internal challenges with which it was confronted.[6] For all its limitations, coercive power played its part, even if the Spanish military establishment, however impressive in contemporary eyes, remained small relative to the extent of the Monarchy, and was largely concentrated in Milan and the Netherlands. But the knowledge that, sooner or later, the king could bring overwhelming power to bear was an obvious deterrent to precipitate revolt. Nor did it escape the eyes of the king's subjects that their master's power also possessed its advantages in a hostile world. The fact that, over much of the sixteenth and seventeenth centuries, the king of Spain had greater fiscal and military resources at his command than any other monarch, offered an incentive to the smaller polities within the Monarchy to remain under the shelter of his capacious protective umbrella. Naples and Sicily were unlikely to be tempted to break the ties of allegiance as long as the Turks were on the offensive in the Mediterranean. Influential members of the Portuguese elite in 1580 believed—mistakenly, as it proved—that Portugal's overseas possessions would be safer from enemy attack if they could call on the resources of a king of Castile who was also king of Portugal.

But the threat, and in some instances the hope, of the deployment of armed force was only one of the many elements that helped to hold this dispersed Monarchy together in defiance of the challenges of time and space. If a single, comprehensive explanation of the survival of Spain's worldwide Monarchy and empire were to be sought, it is most likely to be found in the development over time of a community of interests—cultural and economic, ideological and sectional—binding together the centre of the Monarchy and its component parts. The development of such a community of interests came as much in

---

[6] See J. H. Elliott, 'A Formula for Survival: The Spanish Monarchy and Empire', *17° Congreso Internacional de Ciencias Históricas* (Madrid, 1992), Sección cronológica, ii, pp. 722–6.

spite of, as because of, a constitutional structure that, superficially at least, looks like the perfect recipe for political fragmentation.

The principle that informed the government of the Spanish Monarchy as a composite monarchy[7] can best be summed up in the well-known formula enunciated by Juan de Solórzano Pereira in his *Política indiana* of 1647 that its kingdoms should be ruled and governed 'as if the king who holds them all together were king only of each one.'[8] This formula derived from the historical fact that most of the Monarchy's constituent kingdoms and provinces had entered it through a dynastic union under which they were entitled to preserve their traditional laws, rights and privileges. While it was true that some parts of the Monarchy—notably Navarre, the Indies and (some would argue) Naples— were conquered territories, and hence juridically incorporated rather than united on the basis of equal status, each of them in practice came to enjoy distinctive forms of treatment, determined to a greater or lesser degree by local circumstances. If the Indies, as conquests of Castile, were fundamentally governed in accordance with Castilian law, the need to compile in the later seventeenth century a separate codification for America, the *Recopilación de las leyes de Indias*, is evidence of the way in which a distinctive body of law had grown up in response to specifically American conditions.[9] In the event, even this proved insufficient to meet local requirements. In 1685, five years after the publication of the *Recopilación*, the viceroyalty of Peru responded with the publication of its own *Recopilación provincial*, containing viceregal ordinances from the days of viceroy Don Francisco de Toledo onwards.[10] To all intents and purposes the Monarchy on both sides of the Atlantic had come to be governed as if the king of all the kingdoms were king only of each one.

The acceptance of the inherent diversity of the Monarchy by those who governed it for most of its existence—a diversity reflected in the enormous variety of its laws and institutions—reinforced the importance of those few elements within it that made for unity. At the centre was the monarch, the king who was at once king of each and king of all: a sacred monarch elevated and fortified by a religion that was also the common heritage of all his many

---

[7] See J. H. Elliott, 'A Europe of Composite Monarchies', *Past and Present*, 137 (1992), pp. 48–71, reprinted above, ch. 1.

[8] Juan de Solórzano y Pereyra, *Política indiana*, lib. iv, cap. xix, 39 (*Biblioteca de Autores Españoles* 252–6, Madrid, 1972), 254, p. 301, cited above, p. 7.

[9] See José Manuel Pérez Prendes, *La monarquía indiana y el estado de derecho* (Valencia, 1989), pp. 174–81.

[10] Ruggiero Romano, *Conjonctures opposées. La 'Crise' du XVIIe siècle en Europe et en Amérique Ibérique* (Geneva, 1992), p. 187.

subjects. At his disposal was a complex bureaucratic apparatus staffed by ministers and officials, many, although not all of whom, were university-trained *letrados*. These men approached their work with a highly legalistic view of the tasks of government, and were strongly conscious of the need to uphold and exalt the king's authority.[11]

We badly need a prosopographical treatment of these servants of the Monarchy, along the lines of Janine Fayard's study of the councillors of Castile, but more wide-ranging and comprehensive than that valuable work.[12] In particular, it would be of great interest to follow the careers of those who moved from one part of the Monarchy to another, whether as viceroys or as judges of the *audiencias*, or high courts. There is Don Pedro de la Gasca, for instance, a member of the Council of the Inquisition and entrusted with an official visitation to the kingdom of Valencia before being sent by Charles V to suppress the Pizarro rebellion in Peru; or Don Juan Mendoza y Luna, third Marquis of Montesclaros, the Crown's official representative (*asistente*) in Seville in 1600, viceroy of New Spain from 1603 to 1606, and of Peru from 1606 to 1615, before returning to Madrid where he was appointed to the Councils of State, Finance and Aragon.[13] What image did such men have of the Monarchy, and to what extent did they see it as a coherent unit as a result of their experiences on both sides of the Atlantic?

Officials such as these helped to bind together a fragmented Monarchy. So, too, did many other of the king's subjects from different walks of life: soldiers of the elite Castilian regiments, the *tercios* who were stationed in Milan and then were despatched to 'put a pike in Flanders'; members of the religious orders, who had been working without much success to convert the moriscos of Granada and then moved on to evangelise in New Spain or Peru; merchants engaged in the trade between Antwerp and Seville, and between Seville and Vera Cruz; and those thousands of emigrants who crossed the Atlantic to make a better life for themselves, and who sought as best they could to remain in touch with relatives back home in Castile or Extremadura. These people, to borrow the graphic title employed by the compilers of a collection

---

[11] See Richard L. Kagan, *Students and Society in Early Modern Spain* (Baltimore, Md. and London, 1974).

[12] Janine Fayard, *Les Membres du Conseil de Castille à l'époque moderne (1621–1746)* (Geneva and Paris, 1979).

[13] See Teodoro Hampe Martínez, *Don Pedro de la Gasca. Su obra política en España y América* (Lima, 1989); Antonio Herrera Casado, *El gobierno americano del marqués de Montesclaros* (Guadalajara, Spain, 1990).

of transatlantic letters, constituted 'the thread that binds'.[14] The Monarchy was criss-crossed by networks of kinship groups and personal contacts, all of which helped to articulate it and hold it together. Out of these networks emerged special interest groups, all seeking to influence the decisions of the councils in Madrid by intensive lobbying at court.

The Monarchy can therefore be seen as a vast complex of pressure groups and interests, all competing with each other for the attention and favour of the monarch. These interests tended to accumulate over time, locking disparate groups and regions into what was in effect a global system capable of offering substantial benefits to those who found themselves in a position to exploit it. For this reason it is important not to overemphasise the dichotomy between centre and periphery as a critical fault-line in the structure of the Spanish Monarchy.[15] A well-connected Neapolitan noble, or the owner of a Mexican *hacienda,* could make use of his connections, and of the Crown's pressing needs, to negotiate important social and financial advantages for himself if he played the game skilfully and had a little luck. This meant that, while there was much to divide centre and periphery, there was also much to unite them, and if the ties were often invisible and intangible, they none the less constituted a powerful binding force.

More, however, than mere personal or sectional interest was involved, for all its importance in holding together a disparate and fragmented Monarchy. The organic concept of kingship was deeply entrenched throughout the King of Spain's dominions—a concept in which the king and his people jointly constituted a body politic of which every part was essential to its proper functioning, but of which the king was the head. Loyalty was integral to such a concept: loyalty to a monarch who in turn cared benevolently for the well-being of his subjects.

It is impossible to understand the survival of the Monarchy without taking into account this profound and instinctive loyalty to the person of the monarch, which was almost universally maintained for as long as possible in spite of all the indications that he had failed in his duty to his subjects. The

[14] Rocío Sánchez Rubio and Isabel Testón Núñez, *El hilo que une. Las relaciones epistolares en el viejo y el nuevo mundo (siglos XVI–XVIII)* (Mérida, 1999). See also Ida Altman, *Transatlantic Ties in the Spanish Empire: Brihuega, Spain and Puebla, Mexico, 1560–1620* (Stanford, Calif., 2000), and two studies devoted to migration from the Extremaduran town of Trujillo: Ida Altman, *Emigrants and Society: Extremadura and Spanish America in the Sixteenth Century* (Berkeley/Los Angeles, Calif. and London, 1989), and Gregorio Salinero, *Une Ville entre deux mondes. Trujillo d'Espagne et les Indes au XVII siècle* (Madrid, 2006).
[15] As I did, for example, in my *Imperial Spain, 1469–1716* (1st edn, London, 1963; repr. 2002).

revolt of the Netherlands began in 1566, but it was not until 1581 that William
the Silent and the Dutch rebels formally abjured their allegiance to Philip II.
The crowds in the streets of Barcelona in 1640 shouted 'Long live the king and
down with traitors!' ('*Visca el Rei i muiren traïdors!*)[16] The Duke of Arcos,
viceroy of Naples, reported in 1647 that the people 'have truly shown a firm
loyalty and love for Your Majesty's service, rescuing his portraits from the
houses that they themselves have burnt down, dipping their banners in his
honour, and constantly saying "Long live the king and long live Spain. . . ."'[17]
This instinctive loyalty was to be found at every level of society. In 1730 the
mestizo rebels of Cochabamba in Peru are to be found shouting the shout that
was traditionally to be heard at moments of unrest in every corner of the
Monarchy: 'Long live the king and down with bad government!'[18] That this
should be the universal cry of the rebels is evidence of the tenacity in the King
of Spain's dominions of the convenient fiction that it was evil counsellors and
bad ministers who bore responsibility for acts of injustice, and that if the king
were properly informed of what his subordinates were doing in his name he
would immediately intervene to remedy the wrongs.

The old Basque and Castilian formula of obedience but non-compliance—
obedezco pero no cumplo—which safely made the transatlantic crossing to
begin a new life in the Indies, served the same purpose of at once preserving
the appearance of the subject's loyalty and the image of the king.[19] The
assumption underlying these formulas and fictions was that the relationship
between king and people was governed not only by the terms of the natural
relationship between a father and his children but also, in many instances, by
those of a mutually agreed compact. In some parts of the Monarchy, notably
Castile, this compact was essentially tacit, even though the Castilian constitutionalist and contractualist tradition persisted throughout the sixteenth and
seventeenth centuries. It did so in spite of the trend in Madrid towards royal
authoritarianism and the shortcomings of the Castilian Cortes, and it found
outspoken expression in the writings of Juan de Mariana and other political

---

[16] Elliott, *Revolt of the Catalans*, p. 429.

[17] Rosario Villari, *Per il re o per la patria* (Rome, 1994), pp. 150–1 (Duke of Arcos to Philip
IV, 15 July 1647).

[18] Scarlett O'Phelan Godoy, *Rebellions and Revolts in Eighteenth-Century Peru and Upper
Peru* (Cologne and Vienna, 1985), p. 76.

[19] For the formula of obeying but not complying, see Bartolomé Clavero, *Derecho de los
reinos* (Seville, 1980), pp. 125–30; Benjamín González Alonso, 'La formula "Obedézcase,
pero no se cumpla" en el derecho castellano de la baja edad media', *Anuario de Historia del
Derecho Español*, 50 (1980), pp. 469–87; Pérez Prendes, *La monarquía indiana*, pp. 167–8.

theorists of the day.[20] In other kingdoms, as in the Crown of Aragon, it was formulated and enshrined in a set of specific laws, and protected by such institutions as the Catalan *Diputació*, or the *Justicia* of Aragon. The nature of the resulting constitutional compact was spelled out in a Catalan memorial of 1622: 'Between Your Majesty and his vassals there is a reciprocal obligation, whereby as they must obey and serve Your Majesty as their king and lord, so Your Majesty must observe their laws and privileges.'[21]

Such a formula legitimised resistance and, as a last resort, rebellion, and it, too, made the transatlantic crossing, in spite of the refusal of King Ferdinand and Queen Isabella to allow the establishment of Cortes in their kingdoms of the Indies. The idea of a contract was inherent in the *capitulaciones* made first with Christopher Columbus and later with the leaders of the expeditions of conquest, even if these were officially presented as *mercedes* granted by the monarch.[22] The chronological coincidence between the revolt of the Comuneros in Castile and Hernán Cortés' conquest of Mexico provided a further, and possibly decisive, impetus to the successful transfer of contractualist ideas from the Old World to the New.[23] Cortés and other principal conquistadores were well acquainted with the thirteenth-century Castilian legal code of the *Siete Partidas* and the political assumptions that informed them[24]—assumptions that, deriving from Aristotle by way of Aquinas, were to be reformulated at a theoretical level for sixteenth-century Spaniards by the neo-Thomist scholastics of the School of Salamanca. According to these assumptions, prince and subjects together formed a *corpus mysticum*, designed to enable its members to live good and sociable lives conforming to their respective social stations, under the benevolent rule of a monarch who, following the dictates of his conscience, governed in accordance with divine and natural law. It was expected that the prince would not swerve into tyranny, while his subjects for their part would serve, obey and advise him to the best of their ability.

---

[20] See for instance Charles Jago, 'Taxation and Political Culture in Castile, 1590–1640', in Richard L. Kagan and Geoffrey Parker, eds, *Spain, Europe and the Atlantic World: Essays in Honour of John H. Elliott* (Cambridge, 1995), ch. 2. For Mariana see Harald E. Braun, *Juan de Mariana and Early Modern Spanish Political Thought* (Aldershot, 2007).

[21] Cited in Elliott, *Revolt of the Catalans*, p. 45.

[22] For the contractual characteristics of the *capitulaciones*, see Milagros del Vas Mingo, *Las capitulaciones de Indias en el siglo XVI* (Madrid, 1986), ch. 4, and Alfonso García-Gallo, *Los orígenes españoles de las instituciones americanas* (Madrid, 1987), pp. 714–41 ('El pactismo en el reino de Castilla y su proyección en América').

[23] See Manuel Giménez Fernández, *Hernán Cortés y su revolución comunera en la Nueva España* (Seville, 1948).

[24] Víctor Frankl, 'Hernán Cortés y la tradición de las Siete Partidas', *Revista de Historia de América*, 53–4 (1962), pp. 9–74.

As the conquistadores were transformed into settlers, they were no more inclined to abandon these assumptions and the contractual relationship in which they found their outward expression than they were inclined to abandon their natural relationship with a now distant royal father. Although they petitioned in vain for the establishment of Cortes or some form of representative assembly, their failure did not preclude the use of other forums, like town councils, for expressing collective grievances.[25] While the lack of representative assemblies was to cast a long shadow over the history of Spanish America, a set of unwritten rules was gradually developed which was well understood by both parties to the contract. The experience of the New Laws of 1542 and Pizarro's rebellion served as a salutary warning to Crown and colonists alike. On the basis of that unhappy experience they constructed together through mutual, if unacknowledged, compromise a patrimonial state system for Spain's empire of the Indies, which served its purpose in preserving a reasonable degree of political and social stability over enormous distances and across vast territories thousands of miles from Madrid.[26]

In a patrimonial system of government royal absenteeism presents a perennial problem. If Charles V did his best to counteract its political consequences by means of constant, and often frenetic, travel from one kingdom to another of his European empire, the permanent establishment of king and court in Madrid under Philip II ended the era of itinerant monarchy, and emphasised still further the importance of compensatory mechanisms. Institutionally these already existed. The conciliar system and the establishment of viceroyalties, *gobernaciones* and *audiencias* across the Monarchy helped to sustain the fiction that the king was personally present in each of his kingdoms, and was personally attentive to their problems and needs.

In this sense, government of the Indies was no different from that of Naples or Sicily, which were never to see their monarchs after the establishment of the court in Madrid. The same was almost as true of the Iberian Peninsula itself, where royal visits to Catalonia and Valencia, for instance, were to be few and far between. Beyond the Crown of Castile, royal government was absentee government conducted at a distance. But, where the Indies were concerned, the sheer scale of the distances involved created challenges of a magnitude without parallel in Europe. There was always a possibility that Philip II or one

---

[25] Guillermo Lohmann Villena, 'Las Cortes en Indias', *Anuario de Historia del Derecho Español*, 18 (1947), pp. 655–62; Woodrow Borah, 'Representative Institutions in the Spanish Empire in the Sixteenth Century', *The Americas*, 12 (1956), pp. 246–57.
[26] For the patrimonial state in the Indies see especially Mario Góngora, *Studies in the Colonial History of Spanish America* (Cambridge, 1975), ch. 3.

of his successors would go in person to visit his possessions in Italy or the Netherlands, and indeed Philip IV expressed his determination to do so in 1629.[27] But in the Indies the exercise of personal kingship was out of the question from the start. There was no conceivable chance of a monarch crossing the Atlantic to see his loyal subjects of the Indies and attend in person to their government.

As far as administration was concerned, royal absenteeism from the Indies was counterbalanced by the elaborate institutional structure that the Crown succeeded in imposing on the American viceroyalties, and the greater latitude for manoeuvre that it enjoyed as a result of the absence of those representative institutions that tended to hamper its assertion of power in its European territories. This made it possible, at least in theory, for the Crown to deploy in its government of America the absolute royal power, that *poderío real absoluto*, for which Crown jurists had argued in Castile since the fifteenth century.[28] It could also, through the royal *patronato*, call on the support and resources of what was in effect a state Church, without the dangers of interference by papal nuncios.

The valuable reinforcement of royal power provided by a subordinate Church was accompanied by an impressive deployment of the symbols of majesty. In *Los reyes distantes* Víctor Mínguez Cornelles provides some vivid examples of the ways in which the images of kingship were deployed in New Spain.[29] Glittering viceregal courts, imitating at a distance the royal court in Madrid; the splendour of viceregal entries into the towns and cities on the route from Vera Cruz to Mexico City; the ubiquitous presence of royal portraits on public and ceremonial occasions; the pomp and circumstance of ceremonies provoked by the news of royal births, marriages and deaths. All these public and ceremonial representations of majesty suggest how, in the Spanish Monarchy, invisible kingship had been raised to a high art. What is not so clear, and deserves investigation, is whether there was a correlation between the splendour of the ceremonial and the degree of distance from Madrid. The court presided over by Spain's viceroy in Naples was certainly more splendid than the courts of the viceroys of Catalonia or Valencia. But

---

[27] J. H. Elliott and José F. de la Peña, *Memoriales y cartas del Conde Duque de Olivares*, 2 vols, (Madrid, 1978–81), ii, doc. iv.

[28] Luis Sánchez Agesta, 'El "poderío real absoluto" en el testamento de 1554', in *Carlos V. Homenaje de la Universidad de Granada* (Granada, 1958), pp. 439–60.

[29] Víctor Mínguez Cornelles, *Los reyes distantes. Imágenes del poder en el mundo virreinal* (Castelló de la Plana, 1995).

was its splendour eclipsed by that of the still more distant viceregal courts of Mexico City and Lima?[30]

Yet not even the most elaborate ceremonial could entirely conceal the latent tensions in the composite monarchy of the House of Austria. This was not a static system, but one subject to continuous pressures for change and adaptation in a changing world. The principal motor of change throughout the Monarchy was royal fiscalism. The heavy expenses incurred by the Crown in its efforts to defend its worldwide dominions and pursue a set of policies whose costs bore little relation to the resources it could mobilise, generated an endless succession of fiscal measures designed to relieve its acute financial problems. The introduction of new taxes and ingenious fiscal expedients; the alienation of Crown property; the sale of offices and honours—all these measures had profound social, economic and constitutional implications for the Monarchy as a whole. In economic terms, they helped over the course of the sixteenth and seventeenth centuries to change the balance of forces within the Monarchy, weakening territories like Naples and, most notably, Castile, which lacked strong institutional defences against royal fiscalism. Socially, they strengthened those groups in society that could turn the Crown's needs to their own advantage, those 'enemies of the *patria*, local bosses (*los poderosos de los lugares*), and Your Majesty's wicked minor officials', so scathingly denounced by the Count-Duke of Olivares in 1637.[31] The result was a re-inforcement of the forces of oligarchy on both sides of the Atlantic during the seventeenth century. Although the consolidation of oligarchies represented in the long run a serious weakening of the Crown and its authority, in the short term it had the paradoxical effect of strengthening the bonds that tied provincial elites to Madrid. The nobility of Naples, for instance, showed itself almost uniformly hostile to the Neapolitan revolt of 1647–8.[32] Why turn against a Crown that had done so much to reinforce its local and territorial ascendancy?

---

[30] For Naples, see Carlos José Hernández Sánchez, *Castilla y Nápoles en el siglo XVI. El virrey Pedro de Toledo* (Salamanca, 1994), ch. 6, and for Mexico, Alejandro Cañeque, *The King's Living Image: The Culture and Politics of Viceregal Power in Colonial Mexico* (New York and London, 2004). For some valuable reflections on viceregal courts and their diversity, see Xavier Gil Pujol, 'Una cultura cortesana provincial. Patria, comunicación y lenguaje en la Monarquía Hispánica de los Austrias', in Pablo Fernández Albaladejo ed., *Monarquía, imperio y pueblos en la España moderna. Actas de la IV Reunión Científica de la Asociación de Historia Moderna* (Alicante, 1997), pp. 225–57.

[31] Elliott and la Peña, *Memoriales y cartas*, ii, doc. xiv, p. 171.

[32] See Rosario Villari, 'Rivoluzioni periferiche e declino della Monarchia di Spagna', in *La crisis hispánica de 1640. Cuadernos de Historia Moderna*, 11 (1991), pp. 11–19.

The persistent efforts of the Crown to mobilise more effectively the financial resources and manpower of its dominions inevitably imposed strains on their relationship, especially when, as happened during the ministry of Olivares, the Crown was suspected, and with reason, of wishing to rewrite the terms of the relationship in ways that would reinforce its own authority. If the monarch defaulted on his contractual obligations and behaved not as a king but as a tyrant, those kingdoms and provinces whose constitutional arrangements were based on notions of contract could in extreme cases, as in Catalonia in 1640, declare the contract terminated. But this presupposed the existence of an alternative focus of loyalty. This alternative focus was the *patria*. 'Faith should be kept with the *patria* and not with tyrants', declared the author of a *Discorso* written in Naples during the rebellion of 1647.[33]

Properly, the *patria* was an entity consisting of king and people conjoined, with the king as *caput comunitatis*,[34] and it was in these conventional terms that Olivares was thinking when he denounced the 'enemies of the *patria*' in 1637. It was in these terms, too, that the majority of people were still inclined to think, even when, as Catalonia in the spring and summer of 1640, they were being swept along on the tide of revolution. They did not see loyalty to the king as being in conflict with loyalty to the *patria*,[35] and regarded evil ministers and judges as traitors to both. But, very briefly in Barcelona in the autumn and winter of that year, and again in Naples in 1647–8, the previously unthinkable idea of a *patria* without a king was beginning to be thought, as the leaders of rebellion turned for a possible solution to their problems towards a republican system of government, like that enjoyed by Switzerland or Venice or by the Dutch Republic, another society that had defied the King of Spain, and had done so with success.

If republican sentiments were, and remained, unusual in the profoundly monarchical societies of the Spanish Monarchy, the pressures exercised by Madrid helped to strengthen and deepen the notion of the *patria* as a historic and territorial community, whose fundamental interests were not necessarily compatible with those of a state apparatus that claimed to be carrying out the wishes of the king. Since my observations many years ago on the importance of the concept of the *pàtria* in the mentality of seventeenth-century Catalans,[36]

[33] Villari, *Per il re o per la patria*, p. 34.
[34] Antoni Simon i Tarrés, *Els orígens ideològics de la revolució catalana de 1640* (Barcelona, 1999), p. 279.
[35] Luis R. Corteguera, *For the Common Good: Popular Politics in Barcelona, 1580–1640* (Ithaca, N.Y. and London, 2002), p. 153.
[36] Elliott, *Revolt of the Catalans*, pp. 42–3.

notions of the *patria* and patriotism have attracted increasing attention from historians of the Spanish Monarchy and of early modern Europe in general, stimulated, at least in part, by recent discussions of the origins of modern nationalism and by Benedict Anderson's description of nations as 'imagined communities'.[37] James Casey, for example, has examined the nature of patriotism in early modern Valencia, while I. A. A. Thompson has explored the obstacles to the evolution of the concept of the *patria* as a national community in Castile.[38]

The *patria* was as much an idealised as an imagined community. As a community, it was in the first instance local—one's birthplace or home town. Jeroni Pujades, for instance, spoke of 'my *pàtria* and dear city of Barcelona'.[39] But for him it was also the wider community of those born and brought up in the principality of Catalonia, who shared the same dedication to laws and liberties won in the course of centuries of struggle against domestic oppressors and foreign enemies. Notions of nationality, based on shared ethnicity and language, were ill-defined, and lacked the resonance they were to acquire with the advent of the Romantic Movement at the turn of the eighteenth and nineteenth centuries, but this did not preclude the existence of a strong sense of collective identity. For instance, the inhabitants of the principality of Catalonia, like those of other kingdoms or provinces of the Monarchy, liked to think of themselves as dwelling in a uniquely blessed and beautiful land, and they shared not only laws and institutions but collective memories. The qualities that they saw as exemplified in their community might be exaggerated, and its traditions often invented, but centuries of shared experience had given its inhabitants an understandable pride in their creative achievements. Their distance from Madrid made no difference to their perception of themselves. Similarly, the apparently peripheral position of Spain's Italian territories to a Spanish metropolis gave no rise to feelings of inferiority, because, as far as they were concerned, they were the centre. Since, in addition, they boasted the Romans as their ancestors, it was obvious to them that they were second to none.[40]

The inhabitants of the Crown's Italian possessions or of the Iberian kingdoms had enjoyed many centuries in which to develop their sense of collective identity and elaborate their own vision of the *patria*. No doubt it was in

---

[37] Benedict Anderson, *Imagined Communities* (London and New York, 1983). See also Eric Hobsbawm, *Nations and Nationalism since 1780* (Cambridge, 1990).

[38] See Kagan and Parker, *Spain, Europe and the Atlantic World*, chs. 5 and 7.

[39] Cited in Elliott, *Revolt of the Catalans*, p. 42.

[40] Mireille Peytevin, 'Españoles e italianos en Sicilia, Nápoles y Milán durante los siglos XVI y XVII', in *La monarquía española. Grupos políticos locales ante la corte de Madrid* (*Relaciones*, 73, El Colegio de Michoacán, 1998), pp. 88–90.

many respects an elitist vision, and the seventeenth-century revolts in Catalonia and Naples showed up its fragility as a unifying force when peasants or artisans turned their wrath against their own elites. But this does not necessarily mean that they, too, were not animated by loyalty to the *patria*. The upper classes of Catalan society might manipulate the constitutions of Catalonia in their own interest, but this did not prevent the artisans of Barcelona from seeing themselves as members of a community of the free, and thereby entitled to enjoy historic rights.[41] Bitter social division did not of itself rule out all sense of an ideal community, even among the underprivileged and the dispossessed.

In the Old World societies the idea of the *patria*, nourished by the ideals of classical antiquity transmitted by the humanists, had had a long time to take root.[42] But what of the New World societies that were coming into being? On the far shores of the Atlantic the notion of the *patria* had to start from scratch, but in spite of this it came quickly into being.[43] From the moment when Hernán Cortés landed on the shores of Mexico and transformed his expeditionary force into a formally constituted urban community, the Villa Rica de Vera Cruz, a new *patria* began to be both invented and imagined. This imagined community was to be built on the grievances of the conquistadores and their descendants, who believed that they had not received the *mercedes* to which their own services and those of their ancestors had entitled them, and looked to their monarch for redress.[44]

The *patria* in the New World was thus to acquire, at least in the minds of the colonists, a firm constitutional basis, in this instance the laws and rights enjoyed by the king's Castilian subjects. Very soon this polity, founded—or so it was believed—on a compact, was also to acquire, like its Old World equivalents, a geographical and historical dimension. In 1604 Bernardo de Balbuena was proclaiming in his *Grandeza mexicana* the beauties of his native Mexico City and its surrounding countryside. In 1630 Fray Buenaventura de Salinas y Córdova extolled the glories of Peru, its riches and its climate, in terms that echoed those of contemporary patriotic publicists in the Iberian

---

[41] See Corteguera, *For the Common Good*. For Naples see Villari, *Per il re o per la patria*.

[42] See, for example, Xavier Gil Pujol, 'Ciudadanía, patria y humanismo cívico en el Aragón foral: Juan Costa', *Manuscrits*, 19 (2001), pp. 81–101.

[43] For the development of creole patriotism, see especially David Brading, *The First America: The Spanish Monarchy, Creole Patriots and the Liberal State, 1492–1867* (Cambridge, 1991). See also Bernard Lavallé, *Las promesas ambiguas. Criollismo colonial en los Andes* (Lima, 1993).

[44] See, for example, the complaints of Baltasar Dorantes de Carranza, *Sumaria relación de las cosas de la Nueva España* (Mexico City, 1987), pp. 203–4.

kingdoms. 'In summary', he wrote, 'all find themselves in this city of Lima . . . with satisfaction and pleasure, and look on it as their *patria*.'[45] Pride of place—a place uniquely blessed by God—was to be the cornerstone of the increasingly elaborate edifice of creole patriotism.

There still remained the problem of the exact location of the *patria* in space. What were its territorial limits and extent? The Old World societies by now possessed relatively well-determined territorial boundaries. Those of the New World were still in process of definition. The two viceroyalties of New Spain and Peru were simply too vast and diversified to constitute an instinctive focus of loyalty: the *patrias* of a Balbuena or a Salinas were essentially Mexico City and Lima, with hinterlands extending towards distant horizons. Not surprisingly, therefore, local and regional patriotisms began to develop in the Indies. Municipalities, and by degrees also the wider jurisdictional areas of *audiencias* and *gobernaciones*, came to provide them with a territorial framework. In seventeenth-century Quito a creole official from Lima was already liable to be regarded as just as much of a foreigner as an official who had arrived from Madrid.[46]

The endowment of New World *patrias* with a historical dimension was to prove more problematic than their endowment with a geographical dimension, if only because the creole societies were of such recent creation. But this, too, was to be achieved in due course, in the first instance by inserting them into a divine and providentialist history. The legend that St Thomas had once conducted a mission in the New World pointed to a prior process of evangelisation before the advent of the friars. Mexico's providential place in sacred history was in due course satisfactorily confirmed by the apparition of the Virgin of Guadalupe, who in the seventeenth century was to assume her position as the patron and symbol of creole New Spain.[47] In the viceroyalty of Peru, a possible way forward was provided by Garcilaso de la Vega, when he depicted his sun-worshipping Inca ancestors as the forerunners of a Christian Peru to which the Spaniards had brought the inestimable knowledge of the one true God. But in 1671 Peru acquired its own saint—the first to be born in the Indies with the canonization of Isabel Flores de Oliva as Santa Rosa de

---

[45] Fray Buenaventura de Salinas y Córdova, *Memorial de las Historias del Nuevo Mundo Piru* (Lima, 1957), p. 246.

[46] Pilar Ponce Leiva, *Certezas ante la incertidumbre. Elite y cabildo de Quito en el siglo XVII* (Quito, 1998), p. 196.

[47] Francisco de la Maza, *El guadalupanismo méxicano* (Mexico City, 1953); Jacques Lafaye, *Quetzalcóatl et Guadalupe* (Paris, 1974); David Brading, *Mexican Phoenix* (Cambridge, 2001).

Lima, proclaimed by Pope Clement X as 'Universal and principal patron of all America'.[48]

There were obvious problems, however, for creole elites about the incorporation of indigenous societies into their perception of their American *patrias*. In the corporatist conception of the Monarchy, the *república de los indios* could lay claim to its own distinctive space, as legitimate as that of the *república de los españoles*. But for creoles who gloried in being Spaniards, the origins and natural inferiority of the Indians constituted an insuperable bar to their inclusion within the *patria*. Consequently, in their determination to keep their indigenous populations at arms length, the creoles were forced to develop their own distinctive form of patriotism, more hierarchical and more exclusive than its counterpart in metropolitan Spain.

Local conditions in the Indies, however, were changing, and so too were the creoles' perceptions of themselves. As Spaniards who were no longer quite Spaniards but who were resolutely determined not to be Indians, their anxious search for a collective identity was to involve them in a variety of intellectual contortions to fashion a suitable image of themselves.[49] But the image was always bumping up against uncongenial realities. As the new colonial societies developed, and the mestizo element of the population expanded, it became less easy to determine who was a Spaniard and who was not. The growing obsession with the naming and differentiation of *castas* was itself a desperate and futile attempt to preserve distinctions that were now becoming blurred. At the same time, while new generations of creoles continued to insist with, if anything, growing stridency on their Spanish identity,[50] their styles of life were in many respects ceasing to resemble those of their metropolitan Spanish cousins.[51] Not entirely surprisingly, newly arrived *peninsulares* tended to look down on the creoles as having degenerated in an American

---

[48] Carlos Daniel Valcárcel, 'Concepto de la historia en los "Comentarios reales" y en la "Historia General del Perú" ', *Nuevos Estudios sobre el Inca Garcilaso de la Vega* (Lima, 1955), pp. 123–36; Brading, *The First America*, ch. 12. For Santa Rosa de Lima, see Ramón Mujica Pinilla, *Rosa Limensis. Mística, políca e iconografía en torno a la patrona de America*, 2nd edn (Mexico City, 2005).

[49] See Jorge Cañizares-Esguerra, 'New World, New Stars: Patriotic Astrology and the Invention of Indian and Creole Bodies in Colonial Spanish America, 1600–1650', *American Historical Review*, 104 (1999), pp. 329–49, reprinted in his *Nature, Empire and Nation* (Stanford, Calif., 2006), ch. 4; David Brading, *The Origins of Mexican Nationalism* (Centre of Latin American Studies, Cambridge, 1985), and *The First America*; and see below, Ch. X.

[50] Lavallé, *Las promesas ambiguas*, p. 21.

[51] See Solange Alberro, *Les Espagnols dans le Mexique colonial. Histoire d'une acculturation* (Paris, 1992).

environment, and as having been contaminated by the undesirable character-istics of the indigenous population among whom they passed their lives.

The effect of constant disparagement by metropolitan Spaniards was to reinforce not only the insistence of the creoles on their Spanish ancestry, but also their sense of identification with the American world which they had made their own. If they were not yet *americanos*, they were at least being transformed into *españoles americanos*—a term that by the later eighteenth century they were using of themselves.[52] With this gradual process of transfor-mation came a new openness towards a pre-conquest world that was now receding into a distant past. If living Indians remained on the fringes of the *patria*, the way was at least open for the retrospective incorporation into it of those who were safely dead. To the indignation of the viceroy Juan de Palafox, seventeenth-century Mexico City, turning its back on the coat of arms given it by Charles V, began to adorn its buildings with a replacement displaying the eagle and serpent of the pre-conquest Mexica.[53] In 1680 Carlos de Sigüenza y Góngora designed his famous triumphal arch for the entry of the new viceroy, with its statues of the twelve Mexica emperors since the foundation of Tenochtitlán in 1327.[54] In later seventeenth- and eighteenth-century Peru, fiestas in which the Incas were represented in full ceremonial dress helped to nurture visions among creoles, mestizos and Indians alike of an Andean utopia.[55]

By the eighteenth century, therefore, creole *patrias* in New Spain and Peru had acquired legendary or idealised pasts that conferred on them a historical respectability comparable, at least in their own eyes, to that of the *patrias* of the European dominions of the King of Spain. Ethnic divisions may have made these *patrias* even more fragile than those of the European territories, where sharp social divisions so often subverted the ideal of community, but a sufficient sense of collective identity had been achieved in the evolving soci-eties of Spanish America to provide a potential focus of alternative loyalty at moments when the relationship of king and subjects came under strain. That strain was to become acute in the second half of the eighteenth century with the imposition by Madrid of a comprehensive programme of reform.

---

[52] Guillermo Céspedes del Castillo, *América hispánica, 1492–1898* (Madrid, 1983), p. 401.

[53] Enrique Florescano, *La bandera mexicana* (Mexico City, 1998), p. 48.

[54] Carlos de Sigüenza y Góngora, *Theatro de virtudes políticas* (Mexico City, 1680), in his *Obras históricas* (Mexico City, 1983), pp. 225–361.

[55] Karine Perissat, 'Los incas representados (Lima—siglo XVIII): ¿supervivencia o renacimiento?' *Revista de Indias*, 60 (2000), pp. 623–49. For the Andean utopia, Alberto Flores Galindo, *Buscando un inca* (Lima, 1988), ch. 1.

The drama played out in the Indies in the later eighteenth century—a drama whose highpoint was the crisis of the early 1780s with the rising of the Comuneros of New Granada and the rebellion of Túpac Amaru in Peru[56]— can be seen as a belated American version of the drama that had already been enacted in metropolitan Spain. The advent of the Bourbons and their imposition between 1709 and 1716 of a new form of government, the *Nueva Planta*, on the Crown of Aragon effectively marked the end in the Iberian Peninsula, both in theory and practice, of the composite monarchy which the new dynasty had inherited from the House of Austria. Even if Navarre and the Basque provinces still retained their traditional institutions and laws and privileges, or *fueros*, Philip V's victory over the Crown of Aragon signalled the triumph of 'vertical Spain' over the 'horizontal Spain' of the House of Austria.[57] The new metropolitan Spain, a 'vertical Spain', was to be, at least in intention, a centralised and uniform state, in which there would be no institutional, legal or ecclesiastical barriers to the exercise of the sovereign will of the king, and in which loyalty to individual *patrias* was to be subsumed into an all-embracing loyalty to a Spanish nation state.

Sooner or later this new vision of the monarchy was bound to make the transatlantic crossing. There were too many forces, on both sides of the Atlantic, making for change. Impressed by the benefits that the overseas empires of Britain and the Dutch Republic had brought to their respective mother countries, ministers and officials in Madrid were in no doubt of the validity of José del Campillo y Cosío's arguments for what he called a 'new method' of government of the Indies, 'so that we can obtain benefits from such a rich possession'.[58] It is indicative of their changing attitude that ministers under Charles III were beginning to use, at least among themselves, the word *colonias* for what had hitherto been known as the kingdoms (*reinos*) of the Indies.[59] The terminology itself was suggestive of the extent to which the Madrid bureaucracy had turned its back on the ways of thought associated with the composite monarchy of the Habsburgs.

---

[56] For the crisis of the 1780s, see J. H. Elliott, *Empires of the Atlantic World: Britain and Spain in America, 1492–1830* (New Haven, Conn. and London, 2006), pp. 353–68.

[57] The terms coined by Ricardo García Cárcel, *Felipe V y los españoles* (Barcelona, 2002), p. 114; and see above, p. 21.

[58] See José del Campillo y Cosío, *Nuevo sistema de gobierno económico para América*, ed. Manuel Ballesteros Gaibrois (Madrid, 1993), p. 63.

[59] Guillermo Céspedes del Castillo, *Ensayos sobre los reinos castellanos de Indias* (Madrid, 1999), p. 300; Antonio Anino, 'Some Reflections on Spanish-American Constitutional and Political History', *Itinerario*, 19 (1995), pp. 26–43. See p. 37.

It was not only a question of making the Indies more profitable to metropolitan Spain. With the costs of defending the overseas territories rapidly escalating, the case for radical fiscal reform in the American viceroyalties was becoming overwhelming. But it was hard to see how far-reaching reform could effectively be introduced into societies that in practice had fallen into the hands of creole elites. These elites had taken advantage of the Crown's weakness in the seventeenth and early eighteenth centuries to buy their way into judicial and administrative posts. They had succeeded, too, in establishing a complicity with the agents of government which worked to mutual benefit. The result of their tacit understanding was that royal officials, instead of being the effective agents and executors of the central government, had tended to adopt the role of intermediaries between the elites and Madrid.[60]

As befitted the last major survivors of the Habsburg composite monarchy, the kingdoms of the Indies responded to the determination of the Bourbons to set their American house in order by resorting to the weapons of defence traditionally employed in the kingdoms and provinces of the Monarchy when they found themselves under attack. Instinctively the creole elites sought a counterweight to Madrid in the *patria*—an entity that was emotionally and conceptually much richer than it had been a hundred years before. Their response was characterised, too, by a growing resentment against the mother country, which increasingly led the elites to assert the American component of their dual identity.[61] But their loyalty to their monarch remained intact. Devotion to the *patria* was still compatible, as in so many of the revolts in the Habsburg monarchy, with fidelity to the ideal of a universal monarchy firmly based on natural and contractual kingship. In this instance, and for the last time, their faith was justified. The movements of protest and revolt of the 1770s and 1780s were brought to an end by mutual concessions of the kind that had so often brought the monarchy back from the brink of the abyss in the days when it was ruled by the House of Austria.[62]

It was to be the events of 1808 and the constitutional crisis they provoked that fatally disrupted the delicate balance between king and *patria*. In the absence of a king, power reverted to the people, and the juntas formed in the

---

[60] See Horst Pietschmann, 'Actores locales y el poder central. La herencia colonial y el caso de México', *Relaciones*, 73 (1998), pp. 51–83.

[61] Anthony McFarlane, 'Identity, Enlightenment and Political Dissent in Late Colonial Spanish America', *Transactions of the Royal Historical Society*, 6th series, viii (1998), pp. 309–35. See esp. p. 320.

[62] John Leddy Phelan, *The People and the King: The Comunero Revolution in Colombia, 1781* (Madison, Wis., 1978), pp. 239–40.

New World saw themselves as at one with the Spanish *nación* in its struggle against the French.[63] The American deputies to the Cortes of Cádiz in 1810–14 arrived in the peninsula with no aspirations to independence, but instead with hopes for the restoration of a composite monarchy in which the kingdoms of the Indies would be full and equal partners. Their hopes were to be bitterly disappointed. The liberals turned out to be the heirs, not of the 'horizontal Spain' of the House of Austria but of the 'vertical Spain' of the eighteenth-century bureaucrats; and the creoles discovered to their disillusionment that they were fated to be the colonial subjects of a Spanish nation state.[64]

In the circumstances, it is not surprising that the elites in the Indies should have turned towards republicanism. This republicanism juxtaposed in uneasy combination the creole patriotism that had evolved over the course of the preceding three centuries with the virtuous and classicising republicanism of late eighteenth-century France and the British colonies in America, rejecting historic rights in the name of liberty and the natural rights of man.[65] Between 1810 and 1830 republicanism was to triumph over monarchy, and creole *patrias* were to embark on the slow and halting process of transformation into nation states. The Spanish Monarchy as a universal monarchy had finally expired, a victim of the combined onslaughts of rationality, liberalism and the new-style nationalism. As for the composite monarchy, it too was gone. The best part of two centuries would elapse before the 1978 Constitution of the new democratic Spain brought about its restoration.

---

[63] McFarlane, 'Identity, Enlightenment and Political Dissent', p. 329. See below, pp. 220–1.
[64] Timothy Anna, *Spain and the Loss of America* (Lincoln, Nebr., 1983), p. 64.
[65] David A. Brading, 'El patriotismo criollo y la nación mexicana', in David A. Brading et al., *Cinco miradas británicas a la historia de México* (Mexico City, 2000), p. 99; Anthony Pagden, *Spanish Imperialism and the Political Imagination* (New Haven, Conn. and London, 1990), ch. 6 ('The End of Empire: Simón Bolívar and the Liberal Republic').

CHAPTER X

THE SAME WORLD, DIFFERENT WORLDS

A perennial tension has characterised the relationship between Europe and America: the tension between the assumption of similarity and the recognition of difference. On the one hand, Europeans over the course of the centuries have conceptualised the world they christened the 'New World' as an extension of their own. Consequently, the processes by which they imagined, colonised and organised this American world were elaborated on the assumption that it should, and could, be made to conform to European expectations and models. If, in the beginning, as John Locke argued, 'all the world was *America*', there was no reason why, through the superior skills, resources and hard work of Europeans, America itself should not be made over in the image of Europe. On the other hand, from the very earliest days there was an uneasy awareness that America was not quite another Europe, or even a potential Europe, that it was somehow, and for some reason, different—in other words, that *America* was, and was likely to remain, America.

How did Spaniards, as pioneers in the conquest and colonisation of America, react to the dawning and often uncomfortable awareness that America was different? How did they explain that difference, and what did they seek to do about it? And what were the implications of their response for the development of American colonial society and of Spain's relations with the Indies? These are large questions, which have often been addressed, in one form or another, from a variety of angles. But there may be a case at this stage of our knowledge for an attempt to pursue this theme of assumed similarity and perceived (or not perceived) difference over the three centuries of Spanish domination. Although manifesting itself in different ways, it is a theme that constantly recurs over the entire colonial epoch, beginning with the reconnaissance and subjugation of the new lands and their peoples, and then re-emerging as colonial society becomes established, to end in mutual recrimination and misunderstanding which would have revolutionary consequences for both Spain and America.

In *The Old World and the New* I sought to trace the process by which Europeans attempted to comprehend and assimilate into their consciousness the landscapes and peoples of what to them was an unknown region of the globe.[1] My argument was that Europeans, like all those faced with the unfamiliar, necessarily approached it through the organising principles that shaped their own mental worlds. This meant passing strange places and strange peoples through a kind of conceptual grid, so that they could be slotted into pre-existing categories without disturbing the shape and structure of the grid itself. The structure of the conceptual grid of late fifteenth-and sixteenth-century Europeans had been determined by the juxtaposition and interaction of the Judeo-Christian tradition, and the tradition inherited from classical antiquity. On first setting eyes on the New World of America, Columbus and his immediate successors viewed it on the basis of expectations derived from biblical and classical images, amplified by a store of geographical and ethnic information and misinformation derived from travellers' tales and first-hand acquaintance—sometimes close, sometimes distant—with those non-European and non-Christian peoples who had so far come within the European orbit.

The inevitable result of this process of bringing the unfamiliar within the range of the familiar was to blur differences and to find similarity where little or none existed. A classic example of this process is to be found at the end of the second letter of Hernán Cortés from Mexico, where he writes: 'From all I have seen and understood touching the similarity between this land and that of Spain, in its fertility and great size and the cold and other things, it seemed to me that the most suitable name for it was New Spain of the Ocean Sea. . . .'[2] Notoriously, too, and again drawing on the experience of his native land, he described the temple complexes of Mexico as mosques, just as the Hieronymites who governed Hispaniola had described the Indians in 1517 as 'these Moors'.[3]

Yet the Indians were not 'Moors'. Nor, as Columbus had pointed out on his first voyage in 1492, were they 'negroes as in Guinea'. Similarly, he had found

---

[1] J. H. Elliott, *The Old World and the New* (Cambridge, 1970; repr. 1992).
[2] Hernán Cortés, *Letters from Mexico*, trans. and ed. Anthony Pagden (1971; repr. New Haven, Conn. and London, 1986), p. 158.
[3] Erwin Walter Palm, *Los monumentos arquitectónicos de la Española* (Ciudad Trujillo, 1955), vol. 1, p. 18 ('*estos moros*').

no 'human monstrosities',[4] and, in failing to find them, he had opened the way to their acceptance by Europeans as part of the human race. While this acceptance was not automatic, and only received the seal of authority in Pope Paul III's declaration in *Sublimis Deus* of 1537 that 'the Indians are true men', the case for the rationality of the Indians was greatly strengthened by the discovery of the civilisations of Mexico and Peru. But Gonzalo Fernández de Oviedo, whose experience was confined to the Caribbean world, had no hesitation in classifying even the Indians of Hispaniola, whom he observed closely, as rational human beings, and again he described them by reference to European norms: 'the people of this island are smaller in stature than those of Spain commonly are, and are dun-coloured [*de color loros claros*] . . . they have broad foreheads, and black and very smooth hair, and have no beards nor hair on any part of the body, neither men nor women.'[5] As far as their mental capacities were concerned, there existed, as Oviedo saw it, degrees of rationality, but these peoples of the Indies were indubitably members of the human race.

For Oviedo, the American environment was new and strange, but its inhabitants, being undeniably human, were therefore comparable to the other peoples of the world. This same insistence on the novelty of the natural environment of the Indies and, by contrast, the fundamental humanity of its indigenous inhabitants, was echoed by Francisco López de Gómara, who, unlike Oviedo, had no first-hand experience of the New World although he learnt much about it through his close relationship with Hernán Cortés. In the dedication to the Emperor Charles V of the first part of his *Historia general de las Indias* of 1552, Gómara asserts that the New World can justifiably be described as new, 'because all things are very different (*diferentísimas*) from those of our world. The animals in general, although there are few species of them, are different; so too are the fishes in the water, the birds of the air, the trees, fruits, grasses and grain, which is no small consideration on the part of the Creator, since the elements are one and the same there and here.' 'But', he continues, 'the people are like us, except for their colour; otherwise they would be beasts and monsters, and would not descend, as they do, from Adam.'[6]

The fundamental Christian principle of the singularity of creation and the common humanity of the human race was thus preserved. But it would have been more difficult to preserve if European civilisation had not already

---

[4] *The Journal of Christopher Columbus*, trans. Cecil Jane (London, 1960), p. 200.
[5] Gonzalo Fernández de Oviedo, *Sumario de la natural historia de las Indias*, ed. José Miranda (Mexico City, 1950), p. 91.
[6] Francisco López de Gómara, *Primera y segunda parte de la historia general de las Indias* (*Biblioteca de Autores Españoles*, 22, Madrid, 1858), p. 156.

absorbed the concept of an essential *diversity* within an overall framework of unity. Faced with the novelty of strange American flora and fauna, Gómara could fall back on marvelling at the infinite variety and fertility of God's creation. Oviedo responded in a similar way. 'The greater the variety and differences', he wrote, 'the more beautiful is nature.'[7] The immediately obvious physical and cultural differences between the peoples of America and those of the rest of the known world generated a comparable response. The origins of human diversity could be traced back to Noah's ark and the tower of Babel. Moreover, linguistic, political and cultural diversity were facts of medieval European life. All this made it easier for European observers of America to accept the existence of significant differences between the appearance and customs of the peoples of the world, and helped to cushion the impact of the novelty of this strange New World.

Both American nature, therefore, and America's human inhabitants were perhaps too easily inserted into a pre-existing European mental grid to provoke a serious intellectual effort among commentators at the early stages of discovery and settlement to get to grips with the novelty and distinctiveness of America. Even the genuinely novel could be deprived of much of the sting of its novelty by the discovery of some point of reference within Europe's Christian and classical inheritance,[8] just as diversity itself could be presented as an integral feature of God's grand design. A good example of the inability to rise to the challenge presented by American distinctiveness is to be found in the treatise written around 1570 by Tomás López Medel, *De los tres elementos. Tratado sobre la naturaleza y el hombre del nuevo mundo.*[9]

Something of a humanist, López Medel was educated at the University of Seville before moving on to Alcalá de Henares to study canon law. He was in the Indies from 1550 to 1562, serving as a judge first in the Audiencia de los Confines in Guatemala City and then in the Audiencia of New Granada in Santa Fe de Bogotá. His treatise on the *Tres elementos*, which did not appear in print until as late as 1990, is a description of the New World of America, which he rather disarmingly approaches, as might be expected from his title, by way of air, water and earth (the latter including its inhabitants). While clearly fascinated by the *difference* of America, on which he frequently comments, he is incapable of finding explanations for it. Commenting on the absence of wheat

---

[7] Quoted in Antonello Gerbi, *La natura delle Indie Nove* (Milan and Naples, 1975), p. 270.
[8] See Michael T. Ryan, 'Assimilating New Worlds in the Sixteenth and Seventeenth Centuries', *Comparative Studies in Society and History*, 23 (1981), pp. 519–38, at p. 524.
[9] Tomás López Medel, *De los tres elementos. Tratado sobre la naturaleza y el hombre del nuevo mundo*, ed. Berta Ares Queíja (Madrid, 1990).

in the Indies before the arrival of the Spaniards, he writes: 'in everything Nature discriminated so sharply between this world and that one, that it is impossible to contemplate this without amazement.' Similarly, when discussing the absence of so many animals—horses, elephants, camels—in the Indies, he can find no explanation for this, other perhaps than that nature was deliberately holding back, so that they could all be simultaneously introduced following the arrival of the Europeans.[10]

As far as the American environment is concerned, it is only with José de Acosta, at the very end of the sixteenth century, that we find a serious and systematic attempt to grapple with the strangeness of American nature. Fernández de Oviedo, although well aware of the 'newness' of the New World,[11] had been essentially an observer and chronicler in the manner of the elder Pliny, often baffled by his inability to understand, but equating wherever possible the unknown with the known. Acosta, by contrast, struggled both to understand and explain. At times he was painfully conscious of the difference between America and Europe: 'Almost all the land I have seen in the Indies is close to high sierras on one side or the other, and sometimes on all sides. So true is this that many times I used to say during my time there that I wished I were in a place where the horizon ended with the sky and the land was spread out, as one sees in a thousand Spanish fields; but I never remember seeing such a view either in the islands or on the mainland of the Indies. . . .'[12] There is none of the discovery of superficial resemblances between Spain and New Spain that Cortés makes so easily, and where Acosta does find a resemblance he seeks a reason for it: 'The land that most resembles Spain and the other regions of Europe in all the West Indies is the kingdom of Chile, which departs from the norm of those other lands, because it is outside the torrid zone, and is sited in the tropic of Capricorn.'[13]

The description and classification of the natural environment of America was an intellectual challenge for those who, like Acosta, became preoccupied with the disparities between what they saw with their own eyes and what they had been taught by traditional cosmography. But it lacked the urgency and the immediacy of the challenge presented by the nature of the inhabitants of these new lands. These people presented an immediate practical problem. After they

---

[10] *Ibid.*, pp. 155 and 138.

[11] Anthony Pagden, *European Encounters with the New World* (New Haven, Conn. and London, 1993), p. 58.

[12] José de Acosta, *Historia natural y moral de las Indias*, ed. Edmundo O'Gorman, 2nd edn (Mexico City and Buenos Aires, 1962), p. 126 (lib. 3, cap. 19).

[13] *Ibid.*, pp. 130–1 (lib. 3, cap. 22).

had been subjugated, they had to be converted and governed in ways that would make them conform to Christian and European norms and expectations. It soon became apparent, after the first flush of enthusiasm had passed, that this was not as easy as had first been anticipated.

Fray Ramón Pané had already noted in the early days of the settlement of Hispaniola that some of the indigenous inhabitants easily accepted conversion to Christianity, while others did not. With these others, he wrote, 'force and ingenuity are needed, because we are not all of one and the same nature (*naturaleza*)'.[14] This important recognition that 'we are not all of one and the same nature' was to cut both ways. On the one hand it could, and did, inspire serious investigation on the part of the friars into why some peoples of the Americas seemed readier than others to accept the truths of the Christian gospel and conform to Christian standards of behaviour, thus stimulating them to employ 'ingenuity' as well as 'force' in their evangelising efforts. On the other hand it opened up the possibility of drawing a sharp dividing line between Spaniards or people of Spanish ancestry and indigenous peoples who could be indiscriminately lumped together under the brand name of 'Indians', and considered as in some ways defective by 'nature'. Aristotelian doctrines of natural slavery could then be appropriated to justify their treatment as inferior peoples.

The degree of diversity to be found among the peoples of the New World became apparent as soon as Cortés and his followers set foot on the mainland of America. It was obvious to them that the peoples of Yucatán and central Mexico were of a higher order of civility (*policía*) than any others yet encountered by the Spaniards in the course of their discoveries. Faced with an extraordinary range of languages, the first generation of friars was brought face to face with the enormous cultural differences between the peoples committed to their care. Their historical inquiries into the ancient customs and traditions of their flock only served to reinforce the perception of indigenous diversity. This perception in turn would encourage them to grade the peoples of the Americas according to their level of barbarism or civility. Bartolomé de Las Casas, while obsessively arguing for the humanity and rationality of all the peoples of the Americas, was careful to draw distinctions between them as he sought to define the meaning of the term *bárbaro*.[15] In the final years of the century such distinctions encouraged Acosta to propose his evolutionary scale of civilisation.[16]

---

[14] Fray Ramón Pané, *Relación acerca de las antigüedades de los indios*, ed. José Juan Arrom (Mexico City, 1974), p. 55.

[15] Fray Bartolomé de Las Casas, *Apologética historia sumaria*, ed. Edmundo O'Gorman, 2 vols (Mexico City, 1967), ii, pp. 637–48.

[16] Acosta, *Historia natural*, pp. 323–4 (lib. 7, cap. 3).

Yet if the inherent diversity of the peoples of America suggested to more sensitive observers a diversity of approaches towards them in the light of distinctive local situations, the pressures emanating both from Spain itself and from the evolving colonial societies were largely working towards the reduction of this variegated indigenous population to at least a nominal uniformity. The very attempt to Christianise them and induce them to adopt European norms of behaviour necessarily tended to push them in a uniform direction. At the same time, demographic and social change, the fiscal and labour policies of the Crown, and the responses of the indigenous peoples themselves to the dramatic upheavals in their lives, as they moved to the towns and entered into the orbit of the settler community, had the effect of blurring some of the old distinctions and reinforcing a standard image of the 'Indian'. By the early seventeenth century the Dominican Gregorio García could write: 'Anyone who has had dealings with the Indians of Peru and New Spain will find that, reduced to their own nature and customs, all are one and the same Indian. . . .'[17]

During the course of the sixteenth century this image of the standard Indian became increasingly negative in its evaluation both of character and of prospects for improvement. Evangelisation all too often seemed to have gone only skin deep. As the Jesuit Bartolomé Hernández wrote to Juan de Ovando in 1572: 'As regards the Indians Your Excellency can well believe that for the most part they are like the Moors of Granada, and that the majority are only Christian in name and external ceremonies, and inwardly they have no notion of the matters of our faith; and, what is worse, they have no affection for them, but they all do whatever they do simply in order to comply, or out of fear of punishment. . . .'[18] As a result, there was an emerging consensus, among Spanish clerics and officials as well as among the creoles, who had their own good reasons for playing down the capacity of the indigenous population, that, in the words of Alonso de la Vera Cruz, 'even the most outstanding of them, if compared with us Spaniards, are found to be deficient in many respects'.[19] This suggested that the proper response lay in an almost indefinite tutelage for peoples who, at best, were little more than children.

At the very time, therefore, when the progressive intermingling of indigenous and Spanish blood was creating a new race of mestizos, the distinctions

---

[17] Gregorio García, *Origen de los indios de el Nuevo Mundo e Indias Occidentales* (Valencia, 1607), p. 109. (There is a modern edition, ed. C. Baciero et al., Madrid, 2005.)

[18] Antonio de Egaña, 'La visión humanística del indio americano en los primeros Jesuitas peruanos (1568–1576)', *Analecta Gregoriana*, 70 (1954), pp. 291–306, at p. 302.

[19] J. H. Elliott, *Spain and its World, 1500–1700* (New Haven, Conn. and London, 1989), pp. 52–3.

between those of Spanish descent and those categorised as *indios* were becoming more stereotyped and were being more sharply drawn. The attempt to raise the Indians to Spanish levels of civility was, it came to be believed, a doomed enterprise. But why should this be? What prevented the Indians from being transformed into Spaniards?

One possible explanation was the supernatural. The devil stalked America and held the Indians in his thrall, seducing them into idolatry and other vicious practices. But there appeared to be psychological as well as physical differences between the indigenous population and the Spaniards and their American-born descendants. These demanded, and received, a 'natural' explanation. The most immediately obvious difference was, as Gómara had pointed out, that of colour. But although blackness possessed a series of negative connotations in sixteenth-century European thought, and in particular had come to be closely associated with the biblical curse of Ham, the colour of the Indians, described as resembling that of 'stewed quince',[20] did not of itself condemn them to a status of natural inferiority.

Indeed, for López Medel 'those who live away from the tropics differ little from us in colour. And there are many very white peoples and nations, and indeed there would be more if those peoples, all of them, male and female, from their childhood to the day of their deaths, did not labour in the fields. . . .'[21] In so far as their colour was regarded as the result of exposure to the rays of a strong sun beating down upon them, it hardly represented grounds for discrimination. Not everyone, however, was satisfied by the traditional explanation of colour differences. For Gómara, the colour of the Indians came 'from nature, and not from nakedness, as many believed'. Since peoples living in the same latitudes were of different colours, 'there is a view that it goes with the men, and not the land'. 'This could well be', he continued, 'although we are all born of Adam and Eve.' This, however, seemed to him to be not so much a cause for concern as for admiration of God's 'omnipotence and wisdom that there should be such a diversity of colour in mankind.'[22] Once again the acceptance of divinely ordained diversity had come to the rescue.

In the sixteenth century at least it was Christianity and civility, rather than colour, that primarily differentiated Spaniard from Indian in the eyes of the Spaniard. In the attempt to explain why the majority of Indians signally failed

---

[20] López Medel, *De los tres elementos*, p. 204; Juan López de Velasco, *Geografía y descripción universal de las Indias*, ed. Justo Zaragoza (Madrid, 1894), p. 27.

[21] López Medel, *De los tres elementos*, p. 204.

[22] López de Gómara, *Historia general de las Indias* (*Biblioteca de Autores Españoles*, 22), pp. 289–90.

to conform to Spanish standards in either capacity, commentators had increasing recourse, as the century advanced, to a theory that was essentially determinist in character. This was the theory of climate, as adumbrated in particular by Jean Bodin in his *Methodus ad facilem historiarum cognitionem* (1565), and widely diffused from the end of the century by the extremely influential *Relazioni universali* of Giovanni Botero.

Climatic theory as an explanation of the diversity of human nature was nothing new.[23] There was a strong classical and medieval tradition of explaining human diversity on the basis of Hippocratic and Galenic ideas about the inter-action of the constellations, climate and temperament. It was on this tradition that Isabella the Catholic was drawing when, on being informed that the trees on the island of Hispaniola had shallow roots, she made her famous response to Columbus that in lands where trees are not deeply rooted, the inhabitants will be mendacious and shallow.[24] Las Casas, too, had recourse to the environmental theory, although, as might be expected, he read into it quite the reverse of Isabella's interpretation, arguing that the climatic zone in which Hispaniola was located made it an ideal place for the development of the human mind, and hence for the rationality of its indigenous inhabitants.[25]

The inherent determinism of climatic theory as an explanation of human behaviour was to some extent mitigated by the need to introduce cultural vari-ables in order to explain the obvious differences between the customs of different peoples living in similar climatic conditions. It was also occasionally mitigated by the belief that climate itself could be altered by divine intervention. Oviedo, for instance, argued that the weather had improved and hurricanes had ceased since the Holy Sacrament had been placed in the churches and monas-teries of Santo Domingo on the island of Hispanola.[26] But the theory, however crude, was a weapon waiting to be used, and it was to become increasingly influ-ential from the middle decades of the sixteenth century in shaping Spanish assessments not only of the Indians but also of the increasing number of settlers of Spanish descent born in the Indies.

As an example of the potentially devastating consequences of climatic theory for a negative assessment of the Indians and their potential for Christianity and civility, we can take the words written by a Jesuit, Padre Luis López, to St Francis

---

[23] See Marian J. Tooley, 'Bodin and the Medieval Theory of Climate', *Speculum* 28 (1953), pp. 64–83.

[24] Gonzalo Fernández de Oviedo, *Historia general y natural de las Indias* (*Biblioteca de Autores Españoles*, 117–21, Madrid, 1959), p. 91. Cited above, p. 158.

[25] Las Casas, *Apologética historia sumaria*, i, pp. 115ff.; Anthony Pagden, *The Fall of Natural Man* (Cambridge, 1986), pp. 137–9.

[26] Fernández de Oviedo, *Historia general y natural*, i, p. 147.

Borja in 1569. He was pessimistic about the prospects for genuine conversion, partly because of the behaviour of the Spaniards themselves, who regarded the Indians not as men but as beasts, but also because of Indian inconstancy: 'people with an extreme facility for believing, and even greater facility for going back on their beliefs, and totally inconstant, a vice natural to all who are born in this land ... The skies over this land conduce to four main vices in every kind of people born in it, namely sensuality, avarice, pride and instability.'[27]

In the following decades, such doctrine hardened into dogma in relation to the physiology of the Indians. The natural humidity of the Indies, a part of the world that was increasingly perceived to be dominated by negative constella- tions,[28] had emasculated the Indians and made them phlegmatic by tempera- ment. This in turn could be used to justify coercive labour systems. Juan de Solórzano Pereira, for instance, in his influential *Política indiana*, argued that 'the attentive and prudent legislator should vary his decrees in relation to the regions to whose government they are directed'. It was for this reason that the rulers of the Aztecs and the Incas, faced with subjects who were 'very lethargic (*flojos*), drafted them for great public works; and for this reason, too, that Spaniards could reasonably demand labour services of them'.[29]

While this environmental determinism was bad news for the Indians, it was also bad news for the creoles. The word *criollo*, first used of blacks born in the Indies, was beginning to be used in the 1560s not only of blacks, mestizos and mulattos, but also of the American-born children and grandchildren of Spaniards. Spanish officials who came to the Indies in the middle decades of the sixteenth century were starting to draw distinctions between themselves and American-born Spaniards, to the detriment of the latter. For the interim governor of Peru, Lope García de Castro, these creoles of pure Spanish descent were, although Spaniards, Spaniards who had gone downhill (*decaídos*): 'the people of this land are different from what they were before'.[30] What else could be responsible for this decline—a decline both physical and moral—but the American environment, together with the ease and luxury of the lives of the conquistadores' descendants, nurtured and grown to maturity in the New World?

---

[27] Cited in Egaña, 'La visión humanística', pp. 301–2.
[28] For example, José de Acosta, as cited in Jorge Cañizares-Esguerra, 'New World, New Stars: Patriotic Astrology and the Invention of Indian and Creole Bodies in Colonial Spanish America, 1600–1650', *American Historical Review*, 104 (1999), pp. 33–68, at p. 45 (reprinted in his *Nature, Empire and Nation*, Stanford, Calif., 2006, ch. 4).
[29] Juan de Solórzano y Pereyra, *Política indiana* (*Biblioteca de Autores Españoles*, 252–6, Madrid, 1972), i, pp. 174–7. See also Cañizares-Esguerra, 'New World, New Stars', p. 57.
[30] Bernard Lavallé, *Las promesas ambiguas. Criollismo colonial en los Andes* (Lima, 1993), pp. 17–18 (Lope García to the president of the Council of Indies, 4 April 1567).

As early as 1574 Juan López de Velasco, in his *Geografía y descripción universal de las Indias*, had argued that creoles who were born and lived in America had become 'like Indians' because of the influence of the climate.[31] The creoles therefore were now faced with an acute dilemma. On the one hand they were happy to see their own low estimate of Indian capacity confirmed by the increasing acceptance of environmentalist explanations. Yet at the same time they were desperately anxious to avoid being tarred with the same brush as the Indians by peninsular Spaniards who were already seeking to disparage them and deprive them of the offices and honours which they claimed as of right, by virtue of their descent from the conquistadores and first settlers of the Indies. The words of the Spanish Dominican author Juan de la Puente, writing in 1612, are typical of the attitudes of peninsular Spaniards: 'The skies above America conduce to inconstancy, lasciviousness and lying, and the constellations will give these characteristics to Spaniards who are born and bred there.'[32]

It is plausible to assume that the dilemma was made all the more acute for the creoles by the fact that this was the time, at the turn of the sixteenth and seventeenth centuries, when they were beginning to develop their own sense of a distinctive *patria*, like the 'Mexican paradise' of the poet Bernardo de Balbuena. How could they reconcile their own hyperbolic assertions of the glories of their terrestrial paradise with the apparent stigma of the corrupting effects of that paradise on those fortunate enough to inhabit it?

The answer, in so far as it was found, was to lie in a combination of climatic explanation with the Aristotelian concept of nature. In his famous *Examen de ingenios* of 1575, Juan Huarte de San Juan, who had much to say about the relationship between temperament and climate, sought to show, following Aristotle, that 'nature is nothing else than the temperament of the four primary qualities [heat, cold, humidity and dryness], and this is the master who teaches how souls must function'.[33] It is unclear whether the ideas of Huarte de San Juan influenced the Spanish physician Juan de Cárdenas, who published his

---

[31] Joan-Pau Rubiés, 'New Worlds and Renaissance Ethnology', *History and Anthropology*, 6 (1993), pp. 157–97, at p. 189, note 10. Similar sentiments are expressed at around the same time by Fray Bernardino de Sahagún in his *Historia general de las cosas de Nueva España*, ed. Angel María Garibay, 4 vols, 2nd edn (Mexico City, 1969), iii, lib. 10, cap. xxvii, p. 160.

[32] Fray Juan de la Puente, *Tomo primero de la conveniencia de las dos monarquías católicas . . .* (Madrid, 1612), lib. 2, cap, xxxv, p. 363, marginal note. Also cited by D. A. Brading, *The First America: The Spanish Monarchy, Creole Patriots and the Liberal State, 1492–1867* (Cambridge, 1991), p. 298, and Cañizares-Esguerra, 'New World, New Stars', p. 46.

[33] Juan Huarte de San Juan, *Examen de ingenios para las ciencias*, ed. Rodrigo Sanz, 2 vols (Madrid, 1930), i, p. 113.

Problemas y secretos maravillosos de las Indias in Mexico City in 1591;[34] but in that ingenious if often far-fetched work, Cárdenas argued, among other things, that the Indians possessed by nature a phlegmatic constitution. Spaniards, on the other hand, were of a sanguine temperament by nature, and if they established themselves in the Indies, any phlegmatic characteristics developed by them and their descendants as a result of the American environment were no more than accidental. Consequently, for all the impact of environment, their original *naturaleza* remained predominant.

Back in Spain, the Dominican Gregorio García, who had spent nine years in Peru, also sought to grapple with the effects of climate on psychological and physical characteristics in Book II of his *Origen de los indios del nuevo mundo*, published in Valencia in 1607. In this book he examined the theory that the Indians were originally Carthaginians who had crossed the Atlantic on one of their trading expeditions. But one of the objections to this theory, of which he made very heavy weather, was why the modern-day Indians had no beards and were generally hairless. One possibility, on which he dwelt at length, was that little by little the descendants of these first Carthaginian settlers ceased to be hirsute 'through the virtue, influence and constellation of that air and sky, and the temperament of that land . . '. Most of the Indies lay beneath the torrid zone, and were consequently warm: 'The heat that reigns there, and the air of that region, unchanged by the sun that surrounds and envelops the bodies of the Indians, so consumes the humour, or excremental vapour . . . of which the hairs of the beard are formed, that it scarcely leaves matter from which they may be formed; and so few or no hairs sprout . . '.

There was, however, as he pointed out, a possible objection to this theory: 'If the explanation we have advanced for the Indians not having beards were true and certain, it would also apply to the children of Spaniards born in that region, and called *criollos*; they share the same sky, air and constellations, and have the same temperament as the Indians.' One possibility, according to a doctor he had consulted, was that, with time, the creoles would indeed cease to be hirsute. On the other hand, he suggested, since Spain was more temperate, and farther from the torrid zone than Carthage, the Spaniards were more hirsute than the Carthaginians, and therefore ran less danger of losing their beards. In addition, 'the temperance and virtue that Spaniards born in the Indies inherited from their fathers and grandfathers, they continue to

---

[34] A copy of the *Examen de ingenios* is recorded as having arrived in the Indies with the 1583 fleet. See Carlos Alberto González Sánchez, *Los mundos del libro. Medios de difusión de la cultura occidental en las Indias de los siglos XVI y XVII* (Seville, 1999), p. 216.

maintain, thanks to good food and delicacies, like lamb, chicken, turkey, beef, bread and wine, and other substantial delicacies, which the Indians from their earliest years are not accustomed to eating . . .'.[35] Gastronomy, in other words, counteracted climate.

Out of the work of Cárdenas, García and the polemic that they generated, seventeenth-century creole writers like Buenaventura Salinas y Córdoba, Antonio León Pinelo and Antonio de Calancha elaborated a set of theories designed to defend the creoles from environmentalist slurs that would distinguish them from peninsular Spaniards, and reject those aspects of the environmentalist argument that would equate them with the Indians. Since the development of these theories has been traced by Jorge Cañizares-Esguerra, the story need not be rehearsed here.[36] Essentially, as he tells it, the creole writers of the seventeenth century invented a discourse of scientific racism which predated the racist discourse constructed by late eighteenth- and nineteenth-century Europeans, but which would have no European future because it rested on Aristotelian, Galenic and Hippocratic foundations that were already being discredited in seventeenth-century Europe. 'Nature' had made the bodies and physiognomy of the Indians irrevocably different from those that belonged to people of pure Spanish descent, while any physical or temperamental difference between American-born and peninsular-born Spaniards was purely accidental, and might indeed even constitute an improvement on the Spanish original.

Yet even in their own terms, these creole writers had some difficulty in tying up the loose ends. There was, for instance, the problem of the suckling of creole children by their Indian nurses. Did not their milk transmit to their charges those 'defects and perverse customs' that were innate among the Indians?[37] But if the creoles had succeeded by the eighteenth century in establishing to their own satisfaction the innate disparity between themselves and the Indians, they quite failed in their other enterprise—that of persuading peninsular Spaniards that they were no less authentically Spanish than those born and bred in metropolitan Spain.

Significantly, the English colonists of North America were simultaneously battling against the same negative image, and were consumed by the same anxieties. Like the Spaniards, they arrived in America with the usual assumptions about the impact of climate on temperament and the constancy of the climate

---

[35] García, *Origen de los indios del Nuevo Mundo*, lib. 2, cap. 5, pp. 149–54.
[36] Cañizares-Esguerra, 'New World, New Stars'.
[37] See Lavallé, *Promesas ambiguas*, p. 48.

in any given latitude.[38] The discovery that the North American winter was much colder than the European winter raised some difficult questions, but does not seem to have shaken the standard notions. Cotton Mather in a sermon preached in Boston in 1689 spoke ominously of 'the too general want of education in the rising generation, which if not prevented will gradually but speedily dispose us to that sort of Criolian degeneracy observed to deprave the children of the most noble and worthy Europeans when transplanted into America'.[39] The American environment, and proximity to the Indians, were almost universally seen as a threat to European standards and values.

To metropolitan Spaniards, and to peninsular Spaniards (called by the Americans *gachupines)* who crossed the Atlantic to occupy positions that the creoles saw as rightfully theirs, the Indies *were* different, and increasingly so. The sheer fact of the distance between Spain and the Indies—the length and hazards of the journey between one and the other—no doubt played its part in enhancing the sense of difference between the two worlds, although Oviedo has fun mocking those 'ignorant people' who had never been there, and who 'believe that the Indies are like a kingdom of Portugal or Navarre . . .'.[40] But, on first arriving in the Indies, Spaniards who knew them only by hearsay were likely to be in for a surprise, and increasingly so as the new colonial society began to emerge out of the ruins of the pre-conquest world. Juan de Palafox, bishop of Puebla and interim viceroy of New Spain, wrote some revealing words in a letter to Philip IV in 1642: 'I thought that I knew a bit about the Indies, having served Your Majesty in that Council [of the Indies] for thirteen years, but I assure Your Majesty that seeing things is very different (*diferentísimo*) from reading them. . . .'[41]

---

[38] Karen Ordahl Kupperman, 'The Puzzle of the American Climate in the Early Colonial Period', *American Historical Review* (1982), pp. 1,262–89.

[39] Cotton Mather, Election Sermon (1689), in *The Wall and the Garden: Selected Massachusetts Election Sermons 1670–1775*, ed. A. W. Plumstead (Minneapolis, Minn., 1968), p. 137. Some form or other of the word *criollo* had entered the English language by the early seventeenth century, but it seems to have been only in the 1680s that English officials, or newly arrived immigrants, began to apply the term *creole* to their compatriots born in the Caribbean or on the American mainland, or long settled there. As in the early years of Spanish America, it could also be applied to American-born blacks. See Carole Shammas, 'English-Born and Creole Elites in Turn-of-the-Century Virginia', in Thad W. Tate and David L. Ammerman, eds, *The Chesapeake in the Seventeenth Century* (New York and London, 1979), pp. 274–96.

[40] Fernández de Oviedo, *Historia general y natural* (*Biblioteca de Autores Españoles*, 120, Madrid, 1959), p. 300.

[41] Cited in Cayetana Álvarez de Toledo, *Politics and Reform in Spain and Viceregal Mexico: The Life and Thought of Juan de Palafox, 1600–1659* (Oxford, 2004), p. 154.

It was not only the landscapes and the stars, nor even the Indians themselves, that differentiated the New World from the Old, but also the intermingling of races and the character and comportment of those who, in the emerging society of *castas,* were firmly established at the top of the social hierarchy. Some of these people, who claimed to pass as Spaniards, were manifestly not so, thanks to the infusion of Indian blood. In Paraguay, for instance, as we learn from a decree of Philip IV, 'it is the custom from time immemorial in these provinces that the sons of Spaniards, although born of Indian women, should be treated as Spaniards'.[42] But it was not only a question of *mestizaje,* accepted or disguised. These Spanish inhabitants of America, even those of untainted ancestry, had adopted Indian customs as their own, consuming Indian foods, drinking Indian drinks and even, as in Mexico, imitating the Indian habit of taking steam baths, in sharp contrast to the mass rejection in metropolitan Spain, other than in parts of Andalusia, of the bathing habits of the Moors.[43] Here, surely, was vivid proof of the degeneration that overtook Spaniards when they settled in the Indies.

The reactions of *peninsulares* when they saw the Indies for themselves are perfectly comprehensible, even if they often tended to exaggerate the differences between themselves and the creoles for purposes of their own. Colonial society, along with the creoles who dominated it, was diverging in many respects from metropolitan society during the course of the seventeenth century, and the signs of this were everywhere. Even the language spoken by the creoles came to seem excessively ornate and convoluted when compared with metropolitan norms.[44]

The reaction of the creoles to persistent disparagement of their character and lifestyle by Spaniards and *gachupines* was to insist with increasing stridency not only on their rights as descendants of those who had conquered the land, but also on their essential and inalienable *hispanidad.* Rejecting the name of *criollos,* they demanded that they should be known only as *españoles.*[45] 'We are Spaniards', wrote Baltasar Dorantes de Carranza, in his *Sumaria relación de las cosas de la Nueva España* of 1604, a poignant expression of the creole sense of betrayal. 'We are Spaniards, the harvest of Spain and its government, and

---

[42] Lavallé, *Promesas ambiguas,* p. 47.

[43] Solange Alberro, *Les Espagnols dans le Mexique colonial. Histoire d'une acculturation* (Paris, 1992), pp. 39–51.

[44] *Ibid.,* p. 119; Nicholas Canny and Anthony Pagden, eds, *Colonial Identity in the Atlantic World, 1500–1800* (Princeton, N.J., 1987), pp. 88–9.

[45] Lavallé, *Promesas ambiguas,* p. 21. Similarly, it appears that Virginians did not refer to themselves as 'Creoles', apart from an ironical use by William Byrd III, but as 'native' or 'Virginian' (Carole Shammas, 'English-Born and Creole Elites', pp. 284–5, note 21).

under so great a king and sovereign lord that we should be ruled by his laws, in accordance with the *fuero* of Castile, for the laws must be the same. . . .'[46]

The creoles, therefore, were emphasising similarity where metropolitan Spaniards were increasingly emphasising difference. It would not be unreasonable to suspect that the stridency of the creole response was enhanced by the insecurity that derived from at least a subconscious awareness that they were in reality no longer quite the same as their Spanish relatives. One of the early immigrants to the Indies, writing in 1584, put this awareness into words when he wrote to his cousin in Spain that on returning home he would no longer be 'what I was before, because I shall return so different that those who knew me will say that I am not I . . .'.[47] It was a graphic testimonial to the transforming power of the Indies that seventeenth- and eighteenth-century creoles would be at such pains to deny.

Yet hand in hand with the fierce insistence by creoles on their Spanishness went a growing exaltation of the *patria*: an idealised Mexican or Peruvian *patria*, endowed with its own distinctive history and heavily charged with messianic and providentialist overtones.[48] The creoles were mentally taking possession of American space, and appropriating its past, present and future for themselves. In doing so, they were forced, as the eighteenth century progressed, to defend themselves with increasing vigour against a twin assault: on the one hand the intellectual assault of European theorisers on the world in which they lived, and on the other the political assault of the Spanish Bourbons on the position they had secured for themselves in the stratified corporate world of the Spanish Monarchy.

As Antonello Gerbi showed half a century ago, the old theme of the difference of America was given a new lease of life by the Comte de Buffon, in his *Histoire naturelle, générale et particulière* of 1749–78, which endowed the thesis of the inferiority of the American environment with a specious scientific credibility. Montesquieu had already given a new respectability to the theory of climatic determinism, and one element in Buffon's argument for American exceptionalism was the humidity of the environment.[49] The diffusion of Buffon's ideas through the Europe of the Enlightenment had explosive

---

[46] Baltasar Dorantes de Carranza, *Sumaria relación de las cosas de la Nueva España* (Mexico City, 1987), p. 203.

[47] Enrique Otte, ed., *Cartas privadas de emigrantes a Indias* (Seville, 1988), p. 508 (letter 571).

[48] Lavallé, *Promesas ambiguas*, p. 122; Brading, *The First America*, esp. chs 14 and 17; and see above, pp. 186–8.

[49] Antonello Gerbi, *The Dispute of the New World: The History of a Polemic, 1750–1900*, trans. Jeremy Moyle (Pittsburgh, Penn., 1973), pp. 29–30.

consequences. Buffon's assault on America and the miserable species it produced forced creole and expatriate Jesuit writers—just as it forced Thomas Jefferson[50]—to exalt American virtues still further, at a time when the weight of Enlightened opinion was so determined to disparage them.[51] 'If we are to believe Buffon', wrote the Jesuit exile Francisco Javier Clavijero in his robust defence of America, *Historia antigua de México* (1779), 'America is a totally new world, which has scarcely surfaced from beneath the waters that had inundated it . . . an unfortunate land, beneath a "miserly sky", in which all the animals of the old continent have degenerated, and those suited to its climate are small, deformed, weak, and without weapons for self-defence.' Confronted with Buffon's generalisations he had no difficulty in demonstrating that the Americas possessed many different climates, just as they also contained many different peoples, all with their own distinctive characteristics.[52]

Simultaneously, creole societies found themselves under mounting attack from a Spanish Crown which felt the Indies slipping from its grasp. Not only had the creoles taken advantage of the weaknesses of metropolitan Spain to infiltrate into increasing numbers of high-level administrative posts in the Indies but also, in the eyes of Madrid, they were emotionally distancing themselves from the mother country as they exalted the distinctive and superior qualities of their own little *patrias*.

The new concept of the state implicit in the Bourbon attempt to recover control over the empire of the Indies was seen by the creole communities as a betrayal of the fundamental contractual principles on which the viceregal societies had been established, and by which they had been governed during the two centuries of rule by the House of Austria. In the struggle against Madrid they therefore saw themselves as the authentic guardians of the Hispanic community, upholding traditional constitutional ideals and practices, and traditional Spanish values, against those Spaniards who so wantonly wished to overthrow them. They were, in other words, even more Spanish than the Spaniards themselves. The British North American colonists, faced in the aftermath of the Seven Years War with comparable pressures from the metropolis, would react in a similar way, portraying themselves as the true upholders of traditional English liberties.[53]

---

[50] Thomas Jefferson, *Notes on the State of Virginia*, ed. William Peden (Chapel Hill, N.C. and London, 1982), esp. pp. 59–65.

[51] See Gerbi, *The Dispute*, and Brading, *The First America*, chs 19 and 20.

[52] Francisco Javier Clavijero, *Historia antigua de México* (1779), ed. P. Mariano Cuevas, 4 vols, 2nd edn (Mexico City, 1958–9), iv, pp. 79, 93–4, 189.

[53] See J. H. Elliott, *Empires of the Atlantic World: Britain and Spain in America, 1492–1830* (New Haven, Conn. and London, 2006), chs 10 and 11.

But the discourse of sameness was persistently undercut by the simultaneous discourse of difference, as the sense of distinctive identity, or identities,
grew stronger under the impact of the Bourbon reforms. Were Spain and the
Indies one and the same, or were they more different than similar? This was
the question that had exercised minds on both sides of the Atlantic ever since
the first Spaniards established themselves in the Indies. It provoked differing
and contradictory answers at different moments. But it was a question that
refused to go away.

In 1770 Francisco Antonio Lorenzana, archbishop of Mexico, gave the
following answer from the standpoint of a Spaniard: 'God has placed two
worlds in the hands of our Catholic Monarch, and the New World resembles
the Old neither in climate, nor in its customs, nor in its natives: it has another
body of laws, another council to govern it, but always with the object of
making the two worlds resemble each other more closely. In old Spain there is
only one race *(casta)* of men, in New Spain they are many and different.'[54]

As far as the creoles themselves were concerned, the definitive answer to the
longstanding problem of the difference or sameness of America would be
supplied in 1815 by Simón Bolívar. In his 'Letter from Jamaica' he made it
clear that the inhabitants of the New World were not *Spaniards,* as they had
for so long and so vainly been insisting. Nor even, as some of them had tended
in more recent times to call themselves, were they *American Spaniards.* Rather,
they were *Americans,* neither more nor less.[55]

---

[54] From the Introduction (no page numbers) to Francisco Antonio Lorenzano, *Historia de
la Nueva España escrita por su esclarecido conquistador Hernán Cortés* (Mexico City, 1770),
cited by Ilona Katzew, *New World Orders: Casta Painting and Colonial Latin America*
(Americas Society Art Gallery, New York, 1996), p. 108.

[55] Simón Bolívar, 'La carta de Jamaica', in *Escritos del Libertador* (Sociedad Bolivariana de
Venezuela, Caracas, 1972), viii, pp. 222–48. Alexander von Humboldt in his *Ensayo político
sobre el reino de la Nueva España,* (1811), ed. Vito Alessandro Robles, 4 vols (Mexico City,
1941), had already observed that 'the creoles prefer to be called *Americans;* and since the peace
of Versailles, and especially since 1789, they can often be heard to say proudly: "I am not
Spanish; I am American", words which reveal the symptoms of an old resentment' (ii, p. 118).

CHAPTER XI

STARTING AFRESH? THE ECLIPSE OF EMPIRE IN BRITISH AND SPANISH AMERICA*

During the closing decades of the eighteenth century and the opening decades of the nineteenth, old empires went into eclipse, new empires arose, and the sovereign nation state emerged into the full light of day. With the exception of Canada and the West Indies, Great Britain lost its American empire between 1776 and 1783. Spain, in turn, lost *its* American empire, with the exception of Cuba, Puerto Rico and the Pacific outpost of the Philippines, between 1810 and 1825. The fifty years between the revolt of the British colonies and the culmination of the Spanish-American independence movements saw momentous changes not only in the New World, where Portugal, too, lost its empire following Brazil's declaration of independence in 1822, but also in the Old World. The French Revolution and Napoleon's ambitious attempts to create a new European empire at the very moment of imperial eclipse in the Americas unleashed powerful forces—political, social, economic and ideological—that would convulse the western world for two generations.

The interaction of events in Europe and the Americas, and the continuous exchange of information and ideas between the two sides of the Atlantic, have long exercised historians,[1] and the rise of the new 'Atlantic History' has given

---

* This essay was originally prepared as a paper for a conference on 'Imperial Models in the Early Modern World' held at the Clark Library in Los Angeles in April 2007. I am grateful to the directors of the conference, Anthony Pagden and Sanjay Subrahmanyam, for allowing me to publish the essay in this volume, and to Eric Foner for his comments on a subsequent draft.
[1] See especially, for the period before 1800, R. R. Palmer, *The Age of the Democratic Revolution*, 2 vols (Princeton, N.J., 1959–64).

these topics fresh impetus.[2] But, while not ignoring the Atlantic context of events in the Americas, the purpose of this essay is to look more specifically at the eclipse of the British and Spanish empires in America and its aftermath. There were important differences, as well as similarities, in the respective processes of imperial eclipse, as there were also in the character of the empires themselves.[3] Those differences did much to dictate the distinct responses of the two imperial powers to the loss of their American possessions, just as they also helped shape the character of the new states constructed in the Americas on the ruined fragments of empire.

In both British and Spanish America the crisis of empire was precipitated by the reform programmes launched by the imperial governments in London and Madrid following the end of the Seven Years War in 1763. The heavy costs of war and imperial defence compelled both governments to reassess the relationship between the mother country and its overseas possessions. The fiscal measures that arose out of this process of reassessment led in both instances to revolt. Four years after the North American colonies proclaimed their independence from Great Britain, revolt against the reforms introduced by the government of Charles III of Spain swept through the Andes and New Granada, modern-day Colombia. In the words of Alexander von Humboldt, 'The great revolt of 1781 was on the point of snatching from the King of Spain all the mountainous region of Peru at the same time as Great Britain was losing almost all its colonies in the continent of America.'[4] In the event, whereas the British colonies broke free from the mother country, revolt was contained in Spanish America, where another generation passed before independence came.

Although in both instances the events of the 1770s and early 1780s can legitimately be described as the crisis of empire, they could equally well be described as the crisis of composite monarchy. The worldwide empire constructed by the Spanish Habsburgs in the sixteenth century was, in constitutional terms, a composite monarchy, consisting of an agglomeration of different kingdoms and territories, some of which were acquired by inheritance and others by conquest. For the best part of two centuries, Spain's worldwide monarchy was a relatively loose structure, but the situation changed with the

---

[2] For a review of the historiography of Atlantic history, see Bernard Bailyn, *Atlantic History: Concepts and Contours* (Cambridge, Mass. and London, 2005).

[3] For an extended comparison of the two empires and their downfall, see my *Empires of the Atlantic World: Britain and Spain in America, 1492–1830* (New Haven, Conn. and London, 2006).

[4] Cited in *ibid.*, p. 355.

advent of the Bourbon dynasty in 1700. A much more centralised and authoritarian system of government was introduced, and this had implications not only for Spain itself but also for Spain's possessions in the Americas, where creole elites had taken advantage of the Crown's growing fiscal difficulties in the seventeenth century to secure local power and influence. As the Crown sought to recover its authority during the course of the eighteenth century, communities that had come to think proudly of themselves as forming distinctive kingdoms in a composite monarchy (the kingdoms, for instance, of New Spain, Peru and Quito), and enjoying, as such, equal status with the kingdoms of peninsular Spain, now found themselves relegated to the status of mere 'colonies'. The revolts of the early 1780s were, at least in part, a response to this perceived change of status; and although the revolts were eventually suppressed, the creole elites clung fast to the image of a composite monarchy in which they participated on an equal footing and possessed their own distinctive rights.

Since the sixteenth century Britain, too, had been a composite monarchy, although one that evolved in different ways from the Spanish Monarchy. Whereas Spain from the early eighteenth century had moved in an authoritarian direction, the Glorious Revolution of 1688 had established the sovereignty of king in parliament, while the incorporating union of 1707 gave the Scots parliamentary representation at Westminster in compensation for the loss of their own parliament in Edinburgh. The result was a new phenomenon in the history of composite monarchies—a composite parliamentary monarchy, in which sovereignty resided with the king in parliament. But Ireland and the American colonies remained outside this incorporating parliamentary union, and retained elected assemblies of their own.[5] The resulting asymmetry was a potential cause of constitutional conflict, and the potential was realised in the 1760s when a Westminster parliament in which the American territories were not represented began to legislate new tax measures without their consent. Where sovereignty was seen as indivisible, as it was in the mind-set of the British political establishment, there was little or no room for compromise, as becomes clear when even such a friend of the colonies as William Pitt could observe in 1766 that 'when two countries are connected together, like England and her colonies, without being incorporated, the one must necessarily govern; the greater must rule the less . . .'.[6] At the height of the Stamp Act crisis of 1765 Benjamin Franklin toyed with the idea of an incorporating union between the colonies and England on the

---

[5] See *ibid.*, pp. 317–18.
[6] Cited in *ibid.*, p. 318.

Scottish model, only to decide that it was already too late. By now the die was cast, and the British Atlantic community was moving inexorably towards a civil war that would result in victory for one side or the other.

The colonists initially saw that war as a struggle for the retention of their English liberties, which they looked upon as threatened by a tyrannical parliament that had become irredeemably corrupt. As participants in a British composite monarchy that spanned the Atlantic, they claimed equality of status and treatment with their English cousins, just as the creole elites of New Spain or Peru claimed equality of status and treatment with their Spanish cousins. Few North American colonists were thinking of independence before the outbreak of hostilities in 1775, and the majority would no doubt have been happy to go back to the world as it had been in 1763, a time when the colonists rejoiced in belonging to a British empire of the free. But by the early 1770s the concept of the British empire had begun to sour on them. Their last hope lay with the king. In 1775 John Adams, while dismissing the concept of the British empire, could still speak, like his Mexican or Peruvian counterparts, of the American colonies as separate 'realms' of the king's dominions.[7] But when it became apparent that George III was personally determined to see the rebellion of the colonists crushed by force of arms, there could no longer be any going back. For many of them, although by no means all, the last bonds of loyalty were snapped. In 1776, by declaring simultaneously its independence and its statehood, the new American republic took a leap into the dark with incalculable consequences, for the rest of the hemisphere and for the wider world.[8]

It was natural that the British government should initially resort to force in the hope of restoring the colonies to allegiance to the Crown, although always hoping that the colonists would revert to allegiance of their own free will. What is striking, however, is the relative speed with which the imperial government decided to abandon the struggle and leave the mainland colonies to their fate. The doggedness of American resistance, coupled with the intervention of France and Spain, naturally played a major part in the decision to cut and run. But there were other considerations at work, too. In some quarters there had long been doubts about the value to Britain of its American empire, and a certain psychological distancing of the mother country from the mainland colonies may well have occurred even before the outbreak of

---

[7] P. J. Marshall, *The Making and Unmaking of Empires: Britain, India and America, c. 1750–1783* (Oxford, 2005), p. 176.

[8] For the significance of the association made in 1776 between independence and statehood, see David Armitage, *The Declaration of Independence* (Cambridge, Mass., 2007).

revolt.[9] Britain, too, was divided in its views about the proper response to the rebellion, and it never displayed a wholehearted commitment to the war. For its part, the government, as soon as it found itself confronted by a formidable foreign coalition, decided that the retention of the British West Indies was its first priority, while simultaneously hoping that it would also be possible to salvage Quebec and Nova Scotia from the wreck. Beyond such immediate considerations, there was also the emerging prospect of an alternative, and even more profitable, empire in the east to compensate for the prospective loss of empire in the west. 'I am enthusiastic about India', wrote John Robinson, Lord North's secretary to the treasury, in 1781, 'and look up to it as the salvation, as the wealth, the grandeur, the glory of this country.'[10]

Spain, unlike Britain, had no obvious alternative empire in prospect. Its very survival as a major European power depended on the silver and tax revenues that flowed into it from its American possessions. When, therefore, Spain found itself threatened with the loss of some or all of those possessions, first in the revolts of the early 1780s, and then again in the second decade of the nineteenth century, its natural response was not only to fight back but also to continue fighting to the last moment and beyond. Its resignation to the loss of the bulk of its overseas empire would be a prolonged and painful process, although the retention of the Philippines and the dramatic development of Cuba and Puerto Rico as sugar-producing colonies would subsequently allow Spain to reinvent itself as an imperial power and cling to its imperial status until the very end of the nineteenth century.[11]

Britain's adjustment to the loss of the thirteen colonies was made easier by the nature of its economic relationship with the new American republic. Independence brought no immediate reduction of the economic dependency of North America on British manufactures, whereas the immensely valuable Spanish American market for European manufactures had long ago fallen into the hands of Spain's French and British rivals, in spite of the protectionist policies of Madrid. From an economic standpoint, therefore, Britain, unlike Spain, could face the loss of its colonies with a degree of equanimity, since its hold over its American market remained largely unchallenged. Economically, as Britain was well aware, it held the whip hand. The British Orders in Council of the 1780s, by raising prohibitive barriers on American trade with British possessions, made it

---

[9] See Marshall, *Making and Unmaking*, pp. 359–60.

[10] Cited in *ibid.*, p. 368.

[11] For Spain's nineteenth-century empire, see Josep M. Fradera, *Colonias para después de un imperio* (Barcelona, 2005).

harder for American merchants to sell their wares in Britain and the West Indies;[12] and when a commercial treaty between Britain and the United States was finally negotiated in 1794, it was negotiated in Britain's good time, and very much on Britain's terms, rather than on those of the fledgling American republic.[13]

Thanks to a naval supremacy that was only temporarily disrupted, and to its rapidly growing industrial power, Great Britain, in spite of concessions to the Irish Patriots at its moment of maximum weakness in the early 1780s, managed to survive the loss of the thirteen colonies in reasonably good shape.[14] But in the following decades it did much more than survive the loss. As Britain fought its way to victory in the Napoleonic Wars, it succeeded in recasting its empire in ways that promised to serve metropolitan interests better than the empire that preceded it. For Adam Smith, writing in 1776, Britain's empire had until that point existed 'in imagination only'. Britain possessed not an empire, but merely 'the project of an empire'.[15] The moment had come to turn that project into a reality.

The American colonists and the Irish Patriots had cherished the vision of a composite monarchy based on equality of status between its component parts. The loss of the American colonies meant the end of that vision. Its demise was certified by the Act of Union of 1801, an incorporating union on the Scottish model, which stripped Ireland of its independent parliament. The future was to lie not with composite monarchy, nor with an Atlantic community of equals, but with a global and centrally managed empire, albeit an empire in which representative assemblies, as in Canada, were allowed their due place.[16] While committed, as the empire of an assertive English nation state,[17] to such traditional English principles as liberty, the rule of law and the primacy of trade, it would henceforth be subjected to an imperial government more interested than in earlier times in attempting to dictate the terms on which its subjects went about their business. The fact that, as in India, growing numbers of those subjects were not of British origin, and were deemed to need a degree of civilisation that only the British could impart, inevitably strengthened the impulse towards metropolitan control.

---

[12] Cathy D. Matson and Peter S. Onuf, *A Union of Interests: Political and Economic Thought in Revolutionary America* (Lawrence, Kans., 1990), pp. 44–5.

[13] Stanley Elkins and Eric McKitrick, *The Age of Federalism: The Early American Republic, 1788–1800* (New York and Oxford, 1993), pp. 396–414.

[14] Marshall, *Making and Unmaking*, pp. 370–2.

[15] Cited in Elliott, *Empires*, p. 407.

[16] Marshall, *Making and Unmaking*, pp. 373–9.

[17] C. A. Bayly, *Imperial Meridian: The British Empire and the World, 1780–1830* (London and New York, 1989).

The British were compelled by the loss of their American colonies to reconstruct their imperial project from building blocks that were both old and new. But what of their former colonies, suddenly confronted with the challenge of making their own way in a world of nation states and empires? The newly created United States launched out on their independent course under the flag of innovation. 'We have it in our power', as Tom Paine famously wrote, 'to begin the world over again.'[18] The new republic stood for the rejection of the past—a past identified with a Europe all too liable to succumb to arbitrary power, and built on corporate privileges and inequality of status. The time had come to create, in the more propitious environment of the New World, a new form of community that would embody the lofty Enlightenment ideals proclaimed in the ringing words of the Declaration of Independence.

But in reality, as is well known, the founding fathers drew deeply on the old to create the new. They were imbued with English notions of liberty and the rule of law, and their ideal remained the mixed and balanced English constitutional system, shorn of the defects that had left it prone to subversion by unregulated power, exercised either by the monarch in person or by king in parliament. The challenge that faced the founding fathers was to defy the accepted wisdom, as propounded by Montesquieu, that only in small states could republican values, and republican liberty, be preserved.[19] Would it be possible to forge a coherent and enduring republic, and one that looked towards expansion on a continental scale, out of thirteen independent-minded states, each with its own loyalties and forms of government, and its own representative assembly?

The union established in 1777 by the Articles of Confederation proved in the event to be highly precarious. As Turgot argued in 1778, 'the great inequality now existing, and which is likely to increase, between the different states, is a very unfavourable circumstance' for the stability of the union.[20] By the time of the summoning of the Constitutional Convention in 1787, the strains and stresses on the new republic were such that there was talk of the United States splitting into three or more separate confederacies.[21]

---

[18] Thomas Paine, *Common Sense*, ed. Isaac Kramnick (Harmondsworth, 1986), p. 120.

[19] Elliott, *Empires*, p. 346, and the sources there cited.

[20] Cited in Matson and Onuf, *A Union of Interests*, p. 55 (from Richard Price, 'Observations on the Importance of the American Revolution', 1785, in *Richard Price and the Ethical Foundations of the American Revolution*, ed. Bernard Peach, Durham, N.C., 1979, pp. 177–224, at p. 221n).

[21] Matson and Onuf, *A Union of Interests*, p. 83. For dangers to the survival of the union and the debates leading to the creation of the constitution that was designed to save it, see especially, among more recent works, David C. Hendrickson, *Peace Pact: The Lost World of the American Founding* (Lawrence, Kans., 2003).

Disagreements over the western land question, the problem of slavery, the regulation of the economy and the role of the republic in the international order were tearing the fragile union apart. In drafting a constitution, James Madison and his colleagues had somehow to reconcile the aspirations for a strengthened national government with the particularist tendencies of the states. The brilliant balancing act that was the outcome of their efforts was only achieved by a series of compromises, including a compromise over the vexed question of slavery, which was strong enough to postpone, but not to avert, the later disruption of the union.

But the compromises that gave the United States its constitution and transformed it into a sovereign state gave it also a vital breathing space of some seventy years in which to transform the state into a nation. This nation in embryo was a genuinely new phenomenon, although one inspired by traditional themes and aspirations. The men who drafted the constitution succeeded in realising the old dream of the colonists, for full and equal participation in a composite monarchy, by creating a composite republic, a genuine federation of states in which the individual states could participate on a basis of equality while yielding some of their powers to a national government for the good of all. In the dawning age of popular sovereignty proclaimed by the French Revolution, the United States showed itself true both to its own founding principles and to the times by ensuring that the ultimate sanction for the exercise of power rested with the people, although the definition of 'the people' remained problematic. In spite of deep and continuing fears for the survival of the union, this formula provided the cement that held the federal edifice together.

Yet, for all the skills of the constitution-makers, it should be recognised that the forging of a single nation out of the disparate states was enormously helped by good fortune. The new republic was lucky to have, in the person of George Washington, a national hero whose integrity and civic virtues made him a universally acceptable choice for its first president. The republic was fortunate, too, in the timing of its birth. The Revolutionary and Napoleonic Wars diverted European states from interference in its internal affairs and made it possible to arrange for the Louisiana purchase, so decisive for its future growth. Its status as a neutral power provided it with the opportunity, which it seized with both hands, to expand its overseas trade, and launch itself with confidence on the path that led to national prosperity. It was fortunate, also, in the apparently endless possibilities offered by westward expansion. The colonisation of the interior, as Thomas Jefferson foresaw, could be transformed into a genuinely nation-building project, even if at times it seemed to worried policy makers that the project would tear the new nation apart.[22]

But the nation that Jefferson and Madison set out to build was intended to be nothing like the eighteenth-century European fiscal-military state, which to them was anathema.[23] Yet, in turning his back on the European model, it seems at first sight ironic that Jefferson, by casting his vision for the nation in imperial terms, should have resorted to the old Europe in his bid to create the new America. The United States, as he conceived it, was to be not merely a nation but an empire, an 'empire for liberty', an expression that harked back to Britain's 'empire of the free'. In the minds of Jefferson and his Virginian colleagues that empire, to which they had always been proud to belong, had always been something of an idealised empire. They had thought of empire in terms of an association of free peoples, united in defence of common interests and ideals, until the policies of George III brought disillusionment. It was a vision of empire to which Edmund Burke appeared to subscribe when he made his famous speech on conciliation with the American colonies in March 1775. After commending the temporising Spanish system as being the most appropriate for governing an 'extensive and detached empire', he went on to describe empire, as distinguished from a single state or kingdom, as 'the aggregate of many States, under one common head; whether this head be a monarch, or a presiding republick'.[24] In other words, it was a composite, essentially federal, structure, whose survival depended on mutual understanding and respect among its constituent parts.

The enshrinement in the Constitution of 1787 of this federal ideal—an ideal conceived primarily in terms of mutual parity and esteem between the states—made it possible for Jefferson to conceive of the new republic as an empire, although an empire shorn of its European and hegemonic connotations. It differed from the empire of George III in that it was republican, not monarchical, and would genuinely be grounded on the 'federative principle', as George III's was not. This was an empire without 'the one common head', of which Burke had spoken. The federative principle would allow the nation

---

[22] See James E. Lewis Jr, *The American Union and the Problem of Neighborhood, 1783–1829* (Chapel Hill, N.C. and London, 1998).

[23] For Madison's view of the fiscal-military state, as compared with that of Hamilton, see Gordon S. Wood, 'Is There a "James Madison Problem"?', in David Womersley, ed., *Liberty and American Experience in the Eighteenth Century* (Indianapolis, Ind., 2006), pp. 425–47.

[24] Paul Langford, ed., *The Writings and Speeches of Edmund Burke*, iii (Oxford, 1966), pp. 125 and 132. See Hendrickson, *Peace Pact*, p. 101, and also pp. 22–3 for eighteenth-century notions of federalism.

to grow by accretion from a basis of equality between all the states that joined together in union.[25] As the new composite republic of the United States launched out on the arduous task of continental expansion, Jefferson was thus able to bestow upon it the legitimacy of an imperial mission.

The War of 1812, in banishing the spectre of imperial reconquest by Britain, reinforced the sense of national pride in this expanding republic of the United States. At this same moment, far away to the south, the communities that formed Spain's American empire found themselves on the brink of their own journey to statehood, but in circumstances very different from those that faced Britain's former colonies in the 1780s and 1790s. Although the Declaration of Independence and the French Revolution had inspired a handful of radicals, especially in Venezuela, with the idea of emancipation from Spanish rule, Spain would lose its American empire as the result, not of pressures from the periphery, but of collapse at the centre.

Napoleon's invasion of the Iberian Peninsula in 1808 and the forced abdication of Spain's Bourbon rulers created on both sides of the Spanish Atlantic a power vacuum that subjects of the Spanish Crown who found themselves suddenly bereft of their legitimate monarch, struggled to fill. According to Castilian constitutional tradition, at times when kingship was in crisis, sovereignty reverted to the people. In Spain and America alike, this constitutional principle was deemed to sanction the creation of juntas that were more or less populist in character, and claimed to exercise authority in the name of the deposed Ferdinand VII. At this point, traditional constitutionalist theory merged with, and was submerged by, the Revolutionary notion of popular sovereignty. As French troops virtually completed the occupation of Spain, the Hispanic world was caught up in a great debate, similar to the debate unleashed in France in 1789 by the outbreak of revolution, about the true source of authority, the constituents of nationality and the right of representation.[26]

With liberals in the ascendant, the Central Junta convoked a Cortes in Cádiz in 1810 to devise a new constitution. The first act of the new legislative assembly was to proclaim the Revolutionary principle of the sovereignty of the nation. The constitution that the Cádiz Cortes set out to draft was intended to enshrine in

---

[25] 'Who can limit the extent to which the federative principle may operate effectively?', cited from Jefferson's Second Inaugural by Peter S. Onuf, *Jefferson's Empire: The Language of American Nationhood* (Charlottesville, Va. and London, 2000), p. 1. The imperial vocation of the new United States was being proclaimed as early as 1778. See Charles S. Maier, *Among Empires: American Ascendancy and its Predecessors* (Cambridge, Mass., 2006), p. 1.
[26] Antonio Annino and François-Xavier Guerra, eds, *Inventando la nación. Iberoamérica, Siglo XIX* (Mexico City, 2003), p. 134.

Spain and its overseas possessions the liberal ideals embodied in the American and French Revolutions, avoiding the extremes of French-style republicanism, and transforming Spain into a constitutional monarchy on the British model. After a century of authoritarian Bourbon government, the Hispanic world therefore embarked on a major constitutional experiment in circumstances that could hardly have been less propitious. Most of Spain itself was by now in the hands of the French invader, and Spanish America was in ferment.

From the beginning, the American territories were deeply involved in this constitutional experiment. American representatives were called upon to participate in the Cortes, although from the outset there was discontent in the American territories at the number of delegates allotted to them relative to the size of their populations. But the representatives came to Cádiz buoyed up by the hope of realising the old creole dream of participating in a genuinely composite monarchy which would span the Atlantic and give them equal rights with the peninsular kingdoms. The first article of the 1812 Spanish Constitution would in principle seem to have embodied their hope: 'The Spanish nation is the union of all Spaniards of both hemispheres.'[27] An empire was, in effect, being dissolved, to be replaced by a single nation spanning two continents—a nation that would be based on equality of representation in the national assembly, and equality of rights.

But there was to be a wide discrepancy between theory and practice. For all their lip-service to liberal principles, the Spanish deputies to the Cortes, who were in the overwhelming majority, were in many respects the heirs to Bourbon notions of a unitary nation rather than a pluralist monarchy and, in spite of their high-sounding rhetoric about equality, they continued to think in terms of provincial subordination.[28] From the start they displayed an arrogance towards Spanish America that was bound to alienate those whom they wished to attract. Spain had a population of around ten million, as compared with the fifteen or sixteen million inhabitants of Spanish America,[29] and the not unnatural fear of the Spanish deputies that they would be swamped by the Americans led to electoral manipulations designed to reduce the weight of the American representation. Although the Spanish nation was defined in the Constitution as 'the union of all Spaniards of both hemispheres'—a definition that in principle embraced not only creoles, but also Indians, mestizos, *castas*

---

[27] Antonio Fernández García, ed., *La constitución de Cádiz (1812)*, (Madrid, 2002), p. 89.

[28] See F. X. Guerra, 'El ocaso de la monarquía hispánica: revolución y desintegración', in Annino and Guerra, eds, *Inventando la nación*, p. 129.

[29] Elliott, *Empires*, p. 379.

pardas, or the 'dark' castes, and free blacks—the rights to full citizenship of those with African ancestry were progressively whittled down in the course of the document.[30] It was calculated that the effect of this process would be to produce relative parity between Spanish and Spanish American representation in future meetings of the Cortes, although nobody had a clear idea of the size of the populations involved.

In general, the Spanish deputies showed little knowledge of Spanish America or understanding of its legitimate complaints and, as with colonial British America, economic discrimination, in particular, remained a powerful cause for grievance on the American side. The Cádiz merchants, who exercised a powerful influence over the Cortes, were determined to maintain their dominant position in the organisation of the Atlantic trade—a determination that meant the continuing subordination of the American territories to economic control by the mother country.

In spite of its deficiencies, the new Constitution of 1812 was widely hailed in many parts of Spanish America, which now experienced the novelty of elections on a massive scale for the new institutions created by the Constitution and for town councils that had previously been more or less closed corporations.[31] But by the time this extraordinary liberal experiment was under way, disillusionment over the deliberations of the Cortes had increased the number of Spanish Americans who were now inclined to follow the North American example of independence rather than talk the language of unity and equality within a single Spanish nation. The restored monarchy of Ferdinand VII completed the work that the Cortes of Cádiz had unwittingly begun. His return to Spain in March 1814 was followed by his abrupt dissolution of the Cortes in May and a restoration of Bourbon absolutism. In a bid to recover his American empire and refill his empty treasury, Ferdinand set out to crush the independence movements that had sprung up across the continent.

The result was predictable. Resistance stiffened, the continent was plunged into civil war between rebels and loyalists, and even the return of constitutional government after the Spanish liberal Revolution of 1820 failed to save the day. In 1821 the reconvened Spanish Cortes revived a proposal originally put forward by the Count of Aranda in 1783 for the division of Spain's Atlantic empire into three separate kingdoms, each ruled by a prince of the royal house. Like a rather similar proposal made by Lord Shelburne for British

---

[30] Elliott, *Empires*, p. 385.
[31] Jaime E. Rodríguez O., *The Independence of Spanish America* (Cambridge, 1998), pp. 94–103.

America in 1782, it came far too late.[32] One American territory after another had either already proclaimed its independence or was on the point of doing so. The two oldest and most established kingdoms, New Spain and Peru, were among the last to go, with Mexico declaring itself independent in 1821 and Peru in 1824. For Spanish America the age of empire was over, and the age of state and nation building about to begin. But whereas the rebel colonies of British America managed, if with difficulty, to build a national state on the ruins of empire, Spain's American empire fragmented into seventeen different states. In all of them the creation of the institutions of statehood and the development of a sense of national identity proved even more fraught with problems than they had proved in Britain's former colonies. Why should this have been?

If we compare the differing trajectories of post-independence British and Spanish America, a first and obvious clue to their contrasting experiences is the enormous difference in scale between the two empires at the moment of their dissolution. The surface area of Spain's empire of the Indies was more than 5 million square miles, as compared with the 322,000 square miles of the British mainland colonies.[33] Once imperial control was removed, there was no chance of holding this vast area together as a single unit. This did not, of course, eliminate aspirations after unity, if not of the whole empire, at least of vast regions. Simón Bolívar's project for a Gran Colombia stretching from Venezuela to Chile was an attempt, although a vain one, to bind together in a permanent federal union large units of territory that were already dissolving into independent states. In the viceroyalty of New Spain, an empire was proclaimed in 1821 under a former royalist military officer, Agustín de Iturbide. But two years later the empire collapsed, to be replaced by a Mexican federal republic, from which Central America broke loose to create the United Provinces of Central America, a union that itself would later split up into five independent nations.[34] Similarly, Buenos Aires, the capital of the old viceroyalty of La Plata and of the new republic of Argentina, failed to hold on to Paraguay, Uruguay and Bolivia.[35] In Spanish America, therefore, attempts at large-scale federal union, on the

---

[32] For the Cortes proposal of 1821, see Antonio Annino, 'Soberanías en lucha', in Annino and Guerra, eds, *Inventando la nación*, p. 218; for Aranda's and Shelburne's proposals, see Elliott, *Empires*, p. 367.

[33] Elliott, *Empires*, p. 331.

[34] Rodríguez, *Independence of Spanish America*, p. 210; Jordana Dym, *From Sovereign Villages to National States: City, State and Federation in Central America, 1759–1839* (Albuquerque, N. Mex., 2006).

[35] Jeremy Adelman, *Sovereignty and Revolution in the Iberian Atlantic* (Princeton, N.J., 2006), pp. 261–3.

model of the United States, proved insufficient across much of the continent to prevent a fragmentation into smaller political units.[36]

While part of the explanation for the fissiparous character of the old Spanish American empire lies in its sheer magnitude, part also lies in the organisation and character of the defunct empire itself. After three centuries of imperial government, the territorial divisions introduced by the Spaniards had hardened, and intense local loyalties had developed. In the first instance these loyalties tended to centre on individual cities and towns, but they radiated outwards, although with weakening intensity, to the outer limits of the administrative, judicial and fiscal regions to which they belonged.[37] The resulting sense of the *patria* in what had become a multiplicity of *patrias* seems to have been more deeply rooted in Spanish America than it had been in the British colonies at the moment of independence. This local or regional patriotism acquired new and richer overtones in the opening decades of the nineteenth century, as European conceptions of nationality, dressed up in the fashionable garb of Romanticism, were eagerly embraced in America.

Tensions between the different *patrias* were heightened by uncertainties over the exact boundaries of the old Spanish territorial units—a problem compounded by recent administrative restructuring by the later Bourbons, which had created new areas of dispute. In an essentially urban civilisation, too, like that of Spanish America, provincial cities instinctively resented the dominance of capital cities like Mexico City or Buenos Aires, and resisted their claims to speak for the nation as a whole. The collapse of authority over much of the empire gave these cities and towns an unprecedented degree of autonomy, which they were disinclined to surrender when the process of state building began.

In addition, the sheer length and ferocity of the war between loyalists and patriots in comparison with the North American War of Independence encouraged the emergence of *caudillos* with their own strong regional base and extensive clientage networks.[38] Once the loyalists had been defeated, fragile states emerging from the ruins of empire were all too likely to find themselves at the mercy of local or regional *caudillos* who now fancied themselves as national leaders. The inevitable result was a militarisation of politics and a

---

[36] Anthony Pagden, *Lords of All the World* (New Haven, Conn. and London, 1995), p. 196.
[37] For the development of the sense of *patria* in Spanish America, see especially David Brading, *The First America: The Spanish Monarchy, Creole Patriots and the Liberal State, 1492–1867* (Cambridge, 1991), and above, ch. IX.
[38] See John Lynch, *Caudillos in Spanish America 1800–1850* (Oxford, 1992).

consequent undermining of the nascent institutions of the newly independent states. In such circumstances, a victorious *caudillo* could present himself as the only person capable of restoring order and inducing atomised societies to coalesce around some sense of nationhood. The *caudillos* had already proved themselves as heroes of the struggle against Spain. Now, as the new states fell out with their neighbours over boundary lines and the distribution of the Spanish fiscal legacy,[39] they turned the nationalist sentiments generated during the struggle for independence from Spain against closer enemies.

The nascent United States, too, had been afflicted by serious disputes over the old colonial boundaries, but its federal structure, with its implicit tendency to favour compromise for resolving conflicts, helped it to resolve these disputes without resort to fratricidal warfare. At the same time, the fears of social upheaval and of descent into anarchy unleashed by events like Shay's rebellion in western Massachusetts in 1786, persuaded state elites of the need to sink their differences and support the notion of a central government strong enough to help keep the peace. As already noted, the chances of stability were further increased by the fact that the relative brevity of the War of Independence created fewer opportunities than in Spain's colonies, tradition- ally dependent on patronage and clientage, for the rise of *caudillo* figures with strong local followings. Perhaps even more important, the tradition of classical republicanism that had been instilled into North American colonial elites was not conducive to the militarisation of civil society. As amply demonstrated by his abrupt dismissal in 1783 of the Newburgh conspirators—disaffected offi- cers of the Continental Army—George Washington was the embodiment of republican virtue. Even if he had been so inclined, the ingrained distrust of standing armies in the Anglo-American world would have made it difficult, if not impossible, for him to take the road that would later be taken by a Bolívar or an Iturbide.

But fissiparous patriotism and the militarisation of society were not the only problems to complicate the birth of the new Spanish-American states. The 1812 Constitution brought representative institutions to Spanish America, but they arrived very late in the day. In contrast to British colonial America, opportuni- ties for participation in the political process, even for the creole elite, were very limited, and amounted largely to haggling and bargaining with the royal authorities—an exercise at which it became adept. Where each British colony

---

[39] See Regina Grafe and María Alejandra Irigoin, 'The Spanish Empire and its Legacy: Fiscal Redistribution and Political Conflict in Colonial and Post-Colonial Spanish America', *Journal of Global History*, 1 (2006), pp. 241–67.

had its own representative assembly, the Spanish Crown had from the beginning set itself against the transfer of Cortes, or representative assemblies, to America. Their absence not only deprived the elite and wider segments of the population of opportunities for gaining experience in the art of self-government, but also meant that, at least until the later Bourbons created the new administrative units of intendancies, no intermediate body existed at the equivalent of the provincial level to fill the space between town councils and the institutions of royal government.[40]

It is not, therefore, surprising that cities and city governments should have sought to bridge the divide by making claims for authority over extensive areas of territory. In so doing, they inevitably came into conflict with other cities equally bent on establishing their own claims. The existence of representative assemblies at a provincial level during the colonial period would have helped to mediate such internal disputes, and would also have encouraged the practice of searching for consensus. This in turn might later have facilitated the reaching of agreements at the national, and even regional, level. As it was, each city acted as a law unto itself, resisting equally the claims of rival cities and the attempts of weak central governments to establish national sovereignty over the territory as a whole. The struggle between towns and cities competing for preeminence all too often descended into a civil war that threatened fragile new states with dissolution, although in some regions municipal independence could help, as well as hinder, the task of state formation. In Central America, for instance, the vacuum created by the collapse of the institutions of viceregal government left the smaller municipalities searching for an arbiter to mediate in their internal and external disputes, and they instinctively looked to the new state governments to take up the role formerly filled by agents of the Crown.[41] All too often, however, the outcome of the contest between deeply entrenched municipal sovereignty and a national sovereignty that central governments proved incapable of enforcing was federalism by default.

Finally, the process of state building was hampered in the territories of the former Spanish empire by the social and ethnic structure of the societies that had now achieved their independence. Spain's overseas possessions, like Spain itself, were corporatist and hierarchical societies.[42] During the colonial period, creole oligarchies had consolidated their social and economic dominance, and

---

[40] Guerra, 'El ocaso de la monarquía', in Annino and Guerra, eds, *Inventando la nación*, p. 194.
[41] See Dym, *Sovereign Villages to National States*, ch. 8.
[42] For corporatism in New Spain, see Annick Lempérière, *Entre Dieu et le roi, la république. Mexico, XVIe–XIX siècle* (Paris, 2004).

they were not prepared to relinquish this when independence came. Although there was in fact considerable social mobility during the colonial period, and although a process of racial intermingling between people of European, Indian and African ancestry had been under way from the early years of colonisation, social divisions had tended to harden over time along racial lines.

During the years of Spanish rule, Church and Crown had sought with some success to integrate all the diverse elements of society beneath their capacious cloaks, but the collapse of royal government brought longstanding social and ethnic tensions to the surface, and deprived Indian communities of their natural protector against depredations on their lands. At the same time, no racial group was left untouched by the winds of change blowing through the hemisphere, carrying with them fresh notions of nationhood and rights of representation. The constitutional experiments in the decade after 1808, following close on the heels of the Bourbon reforms, had led to profound transformations at every level of society. The old binary system of two separate 'republics' of Spaniards and Indians had effectively collapsed. The new electoral laws had vastly extended the body politic, and creoles, mestizos, Indians and *pardos* were now jostling for place in the governments of the newly unified municipalities, the *ayuntamientos constitucionales*. The newly enfranchised were quick to learn the new language of individual rights and popular sovereignty. In Mexico, the Indians, who constituted 30 per cent of the total population, resorted to the new constitutional doctrines to defend their lands and rights, which they depicted as being inherent in a Mexican nation stretching back to pre-conquest times.[43]

In these circumstances, it would never be easy to fashion cohesive states and nations out of such ethnically variegated polities—more ethnically variegated than the early United States, with its fundamental fault-line of the black-white divide. There was more chance of success in the old-established polities within the Spanish empire, like Mexico, Peru and Chile, than in the newer administrative units of eighteenth-century creation, like the viceroyalties of New Granada and Río de la Plata, which had enjoyed less time in which to develop some sense of collective identity. But ethnic diversity, the continuing strength of traditional corporations and of patron–client relationships, the power of the cities and the weakness of political institutions following the removal of royal government, all made state and nation building an even harder task than it proved to be in the United States. Instability was chronic in the early years of the new independent republics. As John Quincy Adams observed: 'Their

---

[43] Antonio Annino, 'Pueblos, liberalismo y nación en México', in Annino and Guerra, *Inventando la nación*, pp. 414–21.

governments are Chinese Shadows; they rise upon the Stage, and pass off like the images of Banquo's descendants in Macbeth.'[44]

The new republics, still politically unstable and impoverished by internecine warfare, were also forced to operate in a much less benign economic climate than that in which the United States propelled itself along the path that led to nation-hood. It is true that they were now relieved of the fiscal burdens involved in subsi-dising the imperial metropolis, just as they were also relieved of the commercial restrictions imposed by imperial monopoly. But against these benefits must be set the dissolution of the vast customs and monetary union that Spain's American empire had once been, and the difficulties of finding their own niches in a global economy whose commanding heights were dominated by the British, with increasingly self-confident North American merchants treading on their heels.[45]

There is no inevitable historical law of progression from empire to nation state, of the kind that was taken for granted in standard nineteenth- and twentieth-century accounts, which saw the nation state as the logical culmina-tion of a thousand years of European history.[46] What we see in the western world in the late eighteenth and early nineteenth centuries is, rather, a process of polit-ical reconfiguration on a massive scale, as old empires adapt to new challenges, new empires are born, and states painfully construct or reconstruct themselves from fragments of the old imperial ruins. Did the answer lie in the creation of nation states or of larger, composite units, or, as in the United States, in some combination of the two? In so far as the creation of nation states seemed to offer the only way forward after the collapse of Bolívar's plans for large-scale confed-eration, the transition from empire to viable nation state proved more fraught and prolonged in Spain's American territories than in the mainland territories of British America, although even here many decades, and perhaps even a civil war, would be needed to establish a permanent sense of nationhood.

Part of the explanation, as I have suggested, lies in elements of the Spanish imperial legacy. But timing and context were also critical, and they raise the question of whether the transformation of Spain's American empire into seven-teen independent nation states was itself a preordained historical process. In 1808, when Napoleon's forces invaded Spain, only a tiny minority of Spanish

---

[44] Cited in Lewis, *The American Union and the Problem of Neighborhood*, p. 162.

[45] For a recent survey of the differing assessments of the economic consequences of inde-pendence for the nations of Latin America, see Leandro Prados de la Escosura in *The Cambridge Economic History of Latin America*, vol. 1, ch. 13, ed. Victor Bulmer-Thomas, John H. Coatsworth and Roberto Cortés Conde (Cambridge, 2006). See also, Adelman, *Sovereignty and Revolution*, pp. 349–55.

[46] See, most recently, Jeremy Adelman, 'An Age of Imperial Revolutions', *American Historical Review*, 113 (2008), pp. 319–40.

Americans were thinking of independence. In Spanish America, as in British America, the sense of nationhood followed, rather than preceded, the winning of independence. Traditionally, loyalty to the Crown ran deep among the king's Spanish American subjects, and indeed was reinforced by the overthrow of the Bourbon monarchy.

In attempting to transform Spain and Spain's American empire into a single nation ruled by a constitutional monarchy, the Cortes of Cádiz had embarked on a constitutional experiment of enormous, but unrealised, potential. It was an experiment that at least opened the possibility of a way forward from a centrally directed empire to a nation of Atlantic peoples represented in a single parliamentary assembly. It thus combined the two most powerful ideological currents of the age, liberalism and nationalism. But the experiment was aborted by short-sightedness, self-interest and the reactionary policies of a restored monarchy. The experiment lasted long enough, however, to ensure that liberalism would take its place alongside nationalism in the independent Iberian America of the nineteenth century.

But this America was, and remained, vulnerable. It was made vulnerable by the fact that liberalism, in aligning itself with federalism, reduced the chances for the creation of central authorities strong enough to impose themselves on new territorial units that possessed little or no sense of national identity, and were riven by ethnic and social conflict.[47] It was vulnerable to the forces of the international economic order, and it was also vulnerable to the pressures emanating from the powerful new English-speaking nation arising in the northern half of the hemisphere.

In the Mexican-American war of 1846–8 Mexico lost half its territory to the United States. Fifty years later, in 1898, the United States, displaying an increasingly assertive interventionism in Latin-American affairs, went to war with Spain and stripped it of its last American territories, occupying Cuba and taking possession of Puerto Rico and the Philippines. The war of 1898 was traumatic for Spain, which would take the best part of a century to come to terms with the final loss of empire. Shorn of the bulk of its imperial possessions in an age when its European rivals were consolidating or acquiring empires of their own, the country struggled to reinvent itself as a nation state. In the meantime, a victorious United States was brashly setting out, still largely unawares, on the road that led from nation state to worldwide empire.

---

[47] For a suggestive discussion of the problems of state-building in the new Iberian-American republics, see Miguel Angel Centeno, *Blood and Debt: War and the Nation State in Latin America* (University Park, Pa., 2002).

PART III

THE WORLD OF ART

CHAPTER XII

EL GRECO'S MEDITERRANEAN: THE ENCOUNTER OF CIVILISATIONS

The Mediterranean world of the sixteenth century—the world of El Greco—was a world in which three civilisations coexisted, interacted and clashed: the Latin West; the Greek Orthodox East; and the civilisation of Islam. As a Cretan, and hence a subject of the Republic of Venice, Domenikos Theotokopoulos, known as El Greco (1541–1614), belonged both to the Greek East and to Latin Christendom. He and his generation lived much of their lives in the shadow of confrontation between Christendom and Islam.

More than a month's sailing time from Venice,[1] Crete—a Venetian colony since 1211—was, by the sixteenth century, an exposed Christian outpost in an eastern Mediterranean dominated by the Ottoman empire from its capital at Istanbul. The Greek Orthodox inhabitants of Crete, citizens of the Byzantine empire until the island passed into the hands of the Venetians, had continued to look towards Constantinople as their spiritual home until it fell to the Ottoman Turks in 1453. Clinging tenaciously to their Greek culture in the face of a repressive Venetian regime, the Cretans engaged in periodic insurrections against Venetian rule, and fiercely resisted Venetian attempts to impose upon them the measures agreed at the Council of Florence in 1439 to end the schism between the Greek and Latin Churches. By the later fifteenth century, however, the growing threat from the Turks would begin to force on Venice a reassessment of its policies, including its religious policy, towards a resentful colonial population.

---

[1] The 'normal' sailing time from the island's capital, Candia, in the sixteenth century was thirty-three days. See Fernand Braudel, *The Mediterranean and the Mediterranean World in the Age of Philip II*, Eng. trans. S. Reynolds, 2 vols (London, 1972–3), i, p. 362.

If the peasants, extracting a meagre living from the stony soil, remained implacably opposed to their Venetian feudal lords, in the towns at least the once sharp divisions between colonists and colonised were gradually being blurred. Intermarriage at all levels of society had brought the two communities closer, and the Venetian ruling elite, which had accepted the old Cretan nobility into its ranks, was assimilating the Greek language, Greek dress and Greek ways.

Urban life came to reflect the new prosperity of an island that reaped increasing benefits from its participation in Venice's expanding maritime and commercial empire, exporting olive oil, salt and raisins, and serving as a staging-post for Venetian shipping. Cretan families sent their sons to study at Padua University on the Venetian mainland, and Cretan cultural life began to respond to the Renaissance breezes blowing from Venice—a Renaissance that itself was heavily indebted to the Greek refugees who had fled to the west after the fall of Constantinople. Venetian-style buildings and *piazze* began to change the face of the old Byzantine towns, and most notably of the island's capital, Candia (the modern-day Iraklion), which by the later Middle Ages had given its name to the island as a whole. Gradually, in the late fifteenth and early sixteenth centuries, Greek East and Latin West were blending to create a distinctive Venetian-Cretan culture.[2]

It was in the city of Candia (so named after El Khandak, the defensive ditch built by the Arabs during their occupation of Crete during the tenth and eleventh centuries) that Domenikos Theotokopoulos was born in 1541, a member of one of those local families that had prospered as a result of service to the Venetian state. His father, Georgios Theotokopoulos, was a tax-farmer with shipping and trading interests, and his elder brother Manoussos would start by following in their father's footsteps.[3] The family is thought to have been Greek Orthodox, but by the mid-sixteenth century Venice's more relaxed religious policy had dispelled many of the old tensions between the Greek and Latin cults. In the new, more tolerant climate of religious coexistence, the adherents of the two faiths would frequent each other's churches, while both

[2] For Cretan society and culture in this period, see especially David Holton, ed., *Literature and Society in Renaissance Crete* (Cambridge, 1991).

[3] In spite of intensive work in recent years, very little information has been found about El Greco's family or his early life. See the catalogue essay by José Álvarez Lopera, 'The Construction of a Painter: A Century of Searching for and Interpreting El Greco', in José Álvarez Lopera, ed., *El Greco: Identity and Transformation* (Museo Thyssen-Bornemisza, Madrid, 1999), pp. 45–6. For the fortunes and misfortunes of his brother, see Nikolaos M. Panayotakis, 'Manoussos the Pirate: 1571–1572', in Nicos Hadjinicolaou, ed., *El Greco in Italy and Italian Art* (Rethymno, 1999), pp. 17–21.

communities would participate in the innumerable religious processions that enlivened the street life of Candia and the island's other towns, celebrating their shared devotion to the Virgin Mary and St Francis.[4]

Another bridge between the two religious worlds was provided by the portable icon. Cretan workshops of the later fifteenth and early sixteenth centuries enjoyed a flourishing trade in these sacred images, both for the home market and for export to Venice and the eastern Mediterranean. A distinctive school of Cretan icon painting had by now emerged, producing works of a hybrid character, in which Byzantine traditions (Fig. 5) were modified by western influences brought to the island by Venetian prints and paintings or by returning artists (Fig. 6).[5] His obvious artistic talents qualified the young Domenikos Theotokopoulos for training in the workshop of a local icon painter, and by 1563 he was publicly known as a master in the art of painting icons and tempera panels. At this stage of his career, and for someone of his ambitions, a move from the provincial society of Crete to the cultural metropolis of Venice would have offered irresistible attractions. Many of his compatriots had made the same move before him, lured by the greater economic and social opportunities to be found in the city that prided itself on being the 'Queen of the Adriatic', the head of a great maritime empire.

When El Greco moved to Venice in 1567, possibly making use of his family's contacts in the city, he was confronted not only by a heritage of overwhelming visual and architectural beauty but also by the presence of living artists whose style was far removed from that of the Cretan icon painters with their carefully modelled figures set against brilliant gold backgrounds. During his three years in Venice, where he seems to have worked and studied on his own, he gradually assimilated the lessons to be learnt from the artists of the Venetian Renaissance about colour, perspective and the technique of painting in oils. In particular, the two greatest living masters, Titian and Tintoretto, were to have a transforming impact on his work.[6] Those three years of residence in Venice, so fruitful for El Greco's personal development, were, however, years of impending crisis for the republic and its empire—a crisis in which his family in Crete would be fatally engulfed.

---

[4] Chryssan Maltezou, 'The Historical and Social Context', in Holton, *Literature and Society*, pp. 33 and 44.

[5] See Maria Constantoudaki-Kitromilides, 'Cretan Painting during the XV and XVI Centuries', in *El Greco: Identity and Transformations*, pp. 83–93.

[6] Fernando Marías, *Greco. Biographie d'un peintre extravagant* (Paris, 1997), pp. 62–73.

Figure 5 Angelos Akotantos, *The Virgin Kardiotissa* (Byzantine and Christian Museum, Athens).

The city, with a population of some 170,000,[7] had acquired its prosperity, and built up its maritime empire, through skilful exploitation of its geographical position as a meeting point and centre of exchange between Greek East and Latin West.[8] It had survived both the opening by the Portuguese of an overseas

[7] Brian Pullan, *Rich and Poor in Renaissance Venice* (Oxford, 1971), p. 289.
[8] See William H. McNeill, *Venice: The Hinge of Europe, 1081–1797* (Chicago, Ill. and London, 1974).

Figure 6 Attributed to Nikolaos Tsafouris, *The Virgin 'Madre della Consolazione' and Saint Francis of Assisi* (Byzantine and Christian Museum, Athens).

route to the spices of the East and the replacement of the Byzantine empire by that of the Ottoman Turks. It was in the interest of the Turks as much as of the Venetians to maintain the flow of trade, but the Ottomans had developed into a formidable naval power posing a major threat to Christian lands and shipping in the eastern and central Mediterranean. The thrust of Venetian diplomacy was to protect the republic's territorial and commercial interests by staying on good terms with the Ottoman Sultan, Sulaiman the Magnificent and, following Sulaiman's death in 1566, with his successor Selim II.

By the middle years of the sixteenth century Venice, although it maintained a substantial fleet, had become a pygmy in a Mediterranean world dominated by two opposing giants. An expanding Ottoman empire lay to its east, and to its west lay the Spanish Monarchy and empire, of which the government passed in 1556 from Charles V to Philip II. In both the Spanish and the Ottoman empires memories ran deep. The presence on Spanish soil of a large population of Moorish descent, the moriscos—left behind in the peninsula after the completion of the *reconquista* by Christian forces in 1492, and in large part only nominally converted to Christianity—was a persistent reminder of the centuries of hostility between Christendom and Islam. The legacy of religious hatred was compounded by the clash of territorial interests along the North African coast, and by endless skirmishes on the sea and along the shores of the Mediterranean as the Turks and their North African allies attacked Christian shipping and raided Christian villages, while corsairs from Spain and Italy responded in kind.

As the two empires moved towards their decisive confrontation, it required all the skills of Venetian diplomacy to steer a course between them. But in 1565 the Turkish fleet besieged Malta. The eventual raising of the siege of Malta, following the arrival of the Spanish fleet, made it clear that only Spain had the capacity and the resources to protect the central Mediterranean against Ottoman assaults. Having failed at Malta, the Turks, under their new sultan, Selim II, would sooner or later seek their revenge elsewhere, and the Venetian colonies of Cyprus and Crete were the most obvious targets for an attacking fleet. After thirty years of peace, the Venetians still clung to the hope that their own territories would be immune from attack,[9] but in July 1570 Turkish forces invaded Cyprus and laid siege to Famagusta. In Spain at the same time, Don John of Austria, the bastard son of the Emperor Charles V and half-brother of Philip II, was in the final stages of crushing a revolt of the moriscos of Granada after almost two years of savage guerrilla warfare in the Alpujarra mountains.

Pope Pius V, the most austere of Counter-Reformation popes, saw this as the moment for realising his long-cherished dream of organising an alliance of Christian powers against the forces of Islam. Struggling to save Famagusta, the Venetian Republic set aside its objections to a military confrontation with

---

[9] Braudel, *The Mediterranean*, ii, pt 3, provides an extensive narrative of the origins and formation of the Holy League of 20 May 1571 and the movement of the conflict towards its climax at Lepanto in October 1571, as also does Kenneth M. Setton, *The Papacy and the Levant, 1204–1571*, 4 vols (Philadelphia, Pa. 1984), iv, chs 19–24. For a summary account of the confrontation between the Spanish and Ottoman empires, set in a general European context, see J. H. Elliott, *Europe Divided, 1559–1598*, 2nd edn (Oxford, 2000), especially ch. 6.

the Ottoman empire and an alliance with Spain. After protracted negotiations a Holy League was agreed on 20 May 1571. By the terms of the League, Spain, Venice and the papacy were to join forces in a campaign against the Turks, with Spain contributing half the funds, troops and ships, the Venetians a third and the pope a sixth.

By this time El Greco had been in Rome for several months. He had arrived there in the autumn of 1570, bringing with him works he had painted in Venice. The celebrated Croatian miniature painter, Giulio Clovio, impressed by his skill, recommended him to Cardinal Alessandro Farnese (1520–89), the rich and cultivated grandson of Pope Paul III and the greatest Roman patron of artists and men of letters of the age.[10] The Palazzo Farnese, in which El Greco was initially to be given accommodation, had been completed and extensively remodelled by Michelangelo. The great Florentine painter, sculptor and architect had died six years earlier, but his powerful presence was inescapable for El Greco as he walked the streets and visited St Peter's and other city churches. Cardinal Farnese, protector and patron of the Jesuits, and builder of their church of the Gesù, carried over into the more dogmatic age of the Counter-Reformation the values and concerns of Renaissance humanism, and favoured in his artistic tastes a judicious blending of the old and the new. In coming into contact with the cardinal's intellectual circle under the leadership of his humanist librarian, Fulvio Orsini, El Greco therefore found himself once again in an eclectic environment in which different worlds met and fused—in this instance the worlds of Renaissance humanism, pagan antiquity and Catholic Counter-Reformation spirituality, as defined by the decrees promulgated by the Council of Trent on its conclusion in 1563.

The Farnese circle was much frequented by Spaniards, whose presence in the city, in large and growing numbers, was one of its most striking features in the later sixteenth century. In 1582 it was alleged that there were 30,000 Spaniards—clerics, lawyers, merchants, together with artisans and notaries to meet their various needs. If true, this would mean that they represented over a quarter of Rome's estimated population of 115,000.[11] Spanish influence,

---

[10] For El Greco in Rome, see Lionello Puppi, 'El Greco in Italy and Italian Art', in Álvarez Lopera, ed., *El Greco: Identity and Transformation*, pp. 95–103. For Cardinal Farnese and his circle, see Federico Zeri, *Pittura e Controriforma* (Turin, 1957), and Clare Robertson, *'Il Gran Cardinale': Alessandro Farnese, Patron of the Arts* (New Haven, Conn. and London, 1992). See also Clare Robertson, 'El Greco, Fulvio Orsini and Giulio Clovio', in Nicos Hadjinicolau, ed., *El Greco of Crete* (Heraklion, 1995), pp. 215–27.

[11] Thomas James Dandelet, *Spanish Rome, 1500–1700* (New Haven, Conn. and London, 2001), p. 120.

indeed, was all-pervasive in the Rome of the Counter-Reformation papacy. There was a constant coming and going between Madrid and the papal court. Philip II, like Charles V before him, needed a compliant papacy to support his global interests, and approve his ceaseless requests for taxes and financial support from the wealthy Spanish Church. The Spanish ambassador to the Holy See was therefore a dominant figure in the life of the city, distributing pensions to the cardinals, including Cardinal Farnese, to ensure on each papal death the election of a new pontiff favourable to Spain. While Philip II pursued policies that in his eyes were invariably in the best interests of the Church, a judiciously managed patronage system was intended to keep the papacy in line.

In the early summer of 1571, Spain, the papacy and the normally recalcitrant Venetians were at last united against a common enemy. Vast preparations were now under way, and on 7 October the combined allied fleets, under the supreme command of Don John of Austria, met and defeated the Ottoman fleet in Greek waters at Lepanto (present-day Nafpaktos) in the Corinthian Gulf. It was an extraordinary triumph for Christian arms. Of the Ottoman fleet of some 300 ships, 127 were captured by the forces of the Holy League and the Turks lost 30,000 men, as against Christian losses of 15 to 20 ships and perhaps 8,000 men.[12] In Venice, where the news of the victory arrived on 19 October, the Doge and Signoria went at once to St Mark's, where the mass was sung with the *Te Deum Laudamus*. In Rome, where the news was received on 22 October, an elated Pius V and his cardinals gave thanks in St Peter's, and triumphal arches bearing the names of Philip II, the pope and Venice were erected in the streets.[13] As the news spread across Europe the rejoicings were everywhere repeated, and in Toledo, where again a *Te Deum* was celebrated in the great cathedral, Philip II endowed an annual procession to commemorate the victory in perpetuity (Fig. 7).[14]

Although the psychological impact of the victory was enormous, bringing a vast sense of relief to a Christendom that had long felt beleaguered by Islam, its aftermath proved in many respects a sad disappointment. Pius V and Don John of Austria dreamed of a crusade which would see Christian banners flying from the towers of Istanbul and Jerusalem. Greek copyists, poring over their codices in Spain, dreamed of the liberation of their homeland from the

---

[12] The battle and its implications are well described in John Francis Guilmartin Jr, *Gunpowder and Galleys* (Cambridge, 1974), pp. 221–52.
[13] See Setton, *The Papacy and the Levant*, iv, pp. 1,060–3, for the impact of the news in Venice and the papal court; see Dandelet, *Spanish Rome*, p. 70, for the celebrations in Rome.
[14] Gregorio de Andrés, *Helenistas del renacimiento en Toledo. El copista cretense Antonio Calosinás* (Toledo, 1999), p. 67.

Figure 7 Titian, *Philip II Offering Don Fernando to Victory* (Museo del Prado, Madrid).

Turks.[15] But the Venetians were interested only in the fate of Cyprus, which they finally surrendered to the Turks in 1573 in return for peace, and Spain's attention was being diverted from the Mediterranean by its struggle with the Dutch. For Philip II the challenge of Islam was beginning to take second place to the Protestant challenge emanating from the Netherlands, England and France. For its part the Ottoman empire was becoming increasingly absorbed by developments on its Persian front. As a result, the two empires began to disengage, and the great war in the Mediterranean dwindled into a stand-off characterised by corsair attacks and small-scale naval skirmishes.

The dreams of lesser men than the pope and Don John of Austria were also doomed to disappointment. Among them was El Greco's elder brother, Manoussos, who arrived in Venice in October 1571 in the wake of Lepanto to request four armed galleys to launch attacks on Turkish shipping. His enterprise, however, went awry when he made the mistake of attacking a merchant vessel which turned out to be sailing under a Ragusan flag and carrying supplies for the Venetian fleet. Arrested by the Venetian authorities and unable to pay his debts at a time of depression on the island of Crete, he was forced to sell all his property. Years later he would join his younger brother in Toledo, where he died in 1604.[16]

In Rome, El Greco himself was faring little better. Disappointed of Farnese patronage,[17] he secured admission in 1572 to the painter's guild, the Accademia di San Luca, which allowed him to set up his own studio, but he failed to obtain major commissions, and his prickly temperament and outlandish opinions did not help to smoothe his path.[18] Once again he decided to try his luck elsewhere, this time with Titian's royal patron, Philip II of Spain. By June 1577 he was to be found in Madrid.

He was probably hoping to join the Italian artists who were being recruited to work on the decoration of Philip II's monastery-palace of the Escorial, of which the foundation stone had been laid fourteen years earlier, in 1563.[19] Work had now begun on the great basilica at the centre of the monumental complex, and a whole series of *retablos*, or altarpieces, would be needed for its chapels and altars.[20] El Greco's first documented activity, however, was in Toledo, and here he was to remain. For all his efforts, he would never win the favour of the king. In

---

[15] Andrés, *Helenistas*, p. 66.
[16] The story is told by Panayotakis, 'Manoussos the Pirate', in Hadjinicolaou, ed., *El Greco in Italy*, pp. 19–21.
[17] Puppi, 'El Greco in Italy', in Álvarez Lopera, ed., *El Greco: Identity and Transformation*, p. 103.
[18] Marías, *Greco*, p. 117.
[19] José Manuel Pita Andrade, 'El Greco in Spain', in Álvarez Lopera, ed., *El Greco: Identity and Transformation*, pp.131–63, at p.131. See above, p. 31, Fig. 1.
[20] Rosemary Mulcahy, *The Decoration of the Royal Basilica of El Escorial* (Cambridge, 1994).

the *Adoration of the Holy Name of Jesus*, apparently painted in commemoration of Lepanto, he would portray Philip II at prayer, alongside his Holy League allies, the pope and the doge (Fig. 8).[21] Although he eventually managed to secure a commission for the Escorial, his *Martyrdom of St Maurice* (Fig. 9) failed to conform to Tridentine notions of religious propriety, and was deemed unsuitable for the basilica. No further royal commissions were to come his way.[22]

Failing to find employment at the Escorial or with the court in Madrid, El Greco had to make do for the time being with Toledo, the city that had lost out to Madrid in 1561 when Philip II decided that the inconveniences of an itinerant court were too great, and that the time had come to find a permanent location for the seat of government. Among its other disadvantages, Toledo, perched high above the River Tagus, was a city of steep and narrow streets, and offered little scope for expansion (Fig. 10).[23]

All the indications are that El Greco went to Toledo as a result of the friendship he had struck up in Rome with Luis de Castilla, who had gravitated into the Farnese circle on his arrival in the city in 1570.[24] Luis, the illegitimate son of Don Diego de Castilla, dean of the Toledo cathedral chapter, was well placed to obtain commissions for El Greco in his native city. In the event, Don Diego commissioned him not only to paint *The Disrobing of Christ* for the cathedral vestiary (Fig. 11), on which El Greco was already at work in early July 1577, but also eight canvases for the main and side altars of a new church to be constructed for the convent of Santo Domingo el Antiguo. These were to be the first commissions in a Spanish career that was to see the artist working in Toledo for the rest of his life.[25]

Although he had made the acquaintance of Spaniards in Rome, nothing would quite have prepared El Greco for the Spain of Philip II, a country in which artists were still looked down upon as no more than artisans. His formation had been Cretan and Italian, and it is significant that he was known in Spain as 'the Greek' in its Italian form, 'Greco'—the name by which he came

---

[21] For the iconographical background of this painting, and its interpretation, see David Davis, ed., *El Greco* (National Gallery, London, 2003), catalogue entry no. 22.

[22] Mulcahy, *The Decoration*, p. 65. There is a considerable literature on the unfavourable reaction of the king to this work.

[23] Various possible reasons for Philip's selection of Madrid are discussed in Alfredo Alvar Ezquerra, *Felipe II, la Corte y Madrid en 1561* (Madrid, 1985).

[24] For El Greco's move to Toledo, see Pita Andrade, 'El Greco in Spain', in Álvarez Lopera, ed., *El Greco: Identity and Transformation*, p. 134, and Jonathan Brown, 'El Greco and Toledo', in *El Greco of Toledo* (Toledo, Ohio, 1982), ch. 2, pp. 94–5.

[25] For the Santo Domingo el Antiguo commission, see Richard Mann, *El Greco and his Patrons* (Cambridge, 1986), ch. 1.

Figure 8 El Greco, *The Adoration of the Name of Jesus* (Monasterio de El Escorial, Madrid).

to be known in Italy—rather than in its Spanish form (which would have been 'El Griego'), as might have been expected once he had settled in Castile. The parish register of Santo Tomé in Toledo records his death in 1614 under the name of 'Dominico Greco',[26] but he himself, even in his last years, was still signing his pictures in cursive Greek letters either with his initials or else as *Domenikos Theotokopoulos* in full. Although he had learnt enough Spanish by 1582 to be able to act as an interpreter in a case before the Inquisition involving a fellow Greek accused of Islamic practices,[27] he remained, in Spain as elsewhere, something of an outsider, a native of Candia to the end.

The Spain of the 1570s was still basking in the afterglow of Lepanto, and Philip II was the most powerful monarch in Christendom. In 1580, on the extinction of the native royal line, the kingdom of Portugal would be added to his dominions, and the combined Spanish and Portuguese empires stretched round the globe. Vast quantities of silver were flowing in to Seville each year from Spain's viceroyalties of Mexico and Peru, and, in the nervous eyes of her enemies or her uneasy allies, the Spain of Philip II was on the road to universal monarchy.[28] But problems were accumulating for Philip, not least in northern Europe, where the Protestant Dutch rebels were consolidating their position, and Elizabethan England was proving to be an increasingly aggressive and formidable power on the high seas.

Castile, the heart of Spain's Monarchy and empire, saw itself as the Lord's chosen nation and the champion of His cause. But, to retain the divine favour, its religious orthodoxy must be impeccable. Philip II had been prompt to announce his acceptance of the Tridentine decrees, and strenuous efforts were made to raise the educational standards of the clergy, improve the morals and spiritual awareness of the lay population and standardise devotional practices to conform to the new criteria. The religious orders were to be the active instruments of this Catholic reformation, while an intrusive Inquisition vetted books for any expression of heretical propositions, and maintained a network of informers on the lookout for any hint of religious deviation.[29]

Spiritual confidence was therefore accompanied by a deeply defensive mentality which detected enemies at every turn. At the beginning of Philip II's

---

[26] Andrade, 'El Greco in Spain', p. 162.

[27] Andrés, *Helenistas*, p. 101.

[28] A general account of Spain in this period is to be found in J. H. Elliott, *Imperial Spain, 1469–1716* (London, 1963; repr., 2002).

[29] For a succinct and up-to-date account of the Church and religious policy in Spain in this period, see Helen Rawlings, *Church, Religion and Society in Early Modern Spain* (Basingstoke, 2002).

Figure 9 El Greco, *The Martyrdom of St Maurice* (Monasterio de El Escorial, Madrid).

Figure 10 El Greco, *View and Plan of Toledo* (Museo Casa del Greco, Toledo).

reign, 'Lutheran' cells had been discovered and eradicated in Valladolid and Seville, and nobody was safe, not even the primate of Spain. In 1558 the archbishop of Toledo, the Dominican friar Bartolomé de Carranza, was arrested by the Inquisition on the charge of promulgating heresies in a book of *Commentaries* on the catechism. Carranza's orthodoxy was defended before the Inquisition by a distinguished group of supporters, including Don Diego de Castilla, who described him as 'an excellent prelate', and who, as dean of Toledo cathedral, was effectively in charge of it during the archbishop's long imprisonment. Carranza died in Rome in 1576, the year before El Greco's arrival in Toledo, having abjured sixteen suspect propositions, but without being able to return to his see.[30] In the absence of an archbishop the cause of ecclesiastical reform in the archdiocese lagged, and it was left to Carranza's successor, the Inquisitor General Gaspar de Quiroga, to push ahead with the

---

[30] José Ignacio Tellechea Idígoras, *El arzobispo Carranza y su tiempo*, 2 vols (Madrid, 1968), i, p. 80, and Mann, *El Greco and his Patrons*, pp. 6–8.

Figure 11 El Greco, *The Disrobing of Christ* (Upton House, Warwickshire).

work of Counter-Reformation during a tenure that lasted until 1594, although he too was largely an absentee, spending most of his time at court.[31]

The religious purity of Spain was seen to be threatened not only by Protestants whose heresies infiltrated the peninsula through subversive literature but also by the activities of Moors and alleged crypto-Jews. The subjugation of the rebellious moriscos of Granada in 1570 had been followed by their dispersal throughout Castile, a move that only served to exacerbate the problem by spreading northwards the presumed contagion of Islamic beliefs and practices, and creating new pockets of a largely unassimilated ethnic group in Castilian cities like Toledo. Some forty years later, in 1609–11, the government of Philip II's son and successor, Philip III, adopted a radical solution to the festering morisco question by ordering the expulsion from Spain of the entire morisco population, some 300,000 strong.[32]

Once the internal threat from Protestantism had been eradicated, the taint of 'judaising' had moved to the top of the Inquisition's list of concerns. Practising Jews had been expelled from Spain in 1492, but many had converted to Christianity both before and at the time of the expulsion. Unlike the moriscos, who usually held lowly occupations, many of the descendants of these Jews, the so-called *conversos,* or 'new Christians', occupied important positions both in Church and state. In sixteenth-century Toledo *conversos* were to be found in the flourishing merchant community, the cathedral chapter and on the city council.[33] But in 1547, against strong opposition from the dean of the cathedral chapter, Diego de Castilla, Cardinal-Archbishop Siliceo pushed through the chapter a statute of *limpieza de sangre* (purity of blood), excluding from ecclesiastical offices and benefices anyone with a trace of Jewish lineage over four generations. In 1566 the Crown imposed a similar statute on the Toledo city council.[34]

While many descendants of converted Jews succeeded in concealing their family origins by the use of forged genealogies, change of surname and extensive bribery, the spread *of limpieza* statutes in the Castile of Philip II inevitably heightened tensions in a society where the authorities were obsessively preoccupied

---

[31] Richard L. Kagan, 'The Toledo of El Greco', in *El Greco of Toledo,* ch. 1, pp. 54–6.

[32] Bernard Vincent and Antonio Domínguez Ortiz, *Historia de los moriscos* (Madrid, 1978).

[33] Linda Martz, '*Converso* Families in Fifteenth- and Sixteenth-Century Toledo: The Significance of Lineage', *Sefarad,* 48 (1988), pp. 117–96. See also Linda Martz, *A Network of Converso Families in Early Modern Toledo: Assimilating a Minority* (Ann Arbor, Mich. 2003).

[34] Albert A. Sicroff, *Les Controverses des statuts de 'pureté de sang' en Espagne du XVe au XVIIe siècle* (Paris, 1960), chs 3 and 4; see also Linda Martz, 'Pure Blood Statutes in Sixteenth-Century Toledo: Implementation as Opposed to Adoption', *Sefarad,* 54 (1994), pp. 83–107.

with the purity and preservation of the Catholic faith. In a religious climate characterised by repression, growing dogmatism and an insistence on conformity,
humanist scholarship found itself under pressure, heterodox opinions went
underground and highly charged spiritual energy, like that of Saint Teresa—
herself of Jewish ancestry—was not only channelled into public and private
devotion, acts of charity and religious reform, but also found an outlet in the
upsurge of mystical writing that was to be one of the glories of the age.

There is no evidence that El Greco himself had any contact with these
mystical currents or was affected by their influence, but the city in which he
had taken up residence was at the centre of the Spanish Counter-Reformation.
Now that the court had moved to Madrid, Toledo, with a population of some
60,000 inhabitants, was heavily dominated by its ecclesiastical establishment,
although it retained a strong artisan base, consisting primarily of silk and
other textile workers. The 1591 census recorded 739 secular clergy, and 1,942
members of the religious orders, of whom 1,399 were women.[35] The cathedral
alone, with forty canons, had a staff of almost six hundred.[36] The Church was
ubiquitous in this city, and members of the civic elite, who were proud of the
Roman and imperial heritage of their native city, and keen to modernise and
beautify its public buildings, were no less concerned to found and adorn
churches, chapels and convents, which would help to win them a place in
heaven and perpetuate their memory on earth.

As an itinerant foreign artist in search of employment El Greco, therefore,
had chosen his city well, even if he had done so more by accident than design.
Above all, Toledo offered the promise of patronage, both clerical and that of
an educated civic elite. Patrons, or potential patrons, naturally wanted altarpieces for their churches and chapels, and religious pictures for private devotion, and a number of them, too, wanted their portraits painted. However,
while religion was all-pervasive in late sixteenth-century Toledo, and shaped
the character and direction of El Greco's artistic production, the nature and
extent of his own religious commitment are difficult to determine. The
demand for devotional works and altarpieces meant that there was ample
scope for a skilled and accommodating artist, although El Greco, as his Italian
career had already suggested and his Spanish career was to confirm, was the
least accommodating of men. With unconventional and vehemently expressed
views about the visual arts, and an exalted opinion of the artist's calling and

---

[35] Linda Martz, *Poverty and Welfare in Habsburg Spain* (Cambridge, 1983), pp. 98–9.
[36] Richard L. Kagan, 'El Greco y su entorno humano en Toledo', in *El Greco. Obras maestras* (Amigos del Museo del Prado, Madrid, 2003).

his own personal worth, he was quick to engage in litigation and antagonise his patrons. In spite of this, he received enough commissions for altarpieces to keep his studio working, and gradually built up a circle of discerning clients and admirers who appreciated his artistic genius and were prepared to pay for paintings that defied conventional tastes.[37]

These clients and admirers included some of the most learned and intelligent members of Toledo's elite—not only clerics but also merchants, lawyers and professors in the city's university of Santa Catalina. The city could boast several distinguished scholars with classical, philological and historical interests, and there was a particular enthusiasm at this time for the collecting and editing of Greek texts, especially those relating to the early Church councils—a subject of keen interest in a city whose church enjoyed ecclesiastical primacy in Spain, and which was to be the seat of a reforming provincial council in 1582. A number of Greeks were living in Toledo in El Greco's time, some of whom found part-time employment transcribing these texts. Among them was a fellow Cretan, Antonio Calosinás, brought back for this purpose from the Council of Trent by two of Toledo's most distinguished citizens, the brothers Antonio and Diego de Covarrubias, both of them royal councillors.[38] Antonio de Covarrubias, who was later to become a canon of the cathedral and *maestrescuela*, or rector of the university, was to be El Greco's closest known friend (Fig. 12).[39]

It was among such people—scholars, collectors and connoisseurs—that this proud foreigner seems to have felt most at home. His intellectual approach to the arts made their company congenial to him, while they admired his virtuosity. As they sang his praises, so his fame began to spread. This in turn won him new commissions, but the money was never sufficient to pay for the opulent lifestyle to which he felt himself entitled, and which included paid musicians to entertain him at his meals.[40] Conspicuous consumption, however, was nothing unusual in the Spain of Philip II and Philip III. Not only individuals but the whole country lived beyond its means. Yet at least during El Greco's lifetime Toledo remained a prosperous city. It was only in the two or three decades following his death in 1614 that its population began to dwindle and its industries to decline.[41]

Toledo may not have been what El Greco had in mind as his final destination when he left Candia on his westward journey in 1567, but, as a second

---

[37] Kagan, 'El Greco y su entorno'; see also Marías, *Greco*, ch. 5.
[38] Andrés, *Helenistas*, pp. 32 and 36.
[39] Marías, *Greco*, pp. 166–8; see also Kagan, 'The Toledo of El Greco', p. 64.
[40] Marías, *Greco*, p. 178.
[41] Kagan, 'The Toledo of El Greco', p. 40.

Figure 12 El Greco, *Antonio de Covarrubias* (Musée du Louvre, Paris).

best to the courts of popes and kings, the city had its compensations. His travels had brought him to the very heart of Counter-Reformation Spain, to a country and a city with the spiritual energy and material resources to provide an environment that gave him a degree of acceptance, and sufficient employment to provide him with a living. Above all, it offered him the opportunity and the stimulus to resolve with supreme originality the artistic problems arising from the personal encounter of a painter formed in the Greek tradition with the art and artists of the Latin West. In Toledo, as in Rome, the worlds of classical scholarship and Counter-Reformation spirituality met and interacted. In Toledo, as in Venice and his native Candia, Christianity was brought face to face with the potentially galvanising presence of competing traditions and survivals, both Jewish and Moorish. Here, in the imperial city of Toledo, at the conclusion of his long journey through the kaleidoscopic worlds of the sixteenth-century Mediterranean, the uniquely personal world of El Greco at last fell into place.

CHAPTER XIII

COURT SOCIETY IN SEVENTEENTH-CENTURY EUROPE: MADRID, BRUSSELS, LONDON

'. . . I have a horror of courts . . .' wrote Peter Paul Rubens in March 1636 to his French friend Nicolas-Claude Fabri de Peiresc.[1] It was a subject on which Rubens could speak with considerable authority. His experience of courts included the court of the Duke of Mantua in the first years of the century; the Spanish court, first at Valladolid in 1603 and then in Madrid in 1628–9; the court of Louis XIII of France in 1622, where he was working for the Queen Mother, Marie de Médicis; the court of Charles I of England 1629–30; and, most of all, the Brussels court of his revered sovereigns the 'Archdukes' Albert and Isabella, who appointed him their court painter in 1609. Whether Rubens liked it or not, his life was profoundly shaped by court life. So too were the lives of his younger contemporaries, both of them born in 1599: Anthony Van Dyck, who over a period of ten years sampled a variety of courts before settling in London in 1632 as Principal Painter in Ordinary to Charles I,[2] and Diego de Velázquez, who spent thirty-seven of the sixty-one years of his life in the court of Spain, with interruptions only for his Italian tours in 1629–30 and 1648–51, which took him to the papal court and to the courts of a number of Italian princes.

Rubens's 'horror of courts' was no doubt deep and genuine, at least at certain moments in the course of his long career. But it was also typical of a conventional European discourse, of which Antonio de Guevara's *Menosprecio*

---

[1] Rubens to Nicolas-Claude Fabri de Peiresc, 16 March 1636, in Ruth Saunders Magurn, ed., *The Letters of Peter Paul Rubens* (Cambridge, Mass., 1955), p. 402.
[2] Michael Levy, *Painting at Court* (London, 1971), p. 126.

de corte y alabanza de aldea (1539) provides a good example. The discourse drew a sharp contrast between the ambition, intrigue and corruption that characterised court life, and the alleged simplicity and innocence of a quiet life in the country. In theory, this court–country dichotomy ran right through early modern European society; in practice, the dividing line was blurred. Courtiers and great nobles moved to and fro between court and country, while monarchs periodically retreated to country residences to devote themselves to hunting and other rural pursuits, as a break from the constricting ceremonial of court life. Meanwhile, readers in the country avidly followed the news of the court in the *avisos*, gazettes and newsletters which proliferated in seventeenth-century Europe, in full awareness that distance from the court did not necessarily bring immunity from the consequences of great changes in the lives of princes and their servants. Above all, silken ties of patronage and clientage bound court and country to each other in a network of loyalty, friendship and mutual obligation.

However much its manners and morals might be criticised and condemned by those on the outside, the court was inescapably at the centre of the political, social and cultural life of the monarchical societies of seventeenth-century Europe. It was, first of all, the home of the sovereign, whose household servants formed the core of court society. The total number of household officials and service staff on the Spanish court books in 1623 was around 1,700.[3] The household staff of the court of Charles I of England numbered over 1,800.[4] In addition to being the seat of the monarch, the court was also the centre of his government. This meant that court society extended beyond the household to include councillors, royal secretaries and a host of officials, most of whose business was transacted within the precincts of the palace—the Alcázar in Madrid, Whitehall in London and the Coudenberg in Brussels (Figs 13, 14 and 15). On the fringes of the court, too, were the innumerable petitioners who had come in search of offices, honours or pensions, and hung around the palace in the hope of obtaining an audience and some recognition—usually belated—of real or imagined services. Finally, the court was an educational and cultural centre, which acted as a magnet for aspiring young nobles anxious to polish their manners and catch their sovereign's eye, and for poets, playwrights and artists in search of commissions and patronage.

---

[3] See 'The Court of the Spanish Habsburgs: A Peculiar Institution?', in J. H. Elliott, *Spain and its World, 1500–1700* (New Haven, Conn. and London, 1989), pp. 144–5.
[4] G. E. Aylmer, *The King's Servants* (London, 1961), p. 27.

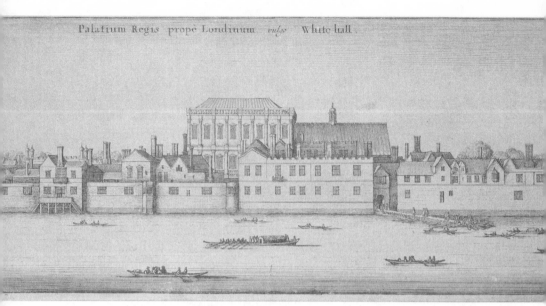

Palatium Regis prope Londinum vulgo White hall.

Figure 13 Wenceslaus Hollar, *View of the Palace of Whitehall from Across The Thames* (British Museum, London).

Figure 14 Attributed to Félix Castelo, *View of the Alcázar Palace in Madrid* (Museo Municipal, Madrid).

Figure 15 Anon., *The Palace of Coudenberg* (Museo del Prado, Madrid).

In all these capacities the court was also a spectacular centre of conspicuous consumption, providing employment for an urban population of artisans, tradesmen and servants which had grown up around it in response to the needs of the elite and their dependants. Of the three court cities of Madrid, Brussels and London, two—Madrid and Brussels—were to a substantial degree created by their courts. When Philip II chose Madrid as the permanent seat of his court in 1561, it was a small town of no more than 10,000 inhabitants at the heart of the Castilian *meseta*, or tableland. By the end of the sixteenth century its population had risen to 90,000. Numbers fell to around 70,000 following the removal of the court to Valladolid in 1601, but the population rapidly picked up after the court's return to Madrid in 1606, and by 1630 had reached around 130,000—a figure at which it remained until well into the eighteenth century.[5] The emergence of Madrid was preceded by that of Brussels, which effectively became a capital city in 1531 when Mary of Hungary, Charles V's governor of the Netherlands, moved there from Malines.[6] When the archdukes, as sovereign rulers of the southern Netherlands, established their court in Brussels in

---

[5] For the growth of Madrid, see José Ignacio Fortea Pérez, ed., *Imágenes de la diversidad. El mundo urbano en la corona de Castilla* (Universidad de Cantabria, 1997), pp. 155–6; Alfredo Alvar Ezquerra, *El nacimiento de una capital europea. Madrid entre 1561 y 1606* (Madrid, 1989); David R. Ringrose, *Madrid and the Spanish Economy, 1560–1850* (Berkeley/Los Angeles, Calif. and London, 1983).

[6] Ghislaine de Boom, *Marie de Hongrie* (Brussels, 1956), p. 55.

1599, the city was still overshadowed by Rubens's native Antwerp. But as the economy and civic life began to revive after the troubles of the later sixteenth century, Brussels attracted a growing number of inhabitants, estimated at 50,000 in 1615 (almost as many as Antwerp) and 78,000 by 1709.[7]

For size of population, however, London was in a class of its own, with some 200,000 inhabitants in 1600, and an astonishing 400,000 in 1650.[8] As a port city, it had a vigorous commercial and urban life of its own, and was less dependent than Brussels and Madrid on the presence of court and government. But they greatly added to London's attractiveness as a centre of entertainment and consumption. By the reign of Charles I it was customary for many country gentry to winter in town; handsome new town houses were under construction, with the city fast expanding into the suburbs to accommodate growing numbers of seasonal or permanent immigrants; and the nobility and gentry acquired a taste for pleasure gardens and parks, transforming Hyde Park, which was still used for hunting in the reign of James I, into a parade ground for their coaches during the reign of his son.[9] The same period saw the embellishment of Madrid as a capital city, as leading members of the nobility built themselves extensive residences surrounded by gardens on the eastern outskirts, and the fashionable world flocked to the Prado de San Jerónimo to take the evening air.

Court cities might differ in size and character, but the courts themselves showed marked similarities. To see one court was, in some ways, to see them all, for the courts of early modern Europe necessarily shared the same essential characteristics. They all revolved around the persons of the monarch and the royal family, and they depended for their smooth functioning on a set of conventions which had crystallised over time into a more or less rigid set of rules governing ceremonial and etiquette. Regularity and repetition were the essence of court life, providing a decorum that was regarded as essential to the conservation of majesty. The Duke of Alba, in a letter to Philip II's secretary, Mateo Vázquez, commented approvingly on the king's request for an account in writing of 'everything relating to the ordering of his household and its cere-monial . . . and also the ceremonial that concerns his royal person'. 'Sir, it seems

---

[7] Figures given in Herman Van der Wee, ed., *The Rise and Decline of Urban Industries in Italy and in the Low Countries* (Louvain, 1988), p. 217. Antwerp had just under 54,000 inhabitants in 1612; see J. A.Van Houtte, 'Economie et societé aux Pays-Bas à l'époque de Rubens', in 'Colloque Rubens', *Bulletin de l'institut historique belge de Rome*, fascicule xlviii–xlix (Brussels and Rome, 1978–9), p. 197.
[8] E. A.Wrigley, 'A Simple Model of London's Importance in Changing English Society and Economy, 1650–1750', *Past and Present*, 37 (1967), pp. 44–70.
[9] See F. J. Fisher, *London and the English Economy, 1500–1700* (London, 1990), ch. 6.

to me very necessary', he wrote, 'that this should both be understood and written down, because in the households of princes it is appropriate that the same customs should always be observed, because their antiquity impresses, and it is impossible to conserve this if they are not written down.'[10] Rules of court etiquette, once codified, were not easily susceptible of change.

The similarity between courts was further enhanced by the fact that the household arrangements and ceremonial of many of the courts of early modern Europe were derived from the same source—the ducal court of fifteenth-century Burgundy. In England, Henry VII continued the innovations in palace ceremonial that had been made by his fifteenth-century predecessor Edward IV 'after the manner of Burgundy'.[11] In 1548 the Holy Roman Emperor Charles V imposed Burgundian ceremonial on the household of Prince Philip, the heir to the throne of Castile; and thereafter the Spanish court, although retaining some strong Castilian characteristics, would conform in its essentials to the Burgundian model.[12] Similarly, when in 1599 Philip II conferred limited sovereignty over the Spanish Netherlands on his daughter Isabel Clara Eugenia and her husband the Archduke Albert, their court in Brussels was set up in accordance with the Burgundian tradition. It was, however, a Burgundian tradition influenced and modified by half a century of Spanish practices, since they had both spent their formative years in the court of Madrid, and were accompanied to Brussels by most of their Spanish servants and officials.[13]

Rubens, therefore, in moving from one court to another, would quickly have found himself at home. There were much the same types of palace officers in each, with the same, or very similar, titles and sets of duties; a court ceremonial

---

[10] British Library, Additional Ms. 28,361, fos 11–12, Duke of Alba to Mateo Vázquez, 15 November 1579.

[11] A. G. Dickens, ed., *The Courts of Europe* (London, 1977), p. 148.

[12] See Elliott, *Spain and its World*, ch. 7 ('The Court of the Spanish Habsburgs'), and M. J. Rodríguez-Salgado, 'The Court of Philip II of Spain', in Ronald G. Asch and Adolf M. Birke, eds, *Princes, Patronage and the Nobility* (Oxford, 1991), pp. 205–44, as also her 'Honour and Profit in the Court of Philip II of Spain', in Maurice Aymard and Marzio A. Romani, eds, *La Cour comme institution économique* (Douzième Congrès International d'Histoire Economique, 1998), pp. 67–86. For a general survey of ceremonial and court culture in the courts of early modern Europe, which updates and complements rather than supplements Dickens, ed., *The Courts of Europe*, see John Adamson, ed., *The Princely Courts of Europe: Ritual, Politics and Culture under the Ancien Régime 1500–1700* (London, 1999). Jeroen Duindam in *Myths of Power* (Amsterdam, 1995) perceptively examines recent scholarship on early modern court culture, much of which was originally inspired by the seminal, if flawed, work of Norbert Elias, translated into English as *The Court Society* (Oxford, 1983).

[13] For the court of the 'Archdukes', see especially Diederick Lanoye, 'Structure and Composition of the Household of the Archdukes', in Werner Thomas and Luc Duerloo, eds, *Albert and Isabella, 1598–1621* (Royal Museums of Art and History, Brussels, 1998), pp. 107–19.

with many of the same practices; and even the layout of the palaces possessed many similar features, as modifications were introduced to provide a sequence of rooms that would meet the ceremonial requirements of the Burgundian-Habsburg court system. The essentials of this system can be deduced both from registers of household servants, and from the household ordinances and rules of etiquette that were periodically issued in order to clarify procedures or modify those currently in operation.[14] The prime purpose of these ordinances and of the procedures and arrangements which they established was to ensure the dignity and safety of a sovereign who was regarded as the vice-regent of God on earth. They were therefore designed to set the ruler apart—a process that was to be carried to its extreme in Spain, where Philip II established a tradition of semi-hidden kingship that was to be perpetuated by his seventeenth-century successors. To reach the monarch's inner sanctum, the *aposento*, it was necessary to pass through a succession of rooms: the large *salón* or *sala*; the *saleta*, the *antecámara* and the *antecamarilla*.[15] Access to these various rooms was regulated by strict rules, dictated by considerations of rank and office, and the ruler was shielded from the world by a group of court functionaries, each with his own carefully defined palace duties.

The three principal functionaries in the courts of Madrid, Brussels and London were the *mayordomo mayor*, or Lord High Steward, responsible for feeding and housing the sovereign; the *camarero mayor*, or Grand Chamberlain, a post that lapsed in Spain, where his duties of attending to the personal service of the ruler were taken over by the *sumiller de corps* or Groom of the Stole until the Count-Duke of Olivares revived the office in his own person in 1636; and the *caballerizo mayor*, or Master of the Horse, who was in charge of the sovereign's stables and transportation. In addition, the royal chaplain, *capellán mayor*, had overall responsibility for the services in the royal chapel and was in charge of the chapel musicians. The organisation of the king's household was replicated in the household of the queen, and in that of the heir to the throne when he became of age to have a household of his own.

---

[14] For Spanish court ceremonial, in addition to the articles cited in note 12, see Antonio Rodríguez Villa, *Etiquetas de la casa de Austria* (Madrid, 1913) and Christina Hofmann, *Das Spanische Hofzeremoniell von 1500–1700* (Frankfurt am Main, 1985). See also Yves Bottineau, 'Aspects de la cour d'Espagne au XVIIe siècle. L'étiquette de la chambre du roi', *Bulletin hispanique*, 74 (1972), pp. 128–57. For the English court as reformed by Charles I, see Kevin Sharpe, *The Personal Rule of Charles I* (New Haven, Conn. and London, 1992), pp. 210–22, and Albert J. Loomie, ed., *Ceremonies of Charles I: The Note Books of John Finet, Master of Ceremonies, 1628–1641* (New York, 1987).
[15] Ludwig Pfandl, 'Philipp II und die Einführung des burgundischen Hofzeremoniells in Spanien', *Historisches Jahrbuch*, 58 (1938), pp. 1–33.

Each of the three great household officials was in charge of his own extensive staff of functionaries. The most coveted posts were those that brought their occupants into closest contact with the sovereign. Competition was therefore especially acute among the nobility for the posts of *mayordomos* (twelve in number in the Spanish court in 1623), *gentileshombres de la casa*, or gentlemen of the household (eighteen on active duty, and another twenty-five who had formerly served and possessed right of entry), and *gentileshombres de la boca* (forty-seven) who served at the royal table. The supreme symbol of access to the royal person was the golden key, and Velázquez's first portrait, painted in 1624, of the Count-Duke of Olivares (Fig. 16) displays prominently the key with which he was entrusted in his capacity as *sumiller de corps*. There was, however, another, if lesser, palace official who enjoyed unique control of the keys. This was the *aposentador mayor de palacio*, the post to which Velázquez would be appointed in 1652. As *aposentador mayor* he was responsible both for the cleanliness and the interior decoration of the palace—a duty that, as exercised by Velázquez, carried with it a wide range of obligations and opportunities[16]—and he not only issued the key to the king's chamber to *gentileshombres de la casa* and the Assistants in the Privy Chamber, *ayudas de cámara*, but also kept in his own pocket a double key which opened all the palace apartments.[17] No doors were closed to Velázquez in the Alcázar of Madrid.

There were, however, a great many doors through which to pass. The Alcázar, the Coudenberg and the palace of Whitehall were like rabbit warrens, added to and modified over time in response to changing needs. Having decided to make Madrid the capital of his Monarchy, Philip II made major structural alterations to the Alcázar, in order to provide it with the private apartments and the grand public rooms that were required by the new Burgundian ceremonial.[18] It remained, however, an inconvenient building. The combination of royal residence with government offices caused continuous confusion, and one reason for the decision taken by the Duke of Lerma to transfer the court to Valladolid in 1601 was to give the king greater seclusion by separating the two.[19] When the Valladolid experiment failed and the court returned to Madrid in 1606, further remodelling was undertaken by the court architects, Francisco

---

[16] See Jonathan Brown, *Velázquez: Painter and Courtier* (New Haven, Conn. and London, 1986), p. 190.
[17] Rodríguez Villa, *Etiquetas*, p. 36.
[18] Rodríguez-Salgado, 'The Court of Philip II', pp. 212–13; Véronique Gerard, *De castillo a palacio. El Alcázar de Madrid en el siglo XVI* (Bilbao, 1984).
[19] See Antonio Feros, *Kingship and Favoritism in the Spain of Philip III, 1598–1621* (Cambridge, 2000), pp. 87–90.

Figure 16 Velázquez, *Count-Duke of Olivares* (Museu de Arte de São Paulo).

de Mora and Juan Gómez de Mora, and the southern facade was reconstructed to give it a more impressive appearance and to provide a new suite of state rooms. But no amount of remodelling could transform the old Alcázar into a palace that conformed to more modern tastes and needs, and it was only with the decision in the 1630s to construct the new pleasure-palace and gardens of the Buen Retiro as a royal retreat on the eastern outskirts of Madrid that these requirements were to some extent satisfied (see Fig. 23).[20]

In Brussels, Archduke Albert began extensive remodelling of the governor's residence on the Coudenberg even before the official entry of the archdukes into the city in 1599.[21] Again it was a question of adapting an old building to meet the requirements of contemporary Spanish court ceremonial. With considerable difficulty a set of state rooms was created on the first floor, with access carefully controlled according to rank, while the Infanta Isabella, as befitted her status as reigning consort, was housed in a suite with an identical number of rooms on the floor above. During the first two decades of the century the archdukes' 'architect generael', Wenzel Coerbergher, was involved in a constant process of embellishment and modernisation of the residence. This work of improvement formed part of a great programme of reconstruction and renovation of the old imperial residences, hunting lodges and gardens, on which the archdukes embarked in order to affirm their status as independent sovereigns ruling over a southern Netherlands with an identity and coherence of its own.

The palace of Whitehall, a rambling series of Tudor buildings, no more lent itself to satisfactory modernisation than the Alcázar and the Coudenberg. But in 1619 fire destroyed the old banqueting house. James I, with his eyes on a possible Spanish marriage for his son and heir, Charles, Prince of Wales, and the need for a ceremonial hall for the celebration of this and other great state occasions, ordered the Surveyor of the King's Works, Inigo Jones, to replace the old hall with a new one. Within three years a handsome new Banqueting House had arisen, the first great building to be completed in England in the Italianate manner of Palladio.[22] Stylistically it stood in splendid isolation,

---

[20] Jonathan Brown and John H. Elliott, *A Palace for a King: The Buen Retiro and the Court of Philip IV*, revised and expanded edn. (New Haven, Conn. and London, 2003).

[21] For the reconstruction of the Coudenberg, see Krista de Jonge et al., 'Building Policy and Urbanisation during the Reign of the Archdukes', in Thomas and Duerloo, eds, *Albert and Isabella*, pp. 191–219.

[22] For a study of the construction of the Banqueting House and its decorative programme, see Per Palme, *Triumph of Peace: A Study of the Whitehall Banqueting House* (Stockholm, 1956).

sharply contrasting with Whitehall's Tudor buildings, but Jones may well have conceived it as the first stage of a grand scheme for a new Whitehall that would be appropriate to James I's exalted vision of the divine majesty of kingship. The construction of this new Whitehall was to be a continuing dream of his son, Charles I, who succeeded him on the throne in 1625. There was never sufficient money to embark on the project, but the king was still to be seen in 1647, by then a captive in the hands of parliament, brooding over plans for his grandiose new palace, which would have been twice the size of the Escorial.[23]

These various projects for the updating and embellishment of old palaces and the construction of new ones were visible expressions of important political, social and cultural developments in Europe during the opening decades of the seventeenth century. The last years of the closing century and the first years of the new one were characterised by a gradual return to peace in Europe after decades of war: peace between France and Spain in 1598; between Spain and England in 1604; and a twelve-year truce between Spain and the nascent Dutch Republic in 1609. One important result of the return to peace was an increase in foreign travel and trade. During the long period of Anglo-Spanish conflict in the later sixteenth century, direct contacts between Spain and England had been few, and each country had relied for knowledge of the other on espionage and second-hand reports. With the coming of peace in 1604, however, trade was re-established and diplomatic relations restored. In 1605 a huge English embassy, led by the Earl of Nottingham, and consisting of five hundred nobles, gentlemen and their servants, arrived in Spain to witness the ratification by Philip III of the recent peace treaty. They were given a magnificent reception in Valladolid, and were treated to a round of festivities in the course of which no pains were spared to impress upon them the wealth and splendour of the Spanish court. While Spain would never equal the attraction of Italy for seventeenth-century British travellers, Nottingham's embassy opened a new phase of Anglo-Spanish relations, bringing closer contacts between the two countries and their courts— contacts that would culminate in the incognito journey of Charles, Prince of Wales, to Madrid in 1623 to seek the hand of the Infanta Maria.[24]

The return to peace also made it possible for the states of western Europe to reduce their military expenses, thus releasing funds for other, less aggressive, pursuits. The first two decades of the seventeenth century, in Spain and England

---

[23] Sharpe, *The Personal Rule of Charles I*, pp. 212–13; Roy Strong, *Britannia Triumphans: Inigo Jones, Rubens and Whitehall Palace* (London, 1980); and see above pp. 30–1.
[24] For Nottingham's embassy and English travellers in Spain, see John Stoye, *English Travellers Abroad, 1604–1667*, revised edn (New Haven, Conn. and London, 1989), ch. 10.

alike, were to be decades of lavish court expenditure. Vast sums were poured into banquets, masques and other court festivities, while courtiers competed in the richness of their clothing, their jewellery and the ostentation of their tables. Tomé Pinheiro da Veiga, a Portuguese visitor to the Spanish court in Valladolid, describes with amazement the lavish banquets laid on by the great nobility: 'Some lords have supremely grand kitchens, in which you can find at any season everything you want. People come to them from outside the city to sell fresh-water fish, salmon, beef, grapes and other fruits out of season . . . and there are more than 150 of these kitchens in Valladolid. All this is needed if they are to spend their immense revenues. They can spend 200,000 *cruzados* and still fall into debt, as they all do, like the Duke of Medina Sidonia with an income of 300,000 *cruzados* and the Duke of Osuna with 150,000, and all the others with incomes hardly any smaller. To spend this kind of money one needs the inventiveness of the kings of Egypt when they built pyramids on the sand. . . .'[25]

To some extent this wave of extravagance in the early seventeenth century may have stemmed not only from the new accessibility of capital and credit but also from a sense of psychological release brought about both by peace and by dynastic change. In 1597, anticipating the death of the ailing Philip II, the Duke of Feria wrote presciently: 'without him we shall be on another stage, as the saying goes, and all the actors in the play will be different.'[26] When Philip died in the following year, the scene-shifters moved in, and new men did indeed appear on centre stage. There was now a young king, Philip III, and every prospect of a livelier court than that of the deceased monarch in his later years. In England, too, the death of Elizabeth in 1603 and her replacement by a male ruler, James VI of Scotland, with a wife and young family, meant a radical change in the character of the court. New monarchs meant new ministers and favourites, and new hopes and expectations. Similarly, in the Spanish Netherlands, the arrival of the Archdukes Albert and Isabella held out the prospect of a new beginning, not least because effectively they were having to build a new country on the ruins of the old.

The nobilities of Spain, Britain and the Netherlands all sought to take advantage of the change of regime. Across the continent illustrious noble families were heavily indebted, and were looking to the Crown for the payment of their debts and the restoration of their fortunes, while aspiring provincial

---

[25] Tomé Pinheiro da Veiga, *Fastiginia. Vida cotidiana en la corte de Valladolid,* Spanish trans. Narciso Alonso Cortés (Valladolid, 1989), pp. 204–5.
[26] Archive of the Archbishopric of Westminster, Ms. E2, fo.15, Duke of Feria to Thomas Fitzherbert, 28 February 1597.

nobles were eager to obtain a share of the spoils. The court therefore became the scene of a new round of intense struggles among noble factions for influence over the monarch, with important consequences for the character of court life. In order to be close to the seat of power, increasing numbers of nobles felt it necessary to acquire temporary or permanent accommodation in the proximity of the court. One highly visible result was the influx of nobles into capital cities, where they rented or built town houses and took up residence for part or most of the year. The convergence of nobles and gentry on the court was an accelerating process, and in Spain the return of the court from Valladolid to Madrid in 1606 marked the beginnings of what has been described as 'an irreversible domestication in the court of the high nobility'. The influx became an avalanche in the 1630s as the economic problems of nobles and gentry multiplied. By the last third of the seventeenth century over two hundred titled nobles were resident in Madrid.[27]

The governments of Philip III and James I were dismayed by the rapid growth of their capital cities, and sought in vain to check a process that threatened grave social dislocation and raised major problems both of provisioning and of public order. The English Privy Council spoke in 1613 of the 'inconveniences which cannot be avoided by the swelling multitudes of people . . . drawn hither from all parts of the kingdom', and published proclamations against the construction of new buildings or the subdivision of old ones.[28] The Council of Castile made repeated attempts to clear the court of its horde of parasites and to halt the depopulation of the countryside by ordering nobles and other persons of quality to return to their estates. In the words of the Junta for Reform of 1619: 'those who should leave are the grandees and lords, together with the gentry and people of similar quality, along with the large number of very rich and powerful widows, and others who are less rich but have come to court with no good cause or on some specious pretext, and also many ecclesiastics whose obligation is to reside in their benefices.'[29]

While the decision of nobles to take up residence in the neighbourhood of the court might be a source of grave concern to governments, it brought to capital cities substantial new spending power, with potentially beneficial consequences for the vitality of urban life. In the first third of the seventeenth

---

[27] José Miguel López Garcia, ed., *El impacto de la corte en Castilla* (Madrid, 1998), pp. 204–5.
[28] Perez Zagorin, *The Court and the Country* (London, 1969), p. 136.
[29] A. González Palencia, *La Junta de Reformación* (Valladolid, 1932), pp. 22–3.

century, for instance, the combined revenues of the nobles resident in Madrid totalled 3.5 million ducats, an average of 33,000 ducats a head, although in practice there were vast inequalities of wealth among the nobility, with incomes ranging from 10,000 or less to the 340,000 of the Duke of Lerma. With much money, too, in the hands of the Crown's bankers, prominent royal officials and the Church and the religious orders, considerable sums were available for the construction of houses and palaces, for the founding and endowment of churches and convents and for urban embellishment. Juan Gómez de Mora's construction of Madrid's new Plaza Mayor between 1617 and 1619 bore witness to this new affluence in a town that was now the capital of a worldwide monarchy, with privileged access to the silver of the Indies.[30]

As Pinheiro da Veiga pointed out, however, the more the nobility spent on conspicuous consumption, the more indebted it became. Growing indebtedness encouraged it to find ways of raiding the royal treasury, but at the same time made it potentially dependent on the favour of the ruler. The Archdukes Albert and Isabella in particular showed considerable skill in turning this potential dependence to their political advantage. The sovereign rights which had been granted them by Philip II included significant powers of patronage, including the power to distribute honours and titles, and to confer membership of the Order of the Golden Fleece. They used these powers of patronage to tie the old nobility of the southern Netherlands to their court.[31] James VI and I, who upon his accession to the English throne in 1603 was followed to London by a hungry horde of Scots nobles and gentlemen eager for English titles and for positions at court, manoeuvred with some success between rival factions, while bestowing special favour on one or two chosen individuals. First there was Robert Carr, whom he created Earl of Somerset, and then the handsome George Villiers, who was to attain great offices of state and reach the highest ranks of the aristocracy as the Duke of Buckingham. Buckingham in turn became a conduit for royal favours, with a widening range of patronage at his disposal. In Spain, where the grandees and titled nobility were pressing hard around the throne, Philip III conferred his favour, and with it extraordinary powers of government, on Francisco Gómez de Sandoval y Rojas, Marquis of Denia, created Duke of Lerma in 1599.

---

[30] For aristocratic incomes, see López García, ed., *El impacto de la corte*, p. 206. For building projects in Philip III's Madrid, see Jesús Escobar, *The Plaza Mayor and the Shaping of Baroque Madrid* (Cambridge, 2003).
[31] See Jonathan Israel, *Conflicts of Empires: Spain, the Low Countries and the Struggle for World Supremacy, 1585–1713* (London, 1997), ch. 1 ('The Court of Albert and Isabella, 1598–1621').

Lerma's elevation to a position of extraordinary preeminence in the court and government, followed some years later by that of Buckingham in England, marked the beginning of a trend of enormous significance for seventeenth-century court life—the rise of the minister-favourite.[32] Exercising, with the consent of Philip III, powers that traditionally formed part of the royal prerogative, including powers of patronage, Lerma dominated a court in which the monarch appeared to have been relegated to the shadows. In the process, he restored the fortunes of his family, the House of Sandoval, built up a wide network of clients and dependants to buttress his position both at court and in the country, and acquired vast revenues which allowed him to spend on a prodigious scale. While he lavished money on hospitality and on court entertainments, he also built or remodelled palaces for himself in Valladolid, Madrid and in his ducal seat of Lerma. He assembled, too, an impressive collection of paintings, for, as Rubens wrote from Valladolid in 1603, 'he is not without knowledge of fine things . . .'.[33]

Lerma's power and wealth put him in a class on his own as a builder and collector, but he was by no means alone. In the courts of early seventeenth-century Madrid, London and Brussels, cultural life acquired a sharp competitive edge as individual nobles and royal officials competed with each other as patrons as well as consumers of culture. On returning in 1615 from the celebration on the border between Spain and France of the Franco-Spanish royal marriages of Louis XIII to Anne of Austria and of her brother Prince Philip to Louis' sister Elizabeth, the Duke of Sessa, flanked by a splendid entourage, entered Madrid with the dramatist and poet Lope de Vega at his side, while the ambitious young Count of Olivares, not to be outdone, was accompanied not by one but two poets.[34] Patronage, too, was often accompanied by increasing sophistication, based on a more informed connoisseurship. This was especially true of Jacobean England, where knowledge of the latest artistic and architectural developments had lagged behind that of continental Europe. In England

---

[32] See J. H. Elliott and L. W. B. Brockliss, *The World of the Favourite* (New Haven, Conn. and London, 1999); and see above, pp. 71–2.

[33] Magurn, ed., *Letters of Peter Paul Rubens*, p. 33 (24 May 1603). For Lerma as a patron of the arts, see Jonathan Brown, *Kings and Connoisseurs* (New Haven, Conn. and London, 1995), pp. 111–14 and Sarah Schroth, 'A New Style of Grandeur: Politics and Patronage at the Court of Philip III', in Sarah Schroth and Ronni Baer, eds, *El Greco to Velázquez: Art during the Reign of Philip III* (Boston, Mass., 2008), pp. 77–120. For Lerma's political career see Patrick Williams, *The Great Favourite* (Manchester, 2006), and, for his manipulation of patronage and clientage systems, see Feros, *Kingship and Favoritism*.

[34] Luis Astrana Marín, ed., *Epistolario completo de Don Francisco de Quevedo Villegas* (Madrid, 1946), letter 10 (21 November 1615).

a wealthy noble, the Earl of Arundel, gave the lead. In 1613 he made an extended tour of the continent in the company of Inigo Jones. His travels took him to Antwerp and Brussels, where he struck up a lasting friendship with Rubens, and then on to Germany and northern Italy, which instilled in him an abiding love of the Venetian school of painting. His continental tour reinforced his position as the arbiter of taste at the English court, and enabled him to become the adviser to a new generation of collectors, including Charles, Prince of Wales, and the Duke of Buckingham.[35]

Arundel's activities point to a feature that was common to the courts of both James I and Philip III. Cultural leadership in both courts came not from the Crown but from a handful of wealthy individuals—Lerma, above all, in Madrid, and Robert Carr (an early British collector of Italian paintings),[36] Arundel and Buckingham in London. There is no indication that either Philip III or James I possessed, or was interested in pursuing, a royal policy favouring the arts, and in so far as any such royal initiative was to be found at the English court, it came from James's elder son, Henry, Prince of Wales, who died prematurely in 1612.[37]

During these first two decades of the seventeenth century only in Brussels was the figure of the sovereign to be found at the heart of cultural life. Partly this reflected Archduke Albert's passionate interest in the visual arts, but it also reflected his determination, together with that of his wife Isabella, to project the splendour of the archducal court as a symbol of the regeneration of the southern Netherlands. Through their ceremonial *Joyeuses entrées* into the different cities of the Netherlands, through their patronage of Netherlands artists like Rubens, Jan Breughel the Elder and Pieter Snayers, through the refurbishment of their palaces, and the construction of the church of Scherpenheuvel as a centre of Marian devotion, they were consciously laying the foundations of a courtly, Counter-Reformation society which would stand in sharp contrast to the upstart Dutch Republic created by the Calvinist rebels of the northern provinces.[38] They were rewarded by an extraordinary upsurge of cultural vitality, sustained not only by court patronage but also by that

---

[35] David Howarth, *Lord Arundel and his Circle* (New Haven, Conn. and London, 1985), pp. 33–6.

[36] See A. R. Braunmuller, 'Robert Carr, Earl of Somerset, as Collector and Patron', in Linda Levy Peck, ed., *The Mental World of the Jacobean Court* (Cambridge, 1991), ch. 13.

[37] See Roy Strong, *Henry, Prince of Wales and England's Lost Renaissance* (London, 1986).

[38] See the various essays in Thomas and Duerloo, eds, *Albert and Isabella*, for different manifestations of archducal cultural activity. For Scherpenheuvel, see the handsomely illustrated work by Luc Duerloo and Marc Wingens, *Scherpenheuvel. Het Jeruzalem van de Lage Landen* (Louvain, 2002).

of the cities and civic elites, and of the Church and the religious orders, in particular the Jesuits.

Archduke Albert died in 1621, a few months after a twelve-year truce expired and hostilities resumed between Spain and the Dutch Republic. With the return of war and the widowhood of Isabella, who henceforth habitually dressed in the habit of the Poor Clares, the court's role in the vigorous cultural life of the Spanish Netherlands became more muted. But the decade of the 1620s was to see important changes in the courts of Madrid and London, bringing them closer to the kind of cultural politics adopted by the court in Brussels under the government of the archdukes. Philip Ill's death preceded by a few months that of the Archduke Albert, and James I died four years later, in 1625. The heirs of both monarchs were to show an acute interest in, and appreciation of, the arts—an interest stimulated by friendly competition and rivalry. The young Philip IV had already shown that he possessed a taste for music and the theatre, and he soon developed a discriminating eye for paintings. He had, too, in the Count-Duke of Olivares, a favourite and first minister who was determined to make his young royal master the supreme monarch in Europe in the arts of peace as well as war. Philip IV, unlike his father, was to be a refined and elegant prince at the centre of a dazzling court—a Planet King who would cast his beams over Europe and whose brilliance would be reflected and disseminated by a host of lesser lights.[39]

Philip's cultural ambitions were sharpened by the 1623 visit to Madrid of Charles, Prince of Wales, five years his senior, whose elegance, refinement and informed appreciation of the arts must have brought home to Philip that he still had much to learn.[40] But if Philip's ambitions to be a connoisseur of painting were sharpened by the presence of the Prince of Wales, Charles for his part was deeply impressed by the great picture collection built up by the Spanish Habsburgs, and on his return to London with gifts from Philip that included two great paintings by Titian and an important Veronese, he began to scour the continent for masterpieces to add to his collection. He was deeply impressed, too, by the formality of Spanish court life. His father's court in London was painfully lacking in the dignity and decorum that he had seen in Madrid, and on coming to the throne in 1625 he took steps to put this right.

---

[39] For Olivares' cultural policies and the creation of the *rey planeta*, see Brown and Elliott, *A Palace for a King*, especially ch. 2; and see below, p. 289.
[40] For the cultural impact of the Prince of Wales's visit to Madrid in 1623, see Jonathan Brown and John Elliott, eds, *The Sale of the Century: Artistic Relations between Spain and Great Britain, 1604–1655* (New Haven, Conn., London and Prado Museum, Madrid, 2002); and see above, pp. 30–1.

Shortly after Charles I's accession the Venetian ambassador reported that 'the king observes a rule of great decorum. The nobles do not enter his apartments in confusion as heretofore, but each rank has its appointed place. . . .'[41] In drawing up new rules for the regulation of the royal household, Charles might claim to be restoring the order and decorum that had characterised the court of Elizabeth, but in the formality and stiffness of its ceremonial his court also had obvious affinities with that of Philip IV.

The affinities, however, ran deeper than rules of etiquette. Although Charles I remained resolutely Anglican in his own personal beliefs, he had in Henrietta Maria a French Catholic wife, and culturally his court shared many of the tastes of the courts of Counter-Reformation Europe. There was a cosmopolitanism about European culture in this period which transcended national, and even to some extent religious, boundaries. Even as the Europe of the 1620s descended once again into war, the lines of communication remained open between the different courts. Diplomats, well aware of the aesthetic interests of their royal masters, kept them abreast not only of political but also of cultural news from the courts of their rivals. 'The Marquis of Leganés', wrote Arthur Hopton, the English agent in Madrid, in a characteristic report dating from 1631, 'is sick of a dangerous *calenture* [fever] which imports this only in His Majesty's service, that he hath some good pictures and statues, which if he should miscarry may be looked out for, if His Majesty shall so ordain.'[42] The ambassadors of Charles I and Philip IV were called upon to serve as unofficial agents for the purchase of important works of art that came onto the market, competing with rival diplomats for paintings and sculptures that would enhance royal and aristo-cratic collections in their home countries. Whether as gifts or eagerly sought purchases, works of art had become by the 1620s and 1630s part of the normal currency of exchange and competition between the courts of Europe.[43]

The competition gave a new prominence to art connoisseurs and middlemen, like the Duke of Buckingham's artistic adviser, the Huguenot-born Balthasar Gerbier, who shunted to and fro between England and the continent, engaging simultaneously in art dealing and informal diplomacy in courts to which his expertise gave him easy entrée.[44] But in this cosmopolitan world

---

[41] Quoted in Sharpe, *The Personal Rule of Charles I*, p. 210.

[42] British Library, Egerton Ms. 1820, fo. 62, Hopton to Lord Dorchester, 11 September 1631.

[43] For royal and aristocratic collecting in this period, see especially Jonathan Brown, *Kings and Connoisseurs*. For diplomacy and gift-giving, see Elizabeth Cropper, ed., *The Diplomacy of Art: Artistic Creation and Politics in Seicento Italy* (Villa Spelman Colloquium, vol. 7, Milan, 2000); José Luis Colomer, ed., *Arte y diplomacia de la monarquía hispánica en el siglo XVII* (Madrid, 2003).

where art and diplomacy walked hand in hand, one figure stood head and shoulders above the others, that of Peter Paul Rubens. Between 1628 and 1630 Rubens linked in his own person the courts of Brussels, Madrid and London, as he sought to lay the diplomatic groundwork for a treaty that would end five years of hostilities between England and Spain. The shared aesthetic tastes of Philip IV and Charles I made Isabella's trusted servant, who was also Europe's most famous living artist, an ideal intermediary for bringing peace to warring nations.

Appropriately, Rubens while in London painted for Charles I his great allegory of peace and war (Fig. 17). He also used the occasion to finalise his magnificent decorative programme to celebrate the triumphs and apotheosis of James I on the ceiling of the Banqueting House in Whitehall. The canvases were completed in the summer of 1634, at around the same time as Velázquez and his team of fellow artists were hard at work on a comparable decorative scheme in Madrid—the series of battle paintings and equestrian royal portraits for Madrid's equivalent of the Banqueting House, the great ceremonial hall of the *Salón de Reinos* in the Palace of the Buen Retiro (see Fig. 24). Rubens's paintings were not, however, finally shipped to London until October 1635, and he declined to accompany them and see to their installation.[45]

Gratified as he was to be the recipient of commissions from so discerning a monarch as Charles I, the constraints normally imposed on court painters were not for Rubens, and now less than ever. His original contract with the Archdukes Albert and Isabella had left him free to live and work in Antwerp rather than at the court in Brussels,[46] and he did much of his work not for the court but for the Church and members of the civic elite. His experiences as a diplomat in Madrid and London only served to reinforce his growing antipathy to courts, and while in Madrid he no doubt played his part in arranging for Velázquez to escape for a time from the confinement of court life and broaden his horizons by visiting the great artistic centres of Italy. Some artists, like Orazio Gentileschi, who arrived in London in 1626,[47] and Rubens's own pupil, Anthony Van Dyck, who became Charles I's court painter in 1632,

---

[44] Brown, *Kings and Connoisseurs*, pp. 24–9; Roger Lockyer, *Buckingham* (London, 1981), pp. 214–15.

[45] Christopher White, *Peter Paul Rubens* (New Haven, Conn. and London, 1987), p. 255. Payments for *The Surrender of Breda* and the other battle paintings run from the summer of 1634 to the summer of 1635 (see Brown and Elliott, *A Palace for a King*, p. 279, note 7).

[46] Christopher Brown, 'Rubens and the Archdukes' in Thomas and Duerloo, eds, *Albert and Isabella*, p. 121.

[47] Gabriele Finaldi, ed., *Orazio Gentileschi at the Court of Charles I* (National Gallery, London, 1999).

Figure 17 Rubens, *Allegory of Peace* (National Gallery, London).

might be willing and even eager to accept this form of servitude, but by this stage of his career Rubens was more than ever anxious to break free. In December 1633 the death of the Infanta Isabella snapped his strongest emotional tie to the Brussels court. A year later he was writing to tell his friend Peiresc that, having been 'away from my home for nine months, and obliged to be present continually at Court', he had made the decision to 'force myself to cut this golden knot of ambition, in order to recover my liberty'.[48] The liberty proved to be less than he might have wished. At short notice Rubens had to organise for the magistrates of Antwerp the great decorative scheme for the ceremonial entry into the city of Isabella's successor, the Cardinal Infante, on 17 April 1635, and he was then commissioned by Philip IV to produce a series of paintings for his hunting lodge, the Torre de la Parada, which would keep the artist busy for the rest of his life.[49] But he sought to steer clear of the

---

[48] Magurn, ed., *The Letters of Peter Paul Rubens*, p. 392 (18 December 1634).
[49] See John Rupert Martin, *The Decorations for the Pompa Introitus Ferdinandi* (London and New York, 1972), and Svetlana Alpers, *The Decoration of the Torre de la Parada* (London and New York, 1971).

court, and would cling to his new-found liberty until the end of his days, in
May 1640.

Rubens's final disillusionment came at a time when court life, both in
London and Madrid, was falling victim to its own artificiality. The court
masque was escapist by nature, and many of the plays performed before
Charles I and his court lacked that sense of contact with the real world that
had given such vitality to Jacobean drama.[50] Performers and audience alike
were transported by the masques into a mythological realm in which chaos
was replaced by order, and tranquillity was restored by a wave of the wand.[51]
Charles saw in these transformations an allegory of his own beneficent rule,
which had turned a troubled land into a royal Arcadia. Anthony Van Dyck,
himself the perfect courtier with his acute delight in fine clothes, fine music
and fine living,[52] was the artist of Arcadia *par excellence*. A stream of dazzling
portraits through the 1630s depicted its inhabitants—the king and his family,
his courtiers and his nobles—as the quintessence of elegance in a timeless
world of courtly refinement (Fig. 18). But by the time of Van Dyck's death in
December 1641, Arcadia was fast disappearing. Rebellion in Scotland, Ireland
and England had brutally dispelled the golden glow of myth.

In Madrid, too, the Buen Retiro, built by the Count-Duke of Olivares for the
king's recreation, became the setting for court festivities and allegorical dramas
which again contrasted sharply with the painful realities of the outside world (see
Fig. 23).[53] Pedro Calderón de La Barca's court spectacle, *El mayor encanto, amor*,
staged in 1635 on the island in the middle of the palace's great lake to the accompaniment of brilliant scenic effects by the Florentine stage designer Cosimo Lotti,
was the story of Ulysses held in thrall by the enchantments of Circe. It was not
hard to read into the performance the story of a monarch held in thrall by his
favourite, when by rights he should have been leading his armies into battle.[54]
While Philip IV had done what Olivares had hoped of him, and created around
himself a brilliant court that could draw on a dazzling array of talent—Lope de

---

[50] Graham Parry, *The Golden Age Restor'd: The Culture of the Stuart Court, 1603–1642*
(Manchester, 1981), p. 203.
[51] Sharpe, *The Personal Rule of Charles I*, p. 183; and see also Kevin Sharpe, *Criticism and
Compliment* (Cambridge, 1987), ch. 5 ('The Caroline Court Masque').
[52] *Anthony Van Dyck* (National Gallery of Art, Washingon, D.C., 1990), pp. 12–13; and see
Oliver Millar's essay in this catalogue, 'Van Dyck in London', for the painter's years at the
English court.
[53] See Brown and Elliott, *A Palace for a King*, ch. 7.
[54] See J. H. Elliott, 'Staying in Power: The Count-Duke of Olivares', in Elliott and Brockliss,
The World of the Favourite, ch. 8, and Margaret Rich Greer, *The Play of Power* (Princeton,
N.J., 1991), pp. 87–94.

Figure 18 Van Dyck, *Lords John and Bernard Stuart* (National Gallery, London).

Vega, Francisco de Quevedo, Calderón, Velázquez—that court, like the court of Charles I, was increasingly living in an enchanted world of its own. The rebellions of Catalonia and Portugal in 1640 brought a rude awakening. Three years later Olivares, the designer and stage manager of the court of the *rey planeta,* was relieved of his duties after twenty-two years in power.

Courts by their nature exalt the majesty of kingship, and the courts of Spain and England fell victim to their own inflated rhetoric. To many of his subjects Charles I's court, with its continental, classicising and popish tastes, stood as the visible manifestation of a form of absolute kingship which threatened to destroy Protestantism and subvert traditional English liberties. Engulfed by the rising tide of dissent, the king failed to understand the grievances of his subjects. In 1649, still uncomprehending, he would walk out onto the scaffold from the window of that same Banqueting House which had been planned to herald the advent of a grander and more majestic monarchy.

Unlike Charles I, Philip IV, in jettisoning Olivares, managed to check the rising tide of dissent and recover the political initiative. In Spain as in England the lifestyle and extravagance of the court had become a major source of popular grievance, and both before and after his fall from power the Count-Duke found himself having to rebut the charges that were swirling around him over the expenditure of large sums on the construction and furnishing of the Buen Retiro.[55] In a symbolic gesture after the fall of his minister-favourite, the king ordered the melting down of the twelve magnificent silver lions which adorned the Hall of Realms.[56] But while Philip sought to change the style of his government in order to assuage political discontent, he did little to change the style of his life. Inevitably the death of his queen in 1644, and of his son and heir, Baltasar Carlos, in 1646, brought a suspension of court festivities, but with the advent of a new queen, Mariana de Austria, in 1649, the court returned to life. The *Avisos* of Jerónimo de Barrionuevo in the 1650s and early 1660s depict a court in which penury and festivity walked hand in hand.

Criticisms of Philip's court expenditure remained continuous, but so too did the expenditure. Similarly, Charles I's Lord Treasurer, Sir Richard Weston, had struggled to reduce the swollen costs of his court, but found himself thwarted by Charles's princely disdain of economy.[57] There was a continuing tension in early modern Europe between the requirements of princely

---

[55] See Brown and Elliott, *A Palace for a King,* pp. 242–8.
[56] *Ibid.,* p. 246.
[57] Michael Van Cleave Alexander, *Charles I's Lord Treasurer: Sir Richard Weston, Earl of Portland, 1577–1635* (London, 1975), p. 158.

magnificence and of princely moderation, a tension that was well caught by Alonso Núñez de Castro when he wrote in his *Libro histórico político. Sólo Madrid es corte:* 'We have seen excess condemned in the apparatus of royalty; we have also seen how necessary it is to maintain respect for some form of exterior display, which is what distinguishes kings from the rest of mankind.'[58]

Philip IV, ever conscious, like Charles I, of the importance of majesty and decorum, brushed the criticisms aside, and created for himself a court setting that reflected his own aesthetic sensibilities and his sense of the splendour and dignity appropriate to a King of Spain. To achieve the setting that he had in mind, he turned more and more in his later years to the man he had appointed as his court painter in 1623, and who had become over the course of time a fixture in his world. It was Velázquez who refurbished the Alcázar and the Escorial in the 1650s, who was constantly refining and re-hanging the royal collection in consultation with the king, and whose duty it was, as *aposentador mayor de palacio,* to make the arrangements for the ceremonial royal journey to the Franco-Spanish frontier in 1660, during the last months of his life. It was Velázquez, too, who oversaw the decoration of the Spanish rooms in the pavilion on the Isle of Pheasants from which Philip presented his daughter María Teresa to her bridegroom, Louis XIV of France.[59]

No painter was every more truly a court painter than Velázquez, in the sense that his life was bound, far more tightly than the lives of Rubens and Van Dyck, to the service of a royal master and to palace rituals. Even when the archducal court made its strongest demands upon Rubens, he preserved a measure of personal liberty by living and working in Antwerp, where his house, with its wonderful collection of paintings and antiquities, allowed him to escape into a world of his own.[60] Van Dyck's first duty in London was to Charles I, who made heavy demands upon him; but he was even more heavily involved in private than in royal commissions, as members of the nobility and gentry from court and country alike flocked to his studio in Blackfriars for portraits that transformed their image of themselves.

To some extent, the different life experiences of Rubens and Van Dyck on the one hand, and Velázquez on the other, were a reflection of the differences between the courts for which they worked. The court of the archdukes, although a hispanicised court, was described by Cardinal Bentivoglio as 'more

---

[58] Alonso Núñez de Castro, *Libro histórico político. Sólo Madrid es corte*, 3rd edn (Madrid, 1675), p. 194.

[59] See Brown, *Velázquez*, chs. 8 and 9. Below, pp. 299–300 and Fig. 30.

[60] See Jeffrey M. Muller, *Rubens: The Artist as Collector* (Princeton, N.J., 1989).

amiable and free' than its Spanish counterpart, and Rubens took advantage of this liberty to undertake commissions other than those specifically associated with the court in Brussels.[61] Although the court of Charles I had acquired a Spanish formality, the English court remained less of a centralised court than a grouping of aristocratic households around the household of the king, and great nobles maintained a strongly independent existence, organising their festivities and bestowing their patronage as they chose.[62] Financially at least, Van Dyck was the beneficiary of this loose intermingling of royal, aristocratic and provincial patronage, although physically and psychologically the burden wore him out. Of all three courts, that of Philip IV most resembled a golden cage, both for those who served the king and for the king himself. This made it no place for a Rubens, with his 'horror of courts' and his thirst for independence. But the career of Velázquez, who spent his life inside the golden cage, is evidence that constraint, as well as liberty, is capable of creating conditions in which genius can flower.

---

[61] Quoted by Diederik Lanoye in Thomas and Duerloo, eds, *Albert and Isabella*, p. 107.
[62] Malcolm Smuts, 'The Political Failure of Stuart Cultural Patronage', in Guy Fitch Lytle and Stephen Orgel, eds, *Patronage in the Renaissance* (Princeton, N.J., 1981), p. 176.

CHAPTER XIV

APPEARANCE AND REALITY IN THE SPAIN OF VELÁZQUEZ

'Reality and Appearance. *Things do not pass for what they are but for what they seem; few look within, and many are satisfied with appearances.*'
(*Baltasar Gracián,* The Oracle, *1647)*[1]

The Spain in which Diego Rodríguez de Silva Velázquez was born in 1599 was a country where appearances showed increasingly ominous signs of being at odds with reality. The old king, Philip II, had died in the previous year, after a reign of forty-two years. The most powerful monarch in Europe, he had left the young Philip III an exhausted realm of Castile, an immense burden of debt, and a faltering mission to preserve his dynastic inheritance intact and rescue Christendom from the advance of heresy. No expense was spared, however, to celebrate the deceased king's exequies in a manner worthy of the ruler of a global empire, officially known as the Spanish Monarchy, the *monarquía española*. Seville, the city of Velázquez's birth, surpassed even its own reputation for lavish display by erecting in its cavernous cathedral a massive catafalque on which the late king's virtues were emblematically represented, his achievements depicted and the extent of his worldwide dominions proclaimed. The crowds gazed in awe at the impressive monument. 'I vow to God', wrote Miguel de Cervantes in a famous sonnet, 'that the grandeur of it terrifies me. . . .' But the irony behind his exaggerated

---

[1] Baltasar Gracián, *The Oracle: A Manual of the Art of Discretion*, trans. L. B. Walton (London, 1953), p. 121 (maxim 99).

reaction to this proud assertion of the king's undying glory did not escape contemporaries.[2]

Seville could no doubt afford the outlay on the catafalque. As the receiving point for the annual remittances of silver from the mines of Mexico and Peru, it was one of the richest cities of the western world. Yet Cervantes was not alone in detecting the disparity between the grandiloquence of the statement made by this ephemeral monument and the realities of the world beyond the doors of the cathedral. A memorialist writing at the turn of the century commented pointedly on the internal contradictions of the Spain of his day. 'Never', he wrote, 'were there vassals so rich as today, and never such poverty as is found among them. Never before was there a king so powerful nor with so many kingdoms and sources of revenue, and never has one embarked on a new reign with his estates so diminished and pledged away.' He attributed this to the fact that the cascade of silver from the Americas had blinded his compatriots to the fundamental truth that the source of genuine wealth was hard work and productive investment. 'And so', he continued, 'the reason why Spain has no money, or gold and silver, is because it has them, and the reason why it is not rich is because it is.' Deluded by its misperceptions, Spain had become 'a republic of enchanted men, living outside the natural order of things'.[3]

It was in this Spain, and in Seville, the richest—and poorest—of its cities, that the young Diego Velázquez, the grandson of Portuguese immigrants from Oporto and the son of the notary in charge of the cathedral chapter's tribunal for dealing with testamentary provisions,[4] embarked on his artistic career and grew to maturity. It was a Spain in which the new ministers of a new monarch struggled to conserve a burdensome legacy. In spite of the silver from the Indies still reaching Seville in massive quantities, the Crown's finances were in no state to sustain the vastly expensive military and foreign policy commitments incurred by Philip II. Reluctantly the new regime, headed by Philip III's favourite and first minister, the Duke of Lerma, beat a phased retreat. Sixteen years of open war with the England of Elizabeth I were ended by a treaty concluded in 1604 with her successor, James VI and I; and five years later the government in Madrid agreed to a twelve years' truce with Philip III's

---

[2] Francisco Gerónimo Collado, *Descripción del túmulo y relación de las exequías que hizo la ciudad de Sevilla en la muerte del rey don Felipe segundo*, ed. F. de B. Palomo (Seville, 1869); Melveena McKendrick, *Cervantes* (Boston, Mass. and Toronto, 1980), p. 185.
[3] Martin González de Cellorigo, *Memorial de la política necesaria y útil restauración a la república de España* (Valladolid, 1600), fos 29 and 25v. See also above, pp. 140 and 142.
[4] Luis Méndez Rodríguez, 'La familia de Velázquez. Una falsa hidalguía', in *Velázquez y Sevilla. Estudios* (Seville, 1999), pp. 33–49.

rebellious subjects in the Netherlands, where Spain's impressive army of Flanders was bogged down in an immensely costly, and apparently unwinnable, war to bring the revolt to an end. The government in Madrid sought to distract attention from the humiliations of a truce signed with heretics and rebels by ordering on the same day the expulsion from Spain of its population of some 300,000 moriscos, the nominally Christianised Moors who had remained in the peninsula after the surrender of the last Moorish king of Granada in 1492. As a boy in 1610, Velázquez would have seen the straggling line of around 18,000 moriscos on their way to embark in Seville for the ports of North Africa.[5] Seventeen years later in 1627, Philip's son and successor, Philip IV, chose this supreme act of royal piety as the subject for a competition between his court artists. The competition was won by Velázquez with a painting, *Expulsion of the Moriscos*, now lost, that showed Philip III in armour pointing with his baton at a group of weeping men, women and children, with the majestic and matronly figure of Spain seated on his right.[6]

An act that can be interpreted as an example of Spain's dedication to the cause of pure religion, or as a necessary solution to an intractable ethnic problem, was also an assertion of gesture politics. Questions of honour and reputation ran through the life of Spanish as of all European society in this period. 'How to preserve reputation' was the theme of a section of Giovanni Botero's *The Reason of State* (1589),[7] and the ministers of Philip III, as representatives of the greatest monarch in the world, were acutely aware of the importance of maintaining the reputation of their king. The need for this was all the greater at a time when Spain's military power appeared to be flagging, and financial necessity was dictating at least a temporary suspension of arms. Lerma and his colleagues used every art to ensure that the resulting peace would look like peace on their own terms, a *pax hispanica*. Spanish diplomats, assisted by Spanish money, worked with skill and devotion to ensure that the reputation of their royal master was upheld in the courts of European princes, and that Spain's international preeminence would be as readily acknowledged in a time of peace as of war.[8]

By 1618 the storm clouds would again be gathering, and Europe would be on the brink of a new international conflagration, the Thirty Years War. Although

---

[5] Antonio Domínguez Ortiz and Bernard Vincent, *Historia de los moriscos. Vida y tragedia de una minoría* (Madrid, 1978), p. 190.

[6] Steven N. Orso, *Philip IV and the Decoration of the Alcázar of Madrid* (Princeton, N.J., 1986), pp. 52–5.

[7] Giovanni Botero, *The Reason of State*, trans. of *Ragion di Stato* (1589) by P. J. and D. P. Waley (London, 1956), book ii, p. 11.

[8] H. R. Trevor-Roper, 'Spain and Europe 1598–1621', in *The New Cambridge Modern History* (Cambridge, 1970), iv, ch. 9.

the interlude of peace brought some respite, and allowed the court and the aristocracy to indulge in conspicuous consumption on a lavish scale, Madrid depended heavily on artifice and sleight-of-hand diplomacy to maintain the image of overwhelming Spanish power. As the more perceptive of contemporary observers recognised, this image did not accord with the underlying economic and social realities that Lerma's corrupt and profligate government proved reluctant to address. Imagery and rhetoric were no substitutes for reform.[9]

Imagery and rhetoric, however, were integral to Spanish Baroque society, as to that of early seventeenth-century Europe as a whole. This was an age of theatre and illusion, and nowhere more so than in the Seville of Velázquez. In the opening years of the new century the city was the theatrical capital of Spain. Around 1600 it boasted four public theatres, and the Coliseo, a splendid new municipal theatre, opened its doors to the public in 1607.[10] Theatre in Seville, however, was not confined to the *corrales de comedias* (playhouses). The city provided a spectacular backdrop for the street theatre which constituted a permanent accompaniment to civic life. Much of this theatre was religious in character. *Autos sacramentales*, descendants of medieval mystery plays, were performed in public places before large crowds, and the clergy, municipal dignitaries, members of religious confraternities and large numbers of the populace would process through the streets in celebration of a local saint or some great event in the liturgical calendar, such as the feast of Corpus Christi. In these great processions, elaborately carved and painted images of Christ, the Virgin and saints, produced in Seville's numerous workshops, were borne aloft or carried on *pasos*, or religious floats. Sevillians were fervently devoted to the cult of the Virgin, and when the doctrine of her Immaculate Conception was disputed by a Dominican preacher in 1613, the city rose in fury at this stain on her honour. Innumerable masses were performed and sermons preached in support of the controversial doctrine. The painting of the *Inmaculada* by Velázquez in 1619 (Fig. 19) was one among the many images created in a campaign that set religious orders at each other's throats and added further complications to Spain's always complex relations with the papacy.[11]

---

[9] J. H. Elliott, *Spain and its World, 1500–1700* (New Haven, Conn. and London, 1989), ch. 11 ('Self-Perception and Decline in Early Seventeenth-Century Spain').
[10] Víctor Pérez Escolano, *Juan de Oviedo y de la Bandera* (Seville, 1977), pp. 46–7; Francisco J. Cornejo, *Pintura y teatro en la Sevilla del Siglo de Oro. La 'Sacra Monarquía'* (Seville, 2005), pp. 23–5.
[11] See Sara T. Nalle, 'Spanish Religious Life in the Age of Velázquez', in Suzanne L. Stratton-Pruitt, ed., *The Cambridge Companion to Velázquez* (Cambridge, 2002), pp. 114–16 and, more generally, Suzanne L. Stratton, *The Immaculate Conception in Spanish Art* (Cambridge, 1994).

Figure 19 Velázquez, *The Immaculate Conception* (National Gallery, London).

Figure 20 Velázquez, *Christ after the Flagellation Contemplated by the Christian Soul* (National Gallery, London).

It would not be surprising if Velázquez, as an apprentice in the studio of one of the city's leading artists, Francisco Pacheco, was deeply influenced by the theatre that he saw all around him. The description of his lost *Expulsion of the Moriscos* makes it sound like the depiction of a scene from a play. There is a theatrical quality, too, to *Christ after the Flagellation Contemplated by the Christian Soul* (Fig. 20) to some of the portraits, like that of *Pablo de Valladolid* (Fig. 21), standing alone as if on an empty stage.[12]

There was more to Seville, however, than the theatre that shaped and coloured so much of public life. As a great port city, Seville was the meeting-point of several different worlds: the Indies, which were popularly said to have

---

[12] For the development of this argument see Miguel Morán Turina, 'Velázquez, la pintura y el teatro del Siglo de Oro', *Boletín del Museo del Prado*, xix, no. 37 (2001), pp. 47–71.

Figure 21 Velázquez, *The Buffoon Pablo de Valladolid* (Museo del Prado, Madrid).

paved the city's streets with gold; Spain's beleaguered northern outpost of
Flanders, whose merchants constituted an important foreign community in the
city; and Italy, the artistic and spiritual capital of Counter-Reformation Europe,
with which Seville's ties were close.[13] A relatively affluent and well-educated
civic elite, consisting of members of the local nobility, cathedral canons and
other members of the clergy and the professional classes, was therefore exposed
to the many influences entering Seville from abroad. The Casa de Pilatos, the
family home of the Dukes of Alcalá, contained a famous collection of Roman
antiquities, and the third duke, Don Fernando Enríquez Afán de Ribera, maintained the humanist traditions of his predecessors, building up a splendid
library and becoming a notable patron of the arts.[14]

Velázquez's master, Pacheco, who was commissioned by the duke to decorate
his study in the Casa de Pilatos, headed one of the several 'academies' or informal
groups that flourished in the city in the early seventeenth century. Poets, scholars,
artists and men of letters would gather in Pacheco's house and that of other
eminent figures in the city to discuss questions of literary and artistic theory or
of antiquarian concern, and engage in the conceits that so delighted the learned
world of the seventeenth century. Here, in addition to learning the technical skills
required for the licence to practise as a painter, Velázquez was introduced to a
world of ideas that would inform his work as an artist for the remainder of his
life. It was a world that, although imbued with classical learning, was also alive to
recent advances in science and mathematics, and displayed a particular interest
in optics and the laws of perspective. Significantly, Velázquez's personal library
would contain a large number of scientific texts.[15]

The literary and artistic vitality of the Seville of his youth created a prom-
ising environment for the development of a gifted and intelligent young artist.
But as Velázquez set up as a painter in his own right, marrying his master's
daughter, Juana Pacheco, and establishing a growing reputation for himself
in Seville, he came up against limits imposed both by the nature of his

---

[13] For seventeenth-century Seville, see Antonio Domínguez Ortiz, *La Sevilla del siglo XVII*,
3rd edn (Seville, 1984); and, for a brief survey, John H. Elliott, 'The Seville of Velázquez', in
Velázquez in Seville (National Gallery of Scotland, 1996), pp. 15–21.

[14] For the Dukes of Alcalá and the classical tradition in Seville, see especially Vicente Lleó
Cañal, *Nueva Roma. Mitología y humanismo en el renacimiento sevillano* (Seville, 1979), and
Jonathan Brown and Richard L. Kagan, 'The Duke of Alcalá: His Collection and its
Evolution', *Art Bulletin*, 69 (1987), pp. 231–55.

[15] For Pacheco's academy and the cultural interests of the civic elite, see Jonathan Brown,
Images and Ideas in Seventeenth-Century Spanish Painting (Princeton, N.J., 1978), pt 1; Vicente
Lleó Cañal, 'The Cultivated Elite of Velázquez's Seville', in *Velázquez in Seville*, pp. 23–7; Pedro
Ruiz Pérez, *De la pintura y las letras. La biblioteca de Velázquez* (Seville, 1999).

profession and by an environment that ultimately could not give him all he needed if he were to develop his genius to the full. For all its cosmopolitan traits, Seville remained a provincial city at heart. It was in the court of Madrid that the true action lay. Moreover, artists in the Spain of Velázquez were still regarded as no more than artisans, and their social status, as practitioners of what was perceived to be a purely mechanical art, was not high. Velázquez's father-in-law would regard it as his mission to dignify and ennoble the profession: had not Apelles secured the exalted approbation of Alexander the Great, and Titian been knighted by the Emperor Charles V?[16] Only at the court of the king could a great artist win the fame and rewards he deserved, and secure for his profession the elevation of status that had long been its due.

A Velázquez aspiring to greater opportunities than those offered by Seville was fortunate in that his hopes for a career at court coincided with a spectacular change of regime in Madrid. The Duke of Lerma fell from power in 1618, and his successors were struggling helplessly in the face of a rising tide of demands for reform when Philip III died unexpectedly on 31 March 1621 at the age of forty-two. His sixteen-year-old son and heir, now Philip IV, immediately acted to remove his father's ministers from power. As his principal minister he chose an experienced diplomat and councillor, Don Baltasar de Zúñiga, but everybody knew that the power behind the scenes was Zúñiga's nephew, the ambitious Count of Olivares, who had won Philip's favour in 1615 while he was still the heir to the throne. Within little more than a year of Philip IV's accession Zúñiga was dead, and Olivares moved to take over the levers of power, which he would control for the succeeding twenty years.

Although born in Rome, where his father had been the Spanish ambassador, the Count of Olivares—or the 'Count-Duke', as he came to be known following his elevation to a dukedom in 1625—prided himself on being a 'son of Seville', and he lived in the city between 1607 and 1615, the year in which he secured a post in the household of the heir to the throne.[17] In those Seville years Olivares was a noted, and flamboyant, patron of poets and men of learning, and is known to have had his portrait painted by Francisco Pacheco.[18] Velázquez in the days of his apprenticeship may well, therefore,

---

[16] Francisco Pacheco, *El arte de la pintura* (1649), ed. Bonaventura Bassegoda i Hugas (Madrid, 1990), pp. 146–7.

[17] For Olivares's life and political career, see J. H. Elliott, *The Count-Duke of Olivares: The Statesman in an Age of Decline* (New Haven, Conn., and London, 1986).

[18] Duque de Berwick y de Alba, *Discursos leídos ante la Real Academia de Bellas Artes de San Fernando en la recepción pública del Excmo. Sr. Duque de Berwick y de Alba* (Madrid, 1924), pp. 23–4.

have come into contact with the man who would dominate the Spanish political scene during the first half of the reign of Philip IV.

When Olivares captured power at court in 1621 it was natural that his Sevillian friends and acquaintances, together with a host of aspirants, should flock to Madrid in the hope of receiving offices or favours from a man whom they regarded as one of their own. Velázquez was only one among the many ambitious Sevillians who took the road to Madrid in these opening years of the new reign, and although his first visit, in 1622, proved abortive, with the support of friends at court, and presumably with the active approval of Olivares, he was named painter to the king in the following year. It was the beginning of a court career in which, in addition to being the king's favoured artist, he would also move by degrees up the ladder of palace appointments, beginning in 1627 with that of usher in the royal chamber.[19]

These palace appointments—Assistant in the Wardrobe (1636), Assistant in the Privy Chamber (*ayuda de cámara*, 1643)—not only brought Velázquez useful income additional to the stipend he received as painter to the king, but gave him a secure place in the royal household, with all that this meant in terms of access to the royal person, and all the additional benefits that such proximity could entail. Yet while it made him a member of a select group of some 350 principal royal servants in a court that numbered around 1,700 household officials and service staff,[20] it also involved him in time-consuming and increasingly onerous duties, and tied him to the routine of palace life. With the exception of his two visits to Italy, in 1629–31 and 1649–50, and those periods when the king escaped with members of his entourage into the countryside to go hunting, or made a journey further afield, Velázquez was to spend most of the rest of his existence in and around the Alcázar in Madrid.

With the acquisition of power by Olivares and his relatives and dependants, Seville itself may be said to have come to Madrid. The Sevillian tradition of pageantry and patronage brought new vitality to a court at the centre of which now stood a young king who was still unformed, but who already possessed a taste for the theatre and music, and would soon show that he had inherited the Habsburgs' discriminating eye for the visual arts.[21] Olivares, who, in 1621, was

---

[19] Feliciano Barrios, 'Diego Velázquez. Sus oficios palatinos', in Carmen Iglesias, ed., *Velázquez en la corte de Felipe IV* (Madrid, 2003), pp. 61–80.

[20] Elliott, *Spain and its World*, pp. 144–5 (ch. 7, 'The Court of the Spanish Habsburgs: A Peculiar Institution?'); and see above, pp. 260–1, for the structure of the Spanish court in a comparative context.

[21] For the Seville connection and the development of court life under Philip IV, see Jonathan Brown and John H. Elliott, *A Palace for a King: The Buen Retiro and the Court of Philip IV*, rev. and expanded edn (New Haven, Conn. and London, 2003).

thirty-four years old had high ambitions for a royal master who was half his own age. The King of Spain was the greatest monarch on earth, and Philip had to be trained to fill the exalted role to which God had called him. During the 1620s Olivares introduced an initially indolent and pleasure-seeking youth to the business of government, and prepared for him an extensive reading programme to broaden his knowledge of history and the world in which he lived. By the early 1630s, Philip had acquired an impressive and wide-ranging private library in his palace apartments where every day he spent two hours reading after dinner, and set himself to translate books VIII and IX of Francesco Guicciardini's *History of Italy* into Spanish.[22]

A genuinely cultivated king was central to Olivares's ambitions for Spain and its ruler. He and his supporters had come to power with a programme designed to restore the strength and reputation of Spain after what they regarded as the failures and humiliations of the Lerma years. 'I think I can truly assure Your Majesty', wrote Olivares in 1625, looking back to the moment of the king's accession in 1621, 'that the reputation of Spain and its government were as low as the rivals of its greatness could have wished.'[23] The rivalry between the princes of seventeenth-century Europe was not confined to the battlefield. The unexpected visit of Charles, Prince of Wales, to Madrid in 1623 in a bid to win the hand of the king's sister, the Infanta María, brought the king face to face with a prince five years his senior, whose culture and connoisseurship had exposed his own inadequacies.[24] A king of Spain could not afford to remain in second place in the world of the arts. He must be the central luminary in the most brilliant and cultivated court in Europe, the 'Planet King', or *rey planeta*, as he came to be styled by court poets and playwrights. In contemporary cosmology the fourth planet in the hierarchy of the heavens was the sun.

Olivares and the king were fortunate in that the first half of the seventeenth century was a period of brilliant creativity for the arts in Spain, but they used their patronage to ensure that this creativity was concentrated in the court, although Luis de Góngora, whom Velázquez would paint while he was looking for preferment in Madrid, would eventually return home to Córdoba, a

---

[22] Brown and Elliott, *A Palace for a King*, pp. 41–2. The contents of the king's private library are identified and discussed in Fernando Bouza Álvarez, *El libro y el cetro. La biblioteca de Felipe IV en la Torre Alta del Alcázar de Madrid* (Madrid, 2005).

[23] John H. Elliott and José F. de la Peña, *Memoriales y cartas del Conde Duque de Olivares*, 2 vols (Madrid, 1978–81), i, doc. VII, p. 149.

[24] For the Prince of Wales's visit and its consequences, see Jonathan Brown and John Elliott, eds, *The Sale of the Century: Artistic Relations between Spain and Great Britain, 1604–1655* (New Haven, Conn., London and Prado Museum, Madrid, 2002), and Glyn Redworth, *The Prince and the Infanta* (New Haven, Conn. and London 2003). Above, pp. 30–1 and 270–1.

disappointed man (Fig. 22). Others, however, were more successful. The two greatest playwrights of the age, Lope de Vega and Pedro Calderón de la Barca, wrote play after play for court performance; the corrosive wit of Francisco de Quevedo was harnessed, if with difficulty, to the service of the Olivares regime; the Andalusian playwright Luis Vélez de Guevara, appointed a gentleman usher in 1625, delighted the court with plays that created a vogue for works depending for their effects on the deployment of elaborate stage

Figure 22 Velázquez, *Luis de Góngora y Argote* (Museum of Fine Arts, Boston).

machinery; and, rising head and shoulders above the other court artists, Velázquez created a series of unforgettable images of the king and the royal family.

Velázquez, as part of a tight-knit group of courtiers, palace officials and dependants of the Count-Duke of Olivares, seems to have been very much at home in this court environment. His selection as the king's chosen artist opened doors to him that would otherwise have been closed, and gave him some of the standing for which he craved. It also afforded him the opportunity to study at leisure the works of Titian and other Venetian masters so well represented in the royal collection, and to examine them in the expert company of Peter Paul Rubens when the great Flemish artist visited the court in 1628–9.[25] With a mind sharpened by the debates in Pacheco's academy, Velázquez could enjoy and turn to account the learned allusions and conceptual conceits of Calderón or Quevedo, or of Olivares's erudite librarian Francisco de Rioja, who had been one of the witnesses at the artist's wedding in Seville in 1618.[26] Velázquez even made an appearance as the Countess of Santiesteban, and was given one line to speak, in a burlesque play performed by courtiers on Shrove Tuesday 1638 in which the world was turned upside down and Olivares himself played the part of the porter.[27]

In the 1630s many of the court activities and entertainments moved from the Alcázar to the Buen Retiro (Fig. 23). The palace, officially inaugurated at the end of 1633, overlooked impressive gardens, lakes and fountains, and was designed to display the brilliance of life at the court of the Planet King.[28] Its rooms decorated with costly furnishings, and its walls covered with paintings hastily assembled or commissioned from across the continent by Spanish agents and viceroys, the Buen Retiro also acquired at the end of the decade its own theatre, named the Coliseo, like the theatre in the Count-Duke's Seville.

Even as the new palace rose, however, criticisms were levelled at the expenditure being lavished upon it, and perhaps partly in response to these criticisms its great central hall, the Hall of Realms, was destined for solemn state occasions as well as for court diversions and the staging of plays. Its ceremonial functions were reinforced by the iconographical scheme devised for its

---

[25] See Alexander Vergara, *Rubens and his Spanish Patrons* (Cambridge, 1999).

[26] Lía Schwartz, 'Velázquez and Two Poets of the Baroque', in *The Cambridge Companion to Velázquez*, ch. 8. For Rioja as a witness at the wedding, see Méndez Rodríguez, 'La familia de Velázquez', in *Velázquez y Sevilla. Estudios*, p. 42.

[27] Hannah E. Bergman, 'A Court Entertainment of 1638', *Hispanic Review*, 42 (1974), pp. 67–81.

[28] For the construction of the Buen Retiro and the activities that took place in it, see Brown and Elliott, *A Palace for a King*.

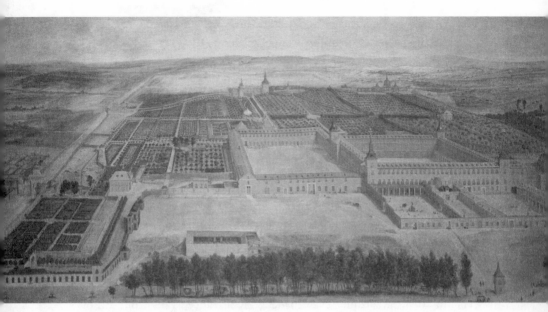

Figure 23 Attributed to Jusepe Leonardo, *Palace of the Buen Retiro in 1636–7* (Palacio Real del Pardo, Madrid).

decoration, and completed in 1635 (Fig. 24). This consisted of three sets of paintings which celebrated the victories won by Philip IV's generals, and proclaimed the glories of the dynasty and its historic continuity. Equally they proclaimed, if more indirectly, the successes of the Olivares regime. Velázquez would certainly have been closely involved in developing the programme and selecting the artists, and he himself was responsible for five of the paintings that adorned the walls—the depiction of one of the most famous victories of the reign, the Surrender of Breda in 1625 to Ambrosio Spínola, commander of the army of Flanders, and the equestrian portraits of Philip III and Philip IV and their respective queens, together with that of the young prince Baltasar Carlos, the heir to the throne and the hope of the dynasty (Fig. 25).[29]

The Duke of Modena was much impressed by the splendours of the Buen Retiro when he was lodged there on his visit to Spain in 1638,[30] but already by then the hollowness of many of the victories depicted in the Hall of Realms was being cruelly exposed and, with it, the defects and failures of a regime whose advent had been greeted across Spain with such high hopes in 1621.

[29] In addition to Brown and Elliott, *A Palace for a King*, see the catalogue of the exhibition held in the Prado Museum in 2005, *Paintings for the Planet King: Philip IV and the Buen Retiro Palace*, ed. Andrés Úbeda de los Cobos (London, 2005).
[30] Salvador Salort Pons, *Velázquez en Italia* (Madrid, 2002), ch. 4.

Figure 24 Virtual reconstruction of the interior of the Hall of Realms.

From the beginning, Olivares's bid to restore Spain's standing in the world involved it in a succession of wars which jeopardised the chances of successful domestic reform. The truce with the Dutch expired in 1621 and was not resumed; Madrid felt in honour bound to come to the aid of the Austrian Habsburgs as they battled against heresy and subversion in the opening stages of the Thirty Years War; England and Spain found themselves at war again in 1625 after the humiliating failure of Charles, Prince of Wales, to bring home his intended Spanish bride from Madrid; and growing tensions between the Spain of Olivares and the France of Cardinal Richelieu culminated in 1635 in open war between the two countries.

While the Spanish government could still lay hands on extensive resources, and Spain achieved some impressive victories, the continuous warfare placed great and growing strains on the Castilian economy and on the fragile constitutional structure of the Spanish Monarchy. The Buen Retiro itself became a symbol of the failures of Olivares and his government: the money so brutally extracted from the Castilian taxpayer was being squandered on frivolities and

Figure 25 Velázquez, *Prince Baltasar Carlos on Horseback* (Museo del Prado, Madrid).

extravagant court spectacles; the king was in retreat (*retiro*), when, like Louis XIII of France, he should have been leading his armies into battle. Above all, there was a widening gulf between rhetoric and reality. On the one hand there was the rhetoric of the regime, as expressed visually in the Hall of Realms and verbally in the apologias written to order by court pamphleteers, and on the other there were the cruel realities of life in a country in which war profiteers and royal officials waxed fat on their illicit gains, while the mass of the population, staggering beneath the burden of an inequitable tax system, was being reduced to starvation and misery.[31]

The crisis came in 1640 when first Catalonia and then Portugal rose in rebellion against the government in Madrid. When the royal army, concentrating first on Catalonia, failed to subdue the rebels, Olivares's days in power were numbered. In January 1643 Philip IV, who had for so long been dominated by the Count-Duke's overbearing personality, gave him leave to retire, and announced that in future he would rule by himself. Symbolically leaving behind the delights of the Buen Retiro, the king joined his army on the Catalan front, and it was in the Aragonese town of Fraga that he was painted by Velázquez in 1644 (Fig. 26), dressed in the costume in which he reviewed the troops at Berbegal.[32]

The high hopes that greeted the king's announcement of his determination to take personal charge of affairs were all too soon to be disappointed. Although he spent long hours at his desk, and was careful to avoid the appearance of giving preeminence to any one minister, much of the business of government slipped by imperceptible degrees into the hands of the Count-Duke's nephew, Don Luis de Haro, whose discretion and smooth affability ensured his survival as the power behind the scenes until his death in 1661.[33] The first priority of Haro and his ministerial colleagues was a general peace settlement, but it proved to be painfully elusive. While Madrid managed to negotiate a peace treaty with the Dutch Republic in 1648, the war with France would continue, with fluctuating fortunes, for another eleven years.

---

[31] For the rhetoric of the regime, see Elliott, *Spain and its World*, ch. 8 ('Power and Propaganda in the Spain of Philip IV').

[32] Jonathan Brown, *Velázquez: Painter and Courtier* (New Haven, Conn. and London, 1986), p. 173.

[33] The second half of Philip IV's reign, much less studied than the first, is covered by Robert Stradling, *Philip IV and the Government of Spain, 1621–1665* (Cambridge, 1988), pt III. The Oxford D. Phil. thesis (1999) of Alistair Malcolm, 'Don Luis de Haro and the Political Elite of the Spanish Monarchy in the Mid-Seventeenth Century', as yet unpublished, is an important study of Haro's political career and his style of government.

Figure 26 Velázquez, *King Philip IV of Spain* (Fraga portrait) (Frick Collection, New York).

For a time, indeed, it looked as if the Spanish Monarchy was on the verge of disintegration. The 1640s in particular were a disastrous decade. Not only were Catalonia and Portugal in revolt, but rebellions also broke out in Sicily and Naples. The king, too, suffered great personal misfortune. His queen, Isabella of Bourbon, died in 1644, and two years later prince Baltasar Carlos died in Zaragoza, where he had accompanied his father for the summer campaign against the Catalans. Although there was also a daughter from the king's marriage, María Teresa, the death of the king's only legitimate son opened the way to a dynastic crisis of immeasurable proportions. After the death of the queen, Philip had made it clear that he had no wish to remarry, but the need for a new male heir forced him to accept the inevitable. He chose as his second wife his young niece, Mariana of Austria, the intended bride of Baltasar Carlos. The new queen, aged barely fifteen, arrived in Spain from Vienna in 1649.

After the years of mourning, the arrival of a young new queen brought a return of life to a gloomy court. Plays and diversions were staged once more in the Buen Retiro, provoking a new round of public criticism; new royal children appeared, and although they were all too often only to be carried away by death, Velázquez had time to paint their portraits. One of the survivors, the Infanta Margarita, provided an enchanting subject for the artist (Fig. 27), but the longed-for son, Felipe Prospero (Fig. 28), was, as Velázquez hints, a frail child, and died before reaching the age of four. Five days later, on 6 November 1661, another sickly son, Carlos, was born. He was to be the last child of Philip IV's second marriage, and in 1665, his life hanging precariously in the balance, Carlos would succeed his father on the Spanish throne.

Meanwhile Philip IV himself, worn down by the long succession of public and personal disasters, which he attributed to his own and his people's sins, was visibly ageing. In 1653 he wrote to a confidante that he was not sending her his portrait 'as it is nine years since one has been done of me, both because I am not inclined to submit myself to the phlegmatic temperament of Velázquez, and because I do not want to see myself growing old'.[34] The artist does, however, seem to have painted around this time the bust portrait of the ageing monarch, which was to become iconic of the king in his later years (Fig. 29). Contemporaries would have seen in this portrait the majesty of the monarch, where later generations have seen instead the frailties and sufferings of the man. Velázquez saw both. The king in fact maintained a dignified and

---

[34] Joaquín Pérez Villanueva, *Felipe IV y Luisa Enríquez Manrique de Lara, Condesa de Paredes de Nava. Un epistolario inédito* (Salamanca, 1986), letter XLIV (8 July 1653).

Figure 27 Velázquez, *Infanta Margarita in a Blue Dress* (Kunsthistorisches Museum, Vienna).

stoical composure in the face of misfortune and defeat. When the Maréchal de Gramont came to Madrid in 1658 to prepare for the peace settlement between France and Spain that would lead a year later to the Treaty of the Pyrenees, he reported that Philip 'had . . . an air of grandeur and majesty that I have seen nowhere else. . . .'[35]

---

[35] *Mémoires du Maréchal de Gramont*, in A. Petitot et H. Monmerqué, *Collections des Mémoires relatifs à l'histoire de la France*, 57 (Paris, 1827), p. 51.

Figure 28 Velázquez, *Prince Felipe Próspero* (Kunsthistorisches Museum, Vienna).

Appearances had at all costs to be preserved, as they were in the ceremony on the Isle of Pheasants on the river Bidasoa that divided France and Spain, when, on 6 June 1660, the seal was set on the Treaty of the Pyrenees as Philip IV handed over his daughter, the Infanta María Teresa, to Louis XIV as his bride (Fig. 30). The scene-setting for the ceremony fell to Velázquez in his capacity as *aposentador mayor de palacio*, a post to which he had been appointed in 1652, and which carried with it not only the routine duties

Figure 29 Velázquez, *Philip IV of Spain* (National Gallery, London).

involved in ensuring that the king's apartments were kept clean, and that accommodation was available for the king and his retinue when they travelled, but also the arrangement of ceremonial events. This important appointment was a tribute to the king's appreciation of his artist, and to the closeness of the relationship that had developed between the two men. Velázquez, now nearly sixty years old, had indeed fulfilled his father-in-law's hope that he would become the Apelles to the king's Alexander. It was only, however, in June 1658 that he at last came within striking distance of the social status to

Figure 30 Charles Le Brun and Adam Frans van der Meulen, *Philip IV and Louis XIV on the Isle of Pheasants, 7 June 1660* (private collection, London).

which he had for so long aspired, when he was nominated by the king for membership in the knightly Order of Santiago.

Even then it was far from certain that his ambition would be realised. There was strong opposition from the Council of Orders to the appointment of a mere artist to such a dignity. Velázquez claimed, unconvincingly, never to have accepted money for his paintings and to be of noble ancestry, with a line of Silvas stretching back to Aeneas Silvius. The customary enquiries were undertaken into his background, and failed to produce the desired results. In a humiliating blow to his reputation, his candidature was rejected on the grounds that his nobility was unproven.

There are strong indications that Velázquez may have falsified the identity of his maternal grandmother in his application for admission to the Order, and that those witnesses who attested to the nobility of his Portuguese ancestors were lying. His maternal grandfather turns out to have been a tailor specialising in the making of breeches, and a merchant in cloths and silks who used his profits to enter the lucrative Seville property market. On the paternal side, too, it is likely that his family were originally in trade, and it is at least possible that, as with so many of the Portuguese immigrants who settled in Seville, Jewish blood ran in his veins.[36] Such an ancestry placed an absolute bar on admission to an order of nobility. Velázquez, like so many others in the Spain of his day, was not what he seemed, or claimed to be. But, as so often, appearances were preserved and reputation was saved. As a result of a special papal dispensation obtained at the personal request of the king, Velázquez was eventually admitted to the Order on 29 November 1659, less than a year before his death.[37]

It was a story characteristic of the society, and the age. But on this occasion the aspirant to social respectability and upward mobility happened also to be a supremely great artist. The artist aspired for recognition, for himself, his family and for the profession he represented and sought to elevate in the public esteem. The only way to this recognition lay through the palace, and in accepting the obligations that went with the honours, Velázquez was paying a necessary price. Yet if the palace confined him, it also opened up for him opportunities as an artist that he could never have enjoyed had he remained in Seville. With the unflagging support of a monarch who could recognise a great artist when he saw one, he was given every opportunity to excel.

Around the time when Velázquez moved to Madrid, a fellow Sevillian, Rodrigo Fernández de Ribera, wrote a satirical work called *Los anteojos de mejor vista* ('Spectacles for Better Vision'), which enabled the wearer to see the reality beneath the appearance.[38] In the Spain of Velázquez, many things, as

---

[36] Kevin Ingram, 'Diego Velázquez's Secret History', *Boletin del Museo del Prado*, xvii, no. 35 (1999), pp. 69–85, based on new archival information, and suggesting Jewish origins. Rafael Cómez, 'La parentela de Velázquez', *Laboratorio de Arte* (University of Seville, 2002), no. 15, pp. 383–8, argues instead for possible Moorish origins. See also Méndez Rodríguez, 'La familia de Velázquez'.
[37] Jaime de Salazar y Acha, 'Velázquez, Caballero de Santiago', in Iglesias, ed., *Velázquez en la corte de Felipe IV*, pp. 95–126.
[38] Rodrigo Fernández de Ribera, *Los anteojos de mejor vista*, ed. Victor Infantes de Miguel (Madrid, 1979); Lleó Cañal, 'The Cultivated Elite', in *Velázquez in Seville*, p. 27.

Baltasar Gracián observed in *The Oracle*, did not 'pass for what they are, but for what they seem'. At both the personal and the national level, immense and often highly successful efforts were made to keep up appearances in the face of the unwelcome intrusion of reality. This was not for nothing the age of elaborate machine-plays, like those that dazzled the court of the Planet King with their artful contrivance and brilliant effects. And, as Gracián added, many were satisfied with appearances but 'few look within'. Diego Velázquez was one of those few.

INDEX